OXFORD STUDIES IN MODERN LEGAL HISTORY

GENERAL EDITOR

A. W. Brian Simpson
Professor of Law, University of Michigan

Private Property and Abuse of Rights in Victorian England

The Story of Edward Pickles and the Bradford Water Supply

MICHAEL TAGGART

OXFORD
UNIVERSITY PRESS

OXFORD
UNIVERSITY PRESS

Great Clarendon Street, Oxford OX2 6DP

Oxford University Press is a department of the University of Oxford.
It furthers the University's objective of excellence in research, scholarship,
and education by publishing worldwide in

Oxford New York

Auckland Bangkok Buenos Aires Cape Town Chennai
Dar es Salaam Delhi Hong Kong Istanbul Karachi Kolkata
Kuala Lumpur Madrid Melbourne Mexico City Mumbai Nairobi
São Paulo Shanghai Taipei Tokyo Toronto

Oxford is a registered trade mark of Oxford University Press
in the UK and in certain other countries

Published in the United States
by Oxford University Press Inc., New York

First published 2002

British Library Cataloguing in Publication Data
Data available

Library of Congress Cataloging in Publication Data
Taggart, Michael.
Private property and abuse of rights in Victorian England: the story of Edward Pickles
and the Bradford water supply / Michael Taggart.
p. cm.
Includes bibliographical references and index.
1. Abuse of rights—England—History. 2. Property—England—History. 3. Water
rights—England—History. 4. Water-supply—England—Bradford—History. I. Title.
KD674.T34 2002
346.4204'32—dc21 2002027425
ISBN 0–19–925687–X

1 3 5 7 9 10 8 6 4 2

Typeset in Palatino by
Cambrian Typesetters, Frimley, Surrey
Printed in Great Britain
on acid-free paper by
T.J. International Ltd, Padstow

To Nicky,
Lisa, Sarah, Richard, and Danny

General Editor's Preface

I first read *Mayor of Bradford v Pickles* nearly fifty years ago when I was studying the law of tort in Oxford under the direction of Tony Honoré. It was studied in relation to two issues which featured in examinations at that time: the relevance of motive, and in particular malicious motive, to tortious liability, and the merits or demerits of adopting a doctrine of abuse of rights into the common law. Like all the best cases it involved an entertaining story, and this provided a vehicle for the discussion of ethical issues of an important and indeed fundamental character as to the proper role of private law. We all, back in those days, particularly enjoyed being introduced to that engaging conception, disinterested malevolence, and would while away our time trying to think of especially unpleasant examples. More recently, in 1994, when I was asked to deliver a lecture for the Selden Society, I decided to spend a short time looking into both the background to the case and the practical consequences of the legal decision of the House of Lords, which appeared to provide a licence to Edward Pickles to hold the inhabitants of Bradford to ransom unless they were willing to see their city become no more than a howling wilderness. Unknown to me at this time, the case had already attracted the interest of Michael Taggart. His researches now present a far more sophisticated study, both of its historical context, and of its legal and social significance, than the short account I provided in the lecture.

The case, to be understood, has to be related to the legal and political history of the Bradford water supply, a local example of the history of the municipalization of utilities in Victorian England, to the general history of water law, in particular the law relating to ground water, as well as to the idiosyncrasies of those directly involved in the long-running dispute—the archetypal Yorkshireman, Edward Pickles (who surely wore a flat hat), and his aggrieved father, Holmes Pickles; his lawyers, in particular his solicitors, George Burr and John Craven, to the Town Clerk of Bradford, William McGowen, and the Bradford Water Engineer, James Watson; and, when the dispute came to litigation, the counsel and judges involved, who included such notable figures as Lords Halsbury and Macnaghten. The second-century Roman jurist, Marcellus, also puts in a ghostly appearance. The analysis of the case involves relating it to the techniques of statutory interpretation adopted by Victorian courts, to disputes as to the role which malice, whatever that really means, should play in tort law, to the possibility of adopting into the common law a doctrine of abuse of rights, to the interrelationship between private and public law, to the proper limits to the despotic dominion of the property owner, and to the legitimacy of greed in a capitalist market based legal system. All these and indeed other issues are discussed by Michael Taggart in a manner which displays both his own fascination with his subject, and his skill in contextual legal history. He brings out, with particular clarity, the fact that the doctrine associated with the case is a product of time and place, and not the expression of some timeless verity. His book is indeed not simply a study of a particular case, but a contribution to general legal theory. It is a pleasure to welcome this highly readable book into the *Oxford Studies in Modern Legal History*.

A.W. Brian Simpson

Preface

This book could not have been written so far from the locus of events without the assistance of an embarrassingly large number of people and institutions.

The archival research was undertaken in Bradford, Leeds, and London. I acknowledge with gratitude the assistance of the staff at the West Yorkshire Archive Service, Bradford Central Public Library, the University of Bradford Library, Yorkshire Water, Keighley Public Library, Leeds Public Library, and the House of Lords' Records Office. The legal research was undertaken principally in Auckland, with sorties to the Bodleian Law Library in the University of Oxford, the Squire Law Library in the University of Cambridge, the Institute of Advanced Legal Studies in the University of London, the Bora Laskin Law Library in the University of Toronto, and the Law Library in the University of Michigan. Special mention is due to Bernice Cole at the Davis Law Library and Janny Jonkers and the staff at the Main Library at the University of Auckland, all of whom processed efficiently and with good cheer more inter-library loan applications than any of us cares to remember. Others assisted by making available material impossible to access in or from New Zealand: including Anna Adams, John Allison, John Barratt, Martin Dockray, Simon Mount, Roderick Munday, and Patrick Polden.

Mrs Hilda Lawn and her son, Mr Herbert Lawn, of East Many Wells Farm kindly allowed me the run of their farm on two occasions to take photos and measurements, and to spy out the lie of the land. Their warm hospitality to a stranger was much appreciated. David Varley at Yorkshire Water arranged for me to inspect inside the waterworks that remain at Hewenden Reservoir and helped me to locate old waterworks plans. Barry Diggle of Bradford generously gave me original copies of the case on appeal to the House of Lords and of the shorthand transcript of the argument before the Court of Appeal. Bradford Art Galleries & Museums kindly gave permission for the reproduction here of the portraits of Messrs McGowen and Burr. Julia Lister, Honorary Secretary to the Keighley and Craven Law Society, helped me trace the law firm of Burr Sugden in Keighley, and John Eteson of that firm searched his firm's archives (alas in vain) on my behalf.

Research funds from the University of Auckland Research Committee and the Faculty of Law were essential to the undertaking and completion of this work. I thank the University of Auckland and Auckland Law School for that financial assistance, and more generally for the support given to me over 25 years. The Centre for Public Law in the University of Cambridge kindly extended invitations to participate in two conferences in 1998 and 1999, which assisted me greatly in obtaining funding to pursue archival and legal research in England, and awarded me a Maines Visiting Fellowship in 2001 that allowed me to put the finishing touches to the typescript. Jack Beatson, Christopher Forsyth, and Ivan Hare were generous to a fault. Murray Hunt and Gráinne de Búrca put me up during my visits to Oxford; as did David Dyzenhaus, Cheryl Misak, and Alexander and Sophie during my visit to Cambridge in 1999.

My thanks to the New Zealand law firm of Chapman Tripp, whose generosity and altruism support the Chapman Tripp Research Scholarship Programme at Auckland Law School. Under the auspices of that programme I benefited from research assistance by Belinda Bagge, Stephen Penk, Bevan Peachey, and Jan Cumming.

I am not a legal historian by trade or training. However, I have had historical 'tendencies' since school, and these were fostered by two inspiring and learned teachers: Ron Hemus at Mt Albert Grammar School and Nadja Tollemache at Auckland Law School. Both of whom were good enough to read the book in draft.

One of the nice things about writing on a subject like this, which straddles so many areas, is that you connect professionally with colleagues working in different specialities from your own. I would like to thank the following colleagues and friends at Auckland for conversations, for reading draft chapters, and for not displaying (too openly) boredom with 'Pickles' over the last few years: Rick Bigwood, Jock Brookfield, Bernard Brown, Brian Coote, Jim Evans, Bill Hodge, Grant Huscroft, Jo Manning, Janet McLean, Paul Rishworth, Rosemary Tobin, John Turner, and Peter Watts. Several of my public law colleagues at Auckland Law School bore the brunt of my absences, and I thank them. Colleagues and friends elsewhere were also good enough to put down their work to assist in improving mine: John Barratt, David Dyzenhaus, David Johnston, and Stephen Waddams. Three legal historians—Stuart Anderson, Connie Backhouse, and Rande Kostal—read a near-completed draft and made many valuable points for improvement, not all of which I was capable of executing.

I delivered a paper based on work in progress in July 1998 at a conference on 'Property and the Constitution' at Victoria University of Wellington, which Stuart Anderson perceptively commented upon. Variations of the paper were presented at staff seminars at Auckland Law School and the Law School at the University of New South Wales in 1998. My thanks to Janet McLean, Mark Aronson, and to the audiences for comments.

Another paper, drawn from Chapters 5 and 6, was presented at a Legal Theory Workshop held at the University of Toronto in January 2001 and at the Centre for Public Law at the University of Cambridge in July 2001. Thanks once again to the audiences for comments.

I would be remiss if I did not single out for special mention A. W. B. (Brian) Simpson. After I had decided to explore the background to the *Pickles* litigation and arranged the first research trip to England, I stumbled by chance on his terrific Selden Society lecture entitled *Victorian Law and the Industrial Spirit*, the first half of which treats the *Pickles* litigation. I was mortified, and nearly abandoned the project there and then. He, however, has encouraged me from that time onwards by sharing his views, and reading and commenting upon drafts. Such is Brian Simpson's reputation that when I have told lawyers what I am working on, the typical response has been 'Oh, you are doing a Simpson'. I wish I could do it as well.

It has been a pleasure to work with John Louth, Danielle Moon, and Geraldine Mangley at OUP, and I thank them for their kindnesses and efficiency.

This book is dedicated to my wife and our children. They have put up with my absences—sometimes physical, but more often of mind—with just the right measures of loving support and annoyance. They will be pleased to see the back of Edward Pickles.

This book has been enjoyable to research and write. I hope it is interesting to read. Feedback is most welcome: c/o Faculty of Law, The University of Auckland, Private Bag 92019, Auckland, New Zealand; e-mail <mb.taggart@auckland.ac.nz>.

Michael Taggart
Auckland, New Zealand
April 2002

Contents

Glossary

B.C.L.	Bradford Central Library, Prince's Way, Bradford BD1 1NN
H.L.R.O.	House of Lords' Record Office, Westminster, London SW1A 0PW
W.Y.A.S.	West Yorkshire Archives Service, 15 Canal Road, Bradford BD1 4AT

Research Note

Almost all of the unpublished material referred to and quoted in this book is held in either the West Yorkshire Archives Service (W.Y.A.S.) or the House of Lords' Record Office (H.L.R.O.). I decided not to burden the footnotes with pinpoint references to box numbers, etc., but instead to refer here to what is held where.

The W.Y.A.S. is at 15 Canal Road, Bradford BD1 4AT, <http://www.archives.wyjs.org.uk>. Most of the correspondence, committee minutes and notes, and notices are held here. The following box references are the most useful:

BBD/1/1/68–72 (papers re *Bradford Corporation v Pickles*, containing affidavits, correspondence between the Corporation and Pickles' solicitor, the Corporation's correspondence with Counsel, etc.)
BBD 1/1/158–162 and 1/1/338–339 (Bradford Waterworks Bill 1852–54; including notices to affected properties, maps, reference books, minutes of evidence on the Bill)
BBD 1/1/640–642 (Bradford Corporation Waterworks Bill 1853–54)
BBD 1/9/3–4 and 1/9/12–16 (Water Committee minutes)
BBD 10/4/39 and 10/4/46–67 (Waterworks Engineer's correspondence)
BBC 4/4/1–14 (Waterworks Committee notes)

The material relating to the litigation is to some extent duplicated in the House of Lords' Record Office at Westminster, London SW1A OPW, <hlro@parliament.uk>. The H.L.R.O. material is in Appeal Cases 1895, Vol. 440, and contains maps, a transcript of argument in the Court of Appeal, affidavits, and appended correspondence. There is also material from the House of Commons Committee's consideration of the Bradford Waterworks Bill on 12 May 1841 (including evidence, petitions in opposition, and attendance details) and of the Bradford Waterworks Bills of 1853 and 1854 (including deposited plans, reference books, and evidence).

Notes to Illustrations

1. (Page 9) A map drawn from the original coloured map of the proposed Bradford Waterworks at Hewenden Beck, drawn in 1840 by George Leather & Son. This map shows the valley, the Spring, and the Hewenden Beck as it was before the waterworks and compensation reservoir were built between 1842 and 1846. This drawing omits all of the lines indicating where the proposed waterworks would be. The original map is appended to Document No. 50 in the *Case on Appeal*, an admitted document. The map was drawn by Ms Susan Hogg, Graphic Designer at the Educational Media Centre in the University of Auckland.

2. (Page 10) A map drawn from the original coloured map of the lands of Edward Pickles and Bradford Corporation drawn by the Bradford Corporation Waterworks Engineer's Office. This drawing omits all of the lines indicating lots of land, fault lines, and other incidental information that obscures the essential features of the landscape. As far as possible the presentation of the map is otherwise in keeping with the original. The original is appended to Document No. 55 in the *Case on Appeal*, an Exhibit to one of the Appellant's affidavits. The map was drawn from the original by Ms Susan Hogg, Graphic Designer at the Educational Media Centre in the University of Auckland.

3. (Page 31) A watercolour of Mr W. T. McGowen, Town Clerk of Bradford, by John Sowden. Reproduced by courtesy of Bradford Art Galleries & Museums.

4. (Page 34) An oil painting of Mr W. G. Burr, Keighley, by Mr J. Bacon. Mr Burr was the senior partner in W. G. Burr & Co., the law firm in Keighley that represented Edward Pickles. Reproduced by courtesy of Bradford Art Galleries & Museums.

5. (Page 37) A photograph of what is left of the waterworks at Hewenden Reservoir on what was formerly Trooper's Farm. In the right of the foreground is a locked metal trap door, and beyond that is the original stone entrance way to Many Wells Spring. In the background, less than 20 yards uphill from the stone entrance way, is the stone wall separating Trooper's Farm from East Many Wells Farm. Take note of the tree on the Trooper's Farm side of the fence and the semi-circle of lighter-coloured stone in the fence to the right of that tree. This provides a point of reference for understanding illustrations 7 and

8 below. The lighter rock is a recent repair to the wall (circa 1999), which had crumbled at that point.

6. (Page 38) A photograph taken from the Trooper's Farm side of the stone wall (shown in illustration 5) looking down on to the top of the stone masonry entrance way, and the concrete and metal trap-door, with Hewenden Reservoir in the background.

7. (Page 39) A photograph taken from East Many Wells Farm with the boundary stone wall on the left. The tree and lighter-colour stone repair work are visible, and are immediately above the Spring (see illustration 5). A tape measure is draped over the wall at that point and lies across the middle of the picture before tapering off in the bottom righthand corner. This tape measures the distance from the boundary to shaft No. 2. The mound in the middle of the picture was artificially made from the tailings from digging the shaft. The large hole in the ground (now covered with undergrowth) is visible on the right-hand side of the picture. The Shaft itself has been covered over and is just to the right of the picture, a little way down the slope. Shaft No. 1 is not visible from the picture but it is 150–200 yards away, heading up the hill to the extreme right of the picture.

8. (Page 40) A photograph taken from the edge of Hewenden Reservoir looking up towards Many Wells Spring and East Many Wells Farm. The tree on the Trooper's Farm side of the stone boundary fence in the middle of the picture, is the one shown in illustration 5. The lighter-coloured stone work in the fence is also visible. The stone masonry around the Spring immediately below is obscured by trees. To the right of the Spring is the original Trooper's Farm cottage and associated buildings.

Table of Cases

Table of Principal Legislation

Prologue

This book tells the story of a water dispute in Bradford, England, in the late nineteenth century. The dispute was finally resolved by the House of Lords in 1895, and the case—*The Mayor, Aldermen and Burgesses of the Borough of Bradford v Pickles* [1895] AC 587—has become a 'leading' one. It is important in legal terms for establishing that it is not unlawful for a property owner to exercise his or her property rights maliciously and to the detriment of others or the public interest. This is accepted by many as a bedrock principle of the common law, and, like bedrock, is often invisible and taken for granted. Both the dispute and its doctrinal significance are explored here.

This introduction is intended to ease the passage of the reader by giving a synopsis of the dispute and providing a guide as to what is treated in each chapter.

Edward Pickles owned land adjoining a spring (Many Wells Spring) that the Corporation of Bradford had used for nearly 40 years to supply water to the town of Bradford seven miles away. The water from the Spring came from underneath Pickles's farm. In the early 1890s, Edward Pickles announced a plan to drain the water in an attempt to mine for flagstone on his land. He had an elaborate plan of shafts and a long tunnel to get rid of the water, with the inevitable consequence that the water would be lost to the Corporation's waterworks.

The plan gave the appearance of a contrivance to force the Corporation to pay a premium for Pickles's land or a water right over it. The Corporation of Bradford took the view that Pickles was acting maliciously. Pickles claimed the right to do whatever he pleased with the water under his land, and if the Corporation wanted him to refrain from draining it away, it would have to compensate him handsomely. The Corporation, in the apparent belief that Pickles's actions were barred by statute or were otherwise unlawful, refused to negotiate with him. Both sides dug in their heels and refused to budge. When Pickles's digging finally fatally threatened the water supply, the Corporation went to court seeking injunctive relief to stop him digging on his own land.

The case went all the way to the House of Lords. Pickles won the legal battle but lost the war. He succeeded in disrupting the water supply (although, it turns out, only temporarily), but the Corporation steadfastly refused to buy his land or his water. A few years later Edward Pickles sold the farm (the Corporation having refused to buy it), and he and his family emigrated to North America and disappeared without trace.

Chapter 1 introduces the nineteenth-century town of Bradford and its water problems. Bradford was the fastest-growing city in Britain (and possibly the world) by the middle of the nineteenth century. It was a product of the Industrial Revolution, and its growing industries and population placed enormous strain on the existing water supply. After considerable difficulties, the Bradford Waterworks Company became incorporated by private Act of Parliament in 1842. The Company was reliant upon water from Many Wells Spring to supply the town. After an expensive tussle between that Company and the Corporation of Bradford in the early 1850s, the Corporation took over the Waterworks Company.

As noted above, the water from Many Wells Spring flowed underneath neighbouring East Many Wells Farm, owned by the Pickles family. However, the Pickles family was never paid a penny for the use of that water, which first the Bradford Waterworks Company (1846–54) and then the Corporation of Bradford (1854 onwards) piped to Bradford. Miffed by this, two generations of Pickles (father and son) attempted by different means and at different times (in 1865 and again in the early 1890s) to extract payment from the Corporation of Bradford for use of the water. The story is told in Chapter 2.

On the second attempt by Edward Pickles to gain recompense, the Corporation resisted. The dispute, which had been simmering since May 1890, boiled over into litigation two years later. Chapter 3 chronicles the case's journey up the English court hierarchy, from the Chancery Division, to the Court of Appeal, and, ultimately, to the House of Lords.

The Corporation succeeded in obtaining injunctive relief at first instance based on an interpretation of the Bradford Waterworks Act 1854. The trial judge held also that Pickles's works were contrived and actuated by malice, but concluded that there was no authority to restrain a landowner from exercising his or her property rights in bad faith. On appeal, the Court of Appeal upheld the trial judge's finding in law on the malice point but reversed his decision on the statutory interpretation point. It held that there was nothing wrong with securing a benefit by virtue of an advantageous geographical position. Purporting to follow earlier House of Lords' authority, the Court of Appeal held that Pickles could remove percolating underground water, even for selfish or vexatious purposes. The House of Lords upheld the Court of Appeal's decision, holding that the Corporation had no right to receive percolating but unchannelled underground water from a neighbour. Pickles was therefore acting within his rights. However, by the mid-1890s Bradford no longer needed the water from Many Wells Spring, and Pickles never convinced the Corporation to buy his land or to pay for his water.

There is no ideal order in which to treat the interrelated but separate aspects of the case discussed in Chapters 4–7. Each aspect depends to some extent on some knowledge of the other topics treated in other chapters. Hence some repetition is unavoidable. For the convenience of those who will dip into this book rather than read the chapters sequentially, as far as possible these chapters have been written as stand-alone treatments of the topic.

The Corporation of Bradford took its stand against Edward Pickles on a statutory provision that dated back to 1842. Part of the case's enduring influence lies in its illustration of the nineteenth-century judges' solicitude towards private property. *Pickles* illustrates the potency of the common law principle that whenever possible (and perhaps even when it is not possible) statutes will be interpreted by the courts to protect the property interests of individuals. Chapter 4 places the key provision (section 49) in the context of the Bradford Waterworks legislation as a whole and the common law approach to statutory interpretation.

Chapter 5 deals with the dry subject of water law. It examines the legal uncertainty surrounding subterranean water rights in the first half of the nineteenth century. When much of that uncertainty was removed by a House of Lords decision in 1859, that in turn caused problems in interpreting a statutory provision drafted much earlier against a then uncertain legal backdrop. This chapter attempts to explain why the courts ultimately declared use rights in underground percolating water to be absolute, and addresses some of the implications of that absolutism.

Famously, the House of Lords in *Pickles* refused to qualify that absolutism with an exception for malice. The judges ignored or dismissed earlier dicta supporting such a limitation in English, American, and Scottish cases, as well as in Roman law. In Continental Europe these Roman law seeds have flowered into a doctrine of abuse of rights, that first took hold in France in the nineteenth century and has since spread like wildfire throughout the civil law. This doctrine provides a means of circumscribing absolute rights in the interests of justice. In French cases, not dissimilar to *Pickles*, it has been held that the landowner had abused his rights and has been held liable in damages. The House of Lords turned its back on any such doctrine in *Pickles*. Chapter 6 attempts to explain why.

The place of malice in the law of torts is the subject of Chapter 7. This was a contested issue in the later part of the nineteenth century in both Great Britain and the United States of America. The vehicle for exploring this issue is the writings of Sir Frederick Pollock in England and Oliver Wendell Holmes Jr in the United States; both of whom doubted the view that malice was always irrelevant to civil liability. Before *Pickles* was decided, Pollock regarded it as an open question in English law. However, he accepted that *Pickles* decisively shut the door on the possibility of having a malice exception in English property law. This was not the case in the United States, where the courts followed the lead of Holmes and developed a prima facie tort capable of attacking malicious exercise of power. This chapter also traces the early cases that could have supported such a cause of action in English law, but which the late Victorian judges shied away from.

In the Epilogue the relevance of *Pickles* to the modern distinction between private and public law is sketched.

1

Bradford and its Water Supply

Bradford and the Water Supply

The broad pattern of water supply in Great Britain up to the end of the nineteenth century falls into three periods.[1] Up to the eighteenth century, natural sources of water—rivers, ponds, springs, and wells—provided a generally adequate supply, which was safeguarded by the community. The development of larger urban centres in the eighteenth century put greater demands on these traditional sources of water. Inadequate supply and pollution became major problems, and most local authorities were unable or unwilling to make the investments necessary to increase supply. So from the late eighteenth century through to about 1870, this prime necessity of life came increasingly to be provided by private enterprise. For a variety of reasons the private provision of water in turn was found wanting, and the final phase of the development was the resumption of collective responsibility for water supply. This so-called 'municipalization' of water supply—describing the purchase of these private water companies by local authorities—began in earnest around mid-century and escalated as the century progressed.[2] The experience of water supply in Bradford conforms to this pattern.

At the end of the eighteenth century Bradford was little more than a village, with a population of approximately 6,000 residents.[3] The residents

[1] There is a reasonably large literature on water supplies in various towns and areas in nineteenth-century Great Britain. The summary and periodization in this paragraph is drawn from J. A. Hassan, 'The Growth and Impact of the British Water Industry in the Nineteenth Century' (1985) 38 *Economic History Review*, 2d ser. 531, and J. A. Hassan, 'The impact and development of the water supply in Manchester, 1568–1882' (1983–84) 133 *Transactions of the Historic Society of Lancashire & Cheshire* 25. See also W. M. Stern, 'Water Supply in Britain: The Development of a Public Service' (1954) 74 *Journal of the Royal Sanitary Institute* 998, 999, and J. Sheldrake, 'The Water Industry: A Brief Review of its Development and Prospects' (1985) 17 *London Rev. of Pub. Admin.* 8. As a broad generalization it rings true with most of the local historical treatments of water supplies I have read. London, as one might expect, is a rather large exception. See generally A. K. Mukhopadhyay, *Politics of Water Supply: The Case of Victorian London* (The World Press Private Ltd, Calcutta, 1981) and B. Rudden, *The New River: A Legal History* (Clarendon Press, Oxford, 1985).

[2] On 'municipalization', see below and Chapter 4.

[3] The population figures vary considerably. Many writers use the figure of 13,264 from the 1801 Census, but this includes the townships of Bowling, Bradford, Horton, and Manningham. The figure for the town of Bradford is 6,393. See J. Fawcett, 'The Rise and Progress of the Town and Borough of Bradford', in A. Holroyd (ed.), *Collectanea Bradfordiana:*

drew their water from pumps or wells,[4] or gained supply from a small reservoir west of the town at Westgate. The population increased exponentially in the first half of the nineteenth century, principally to service the booming worsted industry.[5] By mid-century Bradford was the ninth largest city in England and the fastest-growing city in the British Isles, and possibly in the world.[6] Bradford was very much a product of the Industrial Revolution,[7] exhibiting the best and worst features of that phenomenal period of economic growth and social change. Throughout this period the city faced problems of water supply, sanitation, and maintenance of law and order.

Scarcity of pure water dogged Bradford from its very beginnings as an industrial centre. For almost the entire nineteenth century, demand for water outstripped supply.[8] In common with other industrial centres, an abundant supply of pure water for both domestic and industrial use was vitally important for the continued growth of Bradford and its industries.[9]

The earliest successful scheme to provide the town of Bradford with water dates from 1744, when a small co-partnership was formed to convey water from a 'sough' or coal drain in Little Horton, by a combination of wooden pipes, trough, and lead pipes, to a small reservoir at

A Collection of Papers on the History of Bradford and the Neighbourhood (Abraham Holroyd, Saltaire, 1873), 120, 122.

4 J. Fieldhouse, *Bradford* (Longman Group Ltd, London, 1972), 78–9.

5 See generally G. Firth, *Bradford and the Industrial Revolution: An economic history 1760–1840* (Ryburn Publishing, Halifax, 1990), ch. 6. A considerable amount has been written on the history and development of the worsted industry in the West Riding of Yorkshire. A good introductory treatment can be found in E. M. Sigsworth, *Black Dyke Mills: A History* (University of Liverpool, Liverpool, 1958), chs 1–3. Worsted is one of two methods by which wool could be made into cloth, and denotes that the wool is combed before it is spun: M. C. D. Law, *The Story of Bradford* (Sir Isaac Pitman & Sons, London, 1912), 133.

6 T. Koditschek, 'The dynamics of class formation in nineteenth-century Bradford', in A. L. Beier, D. Cannadine, and J. M. Rosenheim (eds), *The First Modern Society: Essays in English History in Honour of Lawrence Stone* (Cambridge University Press, Cambridge, 1989), 511, 514. See also J. F. C. Harrison, *The Early Victorians 1832–1851* (Weidenfeld & Nicolson, London, 1971), 14, and A. Briggs, *Victorian Cities* (2nd edn 1970; republished by University of California Press, Berkeley, San Francisco, 1993), 140. Cf. J. G. Williamson, *Coping with City Growth During the British Industrial Revolution* (Cambridge University Press, Cambridge, 1990), 2–5.

7 A. Elliott, 'The Incorporation of Bradford' (1979) 15 *Northern History* 156.

8 Fieldhouse, above at note 4, 136; C. Richardson, *A Geography of Bradford* (University of Bradford, Bradford, 1976), 116; *The Centenary Book of Bradford* (William Byles & Sons, Bradford, 1947), 21.

9 For some industrial purposes, especially for the washing and dyeing or bleaching of wool, a soft water is essential. See Hassan, above at note 1, 36–7; J. Tann, 'The Bleaching of Woollen and Worsted Goods 1740–1860' (1968–70) 1 *Textile History* 158; T. Addy and G. F. Renton, 'Bradford Corporation Waterworks 1855–1955: A Review' (1956) 38 *Journal of the Association of British Waterworks* 302, 314–15; C. Gott, 'On the Bradford Waterworks', in *Report of the British Association for the Advancement of Science* (1873), 451, 458 (held in B.C.L.).

Westgate, west of the Township.[10] This was done without the need for statutory authority, as the company contracted for the supply of water and made satisfactory arrangements for the laying and maintenance of pipes with local landowners.[11] Despite some strong local opposition, in 1790 the then shareholders gained incorporation by Act of Parliament as 'The Company of Proprietors of Bradford Waterworks' with a view to borrowing money to improve the works.[12] However, the supply of water, which had always been 'scanty', was little improved.[13]

By the 1830s water shortages were notorious, and the subject of much public dissatisfaction. The population of Bradford had grown to around 50,000 by 1837 and the Company of Proprietors could supply the water needs of only a minority of that number,[14] the rest obtaining water from wells, springs, or increasingly from private water carts.[15] It took a drought, the resulting dust bowl conditions, and a campaign by the editor of *The Bradford Observer* finally to stir the local bourgeoisie to action.[16] A series of public meetings followed and a committee was set up to investigate future water supply for the town. This committee considered several

[10] W. Cudworth, 'The First Bradford Waterworks' (1905) 4 *Bradford Antiquary* 353.

[11] Ibid., 353–4.

[12] 30 Geo. III, ch. lxiii. Preamble.

[13] Cudworth, above at note 10, 354 and 357; A. Elliott, 'Municipal government in Bradford in the mid-nineteenth century', in D. Fraser (ed.), *Municipal reform and the industrial city* (Leicester University Press, Leicester, 1982), 112, 119; G. F. Renton, 'Water Supply of Bradford', undated and unpublished typescript, deposited in the B.C.L. Mr G. F. Renton was the Water Engineer in Bradford in the 1950s, and co-wrote two published historical accounts of the Bradford water supply. This typescript is more extensive than the published accounts and may be his typed research notes.

[14] Needless to say, only the better off sections of society were served, and even they had cause for complaint. It is said that the few fortunate customers still received water for only 30 minutes on three days a week, and even then were at the mercy of an old woman who pleased herself when she turned the water on and off! See Elliott, above at note 7, 159, and above at note 13, 119. The problem of intermittent, poor quality service to a well-off minority was common to much of England: J. Hassan, *A history of water in modern England and Wales* (Manchester University Press, Manchester, 1998), 17.

[15] See W. H. Leatham, J. Ruscoe, and G. F. Renton, *Bradford Corporation Waterworks Department: 1855–1955 Centenary* (Bradford, 1955), 11, and R. (Bob) West, 'Worstedopolis and the Water Works: Bradford Water Works Company 1837–1855' (unpublished B.A. dissertation, University of Bradford, 1980), 4; copy deposited in the B.C.L. (hereafter referred to as West, *Worstedopolis*). The cost of water was yet another burden shouldered by the poorer sections of the community—those least well served by the water supply company. At the time of the Health of Towns' Commissioner's visit to Bradford in 1844, the cost of water from a carrier was a halfpenny for three gallons, which the Commissioner considered 'most expensive. . . and forces an economy. . . [which is] . . . highly injurious to health, cleanliness, and comfort': quoted in B. Thompson, 'Infant mortality in nineteenth-century Bradford', in R. Woods and J. Woodward (eds), *Urban Disease and Mortality in Nineteenth-Century England* (St Martin's Press, New York, 1984), 120, 123.

[16] West, *Worstedopolis*, 5–7. On the crusading zeal of the Liberal *Bradford Observer* and its editor, see D. James, 'William Byles and the *Bradford Observer*', in D. G. Wright and J. A. Jowitt (eds), *Victorian Bradford: Essays in Honour of Jack Reynolds* (City of Bradford Metropolitan Council, Bradford, 1981), 115.

proposals, but eventually settled on a grandiose scheme envisaging 12 reservoirs to the west of Bradford. A new Bradford Water Company was provisionally formed in 1838 with a capital of £40,000 to promote the scheme. This involved seeking incorporation by Act of Parliament and the necessary statutory powers to build the water works.[17] However, the initial application to Parliament for a Bill failed in 1838 on a technicality.[18]

Many Wells Spring

Amid this costly Parliamentary fiasco, J. Wignall Leather, an engineer from Leeds, was engaged to survey the quantity and quality of available water. It was his identification of Many Wells Spring[19] as a copious source of supply that led the Company to abandon its grander plans and to concentrate on this single source.[20] A local antiquary gave this description of Many Wells Spring in 1876:[21]

> [T]he famous Manywells Spring . . . issues from the side of a steep hill in Trooper or Manywells farm. . . . This spring is one of the most extraordinary in the kingdom, its volume, unceasingly poured forth, having been computed at above half a million gallons a day. The quality of the water is well known—it is as cold as ice and as clear as crystal. This priceless spring has been found to issue from a fissure in the rock a short distance from the surface whence it literally belches forth into a massive rock basin and flows to Bradford seven miles away . . .—almost the only

[17] Addy and Renton, above at note 9, 302.

[18] That application seems to have been tainted by vehement opposition by landed gentry and mill-owners to the Directors' new scheme to supply all industrial users, as well as the originally envisaged domestic supply. In light of the strength of the opposition this scheme was soon abandoned, and the Directors reverted to the more modest and original scheme for domestic supply. But this came too late to ensure plain Parliamentary sailing for the Bill. For details of the expanded aspirations of the Directors and the fierce opposition, see West, *Worstedopolis*, 14–18. For a good discussion of the often conflicting interests of industrialists and urban water supply companies in this period, see J. Hassan and P. Taylor, ' The Politics of Water in Early and Mid-Victorian England: The Experience of Bolton' (1998) 148 *Transactions of the Historic Society of Lancashire and Cheshire* 119.

[19] The Spring was also known locally as Seth Springs (after the previous owner, Seth Wright), and earlier still as Manuels or Emanuels. I have used Spring rather than Springs throughout, except in quotations. I have also followed the preferred nineteenth-century spelling of 'Many Wells' as two words; whereas the modern convention, followed in the town of Cullingworth, is to run the two words together into one.

[20] West, *Worstedopolis*, 19.

[21] W. Cudworth, *Round About Bradford: A Series of Sketches (Descriptive and Semi-Historical) of Forty-Two Places Within Six Miles of Bradford* (1876; reprinted by Mountain Press, Queensbury, 1968), 225–6. In 1900 the then Bradford Waterworks Engineer estimated that between 1846 and 1895 the Many Wells Spring supplied Bradford with a daily average of nearly 300,000 gallons of water. See J. Watson, *Water Supply, with a description of the Bradford Waterworks (Old and New)* (Peter Lund, Humphries & Co., Bradford, 1900), 15–16 (being a printed lecture delivered to the British Academy for the Advancement of Science, at its Bradford meeting in September 1900).

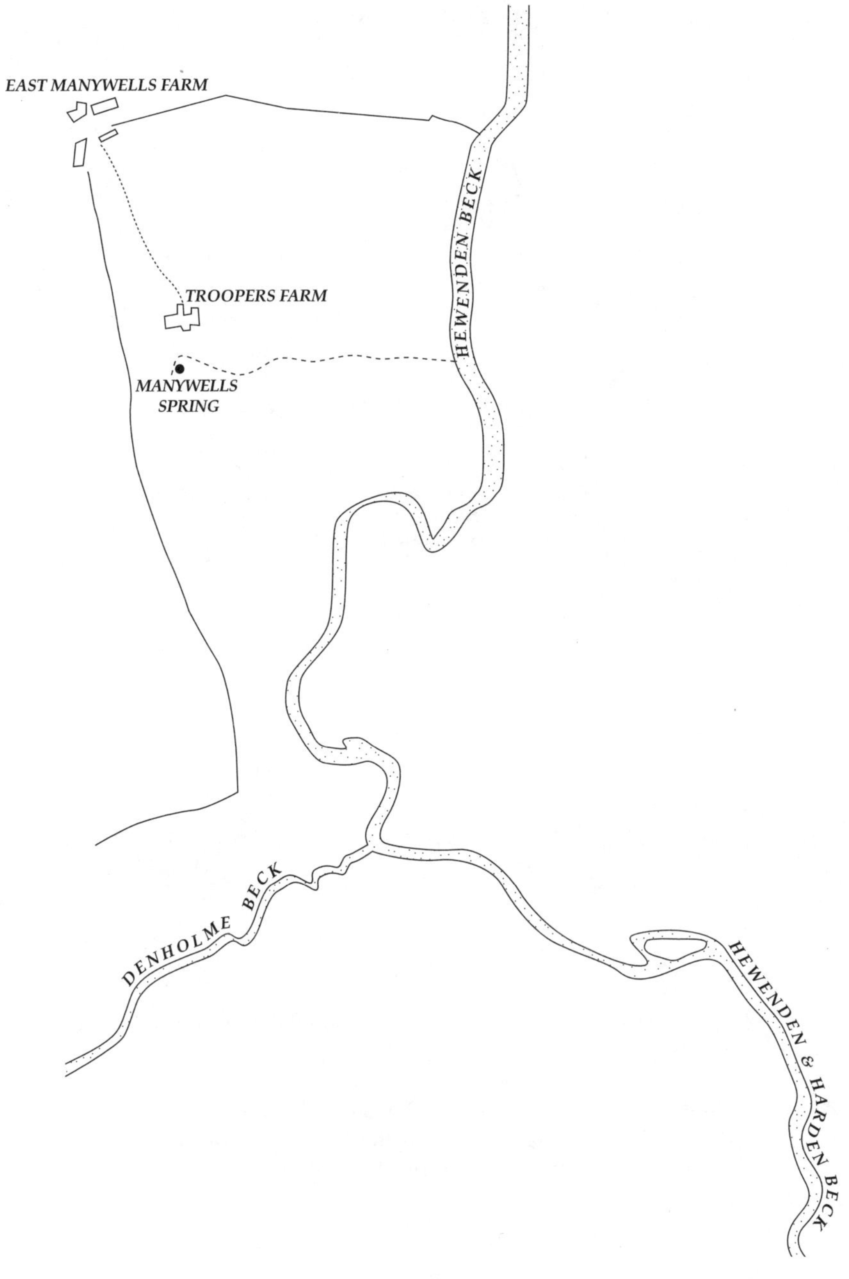

Figure 1. Many Wells Spring and Hewenden Beck in 1840 (see Note on p. xvii).

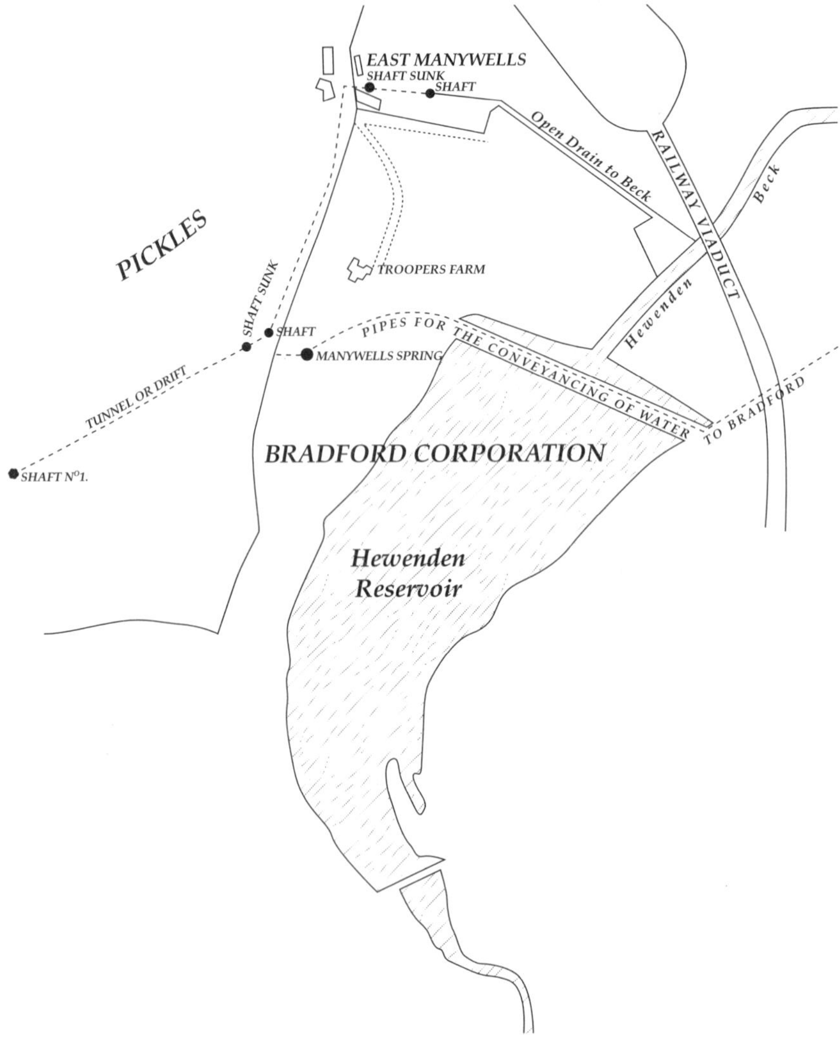

Figure 2. A map of Many Wells Spring and Hewenden Reservoir indicating the line of the tunnelling (see Note on p. xvii).

source of supply. . . . What an inexhaustible store this must have seemed to the Bradfordians of 1850, in comparison with the 15,000 gallons stored in the little reservoir . . . in Westgate, previous to the establishment of the Bradford Water Company in 1842.

When Wignall Leather's reconnaissance of potential water supplies persuaded the Company that Many Wells Spring was the best source of clean water to supply Bradford, his firm—George Leather & Co—was instructed to complete the Parliamentary plans for the project.[22] The Company signed a memorandum for purchase with the owner of Trooper's Farm on 11 January 1838. The cost of the farm (including the Spring) was £2,000.[23]

At this point something more must be said about the position of the Many Wells Spring. The Spring came to the surface on the side of a hill on Trooper's Farm, and spilled down the hillside a couple of hundred yards to the valley floor, augmenting a stream called Hewenden Beck.[24] From there the Beck flowed downstream and from time immemorial had supported water-powered mills.[25] One of the earliest worsted mills in the Bradford area was built on Hewenden Beck in 1792,[26] and by the 1830s the Beck downstream of Many Wells Spring supported several manufacturing mills.[27] The mill-owners were rightly concerned that the Company's plan to pipe water from the Spring to Bradford would adversely affect the flow of water to their mills. To appease the mill-owners and dissuade them from objecting before the Parliamentary Select Committee, the Company proposed to construct a compensation reservoir.[28] This reservoir on Trooper's Farm (just below Many Wells Spring) was to be used exclusively by the downstream mill-owners, who would regulate the flow of water down Hewenden Beck in accordance with an agreed schedule. The reservoir was estimated to cost £6,500 to construct and, when completed in 1845, covered an area of 16 acres and contained,

[22] Despite considerable ability, Leather's career nevertheless was dogged by controversy, not least because his reservoirs often leaked. Several of his Bradford reservoirs gave trouble in that regard, including Hewenden Reservoir. See 'John Wignall Leather (1810–87) and the Bradford Waterworks', in G. M. Binnie, *Early Victorian Water Engineers* (Thomas Telford Ltd, London, 1981), ch. 7, and West, *Worstedopolis*, 48. (For further details, see Appendix, note 1.)

[23] Somewhat surprisingly, the agreement does not appear to have been made conditional upon receiving statutory powers to commence the project. Nevertheless, the completed conveyance was not signed until 19 January 1843, by which time the Bill was enacted. This delay is said to have arisen 'from protracted legal considerations which had to be given to making a correct Title for the property': Renton, above at note 13, 50.

[24] This estimate is based on an undated surveyor's map of the area made prior to construction of the reservoir.

[25] There is evidence of a water-powered corn-mill there as early as 1290. See R. H. Fawcett, 'The Story of Wilsden' (1976) 11 *Bradford Antiquary* 131, 147 (Part II of a three part article).

[26] See the list of Yorkshire Worsted Mills in the second appendix to D. Jenkins, 'Early factory development in the West Riding of Yorkshire, 1770–1800', in N. B. Harte and K. G. Ponting (eds), *Textile History and Economic History: Essays in Honour of Miss Julia de Lacy Mann* (Manchester University Press, Manchester, 1973), 247, 280.

[27] Fawcett, above at note 25, 187, 189–94 (Part III).

[28] The provision of 'compensation water' was a commonplace statutory requirement in the nineteenth century when large water supply schemes threatened to interfere with the riparian rights of downstream users. See K. Smith, *Water in Britain: A Study in Applied Hydrology and Resource Geography* (Macmillan Press, London, 1972), 26–7.

when full, 62 million gallons of water held behind a 230-yard-wide and 16-yard-high earthwork embankment.[29]

East Many Wells Farm

Where did the water feeding this prodigious Spring come from? Less than 19 yards on the up-hill side of the Spring is the boundary stone wall separating Trooper's Farm from its neighbour, East Many Wells Farm. Obviously that farm derived its name from its proximity and bearing to the Spring.[30] The Pickles family had owned East Many Wells Farm since the late eighteenth century.[31] The water feeding this Spring gathered under the Pickles' farm land and was stopped from escaping by coal and rock seams on either side and an impervious substratum. It was like a water bowl under the hillside from which the water ran toward and out the Spring. The extremely close proximity of the Spring to the boundary, and the Spring's position on the hillside, could leave no one in any doubt as to where the Spring water came from: it came from under East Many Wells Farm.[32]

The Company planned to pipe water from Many Wells Spring to the Town of Bradford, some seven miles away. In accordance with Parliamentary Standing Orders at that time, a plan describing the line of the works was prepared and a so-called 'Book of Reference' was compiled, containing a list of all the owners, lessees, and occupiers of 'such Lands' as the works went through.[33] The referent for this book was the plan, which numbered every plot of land in every Township touched

[29] Leatham, Ruscoe, and Renton, above at note 15, 42. The reservoir was not actually completed until late 1845.

[30] No matter that by almost every map I have consulted the farm is shown to the west of Many Wells Spring!

[31] Affidavit of George Burr, No. 34 of the Respondent's Documents in the Case on Appeal to the House of Lords, para. 3 (hereafter referred to as *Case on Appeal*). Ownership of the farm has been traced back to Elizabethan times: Renton, above at note 13, 50.

[32] The extent of the Pickles' landholding in the early part of the nineteenth century is unclear. It was likely closer to 300 acres than 200. The first Edward Pickles is reported to have bought adjoining land when it came available: Cudworth, above at note 21, 247. This landholding accounted for much of the water catchment but not all. The estimated catchment area for Many Wells Spring was 530 acres: Gott, above at note 9, 453.

[33] This was a considerable, and costly, undertaking. Respect for property rights demanded exactitude. 'In order to establish the extent of [this expropriation] . . . beyond any possibility of confusion, it was essential for the engineer in charge of each project to define precisely the line of the proposed route and the amount of land on either side which it would be necessary to acquire': R. A. Buchanan, 'Engineers and government in nineteenth-century Britain', in R. MacLead (ed.), *Government and Enterprise: Specialists, administrators and professionals, 1860–1919* (Cambridge University Press, Cambridge, 1988), 41, 44.

by the works. In this way the plan was available for public inspection and examination by Parliamentary Committee.[34]

Notice of the proposed works and of the proposed Act had to be served on all owners of lands touched by the works. The printed notice (with handwritten additions) described the proposal and the effect it would have on the particular plot of land, and gave the owner etc., the opportunity to assent, object, or remain 'neuter'. The response of each owner was recorded in a book of assents/dissents. This book was filed as evidence in the hearing before the Parliamentary Select Committees, which heard argument in support of and against the passage of the Bill or certain of its provisions. Anyone who objected had the opportunity, at least in theory, to pursue the objection before the Private Bill Committees of the Houses of Parliament. The expense of so doing was enormous, however, and beyond the means of even most well-off landowners.[35] Nevertheless, many provisions of the Parliamentary Standing Orders were 'designed to protect the rights (or usually the property rights) of those who would be affected by a bill, or the interest of users of proposed services'.[36]

In 1842 the legal owner of East Many Wells Farm was (the second) Edward Pickles.[37] His name does not appear in the Book of Reference or in the book of assents/dissents as a person served with notice of the waterworks, neither is his farm indicated in any way, let alone numbered or described, on the plan of the proposed works.[38] The plan, which is held in the House of Lords' Record Office in Westminster, shows a boundary line to the left of the depicted Trooper farmhouse and Spring. Beyond that

[34] Furthermore, the Bradford Waterworks Act 1842 required this plan and Book of Reference to be deposited at the Office of the Clerk of the Peace of the West Riding of the County of York, where it was to be open for inspection and copying, for a fee (section 219). It was further provided that certified copies of these documents shall be received in all courts as evidence of their contents (section 231).

[35] On the excessive costs of carrying a private Bill through Parliament, see E. L. Pemberton, 'Private Bill Legislation' (1885) 38 *Fortnightly Review* (new ser.) 228, 231–2; A. Pulling, *Private Bill Legislation: Can anything be now done to improve it* (Long, Brown, Green, Longmans, & Roberts, London, 1859); J. Prest, *Liberty and Locality: Parliament, Permissive Legislation, and Ratepayers' Democracies in the Nineteenth Century* (Clarendon Press, Oxford, 1990), 5.

[36] D. L. Rydz, *The Parliamentary Agents: A History* (Royal Historical Society, London, 1979), 5.

[37] The farm was purchased by the first Edward Pickles in the 1790s, and upon his death in 1829 passed to his son and namesake, and in turn passed to the second Edward's only son, Holmes, in 1851. Holmes died intestate in 1874 at the age of 42, leaving his widow (Sarah) and five children—three daughters and two sons, ranging in age from 5 to 19. Edward, then aged 9, was the oldest boy and heir at law.

[38] For completeness, it should be noted that Pickles is a common Yorkshire name, and unsurprisingly there is recorded a John Pickles living close to the Township of Wilsden and a William Pickles Senior living East of Wilsden, whose lands were touched by the works and who were served with notices. Furthermore, the names of John and Eli Pickles appear with others as owners of 'Cottage, Garden and Out buildings' in Schedule H of the Act of 1842. None of these references is to Edward Pickles or his wife Mary, or East Many Wells Farm.

boundary lies East Many Wells Farm, but that is not indicated on the plan. It appears that as the Pickles' land was not taken or physically affected, they were neither notified formally nor given the chance to object.[39]

Bradford Waterworks Act 1842

The Company applied again to Parliament in the 1841–2 session, and this time had bought off or otherwise accommodated most of the potential objectors with the wherewithal to oppose the Bill before the Parliamentary Select Committees.[40] The downstream mill-owners were to be 'compensated' by the promised reservoir on Hewenden Beck (hence the name 'compensation reservoir').[41] The old Company of Proprietors (incorporated in 1790), which in 1838 had attempted to head off the Company's initial proposal by petitioning Parliament for an extension of its own powers while simultaneously objecting to the proposed Bill to incorporate the new Bradford Waterworks Company, withdrew its proposal and opposition in 1839 in return for the new Company's agreement to buy its undertaking for £4,000. The remaining objectors were chiefly wealthy individual landowners, most of whom succeeded in protecting their interests without impeding the enactment of the Bill.

On 22 April 1842 the Bradford Waterworks Act received the Royal Assent.[42] The preamble declared that the inhabitants of the Town of Bradford and its surrounding area were 'very inadequately supplied with Water', and that 'a sufficient and constant Supply of pure and wholesome Water would be of great Advantage to the Inhabitants . . .'. It went on to record that certain individuals had agreed to come together into a company in order to provide that water supply at their own expense, but required

[39] It is likely that the Pickles family would have had locus standi to object before the Parliamentary Select Committees, even without receiving notice. Cf. *Cambridge University and Town Waterworks Bill* (1866) 14 LT Rep N.S. 31 (Court of Referees on Private Bills); *South Staffordshire Waterworks Bill* (1866) 14 LT Rep N.S. 236 (Court of Referees on Private Bills); *Bradford Waterworks Bill* (1869) 20 LT Rep N.S. 459 (Court of Referees on Private Bills).

[40] The records of the House of Commons' Committee on the Bradford Waterworks Bill (dated 12 May 1841) disclose only seven petitions in opposition to the Bill: namely, from the inhabitants of Bingley; Sarah Ferrand and her son, William Busfield Ferrand; John George Smith; Bradford Gas Company (no appearance of counsel); certain mill-owners in the Parish of Bradford (no appearance of counsel); George Thompson Lister (no appearance of counsel). For details of some of these objections, see West, *Worstedopolis*, 24–5. Opposition in this high-stakes legal game could be remarkably successful, as can be seen from the detailed provisions in Bradford Waterworks Act 1842 protecting the position of John George Smith (sections 270–3) and Sarah Ferrand (sections 275–83 and 361).

[41] This form of 'compensation', protecting the riparian rights of downstream mill-owners and other industrialists, was very common and also very generous in terms of the amount of water reserved for such use. See Hassan, above at note 14, 42–3.

[42] 5 and 6 Vict. ch. vi.

legislative authority to incorporate and exercise the necessary powers. The private Act runs to 368 sections, occupying 94 pages of the statute book.

A detailed consideration of the Act of 1842 would be out of place here, and is postponed until Chapter 4. It is necessary, however, to quote the specific provision made for the purchase of Many Wells Spring and to anticipate some of the general conclusions drawn from the later examination of the Act as a whole.

The specific provisions relating to Many Wells Spring are as follows:

CCXXXIII. [section 233] And be it enacted, That, subject to the Restrictions and Provisions in this Act, it shall be lawful for the Company from Time to Time to divert or alter the Course of a certain Beck called *Hewenden Beck* or *Harden Beck*, and also to divert and to take the Water from the several Streams and Springs herein-after mentioned; (that is to say,)

> The Springs and Streams of Water called '*Many Wells*,' arising or flowing in and through a certain Farm, Lands, and Grounds called *Trooper* or *Many Wells Farm*, situated in the Township of *Wilsden* in the Parish of *Bradford* in the West Riding of *Yorkshire*.

CCXXXIV. [section 234] And be it enacted, That after the said *Many Wells* Springs have been purchased by the Company, it shall not be lawful for any Person other than the said Company to divert, alter, or appropriate in any other Manner than by Law they may be legally entitled, any of the Waters now supplying or flowing from the same, or to sink any Well or Pit, or do any Act, Matter, or Thing whereby the Waters of the said Springs may be drawn off or diminished in Quantity; and if any Person shall illegally divert, alter, or appropriate the said Waters, or any Part thereof, or sink any such Well or Pit, or shall do any such Act, Matter, or Thing whereby the said Waters may be drawn off or diminished in Quantity, and shall not, immediately on being required so to do by the said Company, repair the Injury done by him, so as to restore the said Springs and the Waters thereof to the State in which they were before such illegal Act as aforesaid, they shall forfeit to the said Company any Sum not exceeding Five Pounds for every Day during which the said Supply of Water shall be diverted or diminished by reason of any Work done or Act performed by or by the Authority of such Person, in addition to the Damage which the Company may sustain by reason of their Supply of Water being diminished.

As we will see in Chapters 2 and 3, it is this latter provision (section 234) which was at the forefront of the Corporation's case to prevent Holmes Pickles's son, Edward Pickles, from digging shafts and tunnelling on East Many Wells Farm in the early 1890s.

Several provisions in the Act of 1842 underline the importance Parliament placed on the necessity for clear statutory authorization for interference with property rights.[43] For example, Schedule H to the Act

[43] See the extended treatment in Chapter 4.

identifies and briefly describes all the properties (and the owners, lessees, and occupiers thereof) which are to be taken or affected by the proposed waterworks.[44] Except as so provided in Schedule H or with the consent of the owners, section 236 enjoins the Company from taking or injuring 'any Property of the following Kinds': any house or building erected before a specified date in 1840; and any ground enclosed or set aside as a garden, orchard, nursery, yard, paddock, plantation, planted wood, or avenue to a house before that same date.[45] Schedule H makes no mention of Edward Pickles or his wife Mary, or East Many Wells Farm. In order to understand why that is so, it is necessary to recall what was said earlier about the mechanics of the preparation of private Acts of incorporation. The Company planned to pipe water from Many Wells Spring to the Town of Bradford, some seven miles away. It was a prerequisite of Parliamentary approval that a plan describing the line of the works be prepared and a so-called 'Book of Reference' compiled, containing a list of the owners, lessees, and occupiers of 'such Lands' as the works went through. The referent for this book was the plan, which numbered every plot of land in every Township touched by the works. It was from those submitted plans and books that the list of properties and owners in Schedule H was compiled.

The detailed examination of the provisions of the Act of 1842 undertaken in Chapter 4 reveals two matters relevant to this discussion. The first is the Legislature's solicitude about protecting private property as far as it was possible to do so while authorizing the proposed waterworks. This is of a piece with the protections built into the Parliamentary Standing Orders and the process of pre-legislative scrutiny, discussed above. The second is that the Company had ample opportunity to press for compulsory acquisition of East Many Wells Farm at that time, if the Company had wanted to do so. Its failure to press for expropriation of the farm (with compensation, of course) or any water right did not stem from any lack of opportunity.

[44] Twenty-eight owners are listed, although several own more than one property. Ninety-three properties are separately described in the Schedule.

[45] A significant proviso follows: 'Provided always, that it shall not be lawful for the Company to take or diminish any water of any of the Becks or Streams of Waters mentioned in such Schedule, or any of the Springs or Feeders thereto, except as herein specifically authorized.' The becks or streams mentioned in the Schedule are Hewenden or Harden Beck, Denholme Beck, Sow Dyke Beck, Pyehole Beck, and Chellow Dean Beck. Two entries refer to 'Beck or Stream of Water' or 'Beck or Water', without identifying by name, but all the rest name the beck or stream. The only reference to 'Springs of Water' in the Schedule is under the entry for Seth Wright, who owned and occupied Trooper or Many Wells Farm, which the Company had agreed to buy for £2,000 in January 1838.

The Incorporation of Bradford

The great municipal reform legislation of 1835 cleaved local government into two distinct groups: incorporated towns and those unincorporated. The Municipal Corporations Act 1835 reformed the government of 178 named incorporated boroughs. Bradford was not one of them. Importantly, however, the Act provided a mechanism by which unincorporated towns could gain a charter, and many subsequently took up this opportunity.[46] Unincorporated towns were often subjected to ineffectual administration by numerous separate authorities exercising overlapping jurisdictions. Bradford was no exception.

Adrian Elliott has described the government of Bradford prior to incorporation as 'chaotic', and the several authorities with particular responsibilities were ill equipped 'to deal with the social disorder and disease which were so rife in the town'.[47] Indeed, it is difficult to paint too gloomy a picture of the living conditions in Bradford for much of the nineteenth century. By any measure—be it infant or adult mortality, sanitation, housing standards, atmospheric or water pollution—Bradford was constantly at or very near the bottom of the 'league tables'.[48] For the majority of the population it was a short life of hardship and deprivation.

In 1847 the Borough was incorporated, combining the townships of Bradford, Bowling, Horton, and Manningham. Incorporation was no magic wand, however, and improvements were hard-fought and slow in coming. The ratepayers were always attentive to the costs of improvements, which they knew would ultimately fall on them.[49]

Becoming incorporated was one thing; acquiring the necessary powers to regulate and improve was quite another. The powers the new Council acquired upon incorporation in 1847 were 'very limited'.[50] In common with other municipalities, Bradford had to acquire the necessary powers

46 See D. Fraser, *Power and Authority in the Victorian City* (St Martin's Press, New York 1979), 1, and D. Fraser, 'Introduction: Municipal reform in historical perspective', in Fraser, above at note 13, 2.

47 Elliott, above at note 7, 157.

48 There is much written on these topics. The best introductory treatment I have read is by Thompson, above at note 15. This degradation and grinding poverty were 'put out of sight and out of mind by the upper classes': D. G. Wright, 'Mid-Victorian Bradford: 1850–1880' (1982) 47 *Bradford Antiquary* (new ser.) 65, 70.

49 'The apparent lethargy of the Town Council is to some extent explained by a reluctance on the part of many ratepayers (not all of whom were wealthy) to add to the already considerable burden of municipal debt incurred during the provision of a basic infrastructure of public utilities': Thompson, above at note 15, 146. See generally N. McCord, 'Ratepayers and Social Policy', in P. Thane (ed.), *The Origins of British Social Policy* (Croom Helm, London, 1978), 21.

50 Fraser, above at note 46, 164. I draw heavily in this paragraph on Derek Fraser's treatment of 'The creation and accumulation of powers' by Victorian cities: ibid., 163–7.

by other means. There were some permissive acts, which local authorities could adapt or incorporate in their own local acts. And later in the century compulsory duties were imposed increasingly by legislation. But the principal vehicle for acquiring powers was by locally initiated private bill legislation. Largely hidden from sight today, the system of private bill legislation was not only very well established but also a boon for the Parliamentary agents, barristers, and solicitors whose job it was to grease the Parliamentary wheels.

The history of the water supply in Bradford is largely the history of privately sponsored legislation: from incorporation and empowerment of private companies in 1790 and 1842, to the steady succession of private bill legislation sponsored by the Corporation; first in 1854, permitting it to buy the private company, and thereafter to augment its powers and to permit further expansion of the works. Between 1855 and 1892 the Corporation went to Parliament 13 times for powers to increase the water supply.[51] This locally sponsored legislation was a source of pride and an assertion of sovereignty. In a real sense it comprised the Victorian town's constitution.[52] This goes a long way to explain the proud possessiveness that the guardians of the Town had towards what to modern eyes looks like a miserable miscellany of statutory provisions.

The Municipalization of Water Supply

By the early 1850s there was much dissatisfaction with the performance of the Bradford Waterworks Company. It had taken the Company nearly four years to complete the works, which did not come on stream until early 1846, and such was the spectacular growth of Bradford in this period that the Company 'never supplied more than half the total population, as defined by the census figures'.[53] Things were brought to a head

[51] Addy and Renton, above at note 9, 305.

[52] Speaking of Bradford's larger neighbour, B. J. Barber said of Leeds' accumulation of local improvement Acts that 'in the process [it] endowed itself with what was virtually its own constitutional history': 'Aspects of municipal government, 1835–1914', in D. Fraser (ed.), *A history of modern Leeds* (Manchester University Press, Manchester, 1980), 301. See also Fraser, above at note 46, 166–7, on the underestimation of the importance of local pride, local knowledge, and the desire for local control.

[53] West, *Worstedopolis*, 59. William Robson's scathing depiction of the national scene was right on the mark as far as Bradford was concerned: 'The water supply in the largest towns until nearly the middle of the nineteenth century was thus nothing short of deplorable. With few exceptions the supply was in the hands of private companies or persons; high prices and large profits were common; the supply was utterly inadequate in extent, and often defective in quality or contaminated; and to the poorer classes of the community—that is, the vast majority of the citizens—water was in many places a luxury which could only be obtained by begging, borrowing, or stealing. At best they were compelled to fetch and carry water

by the severe drought of 1851–2, which caused serious water shortages. Those shortages and complaints about the actions of the Company attracted the attention of the Corporation of Bradford. The Corporation at first seemed to favour 'municipalization' of the water supply by taking over the existing waterworks, but this soon progressed to proposing an extensive rival scheme and the active sponsorship of a Bill authorizing the same.

The Bradford Waterworks Company did not take this threat lying down, and an acrimonious and incredibly costly legal battle raged for more than two years, with the Company and the Corporation simultaneously promoting their own schemes and Bills, and opposing those of the other.[54] In the end both Bills were thrown out of the House of Commons for different reasons.[55] As a result, both sides were forced to negotiate a settlement. The Corporation agreed to buy the Company for £165,000 and to pay £23,000 for its liabilities,[56] and to take over the Company's proposed scheme to expand supply (estimated to cost £240,000).[57] It was agreed that each would apply to Parliament in turn: the Company for powers to construct the proposed works; and the Corporation for powers to purchase the Company and to build the proposed works.[58] This consensus ensured smooth passage through the Parliamentary Select Committee process of two pieces of legislation: the Bradford Waterworks Act 1854,[59] authorizing the Company to expand existing works and to create new ones; and the Bradford Corporation Waterworks Act 1854,[60] authorizing the municipality to purchase the waterworks and to execute the works. By virtue of this convoluted process the Corporation of Bradford received all the property and statutory powers and protections

long distances to their own dwellings. The bad water supply was definitely a contributing factor to the disease prevalent among the poor.' (W. A. Robson, 'The Public Utility Services', in H. J. Laski, W. I. Jennings, and W. A. Robson (eds), *A Century of Municipal Progress—The Last Hundred Years* (George Allen & Unwin Ltd, London, 1935), 299, 314.)

54 For a detailed treatment of this Parliamentary battle, see A. Elliott, 'The Establishment of Municipal Government 1837–57', Ph.D. thesis, University of Bradford, 1976, ch. 6.

55 West, *Worstedopolis*, 84–96.

56 This amount was probably more than the company was worth: D. James, *Bradford* (Ryburn Publishing, Halifax, 1990), 95.

57 The Corporation jettisoned its own more ambitious scheme, and its consultant engineers, and took over the services of the Company's water engineer, J. Wignall Leather of George Leather & Co., Leeds. From that time until the mid-1860s Leather was responsible for the construction of all Bradford reservoirs. On J. Wignall Leather, see above at note 22. The water engineer jettisoned by the Corporation, J. F. Bateman of Manchester, was one of the leading water engineers of the nineteenth century. Bateman was involved in many great hydraulic projects, but his glory was the Longdendale water scheme. See J. A. Hassan and E. R. Wilson, 'The Longdendale water scheme 1848–1884' (1979) 14 *Industrial Archaeology* 102.

58 West, *Worstedopolis*, 102.

59 17 and 18 Vict. ch. cxxiv. Date of Royal Assent: 3 July 1854.

60 17 and 18 Vict. ch. cxxix. Date of Royal Assent: 3 July 1854.

formerly possessed by the Bradford Water Company.[61] The purchase has been described by a noted local historian as '[b]y far the most important municipal achievement in the Council's early years'.[62]

The Attitude of the Pickles Family

There is an interesting sidelight on the attitude of the Pickles to these plans to expand the existing works around Hewenden Reservoir. As noted above, the Company and the Corporation each had rival plans to expand supply from existing sources, and both plans involved new pipe-work westward over the Pickles' farm. The Company gave public notice on 10 November 1852 of its intention to seek legislative authorization to, amongst other things, 'lay down other and additional aqueducts and conduits' between Trooper's Farm and newly constructed reservoirs. This required a plan to be prepared and a book of reference noting the views of all the affected landowners. Unlike in 1842, this time the Pickles' farm was physically affected by the pipe laying, and Holmes Pickles and his mother Mary Pickles received two notices[63] indicating the proposed line of the 'conduit' through seventeen numbered plots of their land.[64] The Pickles registered their opposition to the proposals, and their 'dissent' is recorded.[65] Perhaps this was a foretaste of the family's future attitude and behaviour.

The competing proposal by the Corporation for a private Act likewise had to comply with Standing Orders, which required depositing a plan, creating a book of reference, giving notices, and recording assents and dissents, etc. The only surviving document in either the West Yorkshire Archives Service or the House of Lords' Record Office is the 'Book of Reference 1853' for the Bradford Corporation Waterworks Bill. There is detailed reference to 29 lots of land owned by the Pickles, much of it occu-

[61] For detail see Chapter 4 below.

[62] Fraser, above at note 46, 136, and 138. Fraser points out also the symbolic importance of the purchase, demonstrating the Corporation's commitment to 'a positive and collective role': ibid., 138.

[63] In the trial of the Pickles action, the Pickles family solicitor swore an affidavit that the Pickles had never received any notice as to the proposed works: Affidavit of George Burr, Affidavit No. 34, para. 9, in 'Respondent's Affidavits' in the High Court of Justice. This he subsequently corrected in a further affidavit.

[64] Ten plots described as 'Field', two as 'Field and Woody Ground', one as 'Field and Rough Ground', one as 'Occupation Road and Public Footpath', one as 'Rough Ground', one as 'Plantation', and another as 'House, Stable, Outbuildings and Garden'. The Notices are numbered 12 and 13 and dated 1 December 1852. The entries in the *Bradford Water Works: Book of Reference to Plans of Proposed Additional Works* are less detailed, listing ten plots of land affected (eight of which are described as fields, one as occupation road, and the other as field, occupation road and quarries).

[65] In the 'Bradford Water Works: List of Owners Assents Dissents Neuters etc.', pencilled pagination, p. 15.

pied by others. There is no surviving plan, neither, is it discoverable whether the Pickles objected to this proposal. There is no reason to believe that the Corporation's plan to lay water pipes over East Many Wells Farm would have been any less objectionable to the Pickles than the Company's proposal. It is highly likely Holmes and his mother Mary objected to the Corporation's plan as well.

Many Wells Spring and the Bradford Water Supply

In the 1850s the waterworks at Many Wells Spring were the mainstay of the Bradford water supply. Averaged over the entire year, the daily water supply figures (in gallons) for 1854 to 1859 were as follows: 343,930 (1854); 411,160 (1855); 480,933 (1856); 462,720 (1857); 358,316 (1858); 531,480 (1859).[66] Nevertheless, the rapid expansion of Bradford's population had rendered this supply inadequate by the time of the municipal take-over.[67] The Corporation set about expanding the water supply. Initially this was done by implementing Wignall Leather's plans, which had originally been devised for the Bradford Waterworks Company in its Parliamentary contest with the Corporation but had been taken over by the Corporation, and approved by Parliament in the Acts of 1854. The next 40 years saw a steady procession of private Waterworks Bills from Bradford to Westminster, each seeking authorization to construct new waterworks and/or to enlarge the area of water supply. Ensuring an adequate, regular, and pure supply of water to Bradford and its surrounding areas was a high priority for the Corporation of Bradford. Much of the burden fell on its hard-working Waterworks Committee, a succession of able water engineers and the long-serving Town Clerk, who did much of the preparatory work on the Waterworks Bills. By the mid-1880s, Many Wells Spring was contributing on average 300,000 gallons a day to the daily supply of 8.8 million gallons.[68] But it was not until the beginning of the twentieth century, when the massive Nidd Valley scheme was fully operational, that the city 'enter[ed] upon a period of immunity from [water] shortage'.[69]

66 These figures are derived from a document entitled 'Depth & Quantity of water flowing from Manywells Springs', at p. 115 of a bound volume of Correspondence of the Bradford Water Engineer, BBD 10/4/39, W.Y.A.S.

67 See Gott, above at note 9, 451.

68 The figure is taken from A. Silverthorne, *London and Provincial Water Supplies with the Latest Statistics of Metropolitan and Provincial Water Works* (Crosby Lockwood & Co., London, 1884), 64. Domestic supply accounted for 4,574,000 gallons and the rest went on 'Trade Purposes' and 'Flushing &c'.

69 *The Centenary Book of Bradford* (William Byles & Sons, Bradford, 1947), 22. For a comprehensive discussion of the water resources of the Nidd Valley and the role of Bradford in its development, see K. Smith, *The Water Resources of Nidderdale* (Department of Geography, University of Liverpool, Research Paper No. 4, 1965).

Bradford of the nineteenth century was an extraordinary place. Its phenomenal development as the worsted capital of the world depended crucially on an expanding water supply. Many Wells Spring played a pivotal early role in that supply, and consequently in the development of Bradford. It is time to turn attention to the events that led in the 1890s to that supply being lost to the Corporation.

2

Coal, Stone, and Water at East Many Wells Farm

Coal and Stone

The Bradford district had been known for its coal deposits since the Middle Ages,[1] and useful quantities of coal existed in the Parish of Wilsden, particularly around Many Wells.[2] The demand for coal increased dramatically from the 1840s onwards with the widespread use of steam engines in the woollen textile mills.[3] Many Yorkshire landowners—from the great estate holders down to the small-scale farmers—supplemented their incomes by mining for coal or stone, or leasing to miners.[4] So it was with the Pickles family.

Maps of East Many Wells Farm disclose the scars of quarrying for coal and stone in several locations. Both Edward's father and grandfather exploited the coal and stone under their land. The only instance of mining about which records survive took place in the 1860s, and had an important bearing on the litigation 30 years later.

The detail of the episode is as follows. In November 1861, before Edward was born, Holmes Pickles agreed to sell the 'soft' coal under part of his land to Edward Townsend, a local manufacturer.[5] It appears that

[1] See H. J. M. Maltby, 'The Coal Industry of the Bradford District', in *The Book of Bradford* (W. H. Brocklehurst, Bradford, 1924), 99 (being the proceedings of the British Medical Association's 92nd Annual Meeting at Bradford, July 1924); G. Firth, *Bradford and the Industrial Revolution: An economic history 1760–1840* (Ryburn Publishing, Halifax, 1990), ch. 5; C. Richardson, *A Geography of Bradford* (University of Bradford, Bradford, 1976), 3–5, 43 and 61–7.

[2] G. Firth, *Wilsden In Times Past* (Countryside Publications Ltd, Lancashire, 1985), 12.

[3] See generally W. P. Hartley, 'The Development of Coal Mining in the Heavy Woollen District of West Yorkshire During the Nineteenth Century' (1994–95) 14 *Journal of Regional & Local Studies* 25.

[4] On the prevalence of mining under farm land in the West Riding of Yorkshire and its economic significance for the landowners and the region, see J. T. Ward, 'West Riding landowners and mining in the nineteenth century' (1963), reprinted in J. Benson and R. G. Neville (eds), *Studies in the Yorkshire Coal Industry* (Manchester University Press, Manchester, 1976), 45.

[5] The Memorandum of Agreement appears as Document 57 in the Respondent's *Case on Appeal*. Townsend was one of the leading citizens of Cullingworth, and his family was very successful in business there and in Bradford. See generally W. Cudworth, *Round About Bradford: A Series of Sketches (Descriptive and Semi-Historical) of Forty-Two Places Within Six Miles of Bradford* (1876, reprinted by Mountain Press, Queensbury, 1968), 241–55, and J. H. Turner, *Ancient Bingley; or, Bingley, Its History and Scenery* (Thomas Harrison & Sons, Bingley, 1897), 312.

the subsequent coal mining made the Corporation apprehensive that Townsend would remove a seam of coal on the northern side of the Pickles' property which acted as a natural underground reservoir wall, preventing the water escaping from the underground catchment. The Corporation gave Townsend notice under section 49 of the Act of 1854, the same provision invoked against Edward Pickles nearly 30 years later.

This notice to stop mining gave rise to 'divers disputes doubts and differences' between Pickles / Townsend and the Corporation, which were quietened only by the Corporation purchasing a 25-yard-wide strip of lower bed coal running the length of the Pickles' farm from west to east. This strip preserved the integrity of the northern underground wall. The agreement, dated 16 April 1866, provided for a purchase price of £1,000, with Pickles receiving £400 and Townsend £600.[6]

The Corporation's interpretation of section 49 in this dispute in the 1860s appears to be identical to that adopted by it throughout the *Pickles* litigation in the 1890s. The notice given under section 49 is recorded in the conveyance of 1866 as follows: 'not to work the said beds of coal nor to do any other act matter or thing whereby the said waters of the said springs might be drawn off or diminished in quantity.'[7]

Like Father, Like Son

It is clear from archived Corporation papers that one of the reasons, and perhaps initially the principal one, why the Corporation took such a hard line with Edward Pickles in relation to his drilling in 1890 was the belief that he was attempting to emulate his father's (Holmes Pickles) feat many years earlier of forcing the Corporation to pay him not to use his land. This was very much in the mind of the long-time Town Clerk, Mr William McGowen, who had personal knowledge of that episode.[8] McGowen observed in a letter seeking the advice of a barrister:[9]

[6] The agreement appears as Document 58 of the Respondent's Documents, *Case on Appeal*.

[7] To pick up a point explored in Chapter 4, this wording suggests that the Corporation thought even then that the second part of section 49 (dealing with 'well and pit' and 'drawing off and diminution') was not conditioned by illegality (in contrast to the first part dealing with diversion etc.), and that the provision enjoined Holmes Pickles from undertaking any activity on his property, no matter how far from the Trooper Farm boundary, which drew off or diminished the flow of water, without any compensation being payable.

[8] The senior partner of W. & G. Burr & Co., William Burr, deposed to W. T. McGowen (then recently appointed Town Clerk) signing a letter dated 30 April 1866 acknowledging execution of the deed of settlement between Townsend, Pickles, and the Corporation: Affidavit of George Burr, No. 34 of the Respondent's Documents, *Case on Appeal*, para. 14. Burr also had personal knowledge of these events, being at that time managing clerk in what was then his uncle's firm of Weatherhead and Burr: ibid., para. 13.

[9] 'The Corporation of Bradford v Mr Edward Pickles [:] Case for the opinion of Counsel',

In 1865 the Father of Pickles set up a kindred proceeding connected to the present one with the upper lands, only then it was Coal not Stone, which it was alleged would be worked and would cut off the water. This was settled by the Corporation. . . . The success of that proceeding on the part of Pickles' ancestor has no doubt suggested to Pickles—the present man—that he might repeat the operation in another form. But this time the Corporation think he is in the wrong and can be prevented by injunction.

Why did the Corporation not stick to its guns in the mid-1860s, as it did in the 1890s? It is impossible to know, as records do not survive, but it is possible to speculate. First, there appears to be no doubt as to the bona fides of the Pickles/Townsend transaction or as to the existence of a sufficient quality of merchantable coal.[10] Secondly, in the early to mid-1860s the town of Bradford was still heavily reliant on the Many Wells Spring for its water supply. The additional reservoirs and works authorized by the Act of 1854 came into operation in 1860, but the 400,000-plus gallons a day from this Spring were still a mainstay of the supply. This was no longer the case in the 1890s. The Many Wells Spring were a useful, but no longer the dominant, source of water.

The Bradford Waterworks had been busy in between times, as evidenced by the numerous trips to Parliament seeking additional powers to further develop the waterworks.[11] The largest water development projects started in the 1880s did not come on stream until the end of the century, but the existing reservoirs were able to cope when Pickles succeeded in draining the Spring after he won the court case. In the end the different outcomes for father and son may be explained by timing. In the 1860s the Corporation could not do without the Spring water; in the 1890s it was more expendable. But the merits also must have played a part. Holmes Pickles had a stronger claim. The coal was there in sufficient quantity and quality to be attractive to a willing (and reputable) buyer. His son's claims of valuable flagstone deposits were not taken seriously by the Corporation, or by any one else for that matter. Edward Pickles's behaviour was viewed as vexatious, extortionate, amounting to blackmail, and maliciously motivated to harm the public water supply. The sense of righteousness of the Corporation's cause is palpable from the correspondence. In one letter the Town Clerk conveyed the Corporation's

p. 2 (hand-written, undated and over the signature of Mr W. T. McGowen, Town Clerk of the Corporation of Bradford).

10 This appears to be the case, notwithstanding the tone of the Town Clerk's letter many years later (quoted below at text accompanying note 56).

11 The Corporation of Bradford went back to Parliament 13 times between 1855 and 1892 for authorization to construct new works and/or to enlarge the water supply area. For a comprehensive list of these Acts, there is a bound and indexed volume entitled *Bradford Local Acts 1842–1903*, held in the library of Yorkshire Water, Western House, Western Road, Halifax, Bradford BD6 2LZ.

view that 'they would be grossly wanting in their duty to the public if they submitted to this injustice' (referring to Pickles's demand for payment).[12]

The 'divers disputes doubts and differences' over the coal in the mid-1860s should have given the Corporation warning that the legal position was less than watertight, but the legislation was not amended. It seems, however, that it was not for want of trying. The senior partner in the law firm which had represented the Pickles family for many years, George Burr, deposed that the Corporation tried to insert clauses into the Bradford Waterworks and Improvement Bill, introduced in the Parliamentary session of 1867–8, in an attempt to prevent neighbouring landowners interfering with the underground supply of water before it became the property of the waterworks company.[13] Burr quoted from the Minutes of Evidence of the Select Committee considering the Bill, where a witness for the Corporation was re-called to justify these clauses, in the face of opposition. The witness said:

> The Waterworks Clauses Act gives no protection to this Corporation or to any Company except after the water has become theirs by its having entered upon their land or works and the difficulty which is now felt by all the Water Companies and other persons having the supply of towns is that the injurious fouling and otherwise dealing with the water above the point at which it becomes their property by entering upon their works is not provided for by the Waterworks Clauses Act[:] that is the construction which has been given to it by this Court and on one occasion we had a great Chancery suit for many years upon the point.

In response to a question from the Committee chairman that this was really a matter for general legislation, the witness agreed but noted that it can take 20 years to get general legislation and in the meantime 'all sorts of things may be done'. The Committee was not persuaded, however, and struck out the clauses on the ground that the parties should be left to seek amendment of the general legislation on the subject.[14] It would appear that that route was never pursued.

Mr Burr had deposed earlier that upon instructions by clients he had at various times—and especially in 1868, 1869, 1873, 1875, and 1881—opposed Waterworks Bills promoted by the Corporation. In relation to

[12] Letter from the Town Clerk to W. & G. Burr & Co., dated 6 April 1892. In this letter reference is made to the earlier episode with Holmes Pickles and it is recorded that 'for the sake of peace' a payment was made 'for a strip of coal which is quite useless to . . . [the Corporation]'.

[13] Affidavit of George Burr, No. 34 in the Respondent's Documents, *Case on Appeal*, para. 16. What follows in this paragraph is taken from the affidavit.

[14] That left section 21 in the Bradford Waterworks and Improvement Act 1868, 31 & 32 Vict., ch. Cxl, which, amongst other things, prohibits anyone polluting or injuriously affecting the colour or quality of any water taken by the Corporation.

the 1868 Bill Mr Burr represented clients other than the Pickles.[15] It seems that the Pickles family never took to the Select Committee whatever objections they harboured to proposed Waterworks Bills. As noted above, no doubt the expense of doing so was prohibitive.

It is not clear why McGowen and the Corporation in 1890 thought that 'this time' Edward Pickles was in the wrong as a matter of law.[16] In the light of the matters deposed to by George Burr, which were not challenged and which had been raised in correspondence much earlier,[17] it at best is puzzling and at worst suggests that there might be some truth to Pickles's claim that the deep-pocketed Corporation had threatened 'to swamp' him with the litigation.[18]

The Town Clerk

One of the dramatis personae in this dispute is the Town Clerk of Bradford, Mr William Thomas McGowen.[19] McGowen is ever present in the water dispute of 1890–5. It is only in the Law Reports that he is not visible.[20] It is he who recorded the minutes of the powerful Waterworks Committee,[21] and conducted all the correspondence with Edward's solicitors. As a solicitor himself, McGowen briefed counsel directly on behalf of the Corporation and gave them instructions. The important matters

15 Above at note 13, paras 2 and 16.

16 Edward Pickles's solicitor took this point. See letter from W. & G. Burr & Co. to W. T. McGowen, 17 June 1890 ('We fail to see any distinction between the respective [legal] positions of Mr Pickles and his father').

17 Letter from W. & G. Burr & Co. to W. T. McGowen, 6 May 1890 ('Our recollection is that in 1868 the Corporation endeavoured to obtain in their Bill of that year of a clause which would have had somewhat of the effect you mention but that certain clients of ours objected to it before a Committee of the House of Commons and we are not aware that the Corporation had subsequently obtained that power').

18 In a letter from W. & G. Burr & Co. to the Town Clerk, dated 11 October 1890, Pickles's solicitor, John W. Craven, wrote: '[Pickles] is annoyed by the assertions which have been made to the effect that the Corporation have [*sic*] more money than he has, and that they will consequently swamp him'. In reply, dated 27 October 1890, McGowen denied the Corporation was capable of 'such a vulgar threat'. By return letter the next day Craven records his client's disagreement as to the Corporation's alleged incapacity to make such threats, and said: '[t]he issue is well known to both parties yet the Bradford Corporation simply repeats the threats already made.'

19 The spelling of his surname is not consistent in Council documents, correspondence, and newspaper reports—McGowen and McGowan are used often interchangeably. I use McGowen as that was the spelling in his death notice.

20 Except, that is, as the instructing solicitor, named as a matter of convention at the end of each reported judgment.

21 For an overview of the relationship between Council and its Committees during this period, see H. J. Laski, 'The Committee System in Local Government', in H. J. Laski, W. I. Jennings, and W. A. Robson (eds), *A Century of Municipal Progress, 1835–1935* (George Allen & Unwin Ltd, London, 1935), 82.

were taken back to Committee or Council, but one is left in little doubt as to who was calling the tune.[22] Pickles's legal adversary was the Corporation, but its human face most often was that of the ubiquitous Town Clerk.

The office of Town Clerk transformed in the course of the nineteenth century. In the first half of the century Town Clerks were usually solicitors, who acted as legal advisers to the town and as record-keepers. They often received a nominal salary but were paid for their legal work on the usual scale of professional fees. It was very much a part-time job.[23] The increasing complexity of local governance led to the emergence of full-time professional managers; for example, public officers of health, surveyors, engineers, etc. Foremost amongst this new professional class was the Town Clerk. The Town Clerk became the hub around which the multifarious activities of the Council took place. The important roles of coordination and oversight were maintained by the Clerk's duty to record and minute Council and Committee proceedings, and to conduct all of the Council's correspondence.[24] As John Garrand has noted:[25]

> The town clerk was a crucial figure from the start. He was accorded considerable respect within the council and without. His legal expertise gave him an important role in shaping local improvement bills—a source of advice not merely on the wording of particular clauses but more generally upon what powers could be obtained from Parliament, and how. . . . Furthermore, as councils moved increasingly into the land market to find sites for town halls, baths, parks and cemeteries the town clerk became an important, and often sought after, source of advice on complex and confusing [legal] issues. . . .

The Town Clerkship was a position of high visibility, and long-serving clerks became part of 'the local political elite'.[26] The Clerk functioned, in Headrick's words, as lawyer, secretary and spokesman for the Council.[27]

William McGowen became Town Clerk on 17 April 1866,[28] and held

[22] In one letter to Pickles's solicitors, McGowen said '[a]t the commencement of our controversy the usual authority was given me to take all steps as were necessary for the interests of the Corporation and that you have known from the first . . .': letter dated 27 April 1892 from W. T. McGowen to W. & G. Burr & Co.

[23] See T. E. Headrick, *The Town Clerk in English Local Government* (George Allen & Unwin Ltd, London, 1962), 18–22.

[24] Ibid., 23.

[25] J. Garrand, *Leadership and power in Victorian industrial towns, 1830–80* (Manchester University Press, Manchester, 1983), 76.

[26] Ibid., 82.

[27] Headrick, above at note 23, 30.

[28] There is an interesting story behind his appointment. Born in London of Scottish descent in 1814, McGowen had the benefit of a liberal education and entered the legal profession. He became Deputy Town Clerk in Liverpool in 1853, and applied unsuccessfully for the vacant Town Clerkship of Bradford in 1861. He lost out to Mr Joseph Rayner of Brighouse, and stayed put in Liverpool. In 1866 the Town Clerkship in Liverpool fall vacant.

this office for over 30 years until his death on 18 July 1896 in his eighty-second year. His was a remarkable record of service.[29] He ran a tight ship—the envy of many other local authorities[30]—and was largely responsible for the expansion of Bradford's parliamentary powers, its enhanced civic amenities, and strong financial position. He was described as 'a man of legal acumen, with a good constitution and full of energy'.[31] One of the new breed of professional, full-time Town Clerks, McGowen was a dominating figure in the life of Bradford. His predecessor combined the Town Clerkship with private legal practice, but the job had McGowen's undivided attention. He did as much of the legal work as he could himself, and by doing so 'saved the borough thousands of pounds' in legal fees. His salary started at £900 but quickly went up to £1,200, and ultimately to £1,500. He was revered by Councillors, officials, and the public.[32] Upon completion of 25 years' service in 1891, McGowen was presented with an illuminated address and a purse of 3,000 guineas subscribed to by the public.[33] The local artist John Sowden, who immortalized in watercolours both the 'worthies' and street 'characters' of nineteenth-century Bradford, executed a nice watercolour of McGowen in 1888. Sowden, himself a remarkable man, only painted 'worthies' of

McGowen applied for his boss's job only to miss out (again) to Mr Rayner. Apparently McGowen was the selection committee's first choice, but political considerations favoured Rayner in the Council vote. This left the Town Clerkship in Bradford open, but McGowen did not apply. However, some Councillors remembered his strong candidacy of five years before, and he was approached and prevailed upon to apply, and he did so at the very last minute. He was appointed on 17 April 1866 at age 52. This account is taken from H. Hird, *How a City Grows: Historical Notes on the City of Bradford* (privately published by Horace Hird, Bradford, 1966), 22–3, and the obituary in *The Bradford Observer*, Monday, 20 July 1896.

29 McGowen was a man of considerable literary attainments also, and was the first President of the Bradford Literary Society in 1876, as well as connected with the Bradford Scientific Association and the Church Institute.

30 The impression left on a visiting American scholar was of excellent local governance in Bradford, stemming in large part from the beneficial influence wielded by its salaried officials: A. L. Lovell, *The Government of England* (New York, 1908), vol. 2, 178–80, quoted in A. Briggs, *Victorian Cities* (2nd edn 1970; republished by University of California, Berkeley, San Francisco, 1993), 238.

31 W. Hustwick, 'Bradford Characters' (undated newspaper article, on file at the Local Studies section of the B.C.L., under the 'Celebrities' section under 'W. T. McGowen').

32 In the Local Studies section of the B.C.L. there is a booklet entitled *The Death and Funeral of the Town Clerk of Bradford* which contains newspaper clippings of the obituaries and orations at the time of his death and at his funeral. There is no reason to disagree with the judgement that he 'was liked by all and beloved by many of those with whom he had to do': *The Bradford Observer*, Monday, 20 July 1896.

33 The address is reproduced in 'Public Presentation To Mr W. T. McGowen', *The Bradford Observer*, Saturday, 7 November 1891. The purse, subscribed to by 245 citizens who knew and admired the Town Clerk, represented two years' salary. His grandson donated the address to the City in 1979. See 'Book of memory handed back to city', *The Telegraph & Argus*, 23 July 1979, and 'Liked by all and beloved by many', *The Telegraph & Argus*, 2 August 1979. See also 'Why This Testimonial?', *The Yorkshireman*, 11 November 1891, p. 324.

whom he approved,[34] and persisted with McGowen, despite his missing several sittings. Finally, Sowden resorted to painting McGowen at work! The watercolour is reproduced on p. 31.

The only controversy I know of attaching to McGowen stemmed from a well-intentioned offer by him to take on the additional duties of the new post of Clerk of the Peace when a Court of Quarter Sessions was created in Bradford in 1877.[35] Apparently, due to a 'regrettable misunderstanding', some believed (apparently incorrectly) that McGowen intended thereby to retain the emolument (approximately £150 per annum) that went with the post. 'Hard words were spoken and spoken unfairly both in the Council Chamber and out of it and consequently he withdrew his offer.'

The date of McGowen's appointment as Town Clerk—17 April 1866—is important. Just one day earlier, the Corporation entered into the deed settling the dispute with Edward's father, Holmes Pickles, and Edward Townsend, and a couple of weeks later McGowen wrote to them confirming execution of the deed. As we have seen, when Edward began drilling a quarter of a century later, the long-serving Town Clerk readily recalled the earlier episode.

By dint of his position and distinguished service, McGowen must have been a formidable opponent. Neither was he completely disinterested in the dispute. Given the Clerk's primary role as legal adviser to the Council and its committees,[36] it is reasonable to assume that McGowen initially advised the Waterworks Committee as to the illegality of the proposed drilling at East Many Wells Farm.[37] The Committee and the Council held fast to that position throughout the long and expensive litigation. So, in addition to the interests of the Corporation, McGowen had a personal interest in the vindication of his legal advice. Furthermore, as the correspondence between him and Pickles's solicitor became more and more heated, it would have been difficult for anyone to remain objective and neutral.

There is a less obvious respect in which McGowen had a professional interest in the outcome of the dispute. The Town Clerk is involved at

[34] See A. Bickley, 'The Sowden Watercolours', in G. Firth (ed.), *Street Characters of a Victorian City: John Sowden's Bradford* (Arts, Museums and Libraries Division, City of Bradford Metropolitan Council, Bradford, 1993), ix.

[35] I have relied in this paragraph on H. Hird, *Bradford in History: Twenty-four Essays on the Life by the Broad Ford from the Celtic Age to the Present Day* (privately published by Horace Hird, Bradford, 1968), 127–8. The quotations are from there. The salary figure is taken from p. 133, n. 2.

[36] Headrick, above at note 23, 104–5 (discussing the Town Clerk's role in Committee work).

[37] It was many months after the Waterworks Committee ordered Edward to cease drilling that the opinion of counsel was sought.

Figure 3. Mr W. T. McGowen (see Note on p. xvii).

every stage in the preparation of private bill legislation,[38] which was a major activity for local authorities such as Bradford in the nineteenth century. Initially the Waterworks Committee and the Council took their stand against Pickles squarely on the language of the Act of 1854 (which had been sponsored by the Borough and drafted by its Parliamentary agents). It was assumed that that Act (and the identical terms of its predecessors) protected the Corporation's vital interest in continued water flow to the waterworks at Trooper's Farm. McGowen's predecessor as Town Clerk would have had prime responsibility for ensuring that such

[38] Headrick, above at note 23, 188–9.

crucially important details were attended to by the Parliamentary agents. McGowen's incredulity that this matter could have been left in any doubt is evident from the correspondence. It appears that he was unwilling to believe that his predecessor could have made such a slip. He was certainly not going to concede the point. And he was unlikely to advise any backdown, as occurred in the mid-1860s with Pickles's father.

Edward Pickles

We know next to nothing about Edward Pickles the man. One thing we do know, however, is to his credit. His father, Holmes Pickles, died in 1874 at age 42, leaving his widow Sarah and six children—Louisa (17), Mary (13), Ada Elma (11), Edward (9), Susannah (6), and Herbert (5).[39] As the oldest son, Edward was the heir in law. On reaching the age of majority in 1886 he set about making adequate provision for his mother, sisters, and younger brother. He did this by selling some of the land and mortgaging some. Edward was left with 140 acres, most of which he leased out, and he was determined to make the best of what he had left.

Pickles's Solicitors

The Pickles' family solicitors were W. & G. Burr & Co. of Keighley. The town of Keighley is about half the distance away from Cullingworth that Bradford is. From the mid-1880s the Great Northern line ran from Halifax to Keighley, via Cullingworth, making daily communication quicker and more convenient.[40] This is evident in the speed with which each side returned correspondence.

Pickles was fortunate in his forebear's choice of solicitors. The senior partner in the firm at the time of the dispute was Mr George Burr. His record of public service in Keighley rivalled that of McGowen in Bradford. Burr was born in 1840 and moved to Keighley at age 17 to serve under articles with his uncle, William Burr, in the Keighley office of the

[39] The only direct relative of Edward's of whom I have found any trace is Herbert, and even here I cannot be sure. There is a death notice in *The Keighley News*, 25 May 1935, for a 'Herbert Pickles'. He was an assistant master at Leeds Modern School for 36 years, who retired in 1934. Assuming he retired at 65, that would put his date of birth in 1869, the same year as Edward's younger brother. There is no mention of family or kin in the obituary. I have found a square headstone in the churchyard of St John's the Evangelist, Cullingworth, engraved with 'E. Pickles Owner'. It may be that of Edward's great-grandfather or grandfather, but the Church records do not disclose any details.

[40] Indeed, the Great Northern Railway dominates the landscape still in the form of an impressive viaduct built in the early 1880s. It stands over Hewenden Beck a few hundred yards down stream from Hewenden Reservoir (indicated on Illustration 2 at p. 10).

firm of Weatherhead & Burr. George was admitted as a solicitor in 1863. George's uncle was the Clerk to the Keighley Local Board of Health, and from 1857 to 1882 (when the Borough was incorporated) George acted as 'joint clerk' of that body with his uncle.[41] Upon incorporation, George Burr was the natural choice as Town Clerk, and he discharged this office with distinction and dedication until his death in July 1906.[42] In addition, Burr served on and advised numerous other public bodies.

By all accounts George Burr was a remarkable man. He possessed 'a wonderful memory' and 'his acquaintance with local affairs was as minute as his mastery [of] municipal law'.[43] His reputation locally knew no bounds. He was credited with beating off the determined attempt by Bradford in the late 1860s to take over the water supply to Keighley.[44] The rivalry between the smaller Keighley and its larger, and ever expanding, neighbour was keen and long-standing. (It will be recalled that the town of Keighley was one of the more determined opponents of Bradford's ultimately successful buy-out of the Bradford Waterworks Company in 1854.)[45] It is clear from the local press reports of what became known as the 'great fight of 1867–69' that Burr and McGowen had clashed swords then. It is reported that the 'worthy' Town Clerk of Bradford came to Keighley to sign up locals in favour of the Bradford proposal to supply water to Keighley, but got only one signature, and that from someone disaffected with the town council! In the *Pickles* litigation, it will be recalled, Burr deposed to opposing Bradford Waterworks Bills on numerous occasions, on behalf of both the Corporation of Keighley and private individuals. Unlike McGowen, Burr combined his duties as Town Clerk with active private practice. Indeed, all the Corporation's legal work was done through Burr's firm until 1900, when it was transferred 'in-house'.

George Burr was remarkable in one other respect. For the last ten years of his life he was bed-ridden by arthritis. He conducted all of his duties as Town Clerk from his house, attending the Corporation's offices or that of his law firm on very rare occasions. He had offered to resign on several occasions, but the Corporation declined to accept. Despite his physical infirmities, Burr was mentally sharp until the end and his advice was 'almost invaluable'.[46] In recognition of his service to the town, in 1893 the Mayor presented Burr with his own portrait in oils. This is reproduced on p. 34.

[41] *The Keighley News*, 'Death of Keighley Town Clerk—Nearly Half a Century of Public Service', Saturday, 21 July 1906, p. 5.

[42] Idem.

[43] Idem; 'Local Topics', ibid., p. 4.

[44] For a brief discussion of Keighley's water supply in the nineteenth century, see I. Dewhurst, *A History of Keighley* (Keighley Corporation, Keighley, 1974), 72–4.

[45] For details, see A. Elliott, 'The Establishment of Municipal Government in Bradford 1837–57', Ph.D thesis, University of Bradford, 1976, pp. 175–80.

[46] Above at note 41.

Figure 4. Mr W. G. Burr (see Note on p. xvii).

William Burr died in 1882, and in 1889 George Burr took his cousin, Thomas Henry Burr, and his former articled clerk, John Whipp Craven, into partnership with him; as a consequence the firm name was changed to W. & G. Burr & Co.[47] John Craven was the solicitor on the record in the *Pickles* litigation. Craven is a famous name in Keighley, as one branch of the family were leading industrialists in the town. John W. Craven was admitted as a solicitor in 1884, and upon entering partnership headed up

[47] The information in this paragraph about John W. Craven is taken from the obituaries which appear in *The Keighley Herald*, Friday, 30 May 1894, p. 5. Intriguingly, one of the clerks in the firm who attended Craven's funeral was 'W. Pickles'. I have not been able to establish whether he was any relation of Edward.

the common law and chancery departments of the firm, as well as holding the position of Deputy Town Clerk. He was an energetic, tenacious, and able lawyer. These qualities are evident in the blistering correspondence exchanged between Craven and McGowen between 1890 and 1894. Tragically Craven died suddenly in March 1894, the result of a chill that turned from influenza to pneumonia. His death occurred three months before the Corporation's application for an injunction came on for hearing. This must have upset preparation for trial, but as no papers exist it is not possible to say more or to find out who took over the prime responsibility for conduct of the litigation.

In George Burr and John W. Craven, Edward Pickles had a formidable legal team, combining youthful tenacity with mastery of local politics and local government law. George Burr had mixed it with the larger neighbouring Corporation, and his counterpart, before and won. Edward Pickles had proceeded at every stage with legal advice, and he had good reason to have faith in his solicitors.

'. . . the ordinary rights of a Landowner'

A constant refrain of Edward Pickles and his solicitor in the long-running dispute with the Corporation was that all Pickles wanted to do was 'to work [his] stone and minerals as an ordinary land owner . . .'.[48] In his affidavit Edward described his occupation as 'Quarry Owner', and he deposed to his father (Holmes) and grandfather (Edward) 'deriving good incomes from the working of stone on [the] Estate'.[49] Evidently Edward wanted to follow in their footsteps.

Edward Pickles claimed that there was valuable flagstone underneath his property close to the boundary with the Corporation's waterworks. There was considerable demand at the time for flagstone for street improvements.[50] The stone could not be mined due to the inundation of underground water, so in order to exploit the minerals an elaborate plan was devised supposedly to get rid of the water. Essentially, Edward planned to sink several shafts to a depth lower than the neighbouring Spring and to link all the shafts by a 600-yard-long tunnel, which would

[48] Letter from W. & G. Burr & Co. to the Town Clerk, W. T. McGowen, dated 6 May 1890. In his affidavit, dated 30 January 1893, Edward deposed: 'I am only seeking to exercise an ordinary landowner's rights . . .': Affidavit of Edward Pickles, No. 33 of the Respondent's Documents, *Case on Appeal*, para. 4.

[49] Affidavit of Edward Pickles, ibid., para. 1.

[50] A. W. B. Simpson, *Victorian Law and the Industrial Spirit* (Seldon Society, London, 1995), 10. Demand for stone increased dramatically during the nineteenth century, especially for street improvements and monuments: D. J. Smith, 'Victorian Valuations' (1995–6) 18 *Transactions of the Hunter Archeological Society* 35, 43.

carry the water under his land to a point where it would run off down an open drain into Hewenden Beck, downstream of the 'compensation' reservoir and the Corporation's water pipes.

The broken lines on Figure 2 on p. 10 indicate the proposed line of the tunnel. Edward commenced the first 'trial' shaft, some 150 yards to the southwest of the Spring, in early 1890. He claimed that this drilling indicated that that there was valuable stone, although he kept no records of the digging. However, he encountered difficulties with water inundating these trial drill holes, and sought professional advice from a Bradford engineer, Mr John Woodhead. It was apparently Woodhead who came up with the elaborate and unprecedented plan to run a 3 foot by 3 foot tunnel for 525 yards underground, connecting three shafts of the following depths: shaft No. 1 in the southwest (120 feet deep); shaft No. 2, directly opposite the Spring (80 feet deep); shaft No. 3 (18 feet deep). This tunnel came out at ground level past East Many Wells Farm and connected to an open drain that would discharge the water into Hewenden Beck below the Corporation's waterworks.

This plan was disclosed to the Corporation on 5 December 1891, but it was apprehensive about the digging from the outset. The digging of the initial trial shaft, some 150 yards from the Spring, came to the attention of the Waterworks Committee of the Corporation on 2 May 1890. The Committee took a dim view of this development. The Committee minutes record the view that this contravened the Corporation's legal rights, and the Town Clerk was instructed to write to Pickles warning him that unless he stopped forthwith the Corporation would take legal action.[51] Thus was fired the first shot in a long and acrimonious exchange of correspondence.[52]

The Corporation dealt with this matter largely through its Waterworks Committee, and the minutes of that Committee are formal and bloodless. Not so, however, the correspondence between Pickles's solicitor, Mr John Whipp Craven, and the experienced Town Clerk, who was deputed to correspond with Edward's solicitors. Moreover, the handwritten notes of the meetings are more revealing of the temper of the Waterworks Committee, and of the important role played by the Town Clerk.[53]

From the start the Town Clerk saw Edward's motive as blackmail, pure and simple. In a letter briefing counsel in 1892, McGowen wrote:[54]

[51] Bradford Corp. Waterworks Committee Minutes Book, 2 May 1890, p. 4.

[52] Some, but by no means all, of the correspondence is printed as exhibits to the affidavits of deponents on both sides in the *Case on Appeal*.

[53] The Waterworks Committee Notes are paginated in BBC 4/4/8, W.Y.A.S. The Notes are mostly in the handwriting of William McGowen, but occasionally the writing is of another.

[54] McGowen, above at note 9, p. 2.

This stone is known throughout the district to be of such inferior quality that it cannot repay the cost [of] working but the real object of Pickles is to coerce the Corporation into paying him blackmail to stay his hand under the threat of the entire loss of their water by his proposed works. . . .

Figure 5. The remnants of the Waterworks at Many Wells Spring (see Note on p. xvii).

Figure 6. The view from East Many Wells Farm down to Hewenden Reservoir (see Note on p. xviii).

This was a view he had been pressing on the Waterworks Committee since early in 1891.[55]

[55] Waterworks Committee Notes, p. 273, 13 February 1891 ('The Town Clerk explained matters with Pickles to show that the man was seeking to get money'); ibid., p. 294, 10

Figure 7. The distance between shaft No. 2 and the boundary fence (see Note on p. xviii).

The Water Engineer, James Watson, was instructed to keep a watching brief on the mining operations in early March 1892. A special meeting was called on 25 March 1892 to deal with imminent danger to the water supply at Hewenden. The Notes of the meeting provide in relevant part:[56]

> The T.C. [Town Clerk] read extracts from various Acts of Parliament showing what the powers of the Corporation were—He considered that Pickles had no right to the claim which he has made. Some years ago £2000 [*sic*] was paid for coal which had been shuck—C[ouncillo]r Robb Pratt proposed that the T.C. be instructed to take all necessary proceedings for the protection of the Corporation.

About this time desultory negotiations commenced. The amount proposed by Edward varied considerably. In early April 1892 the sum of £3,000 for the minerals was mentioned, but by July this had increased to £18,000 for the land or a mere £11,000 for the minerals thereunder and

December 1891 ('The Town Clerk reported on this matter [sc. Pickles-Quarrying operations]—It being believed that Pickles was not in earnest in seeking to get stone as it was not worthwhile to quarry there being no good stone').

56 Waterworks Committee Notes, pp. 299–300, 25 March 1892. The settlement figure was £1,000. By 'shuck', McGowen was probably intending to say that the coal was worthless to the Corporation because it could not be mined, rather than that the coal was of worthless quality. That is really beside the point, however. What the Corporation purchased was peace of mind that the fault would not be breached by coal mining.

Figure 8. Looking up at East Many Wells Farm from Hewenden Reservoir (see Note on p. xviii).

water rights.[57] This offer was described as 'ridiculously extravagant'[58] and was rejected by the Waterworks Committee. Shortly thereafter Pickles withdrew the offer in retaliation.[59]

The Notes of a special meeting of the Committee on Monday, 15 August 1892, disclose for the first time an elected Committee member contributing to the recorded discussion.[60] The Chairman of the Committee, Alderman Smith Feather, is recorded as saying he would not give Pickles anything but thought he should be left alone as he could not do much harm.[61] The Town Clerk pointed out that the Spring yielded about £2,000 worth of water a year.[62] The Water Engineer raised a contingency plan in case Pickles did tap the water; namely, to dig down further

[57] Letter from W. & G. Burr & Co. to Town Clerk, dated 18 July 1892.

[58] McGowen, above at note 9, p. 11.

[59] Simpson gives the dates for the Committee's rejection as 17 August 1892 and for the withdrawal as 24 August 1892: above at note 50, p. 13. In fact, the sub-committee formally resolved not to recommend purchase of Pickles's land on 17 August 1892, and this recommendation was approved of by the full Waterworks Committee on 19 August 1892.

[60] Waterworks Committee Notes, p. 309, 15 August 1892.

[61] Alderman Feather must have been sitting in for the absent Chairman of the Committee, Alderman William Holdsworth, who chaired the Committee for nearly 20 years (1892–1910). For a profile of Alderman Smith Feather J.P., depicting a quiet, retiring, and humane man, see W. Cudworth, *Bradford Portraits* (Bradford, 1892), 58.

[62] McGowen also made the point that 'Pickles had not given notice to begin the work as required by Act of Parliament.' See further below at text accompanying notes 78–87.

and recover the supply. It was resolved that a sub-committee of ten members would visit Hewenden Reservoir and inspect Pickles's mining operation.[63]

The site visit took place on Wednesday, 17 August, and this report appeared in the leading Bradford paper, *The Bradford Observer*, the next day:[64]

MANY WELLS SPRINGS.—A sub-committee of the Bradford Waterworks Committee yesterday afternoon made an inspection of Many Wells Springs with the object of assisting them to form a decision as to the course which they shall take to preserve that source of supply. Interference with this supply has been imminent before, but was staved off by the Corporation paying a considerable sum for a strip of coal which the owner desired to work. A gentleman belonging to the same family has now once more produced a similar difficulty. He says he is only seeking to work his quarries, and contends that the Corporation should buy him out if they object to his operations. The question before the sub-committee is whether they shall take legal proceedings if the supply be interfered with, or whether they shall dispose of the difficulty by purchasing the property.

Not surprisingly, Pickles detected the voice of the Corporation behind this account, and characteristically immediately fired this salvo off to the Editor:[65]

SIR,—I have seen the paragraph in the 'Observer' of yesterday referring to the Many Wells Springs, and I reply to it because the information appears to be have been given to you in the interests of the Bradford Corporation.

I am not anxious to sell my land to the Corporation, but would much prefer to have my quarries worked as I have always intended. I only offered to sell after the Corporation had very much pressed me to fix a price. There is no question of legal proceedings, because the Corporation know perfectly well that they have no ground on which they can take any such proceedings as those referred to in the paragraph, and it is ridiculous to refer to them, because nearly two years ago the Corporation threatened to commence proceedings, and my solicitors pointed out that I was only doing what I am entitled to do. The fact that this threat has not been acted upon shows that the Corporation have no right to stop me doing what every landowner may do, viz., get stone from out of his land.—

I am, &c, EDWARD PICKLES.

East Many Wells, 19th August, 1892

It is possible that Pickles wrote that letter knowing that the sub-committee had already resolved not to recommend to the full Committee purchase of his farm or the water and mineral rights.

The sub-committee had visited Hewenden Reservoir and inspected

[63] Waterworks Committee Minute Book, BBC/1/9/12, p. 289.

[64] *The Bradford Observer*, Thursday, 18 August 1892, p. 7, col. 1.

[65] Ibid., Saturday, 20 August 1892, p. 9, col. 2.

Pickles's land on Wednesday, 17 August 1892. That same afternoon the sub-committee met at the Town Hall at 3 p.m. and resolved, '[a]fter full consideration', not to recommend purchase.[66] The reason for thinking that Pickles might have learnt by the following Friday of that recommendation is that the minutes record the instruction to the Town Clerk to communicate this to Mr Burr (who, one infers, picked up this file after the sudden death of John Craven in March that year). The recommendation of the sub-committee was put before the full Waterworks Committee at a meeting on Friday, 19 August, which approved its recommendation.[67] Committee members who read Pickles's letter the next day no doubt felt confirmed in the correctness of their view.

According to *The Bradford Observer* account of the Committee's deliberations, the stumbling block was price: 'What the Corporation believe is that, the sums asked for the minerals and the land are far too great: while the owner is of the opinion that rather more than sixpence per square yard is not by any means too high a figure to pay for purchase outright.'[68]

The attitude to the dispute displayed by the leading Bradford daily newspaper contrasts starkly with that exhibited in the *Leeds Evening Express*. In an uninhibited column by 'The Expressman', this was said on 26 April 1892:[69]

> I hear that the Waterworks Committee of a neighbouring borough has managed to get into a somewhat serious fix. Over £200,000 have been spent in storage and compensation works for the purpose of utilising a single spring of water. Now it seems there is an immediate danger of losing every drop of it. It is the old story of 'penny wise and pound foolish' policy. I hope they will get out of the difficulty soon. I shall have more to tell shortly.

Good as his word, the well-informed 'Expressman' told more on the same day as Edward Pickles's letter appeared in the Bradford paper:[70]

> Some time ago I referred to the attitude of the Bradford Corporation with reference to their waterworks at Hewenden. I now learn that the Waterworks Committee have decided to recommend the Corporation not to purchase. This means that Bradford will run the risk of losing a spring of pure water which has cost about £200,000. Would it not be better to look after the water they have instead of spending so much money on imaginary water schemes and picnics into the country with landaus and pairs?

66 Waterworks Committee Minute Book, BBC/1/9/12, p. 291.

67 Ibid., p. 292.

68 'The Bradford Corporation and Many Wells Springs', *The Bradford Observer*, Saturday, 27 August 1892, p. 7, col. 2. Perhaps pricked by Pickles's scarcely veiled allegation of partiality in his letter to the Editor a week earlier, this long article is very informative and balanced, putting both sides fairly.

69 'Notions', *Leeds Evening Express*, Tuesday, 26 April 1892, p. 1, col. 7.

70 Ibid., Saturday, 20 August 1892, p. 1, col. 7.

The Town Clerk, McGowen, saw Pickles's hand behind this campaign and told his solicitor so.[71]

It is unwise to be dogmatic, but reading the surviving correspondence, minutes, and newspaper accounts, the strong impression given is that the Corporation was not minded to settle. The incendiary correspondence, the lack of cooperation in arranging site visits, and the consequent frustration over a long period probably foredoomed settlement. Moreover, the spectre of Holmes Pickles and his earlier victory haunted the Town Clerk, if not the Waterworks Committee and the Corporation. So two and a half years after the matter was first brought to the attention of the Waterworks Committee, the Town Clerk was instructed on 25 November 1892 to commence proceedings against Pickles to prevent him continuing with the works at East Many Wells Farm.[72] The Corporation went to Law.

Blackmail?

Was Pickles really a blackmailer? Apart from McGowen's description of Pickles as such in private and privileged correspondence, there is no other suggestion that he was guilty of criminal blackmail. It seems that the Town Clerk was not using the term 'blackmail' in its legal sense; for it is difficult to believe that a man like McGowen would have let the issue rest if he had thought it was arguable. So McGowen appears to have used the term in the lay sense of a demand for payment by an unprincipled person who had it in his power to injure the entity of which the demand was made.[73]

But nothing about the law of blackmail is straightforward, then or now. The law of blackmail suffers from the oft-remarked upon paradox that when one adds together two acts lawful in themselves—threatening to do a lawful act and the request for payment—it produces the criminal act of blackmail.[74] It is not easy to explain why Pickles's actions did not amount to criminal blackmail.

As the law of blackmail stood in the mid-1890s, it was a crime to

[71] Letter from W. T. McGowen to W. & G. Burr & Co. dated 27 April 1892. After pointing out that the Corporation was not responsible for what was reported in the *Bradford Observer*—'neither of us can escape the vicious meddlesomeness of the reporters'—McGowen inquired whether Mr Craven happened to know the informants behind the story (supporting Pickles) in the *Leeds Evening Express* (quoted above in the text accompanying note 69).

[72] Waterworks Committee Minutes Book, 25 November 1892.

[73] See *Oxford English Dictionary* (Oxford University Press, Oxford, 2nd edn, 1989), vol. 2, 250.

[74] There is a large body of literature on the subject, but a good introduction to the major lines of debate is in a symposium published in (1993) 141 UPaLR 1565–1988.

demand money with menaces and without reasonable or probable cause.[75] In the reported cases the threat was almost always to disclose disreputable information to a third party. Threats to exercise legal rights in land or contract in order to extract payment were unheard of in the nineteenth century. The law of blackmail has developed considerably in this direction since then, but in the 1890s it appears that Pickles's demand for purchase of his land or he would interrupt the water supply would have been seen neither as menacing nor as lacking reasonable cause.[76] It appears to have been assumed that a landowner could not commit blackmail by attempting to make the most of what he had.[77]

Too Clever by Half?

There is a piece of the story not easily discernible from the law reports that is interesting in its own right, and also throws some light on Edward Pickles's motivation. Every step he took was deliberate and preceded by taking professional advice, be it legal or engineering advice. When Edward sunk the second shaft opposite the Spring in August 1892 the placement of the shaft was exact. It was 40 yards and 6 inches from the visible waterworks on the Corporation's land. There was a very good reason for this exactitude.

As described more fully in Chapter 4, section 196 of the Act of 1842 protected the waterworks from apprehended danger from mining within 40 yards of any works. It represented an ingenious compromise of the competing interests.[78] Any owner desiring to mine within that proximity was required to give the Company notice. Within 30 days of receipt of notice the Company was empowered to inspect the mine to assess the likelihood of damage to the works. If the Company thought that damage was likely *and* was prepared to compensate the owner for his inability to work the mine, the owner was enjoined not to work the mine. In case of disagreement as to the amount of compensation, this was to be settled according to the procedure laid down earlier in the Act.[79] If the Company did not state its willingness to treat within the 30-day period, the owner was entitled to work the mines 'in such a Manner as may be proper and

[75] See W. H. D. Winder, 'The Development of Blackmail' (1941) 5 MLR 21.

[76] See *R v Walton & Ogden* (1863) Le. & Ca. 288, 297; 169 E.R. 1399, 1403. Sometime later it was held to be no defence to a charge of blackmail that you honestly believed that the demand was reasonable: *R v Dymond* [1920] 2 KB 260 (CA).

[77] This sits comfortably with the notion that a landowner cannot exercise any absolute legal rights maliciously, which is discussed below in Chapter 7.

[78] This is discussed more fully below in Chapter 4.

[79] Bradford Waterworks Act 1842, section 196.

necessary for the beneficial working thereof . . .'.[80] However, 'improper working' of such mines was a different matter entirely. In that event, the Company was given power to inspect, to give notice of remedial action required to prevent injury, and, in lieu of action, to undertake that work at the owner's expense.[81]

These provisions concern the working of mines within 40 yards of any waterworks. Outside that radius any owner would be free to mine or work existing mines without fear of restraint under this Part of the Act.[82] Outside that radius the owner desirous of mining was not required to give the Waterworks Company any notice of intent to commence mining operations. Should such operations come to the attention of the Company and cause concern, the Company had no statutory authority under this Part of the Act to elect to prevent the mining upon payment of compensation. That would be a matter for negotiation, or of reliance by the Company on any other powers of acquisition in the Act of 1842 or elsewhere.

Thus, if the work is within the 40-yard radius, the owner of the mines or minerals either will be able to mine (in a proper fashion), or will be compensated for not being able to do so where the Company thinks damage to the works is likely. The decision lies with the Company to weigh up the risk of damage against the enforced expenditure of compensation, which, if disputed, will be determined by justices or a jury (depending on the amount claimed). If the Company weighs up the risk and decides within the timeframe not to compensate the owner, the only limitation on the owner's working of the mine within 40 yards of the waterworks is that it be 'properly' mined, whatever that means.[83]

Now we can see why Edward was so careful with his measurements.[84] If he had drilled within the 40-yard radius he could have been compelled to sell to the Corporation at a price set by a jury. By this procedure he would have been put to the proof of the value of the mineral deposits. Even making every assumption in his favour—that he had found evidence of flagstone, that the vein was likely extensive and of good quality, and that his preference was to mine his lands rather than sell them at a vast profit—Edward may have been wary of losing control of the situation by falling under the regime laid down by section 196.

Before he sunk his second shaft opposite the Spring, Edward gave notice to the Corporation of his proposed drilling and tunnelling, attaching a

[80] Ibid., section 197.

[81] Ibid., sections 198–9.

[82] There may, of course, be common law restrictions.

[83] The only indication of what might amount to 'improper working' appears from a juxtaposition in section 197 with lawful working in a proper and necessary manner for the beneficial working of the mines.

[84] This was the view of the trial judge as well: [1894] 3 Ch 53, 64.

plan. This notice was in the form laid down in the statute, but was said to be given out of courtesy and was not to be deemed to be an admission that the Corporation had any right to such notice under the Act of 1842, the Waterworks Clauses Act 1847, or any other Act.[85] This notice brought home to the Corporation the fatally serious threat that Edward's works posed to its water supply. However, because he claimed to be outside the 40-yard radius the tight statutory timetable did not operate, and the dealings limped along, as indicated above.[86]

There was dispute as to whether Edward's shaft was outside the 40-yard radius. Some underground waterworks were discovered closer to East Many Wells Farm and, if the measurement was taken from them, his shaft would have fallen within the radius. This point was raised off and on, but mostly lurked in the background. Neither side acted as if the proposed works were within the statute.

With the considerable benefit of hindsight, the placement of the shaft six inches outside the 40-yard radius was a mistake. It bought Edward an expensive lawsuit which, even thought he ultimately won it, extracted not a penny out of the Corporation for his land or water. It might be said that it was a mistake only if Edward really wanted to sell. That is true, but there can be no doubt that he wanted to do so. He had to go out of his way to route the tunnel so close to the boundary and Many Wells Spring. There was no legitimate engineering or other purpose in deviating from a straight line between his first shaft and the third one by the farmhouse. The proposed route was 40 yards longer than if it had gone in a straight line from the most distant (No. 1) shaft to the farmhouse, and hence was more expensive. It was on this basis that the trial judge found Edward not to be acting in good faith,[87] as we will see in the next chapter.

It is difficult to avoid the conclusion that Edward was just a little too clever or calculating for his own good. He was certainly greedy. If his digging had fallen within the 40-yard radius, and the statutory scheme, he would have likely received generous compensation from the jury

[85] The notice was dated 5 December 1891.

[86] At first instance, North J. did not think that these provisions had any application for the different reason that the digging, even if within 40 yards of the waterworks, did not interfere with the 'support' of the reservoir or buildings: [1894] 3 Ch 53, 64. It is difficult to square this with the terms of sections 196–200 of the Bradford Waterworks Act 1842.

[87] A straight line from shaft No. 1 to the farmhouse was 485 yards, and so directed the tunnel would have passed 90 yards to the west of the Spring. The actual dog-legged route, which took the drift to within 40 yards and 6 inches of the Spring, increased the length of the tunnel to 525 yards. These measurements are taken from the unreported sections of the first instance judgment: A *Transcript of Shorthand Notes of Judgment of Mr Justice North* appears as Item No. 10 in Appendix A (pp. 22, 26–7) of the printed and bound Appeal Book filed with the House of Lords (undated) (hereafter referred to as *Case on Appeal, App. A*).

(failure to agree compensation being a certainty in this case), but it is reasonable to assume it would not have come close to the £11,000 Edward wanted for the water and mineral rights. It should not be forgotten that section 196 did not authorize the expropriation of the land itself; neither would it permit compensation for the water use. It allowed compensation only for the loss caused by the inability to mine minerals, in this case flagstone.

3

To Court

The Litigation at First Instance

The Corporation engaged one of the leading Chancery silks of the day, Herbert Cozens-Hardy Q.C., to argue its case.[1] His adversary, instructed by Pickles's Keighley solicitors, was Francis Everitt Q.C.[2] The two silks were both members of Lincoln's Inn and were called to the Inner Bar on the same day.[3] Cozens-Hardy's name is still encountered today through his judicial decisions, for he was appointed to the bench in 1899 and served as Master of the Rolls from 1907 to 1918. Denied the partial immortality that judicial service provides, Everitt passed into oblivion. Throughout the litigation, however, Francis Everitt Q.C. proved a tenacious and shrewd advocate, who in many ways outshone his more illustrious opponent.

The Corporation won at first instance. North J. of the Chancery Division granted an injunction restraining Edward from continuing with the works.[4] The judge viewed section 49 of the Act of 1854 as the identical successor to section 234 of the original Bradford Waterworks Act 1842, and interpreted that provision as preventing Pickles's appropriation of the underground water before it united into a defined stream or entered the Corporation's land. Pickles's counsel had argued in vain that the private Acts had to be very strictly construed and prima facie were not to be interpreted as to affect property rights, where the land had not been taken and no compensation was ever paid for the abridgement of those rights.[5]

[1] See A. W. B. Simpson (ed.), *Biographical Dictionary of the Common Law* (Butterworths, London, 1984), 134.

[2] Francis William Everitt Everitt was born in 1830 and died on 9 March 1904. See A. B. Schofield, *Dictionary of Legal Biography, 1845–1945* (Barry Rose Law Publishers Ltd, Chichester, 1998), 141.

[3] J. Sainty, *A List of English Law Officers, King's Counsel and Holders of the Patents of Precedence* (Seldon Society, London, 1987), 135 (called on 18 January 1882).

[4] *Corporation of Bradford v Pickles* [1894] 3 Ch 53. As the Corporation was seeking the equitable remedy of injunction the proceedings were commenced in the Chancery Division. For discussion of the ambit of equity, see Chapter 6. In terms of the dichotomy between property rules and liability rules identified in the famous article by G. Calabresi and A. D. Melamed ('Property Rules, Liability Rules, and Inalienability: One View of the Cathedral' (1972) 85 Harv LR 1089), the Corporation was seeking to protect its 'entitlement' under a property rule. The issue of who had property in the underground water was a major one in the litigation and is explored in Chapter 5.

[5] *Pickles*, 63. Pickles's counsel were Everitt Q.C., Tindal Atkinson, and Butcher.

North J. recognized this as 'a very weighty argument', supported by considerable authority, but held that it must give way to Parliamentary sovereignty in this case as the statute was so clearly worded. Neither did North J. think that this interpretation caused any injustice to Pickles, as it did not deprive him 'of anything which was of the slightest value'.[6] This was because the judge accepted evidence that the flagstone deposits were either non-existent or worthless.

It should be noted that of the total of eight judges in the three levels of court to consider this case, North J. was the only one to find for the Corporation on the interpretation point.[7] The finer points of statutory interpretation are discussed in the next chapter.

Although the Corporation had succeeded on the statutory interpretation point, it had another string to its legal bow, and North J. went on to consider it. The Corporation claimed that the exercise of Pickles's rights as a landowner was malicious and a breach of the common law. It was said his 'object [was] not to get his own minerals but to injure the Plaintiffs by carrying off the water, and compelling them to buy him off in order to avert this'.[8] The Corporation sought an injunction on this ground. Alert to the possibility of an appeal, North J. felt bound to record his view of the evidence on this issue.

Lack of Good Faith

The gravamen of the Corporation's case was to show that Pickles's proposed works were so unprecedented, inefficient, and contrived that the only possible inference was that he wanted to divert the water in order to injure the Corporation and thereby force it to buy his land at a premium.[9] North J. found 'this charge against the Defendant . . . well founded'.[10] He had earlier found that the tunnel scheme was deliberately planned to carry off the Spring water.[11] North J. surveyed evidence

[6] *Pickles*, 67.

[7] Sir Ford North is not remembered as a distinguished judge. He was a Chancery silk who was appointed to the Queen's Bench Division at the time of merger of common law and equity. Apparently, the appointment was not a success and he was transferred to the Chancery Division within 18 months. R. F. V. Heuston unflatteringly lumps Sir Ford North in with other, long since forgotten (common law) trial judges, after observing that the quality of the Queen's Bench had declined in the 1890s. See R. F. V. Heuston, 'Judicial Prosopography' (1986) 102 LQR 90, 102 and 106.

[8] Above at note 4, 68.

[9] A large amount of evidence was heard on this point. The Corporation appeared to leave nothing to chance and spared no expense filing affidavits from a Professor of Geology at the University of Oxford and from several leading local stone merchants and quarry owners. The deponents for Pickles paled in comparison to the expertise, experience, and objectivity of the plaintiff's deponents.

[10] Above at note 4, 68.

[11] Ibid., 65.

pertaining to the location of shaft No. 2 so close to the Spring and showing that no adequate steps had ever been taken to locate and appraise any stone beds below the level of the Spring.[12] 'These are the principal grounds', North J. concluded, 'which have led me to the conclusion that the Defendant has not been acting in good faith in this matter, and that the avowed ground for the construction of the drift is not the true reason'.[13] By lack of good faith North J. meant Pickles's efforts to divert the water in order to pressure the Corporation into buying his land at a premium.

North J. went on 'to consider whether, the facts being as I have just stated, the Defendant can be restrained from making the tunnel proposed, on the ground that he is not acting *bona fide*'.[14] This was a novel point of English law. Counsel had cited no English case on the point, and the judge 'after much research' could find none. (This may explain the 11-month delay between the trial and delivery of judgment.) In time-honoured fashion, faced with a novel point and 'a great dearth' of common law authority, North J. turned to Roman and civil law.

Marcellus' Morsel

North J. began by citing the view of Marcellus recorded in *The Digest of Justinian*:[15]

[12] This part of the judgment is unreported. A *Transcript of Shorthand Notes of Judgment of Mr Justice North* appears as Item No. 10 in Appendix A (pp. 22–39) of the printed and bound Appeal Book filed with the House of Lords (undated) (hereafter referred to as *Case on Appeal, App. A*). I have relied on this source. The judgment was quoted from extensively by Mr Cozens-Hardy Q.C. in his submissions to the Court of Appeal. See *Transcript from Shorthand Notes of Argument before Court of Appeal, on 30th and 31st of October, 1894, and Notes of offer made by the Lord Chancellor on the 5th November, 1894, as to application to Parliament for powers to purchase* (hereafter referred to as *Shorthand Notes of Argument before Court of Appeal*).

[13] *Case on Appeal, App. A*, pp. 35–6.

[14] Ibid., p. 36.

[15] T. Mommsen, P. Krueger, and A. Watson, *The Digest of Justinian* (University of Pennsylvania Press, Pennsylvania, 1985), vol. 3, 396 (D. 39.3.1.12). The articles prior and subsequent to this one in the *Digest* speak of surface water and the action to ward off rainwater. A contextual reading would interpret 'water supply' in this light, but it has been read invariably as covering subterranean water supply. See further Chapter 5. Marcellus lived in the second century AD, and his extensive writings on Roman law were influential and frequently copied. See D. M. Walker, *The Oxford Companion to Law* (Oxford University Press, Oxford, 1980), 804. It has been suggested, however, that Ulpian is responsible for the qualification as to malice. This is the view of Innes C.J. in *Union Government (Minister of Railways and Harbours) v Marais* 1920 AD 240, 247, and is supported by Visser: F. Visser, 'Ground-water law in South Africa' (1987) 50 *Tydskrif Vir Hedendaagе Romeins-Hollandse Reg* 412, 420, n. 64. See also F. Pringsheim, '*Animus* in Roman Law' (1933) 49 LQR 43, 51–2. Cf. W. W. Buckland and A. D. McNair (rev. edn by F. H. Lawson), *Roman Law & Common Law: A Comparison in Outline* (Cambridge University Press, Cambridge, 2nd rev. edn, 1952), 97. Ulpian's writings comprise well over a third of the *Digest* and are of high authority: Walker, *op. cit.* above, 1246. Notwithstanding the uncertainty over authorship, I will attribute this passage to

Next, Marcellus writes that no action, not even the action for fraud, can be brought against a person who, while digging on his own land, diverts his neighbour's water supply. And of course the latter ought not to have even the action for fraud, assuming that the other person acted not with the intention of harming his neighbour, but with that of improving his own field.

This passage indicated to North J. that an action might lie if an act was done causing damage to a neighbour, not for the improvement of one's own property, but for the purpose of 'levying blackmail upon the neighbour'.[16] However, as North J. pointed out, this passage from the *Digest* had had something of a chequered career in the English courts.

The Roman and English law of water is discussed in a later chapter.[17] It is necessary here only to say enough so that the broad outline of the legal arguments is perceptible. *Acton v Blundell* (1843)[18] was the first English case to concern interference with underground water supply caused by a neighbour's mining. In that case, counsel for the plaintiff cited a number of Roman law texts to support his client's claim to an undisturbed flow of underground water to his water-powered mill. In a famous interjection Maule J. said: 'It seems to me that what Marcellus says is against you. The English of it I take to be this: if a man digs a well in his own field, and thereby drains his neighbour's, he may do so, unless he does so maliciously.'[19] And in the judgment, while recognizing that Roman law guides rather than binds English courts in determining novel points of law, the Court of Exchequer Chamber quoted the opinion of Marcellus and said that it was 'decisive upon the point in favour of the defendants'.[20]

As North J. correctly noted at first instance in *Pickles*, maliciousness was not alleged in *Acton*'s case and so approval of the malice qualification is only *obiter*.[21]

Subsequent to *Acton*'s case judges disagreed over the law relating to percolating subterranean waters[22] and the legal position was not authoritatively settled until the great case of *Chasemore v Richards*[23] in 1859. The plaintiff in that case was a mill-owner who for a long time had enjoyed

Marcellus. My primary reason for doing so is that at the time *Pickles* was decided no one appeared to dispute Marcellus' authorship.

[16] Above at note 4, 68.

[17] See Chapter 5.

[18] (1843) 12 M. & W. 324; 152 E.R. 1223.

[19] Ibid., 336; 1228. See A. D. E. Lewis, ' "What Marcellus says is against you": Roman Law and Common Law', in A. D. E. Lewis and D. J. Ibbetson (eds), *The Roman Law Tradition* (Cambridge University Press, Cambridge, 1994), 199.

[20] *Acton v Blundell*, 353; 1235.

[21] Above at note 4, 67.

[22] The important cases between 1843 and 1859 include: *Dickinson v The Grand Junction Canal Company* (1852) 7 Exch. 282, 155 E.R. 953 (Ex.); *Rawstron v Taylor* (1855) 11 Exch. 369, 156 E.R. 873 (Ex.); and *Broadbent v Ramsbotham* (1856) 11 Exch. 602, 156 E.R. 971 (Ex.). (For further details, see Appendix, note 2.)

[23] (1859) 7 HLC 349; 11 E.R. 140.

the use of a river, which was fed by percolating underground water. The defendant was a Local Board of Health which had sunk a large well on its own land and extracted by steam-driven pumps a very large quantity of underground water for town supply, thereby diminishing the underground water supply to the river and causing damage to the plaintiff. The amount of water pumped daily from the ground was between 500,000 and 600,0000 gallons, and it was piped some distance to supply the entire population of Croydon. The case stated on appeal recorded that the Local Board of Health was not actuated by malice, and neither did it intend to diminish in any way the water feeding the river or to injure anyone, although the Board had reasonable means of finding out the probable effects of its scheme.[24]

One of the reasons this is a landmark case is the amount of judicial consideration it received. The Court of Exchequer held against the plaintiff.[25] The Exchequer Chamber affirmed that decision by a majority of six to one.[26] As was then common in the most difficult cases, the Lord Chancellor called together the common law judges to listen to the arguments before the House of Lords, and to advise the Lords.[27] The unanimous opinion of the six judges who gathered was delivered by Wightman J. and favoured the position taken in the courts below; basically affirming *Acton v Blundell*.[28] Almost all of their Lordships adopted that advice wholeheartedly.[29] The exception was Lord Wensleydale, who found the issue much less clear-cut and only reluctantly concurred, 'though not without very serious doubts as to the propriety of the conclusion' the other judges reached.[30] A small part of his difficulty was that he had been

24 Ibid., 353–4; 142.

25 The case came on for argument before the Court of Exchequer on 30 April 1856. The judgment is not fully reported and the composition of the Court is not given in any of the reported proceedings. One brief account gives the Court's reasoning as follows: the case was 'very like' *Broadbent v Ramsbotham* (1856) 11 Ex. 602; 156 E.R. 971 (decided by the Court of Exchequer less than four months earlier), and so judgment should accordingly be given for the defendant so that the case could be taken on appeal to the Court of Exchequer Chamber. *Broadbent v Ramsbotham* principally involved surface water not in a defined channel, but interference with underground water flow was involved to a lesser extent.

26 Cresswell J. delivered the majority judgment, agreed in by Wightman, Erle, Williams, Crompton, and Crowder JJ. Coleridge J. dissented.

27 The judges that attended were Crompton, Wightman, and Williams JJ., and Martin, Bramwell, and Watson BB.

28 In his speech Lord Wensleydale made a cryptic remark from which one can infer that Baron Bramwell was not in full agreement with the other judges advising the House of Lords. He said 'Baron Bramwell has had the goodness to communicate to me [an opinion] which he wrote, at the time I suppose a difference of opinion was expected, and I am much indebted to him, as the subject is discussed by him with much ability' (above at note 23, 381; 153).

29 Lord Chelmford L.C., Lords Brougham, Cranworth, and Kingsdown.

30 Above at note 23, 381; 152. Lord Wensleydale was ennobled in 1856 amid controversy. James Parke became a judge of the King's Bench in 1828, and became a Baron of the

a party to a number of the allegedly conflicting decisions of the Court of Exchequer and did not think that they were in conflict.[31] More fundamentally, however, Lord Wensleydale was more attracted to the notion of 'reasonable user' than the others were.

Lord Wensleydale came to this conclusion on the law:[32]

Every man has a right to the natural advantage of his soil—the Plaintiff to the benefit of the flow of water in the river and its natural supplies, the Defendant to the enjoyment of his land, and to the underground waters on it, and he may, in order to obtain that water, sink a well. But according to the rule of reason and law, '*sic utere tuo ut alienum non laedas,*' it seems right to hold, that he ought to exercise his right in a reasonable manner, with as little injury to his neighbour's rights as may be. The civil law deems an act, otherwise lawful in itself, illegal if done with a malicious intent of injuring a neighbour, *animo vicino nocendi*. The same principle is adopted in the laws of Scotland, where an otherwise lawful act is forbidden 'if done *in aemulationem vicini,*'[Bell's Principles, section 966] but this principle has not found a place in our law.

The question in this case, therefore as it seems to me, resolves itself into an inquiry, whether the Defendant exercised his right of enjoying the subterraneous waters in a reasonable manner.

To that question, Lord Wensleydale gave a resounding 'No'. He was of the firm view that to extract large quantities of water for a purpose completely unconnected with the land under which it flowed or the inhabitants of that land, for the use of persons who had no right to use it directly and to the injury of neighbours who had an 'equal right' to the water, was unreasonable and hence unlawful.[33]

Part of the reason for spending a little time on this issue is that it is

Exchequer in 1834. As Baron Parke he sat with great distinction as a judge of the Exchequer for more than 20 years. He resigned in 1855 and was given a life peerage so that he could sit in the House of Lords. The conferral of a life peerage was successfully challenged and he was given a hereditary peerage instead. See Walker, above at note 15, 918.

[31] Above at note 23, 381–2; 153.

[32] Ibid., 388; 155. The maxim *sic utere tuo ut alienum non laedas* translates in English to 'so use your own property as not to injure your neighbour's': G. F. Wharton, *Legal Maxims, with Observations in Two Parts* (Law Times, London, 3rd edn, 1903), 179. For discussion of the maxim and its application to surface and underground water, see R. H. Kersley (ed.), *Broom's Legal Maxims* (Sweet & Maxwell Ltd, London, 10th edn, 1939), 238–56. The Scottish doctrine of *animus vicino nocendi* is discussed below in Chapter 6. It is ironic that Lord Wensleydale is the only judge to refer to Scots law, as in the debate in the House three years earlier over the validity of the life peerage conferred on him (see above at note 30), 'his ignorance of Scots law was recognized to be a disadvantage': R. F. V. Heuston, 'Parke, James (First (and last) Lord Wensleydale)', in Simpson, above at note 1, 401, 403.

[33] Above at note 23, 388–9; 156. This distinction between ordinary uses of water (e.g. domestic purposes, watering cattle), which is justified (reasonable) whatever the effect on the flow, and extraordinary uses, which cannot interfere with the rights of other proprietors, is drawn in many of the surface water cases. See, e.g., *Miner v Gilmour* (1858) 12 Moore PC 131, 156, *per* Lord Kingsdown (PC), and *McCartney v Londonderry & Lough Swilly Railway Co.* [1904] AC 301 (HL). See Chapter 5.

common for judges and commentators to quote out of context the passage about Scots law as to malicious exercise of right not finding a place in English law. Indeed, North J. did just that in *Pickles*.[34] Read in context, however, one can see the connection between a rule prohibiting malicious exercise of right and a rule of reasonable use. On the law as Lord Wensleydale thought it ought to be, there is no need for English law to find a place for the civilian doctrine. Everything that such a doctrine achieves in the civil law can be achieved under the rubric of reasonable use. (This can be seen clearly in the later nuisance cases and in American law.)[35] Without such balancing of interests under a rule of reasonable user, however, the more necessary a doctrine like malicious exercise of rights would be.[36]

But in *Pickles* North J. did not see any connection between Lord Wensleydale's simultaneous rejection of the malice qualification and his championing of a rule of reasonable use. North J. simply viewed the dictum of Lord Wensleydale in the House of Lords as cancelling out the seeming approval by the Court of Exchequer Chamber in *Acton*'s case, again by way of dicta, of Marcellus' qualification as to malice. As there was no English case affirmatively applying the malice qualification, and a more recent dictum from a higher court contradicting the dictum in *Acton*'s case, North J. held that Pickles's 'motive' was not material, and consequently the Corporation was not entitled to injunctive relief as a matter of common law. This assumed no importance to the result at first instance, as breach of the private Act justified injunctive relief. But in the appellate courts, which unanimously repudiated the statutory basis for an injunction, attention focused directly on the common law basis (if any) for an injunction.

In the Court of Appeal

Pickles appealed the decision, arguing that North J. was wrong on the statutory interpretation point and right on the common law point that intention was irrelevant. The Corporation argued the converse.[37] Pickles prevailed on both issues. The statutory interpretation point is treated in the next chapter. The focus here is on the common law point.

The opposing arguments of counsel, as appear in the official law reports, framed the common law issue for the Court of Appeal. Pickles's counsel argued:[38]

[34] Above at note 4, 67.
[35] These are discussed in Chapter 7.
[36] This can be seen clearly in Scots law and the later American law. See further in Chapters 6 and 7.
[37] *Corporation of Bradford v Pickles* [1895] 1 Ch 145.
[38] Ibid., 149–50.

The question whether the object of the Defendant in making the shafts was with the *bona fide* intention of working his stone quarries is immaterial. Every man has a right to make what use he pleases of his own land and of the water that percolates through it; and if the situation of the land gives him a special advantage he has a right to the benefit of it: *Rawstron v Taylor*; *Chasemore v Richards*. But there is in fact no evidence that the Defendant has been acting with *mala fides*.

Counsel for the Corporation began by denying Pickles's common law right to intercept the percolating water, arguing that it was in a defined underground channel and so fell within the surface water/riparianism rule.[39] This had been rejected as a matter of fact at first instance, and, although persisted with, made no greater headway in the appellate court.[40] Counsel continued:[41]

But if [Pickles] had a right at common law to intercept the water percolating through his land, he can only exercise that right *bona fide* for his own benefit, and cannot do so maliciously or in order to force the Plaintiffs to make terms with him. He can only exercise the right subject to the maxim '*Sic utere tuo ut alienum non laedas*': *Acton v Blundell*; *Smith v Kenrick*. The evidence shews that he is not acting with the intention of working his quarries, but to annoy the Plaintiffs and to oblige them to buy him off.

The reported skeletal arguments, however, do not do justice to the wide-ranging discussion between bench and bar lasting two days, recorded in shorthand and printed as part of the case on appeal to the House of Lords.[42] Three matters should be highlighted.

First, Pickles's counsel did not shrink from the logical implications of taking their stand on *Acton v Blundell* and *Chasemore v Richards*. Pickles had the absolute legal right to do what he wished with water percolating under his property. Everitt Q.C. declared: '[W]e could appropriate the whole of the water. We might if we had desired it, apart from any special statute, have dug out a hole and made a great reservoir and accumulated the whole of the surface and percolating water, and supplied that or sold it to anybody.'[43] Where, he taunted, was the equity to restrain his client from doing that or diverting the water?[44]

[39] On this rule, see further in Chapter 5.

[40] In saying that, I am not commenting on the strength of the argument. Indeed, it seems to me a reasonably strong one. Given the geography of the area and the fact that the second shaft (No. 2) was about 40 yards from the mouth of the Spring, it does not seem to require any stretch of the imagination to say that at that point the captive waters were in a defined stream. It may be that not enough evidential attention was devoted to this issue by counsel for the Corporation. In any event, the findings of fact were unhelpful. Despite significant argument on this point before the Court of Appeal the issue was really foreclosed by the findings below. Understandably, the point was not pursued to the House of Lords.

[41] Above at note 37, 150.

[42] *Shorthand Notes of Argument before Court of Appeal*, above at note 12.

[43] Ibid., p. 3.

[44] Ibid., p. 27.

Secondly, the Court of Appeal sought clarification from Pickles's counsel that the Corporation lacked the power to acquire the land or water rights compulsorily, and that this was not a matter that could be forced to arbitration under statute.[45] The assurance was given.

Thirdly, there was much contention as to whether Pickles's right to use the water was a property right in the ordinary sense, or something less than that. Not surprisingly, Pickles's counsel spoke only of a fully fledged property right; whereas the Corporation's counsel characterized it as 'a peculiar sort of right' because there is no property in percolating water until it is appropriated.[46] Because of this peculiar character, the Corporation's leading counsel argued that percolating water could not be dealt with in a malicious fashion so as to damage a neighbour. The following exchange is illuminating:[47]

Mr COZENS-HARDY: . . . you must not in dealing with subterranean water in your own land act maliciously, and therefore damage your neighbour.
The LORD CHANCELLOR: I do not think the principle could be confined to subterranean water. I think if you make it good at all it must be good as to the exercises of rights of property. One can hardly see a reason for an exceptional law.
Mr COZENS-HARDY: Except that subterranean water is of a peculiar character. There is no property in it before it is appropriated and used.
The LORD CHANCELLOR: There is no right to it, but ordinarily speaking the man who has the *solum* to the centre of the earth can do what he likes between these points on his own land. It comes on his land as forming part of it. I suppose there is no property in the percolating water; that is to say when it percolates away the man cannot follow it and say it is mine, but I suppose the water that is in the man's soil is as much a part of his property as the earth or the stone, or anything else while it is there.
Mr COZENS-HARDY: He may have a right to appropriate it for his own legitimate purposes, but he has no further right than that.
The LORD CHANCELLOR: Is not it his?
Mr COZENS-HARDY: I submit not.
The LORD CHANCELLOR: Why is not the water that is there his as much as the gravel, or the earth, or the moss, or anything else?
Mr COZENS-HARDY: Because there is property in the stone. There is no such thing, I submit, as property in the underground water.
The LORD CHANCELLOR: When you say there is property in the stone, supposing the percolating water were to carry with it some of the stones or gravel that was underneath his land on to somebody else's with that percolating water, he would have no more right to follow the gravel than the water?
Mr COZENS-HARDY: He would not.
The LORD CHANCELLOR: Is not it really this, that whether water or gravel, or anything else, so long as it is on his land, it is his to do as he likes with?

[45] Ibid., pp. 22–3 and 32–3. [46] Ibid., p. 53. [47] Ibid., pp. 54–5.

Mr COZENS-HARDY: But not to do it maliciously for the purpose of injuring his neighbour. . . .
The LORD CHANCELLOR: I confess I feel there is a great deal to be said—whether it is the law or not—for the expediency of the law which prevents the assertion of the rights of property not for the benefit of the individual who possesses the right, but to the injury of the neighbour. There is a good deal to be said for that. Whether it is part of our law is another thing.

The Court of Appeal judges found in favour of Pickles and discharged the injunction. Lord Herschell L.C. referred first to the absence of precedent and said '[i]t could hardly be asserted that this was because no person had ever thus exercised his legal rights to the prejudice of his neighbour'.[48] The Lord Chancellor cited 'the high authority' of Lord Wensleydale as against a malicious abuse of rights doctrine. In common with North J. at first instance, Lord Herschell did not stop to observe that this was in the context of Lord Wensleydale advocating a reasonable use rule. Although counsel for the Corporation did not rely on Lord Wensleydale's speech in *Chasemore*'s case (probably because it was effectively a dissenting view) their argument followed it closely, even down to reliance on the Latin maxim *sic utere tuo ut alienum non laedas*. But ultimately Lord Herschell L.C. did not have to reject the doctrine of abuse of rights, because he did not think that Pickles's object could be described as malicious in any event.[49] His object was to secure a benefit to himself by virtue of the advantageous geographic position of his property.

A. L. Smith L.J. reached the same result. He held that it was not malicious for Pickles to seek to benefit himself. Nevertheless, he went further than the Lord Chancellor and rejected any such doctrine of malicious exercise of rights. The statement of Lord Wensleydale in the House of Lords had to be treated as 'decisive' as far as the Court of Appeal was concerned. Lord Justice Smith was well aware that Lord Wensleydale had held out for a rule of reasonable use, applying the maxim *sic utere tuo ut alienum non laedas*, but observed that this found no favour with the rest of the House or the advising judges in *Chasemore's* case.[50] Noting that neither the House nor the assembled judges gave reasons for not applying that maxim, A. L. Smith L.J. opined that:[51]

it may have been so held, upon the ground that an adjacent landowner has no property in or right to subterranean percolating water until it arrives underneath his soil, and that therefore no property or right of his is injured by the abstraction of the percolating water before it arrives under his land. It is not the case of a natural stream flowing either above or below the surface in a definite channel, to which an adjacent owner has a right *ex jure naturae*.

[48] Above at note 37, 157. [49] Ibid., 157–8. [50] Ibid., 163. [51] Idem.

He concluded, 'by the common law of *England* a man may deal with his own in any way he pleases irrespective of what his motive may be as long as he transgresses no statute, no contract, or the maxim above referred to'.[52]

Lindley L.J. concurred in the first instance judge's view of Pickles's conduct but reluctantly was driven to the view that Pickles was not exceeding his legal rights.[53] The legal right to get rid of percolating water came from *Acton v Blundell* and *Chasemore v Richards*, and those cases were viewed as standing for the proposition that the owner can exercise this right selfishly, vexatiously, or even maliciously.[54] Although those cases did not say so, this was taken to be the logical implication of the holdings. 'This is not one of those cases', observed Lindley L.J., 'in which an improper object or motive makes an otherwise lawful act actionable. It is not like libel or malicious prosecution, or what are called frauds on powers.'[55]

Head versus Heart?

Counsels' argument occupied two days at the end of October 1894, and judgment was reserved. Five days later, the Lord Chancellor informed Mr Cozens-Hardy Q.C. that if the Corporation undertook to apply to Parliament for compulsory power to take the water, the Court would allow the *Pickles* appeal 'to stand over' until Parliament determined what should be done. He directed that the other side was to be told of this offer and that the Corporation had to decide quickly as the cut-off for such Bills was just over a week away.[56]

This can only be described as extraordinary. It was a clear signal that the Court of Appeal was going to find for Pickles but that some or all of the members had qualms about doing so. No doubt, they worried about the future supply of water to the inhabitants of Bradford.[57] It would have been easy to gather from the argument of both sets of counsel that the Corporation was, so to speak, 'stuck between a rock and a hard place'.

52 Ibid., 166 (emphasis in the original).

53 Ibid., 158 and 161.

54 Ibid., 159.

55 Idem.

56 This account is taken from the *Shorthand Notes of Argument before Court of Appeal*, above at note 12, p. 78 (note that the date is 5 November 1894, which is correctly stated on the cover sheet but is otherwise on p. 78). Credit for first unearthing this goes to Brian Simpson, *Victorian Law and the Industrial Spirit* (Selden Society, London 1995), 14–15.

57 '[N]ot a little nervous of the possibly appalling practical consequences of their decision', is the way Brian Simpson put the matter: ibid., 14. A competing explanation is that the Court thought that the Corporation should be given the opportunity to pay for the water rights. See B. Rudden, 'Comparative Law in England', in W. E. Butler and V. N. Kudriavtsev (eds), *Comparative Law and Legal System: Historical and Socio-Legal Perspectives* (Oceana Publications Inc., New York, 1985), 75, 83.

The rock being the absence of statutory power to acquire compulsorily the land or the water rights on payment of compensation. The hard place being Edward Pickles, trying to extract an 'extravagant' sum of money for his unwanted water.[58]

The public interest may have found no place in the law (as the judges had, no doubt, decided to state it, if necessary) but the hard-headed common law is not necessarily hard-hearted or unmindful of real world consequences.[59] The Court, however, misjudged the temper of the Corporation.

Leading counsel thought the Corporation would be wise to fall in with the suggestion: '[i]t indicates that the Court of Appeal is against us; but that they think we ought to have parliamentary powers, which will not involve any substantial payment to Pickles.'[60] In making this last comment, Mr Cozens-Hardy probably had in mind a comment the Lord Chancellor made during argument. Lord Herschell L.C. said that if the Corporation had available the statutory power of compulsory purchase, the compensation to Pickles would probably not be a very big sum because he could not use the water himself and there was only one customer who could possibly use it.[61]

The Court's offer was considered at a special meeting of the Waterworks Committee on Thursday, 7 November 1894.[63] The Chairman, Alderman William Holdsworth, strongly urged the Committee to reject the offer.[63] Another member thought the suggestion 'quite preposterous' and 'absurd'. The Committee unanimously decided to decline the offer and to 'fight out' the case. In a letter of that date to Mr Cozens-Hardy Q.C., the Town Clerk said the Corporation's experience of Parliamentary procedure led it to believe that the compensation would be very generous. The Select Committee would say that, unless the parties agreed, the

[58] In their interjections during argument the judges did not disguise their views as to Pickles's demands. Lindley L.J. said that Pickles's object was to sell his rights 'at an extravagant price, it may be': above at note 12, p. 58.

[59] This may be what Jose Harris had in mind when she wrote 'And in the famous case of *Bradford Corporation v Pickles* (often seen as the apogee of judicial support for private property rights), the Court of Appeal clearly supported the claims of the community *against* the individual owner—before the rights of property were reasserted by the House of Lords' (*Private Lives, Public Spirit: Britain, 1870–1914* (Penguin Books, London, 1994), 117)—but, without more, it is incorrect.

[60] Hand-written letter from H. H. Cozens-Hardy Q.C. to the Town Clerk dated 5 November 1894.

[61] Above at note 12, p. 65. See also the references to 'not very much' on p. 66. See also p. 33.

[62] Waterworks Committee Notes, pp. 372–3.

[63] Ibid., p. 372. The Notes record him saying '[h]e would certainly go to the House of Lords—The proceedings were proved up to the hilt to be inequitable as far as Pickles was concerned.' It is difficult to decipher the hand-written last sentence, but that is the best sense I can make of it.

matter would go to arbitration. McGowen wrote that arbitration 'is what Pickles and his advisors desire, and they will do their best to get the largest sum possible, the Corporation bearing all the expenses. The proposal to obtain relief by fresh legislation is considered by [the Corporation] to be hopeless.'[64] Counsel were instructed to take the matter to the House of Lords if the Court of Appeal overturned the injunction granted at first instance.

There was a telling moment in argument at the hearing a few days earlier when leading counsel for the Corporation described the demand for £18,000 in return for the land as 'blackmail'. A. L. Smith L.J. enquired '[a]re you willing to buy at a fair price?'. To which Mr Cozens-Hardy Q.C. replied 'I am really not instructed to answer that question.'[65] The Corporation was not prepared to pay Pickles's price, or a price set in negotiation before a Select Committee, or indeed one settled by arbitration. Much of the evidence from the very first points to the Corporation being unwilling to pay anything at all to Pickles.

Part of it, as we have seen, is that Pickles was considered maliciously opportunistic. But that was not the whole story. The Corporation could not admit to being duped in 1854. A recurring lament in correspondence is that if the statute did not protect the water supply from such diversion then the Corporation paid over £200,000 in 1854 for nothing. Typical was the Corporation's Water Engineer's observation, after reading the Court of Appeal's judgment, that the promoters of the private Bradford Waterworks Company 'must have been little short of simpletons' to have undertaken the works on that basis![66] And so must have been the Councillors and officials who oversaw the Corporation's take-over of the Company in 1854. It was an affront to the intelligence and business acumen of the transferee Corporation to suggest any such thing.

The House of Lords

The Corporation appealed.[67] The reported argument of the Corporation's counsel in the House of Lords focused again on Pickles's unreasonable use of his land and his malicious action. A newspaper report of the argument discloses counsel struggling against a barrage of hostile questioning.[68]

[64] Typewritten copy of a letter from the Town Clerk to H. H. Cozens-Hardy Q.C., dated 7 November 1894.

[65] Above at note 12, p. 57.

[66] Letter to the Town Clerk from Mr James Watson dated 4 April 1895 (quoted by Simpson, above at note 56, 16). (For further details, see Appendix, note 3.)

[67] The injunction was continued pending appeal at the request of the Corporation and by order of the Court of Appeal. (For further details, see Appendix, note 4.)

[68] 'The Manywells Springs Dispute. The Case in the House of Lords. Judgment Reserved.', *The Bradford Observer*, Friday, 10 May 1895, p. 5.

Pickles's counsel were not called upon and the House reserved judgment, which was delivered ten weeks later.[69]

The point of departure for their Lordships was the House of Lords' decision 36 years earlier in *Chasemore's* case. For them that case determined conclusively that the Corporation had no right in the continued flow of the percolating but unchannelled water from its neighbour. To Lord Halsbury, the newly ensconced Lord Chancellor, it was 'absolutely hopeless' to argue against the authority of *Chasemore*'s case, which he said stood for the proposition that 'the landowner had a right to do what he had done whatever his object or purpose might be, and although the purpose might be wholly unconnected with the enjoyment of his own estate'.[70] In other words, there could be no investigation of reasonableness of use, as the Corporation had argued. Pickles's intention to divert the water down into Hewenden Beck, with the consequence of denying water to the inhabitants of Bradford, was just as permissible as the Local Board of Health's appropriation of water in *Chasemore*'s case in order to supply a town's inhabitants.

Lord Watson took the view that the 'Lords . . . in *Chasemore v Richards* held that . . . [Marcellus'] doctrine had no place in the law of England.'[71] It will be remembered that only Lord Wensleydale said that. Like the Lord Chancellor, however, Lord Watson clearly thought that the premise logically excluded an inquiry into malicious exercise of right. As an aside, like Lord Herschell in the Court below, Lord Watson doubted whether this case would have come within the doctrine; but that was neither here nor there.[72]

The House of Lords held Pickles's motive or intention to be 'absolutely irrelevant'.[73] If the act was within his legal rights, however ill Pickles's motives, he had a right to do it. The Lord Chancellor disassociated himself from Lindley L.J.'s moral disapproval of Pickles's actions. Pickles was not obliged to allow the water to flow to 'this trading company'.[74] Lord Halsbury could 'see no reason why he should not insist on their purchasing his interest from which this trading company desires to make

[69] *The Mayor, Aldermen and Burgesses of the Borough of Bradford v Pickles* [1895] AC 587. The case is reported also in the following report series: [1895–99] All ER Rep 985; 64 LJ Ch. 759; 73 L.T. 353; 69 J.P. 3; 44 W.R. 190; 11 T.L.R. 555. Something that is not evident from any of the law reports is that Lord Shand apparently took part in the hearing but, inexplicably, did not participate in the judgment writing. In a newspaper account of the argument before the House of Lords, Lord Shand is recorded present and his questions are reported: above at note 69. For this reason *Pickles* is a judgment of a four-judge bench, which is unusual for a case of this importance. Lord Shand was a Scottish judge, and, if his reported interventions during argument are a reliable guide, he would not have decided any differently than his colleagues.

[70] Ibid., 593.

[71] Ibid., 597.

[72] Idem. This was also the view of Lord Macnaghten: ibid., 601.

[73] Ibid., 594, *per* Lord Halsbury L.C.

[74] Ibid., 595.

a profit'.[75] To the same effect but infinitely more memorable is the response of Lord Macnaghten, which deserves to be quoted in full: [76]

The position of the appellants is one which is not very easy to understand. They cannot dispute the law laid down ... in *Chasemore* ... [b]ut they say that Mr Pickles' action in the matter is malicious, and that because his motive is a bad one, he is not at liberty to do a thing which every landowner in the country may do with impunity if his motives are good. Mr Pickles, it seems, was so alarmed at this view of the case that he tried to persuade the Court that all he wanted to do was to unwater some beds of stone which he thought he could work for profit. In this innocent enterprise the Court found a sinister design. And it may be taken that his real object was to shew that he was master of the situation, and to force the corporation to buy him out at a price satisfactory to himself. Well, he has something to sell, or, at any rate, he has something he can prevent other people enjoying unless he is paid for it. Why should he, he may think, without fee or reward, keep his land as a store-room for a commodity which the corporation dispenses, probably not gratuitously, to the inhabitants of Bradford? He prefers his own interests to the public good. He may be churlish, selfish, and grasping. His conduct may seem shocking to a moral philosopher. But where is the malice? Mr Pickles has no spite against the people of Bradford. He bears no ill-will to the corporation. They are welcome to the water, and to his land too, if they will pay the price for it. So much perhaps might be said in defence or palliation of Mr Pickles' conduct. But the real answer to the claim of the corporation is that in such a case motives are immaterial. It is the act, not the motive for the act, that must be regarded. If the act, apart from motive, gives rise merely to damage without legal injury, the motive, however reprehensible it may be, will not supply that element.

Simpson detects here judicial 'glee at the grasping, greedy behaviour of Edward Pickles'.[77]

The Indigestible Morsel

In *Pickles*, counsel and the judges did not wear whatever Roman and civil law learning they possessed on their sleeves. Marcellus' doctrine and its subsequent treatment in English cases were dutifully trotted out at each level, without any analysis of the place of the doctrine in Roman and civil law or any examination of the scope of the action for fraud. It was given short shrift on the basis of precedent in the courts below. In argument in the Court of Appeal, in response to Everitt Q.C.'s jibe that North J. reserved his judgment in order to search out authorities against Pickles, Lindley L.J. said: 'Our law differs from the law of other countries on that

[75] Idem.

[76] Ibid., 600–1.

[77] Above at note 56, p. 15. Cf. G. H. L. Fridman, 'Motive in the English Law of Nuisance' (1954) 40 Va LR 583, 595.

score. We know that.'[78] This from a lawyer who, as a young man, studied Roman law at Bonn and published an English translation of a leading German codifier of Roman Law under the title *An Introduction to the Study of Jurisprudence*.[79] And one who, late in life, acknowledged his debt to civilian writers in the following terms:[80]

> I owe much to my study of German and French Law Books and to the habit of mastering legal principles before the mode of practically giving effect to them. With us the tendency was to study remedies and learn principles from procedure, which is less scientific and satisfactory in dealing with new and difficult questions.

None of that is evident in *Pickles*.

Neither did Lord Justice Lindley refer to the torts textbook of his former pupil, Frederick Pollock, whom he encouraged to study Roman law, although there is every reason to believe that counsel and the judges would have read it. As we will see in Chapter 7, Pollock referred to Marcellus and Scots law, and pointed out that there was no English authority foreclosing acceptance of the Roman law position.[81]

In the House of Lords, despite the fact that Roman law was at the forefront of the appellant's argument, only Lord Watson referred to it. He doubted whether the doctrine of Marcellus assisted the Corporation, but it was unnecessary to decide the point as he took all of their Lordships (and not just Lord Wensleydale) in *Chasemore*'s case to have held that it was not part of English law. So Lord Watson too decided the matter on precedent.[82] *Chasemore*'s case was decided in 1859. The House of Lords

[78] Above at note 12, p. 21. Lord Herschell L.C. confessed to thinking that there was 'a great deal to be said' for the expediency of a law which prevents the assertion of the rights of property not for the benefit of the individual who possesses the right, but to the injury of the neighbour; but he went on to say '[w]hether it is part of our law is another thing': *Shorthand Notes of Argument before Court of Appeal*, p. 55. See also *Ballard v Tomlinson* (1885) L.R. 29 Ch. 115, 125, *per* Lindley L.J. (CA).

[79] See O. Hood Phillips, 'Legal Authors since 1800', in *Then and Now, 1799–1974: Commemorating 175 years of Law Bookselling and Publishing* (Sweet & Maxwell, London, 1974), 3, 7; P. G. Stein, 'Maine and Legal Education', in A. Diamond (ed.), *The Victorian Achievement of Sir Henry Maine: A centennial reappraisal* (Cambridge University Press, Cambridge, 1991), 195, 200; W. Holdsworth, *A History of English Law* (A. L. Goodhart and H. G. Hambury, eds) (Methuen & Co. Ltd, London, 1965), vol. XV, 357–8. Lindley published his translation of the general part of A. F. J. Thibault's *System des Pandekten Rechts* (1803) in 1855. One possible source of that knowledge was the writings of Lindley's former pupil, Frederick Pollock. For what Pollock had to say about abuse of right at the time of the *Pickles* litigation, see Chapter 7.

[80] Quoted in M. Dockray, 'Savigny and the Squatter' (1985) 6 J Leg Hist 109, 110. I am grateful to Martin Dockray for allowing me to read his copy of Lord Lindley's unpublished autobiography.

[81] See Chapter 7.

[82] Bernard Rudden viewed this as an illustration of 'common law courts selecting those parts of Roman law which support their conclusion and rejecting those qualifications in the same sentence of the author which do not': above at note 56, 83.

held itself to be bound by its own decisions in 1861, and this was reiterated conclusively in 1898.[83] The powerful pull of precedent is not surprising. What is surprising is that Lord Wensleydale's dictum of itself, without analysis or discussion, should have proved decisive.

Notwithstanding Lord Wensleydale's extraordinarily high reputation, it was only a dictum, and one contained in as close to a dissenting judgment as possible without recording a formal dissent.[84] As noted above, Lord Wensleydale clearly favoured the rule of reasonable use exemplified in the maxim *sic utere tuo ut alienum non laedas*. In the paragraph preceding the one mentioning Marcellus in *Chasemore*'s case, Lord Wensleydale had cited from the *Digest* with a view to putting *Acton*'s case on a satisfactory footing. Both in this judgment and an earlier one in the Court of Exchequer, Lord Wensleydale was highly critical of the reasoning in *Acton*'s case.[85] It was because Roman law and the common law were at one (in his dissentient view) in applying the rule of reasonable use to percolating water that English law had not found a place for the more limited doctrine of Marcellus. It was simply not needed! To latch on to the dictum without a thought or care for its meaning in context suggests corner-cutting to reach a desired result.

Why does it matter? It matters because Marcellus' doctrine gave the courts in *Pickles* the chance to think through in a careful way the implications of decisions such as *Acton v Blundell* and *Chasemore v Richards*. The policy reasons supporting the rule are, in essence, two-fold. First, that as by its very nature no one knows where percolating water flows, it would be very undesirable to hold an owner liable for digging in his or her own ground for legitimate purposes, when unbeknownst to him or her this affects someone else's water supply. The archetypal case given is the artesian well which drew its water from up to 40 miles around. Secondly, and

83 The cases are *Beamish v Beamish* (1861) 9 HLC 273; 11 E.R. 735 and *London Tramways Co. v London County Council* [1898] AC 375. See generally J. Evans, 'Change in the Doctrine of Precedent during the Nineteenth century', in L. Goldstein (ed.), *Precedent in Law* (Clarendon Press, Oxford, 1987), 35. David Pugsley cites the *Pickles* case as a 'good example' of the 'overwhelming agreement among the judges that the House of Lords was bound by its own previous decisions' for much of the nineteenth century, but does not take the point that *Chasemore v Richards* was distinguishable. See D. Pugsley, '*London Tramways* (1898)' (1996) 17 J Leg Hist 172, 172–3.

84 This was readily apparent at the time. As can be seen from a case note on *Pickles* under the title 'Malicious Exercise of Rights' (1894) 68 *Justice of the Peace* 814, 815 (reprinted in (1895) 28 *Irish Law Times* 23, 24): 'the Court of Appeal endorse with approval the *dictum* of Lord Wensleydale in *Chasemore v Richards*, which is, in reality, the only previous authority on point, and that *dictum* was in itself spoken *obiter* for the statement of facts in that case expressly negatived any intention to harm the plaintiff'.

85 *Chasemore v Richards*, above at note 23, 387; 155. See also *Broadbent v Ramsbotham* (1856) 25 LJ Exch. 121. The sole dissentient in the court below (the Court of Exchequer Chamber) in *Chasemore v Richards* (1857) 2 H. & N. 168; 157 E.R. 71, Coleridge J. was fortified by the fact that Baron Parke (as Lord Wensleydale was then) took the same view.

related, it is said that any other rule would unreasonably inhibit productive, economic use of land—the obvious illustration being mining, which was the fact situation in *Acton*. As Lord Wensleydale observed, 'the great interests of society require that the cultivation of every man's land should be encouraged, and its natural advantages made available'.[86]

Pickles was a very different case. The policy arguments did not cut against finding for the Corporation. There was an absolute certainty that shaft No. 2 and the associated tunnelling would divert the water going to the Spring and the waterworks. In argument Pickles's counsel cleverly always referred to the hypothetical situation of a diverting well being a long distance off from a spring. The fact was, however, that shaft No. 2 was 40 yards from the Spring![87] The finding of fact at first instance that Pickles was not acting in good faith stemmed in large part from the deliberate placement of shaft No. 2 as close as possible to the Spring.[88] Here there was no legitimate use. This distinguishes *Pickles* starkly from all the other cases, where the use was held or assumed to be legitimate.[89] Pickles was not genuinely engaged in coal mining in a regular and proper way as in *Acton*'s case. Neither was he appropriating the water so as to supply a nearby town as in *Chasemore*'s case. Pickles was going to waste the water by pouring it in Hewenden Beck and had no intention of working his dewatered stone, even if there was some there to work![90] In doing so he endangered a large water supply business, which, in terms of the economic incentive argument, was making the very best use of the water.

Given the rudimentary understanding of the movement of groundwater last century, it is entirely understandable that the judges thought it would be 'unreasonable and unjust'[91] to hold a landowner liable for harm caused to others' water supplies when he was not in a position to predict this effect or to anticipate it in advance. Even at that time, however, when the law was applied in situations where there was

[86] *Chasemore v Richards*, above at note 23, 387; 155.

[87] The distances recorded in the judgments vary a little. Forty yards is the most frequently given distance. In argument in the Court of Appeal, Pickles's counsel constantly speaks hypothetically about distance, most commonly in the order of a mile or two: above at note 12, pp. 6, 9, 13 ('. . . whatever distance up that hill . . .'), 16 and 20 ('It is a long way up the hill to our property'). For actual distances, see Chapter 2.

[88] See above at notes 9–13 and accompanying text.

[89] An identical point is made in relation to a much-criticized Wisconsin case, *Huber v Merkel*, 117 Wis. 355 (1903), allowing an owner to waste water with the intention of harming his neighbours: see D. L. Uelmen, 'The Law of Underground Water; A Half-Century of *Huber v Merkel*' [1953] Wis. LR 491, 494–5.

[90] The lack of adequate inquiry in that regard was the other principal ground for North J. holding that Pickles lacked good faith: above at note 12.

[91] *Acton v Blundell*, above at note 18, 352; 1234. The identical phrase is used in an earlier New York case, *Ellis v Duncan*, 21 Barb. 230, 234 (1855), *per* S. B. Strong J. See also *Bradford Corporation v Ferrand* [1902] 2 Ch 655, 663–4.

absolutely no doubt where the water flowed and what the consequences of digging would be—as in *Pickles*—this policy justification fell to the ground.[92]

The policy reasons given in the earlier case law did not mandate or necessitate the judicial creation of absolute property rights in percolating underground water, so that the neighbour had no legal right whatsoever in the flow no matter what the circumstances. As we will see, the technical, doctrinal reasons justifying the essentially policy decision—principally acquiescence, percolating water is part of the soil, the maxim *cujus est solum, ejus est usque ad coelum et ad inferos*—were hardly legally compelling.[93] It was this challenge that Marcellus' doctrine placed before the judges, but none rose to it. Even allowing for the progressive hardening of the arteries of precedent throughout the nineteenth century, in my opinion, the courts in the *Pickles* litigation were not bound by the earlier case law in the way the judges at every level so readily assumed or asserted. In holding as they did in *Pickles*, the courts were establishing an absolute property right in percolating water such that *in no circumstances* does a neighbour have any right to the flow of percolating and unchannelled water under the land of another.[94] This issue is examined in greater depth in Chapter 5.

The judges in the nineteenth century were not antagonistic to Roman law.[95] They appreciated better than most lawyers today the enormous debt the common law owes Roman and civil law in terms of its superstructure and many of its ideas and doctrines. Typical is the complimentary description of Roman law by Tindal C.J. in *Acton v Blundell*: 'the fruit of the researches of the most learned men, the collective wisdom of ages and the ground work of the municipal law of most of the countries of Europe.'[96] Why, then, did the late Victorian judges in *Pickles* find Marcellus' morsel unappetizing? I speculate in Chapter 6 as to the influences at work.[97]

[92] P. N. Davis, 'Wells and Springs: Relationship at Law' (1972) 37 Missouri LR 189, 202.

[93] See Chapter 5.

[94] J. F. Lever, 'Means, Motives, and Interests in the Law of Torts', in A. G. Guest (ed.), *Oxford Essays in Jurisprudence (First Series)* (Clarendon Press, Oxford, 1964), 50, 59.

[95] However, in the latter part of the century, increasing judicial impatience is evident with arguments based on Roman law: R. Powell, 'Roman Law in Common Law Courts' (1958) 11 Curr Leg Probs 19, 28, and esp. *Keighley, Maxstad & Co. v Durant* [1901] AC 240, 244 (Lord Halsbury) and 262 (Lord Lindley). See generally M. H. Hoeflich, *Roman and Civil Law and the Development of Anglo-American Jurisprudence in the Nineteenth Century* (University of Georgia Press, Athens, 1997), chs 3–4, and M. Graziadei, 'Changing Images of the Law in XIX Century English Legal Thought (The Continental Impulse)', in M. Reimann (ed.), *The Reception of Continental Ideas in the Common Law World, 1820–1920* (Duncker & Humblot, Berlin, 1993), 115.

[96] Above at note 18, 353; 1234. See also *Mason v Hill* (1833) 5 B. & Ad. 1; 110 E.R. 692.

[97] See Chapter 6.

Press Reaction

The National newspaper, *The Times*, reported the House of Lords' decision, without editorial comment.[98] The only substantive comment in the local press appeared in the same two papers that had carried stories about the dispute before it went to court.

The Editorial in *The Bradford Observer* appeared resigned to the result, but sniped at the cost to the ratepayers, deprecated the casuistry of some of the reasoning on the statutory interpretation point, and imagined that both the draughtsman and Parliament intended to protect the waterworks from diminution of supply within a certain area of the Spring's flow underground to the waterworks.[99] The Editorial accepted that the leading case was against such a view, percolating water belonging to 'to the man who can catch it first'. It went on:

> We do not know that it is a bad rule, if it is to apply all round. But on this showing, why has the long-suffering Bradford ratepayer had to pay sundry millions for the construction of compensation reservoirs to recoup riparian owners and occupiers for something not more valuable perhaps than Mr Pickles's minerals?

This is an echo of the privately expressed view of both the Water Engineer, James Watson, and the Town Clerk, William McGowen. That is, why would the Corporation have gone to the expense of buying off other users if it could have bought a small plot of land close to a spring, or otherwise tapped percolating underground water, and taken as much as it desired?

In this account, the Corporation emerged largely unscathed, as it had in the earlier accounts of the dispute in *The Bradford Observer*. The *Leeds Evening Express* also ran true to form. It lambasted the Corporation in an Editorial, describing the behaviour of the Corporation as 'high-handed, overbearing and unreasonable', and the case as illustrating 'the grasping and high-handed methods which some public bodies see fit to adopt'.[100] Praising Pickles for his honesty in laying his plans before the Corporation, the leader went on to say 'that by some occult process of reasoning' the Corporation concluded that he had a sinister motive. That was Bradford's 'great mistake': it was not only legally irrelevant (as their Lordships said), but it was also 'certainly undignified and unfair for a powerful Corporation to adopt such a position simply for the purpose of prejudicing the case'. At the end of this excoriation the Editor put his finger exactly on the crucial point:

[98] *The Times*, 30 July 1895, p. 5.
[99] *The Bradford Observer*, Tuesday, 30 July 1895, p. 4.
[100] *Leeds Evening Express*, Tuesday, 30 July 1895, p. 1, coll. 5 and 6.

The Corporation had no rights over his land—for the absurd clause upon which they relied did not in any way give them more than their common law rights. Bradford had made a mistake in the way in which its waterworks were acquired; and it is nothing but right that Bradford should pay for the mistake. It will now have to do so.

But the Corporation never did pay for its 'mistake' of 1854, and therefore never publicly admitted to making one.

Swamped by Draining Water

Pickles won the litigation battle but lost the war.[101] He set about and completed the tunnelling, and by mid-1897 had completely diverted the water away from the Spring. He continued both before and after that time to attempt to sell his land to the Corporation, but the Waterworks Committee steadfastly refused to deal with Pickles and dismissed his solicitor's several entreaties.[102] The Corporation never paid him a penny for his land or his water. By century's end the one-time mainstay of Bradford's water supply was a very minor contributor. There were evidently enough other sources of supply to make do.

It has always been assumed that that was the end of the water supply. The once prodigious Many Wells Spring has been assumed to have been permanently spiked by Pickles's tunnelling, and the water carried away under and then over his farm and into Hewenden Beck below the Reservoir. In fact, this state of affairs did not last for long.

In 1900, James Watson, the Bradford Water Engineer, told the British Association for the Advancement of Science gathering in Bradford that in the aftermath of the *Pickles* case the Corporation 'sunk in . . . [its] own land a well deeper than Mr Pickles' shaft, and . . . succeeded in recovering a very large quantity of the spring water, which again flows daily to Bradford'.[103] He had had this contingency plan in mind since at least

101 Much of this paragraph is drawn from Simpson's account: above at note 56, pp. 16–18.

102 The Waterworks Committee Notes disclose an approach by someone (name indistinct) from Leeds representing a syndicate formed to work the stone and sell the water at East Many Wells; it was rebuffed: BBC 4/4/9, p. 22, 23 December 1896. Another approach (name again indistinct) asking if the Corporation will purchase was considered by the Committee on 7 January 1898, and declined: Waterworks Committee Notes, ibid., p. 59. At Waterworks Committee meetings on 16 August 1901 and 2 January 1903, letters from W. & G. Burr & Co. offering the farm for sale were considered and rejected: ibid., pp. 171 and 211. The only movement on the part of the Corporation I found was this enigmatic reference: 'Pickles Manywells—Land Exchange, Mr Watson reports further interviews with Mr Pickles—Instructions given for Mr Watson to see Pickles to settle—terms—': ibid., p. 146, 30 November 1900.

103 J. Watson, *Water Supply, with a description of the Bradford Waterworks (Old and New)* (Percy Lund, Humphries & Co. Ltd, Bradford, 1900), 16. James Watson, M. Inst. C.E., was

1892.[104] The drilling of this shaft was authorized by the Waterworks Committee on 4 June 1897.[105] Many of the records have been destroyed, but it is clear from the sundry documents that remain that the recouped water from Many Wells Spring supplied parts of Bradford well into the 1950s. At the time of the centenary of the Corporation of Bradford's ownership of the waterworks in 1955 it was said that Many Wells Spring was still supplying water to nearby Harden.[106] At some point thereafter the supply seems to have become uneconomic and it ceased, and the last vestiges of the waterworks were removed. All that is left is the original masonry around the wellhead, and a locked door leading into a long tunnel containing the pipes that led well back into the hillside and tapped the Spring.[107] In front of the door is a concrete cover, in the place of what was once pipe work, and the steady noise of flowing spring water can be heard underneath, flowing underground down to Hewenden Reservoir below.

As for Pickles's elaborate scheme of tunnels and open drain down to Hewenden Beck, little remains visible. The shafts have been concreted over in the interests of safety, and the pipework leading down to the Beck has been subsequently disturbed by earth and drainage works. But a steady stream of water still discharges out of a pipe at the bottom of Pickles's field below the Reservoir: a testament still to his foolish plan.

Edward Pickles was not a rich man. At trial, after some prevarication under cross-examination, Edward gave evidence that the annual rental received for leased farmland was about £260; although, when pressed for detail, he could account for only £235 10s in rental income.[108] An income of £200 a year in 1900 has been estimated to be the bare minimum necessary for a married man with a family to maintain a 'middle middle-class

born on 18 March 1844 and died on 29 March 1919. He was the Bradford Water Engineer for the duration of the Pickles saga. In this, almost certainly unknowingly, the Water Engineer was following the advice of Baron Bramwell in *Ibbotson v Peat* (1865) 3 H. & C. 644, 50; 159 E.R. 684, 686. There Baron Bramwell discussed hypothetically a situation very similar to *Pickles*, and said the answer for the neighbour deprived of ground water was simply to dig a deeper well.

104 See Waterworks Committee Notes, 13 August 1892.

105 Waterworks Committee Notes, p. 41.

106 W. H. Leatham, J. Ruscoe, and G. F. Renton, *Bradford Corporation Waterworks Department, 1855–1955 Centenary* (Bradford, 1955), 52.

107 See Figure 5 on p. 37. (For further details, see Appendix, note 5.)

108 Transcript of the Evidence given in the Chancery Division, *Case on Appeal*, pp. 337–8. In undated hand-written notes entitled 'Notes for Cross-Examination on Affidavits filed on Defendant's behalf', it was estimated that Edward's rental income was about £170 and noted that '[a]pplying that to the £18,000[,] his price is equal to 106 years' purchase'.
In the earlier negotiations Pickles had lead the Committee to believe that his rental income was £300 a year: Waterworks Committee Notes, p. 309, Monday, 15 August 1892.

way of life'.[109] The costs of the litigation must have put Pickles under enormous financial strain, especially as he had already invested in the exploration and drilling on his land for over two years without seeing any return on his investment. Throughout the litigation, Pickles was represented by at least three counsel (a fourth was added in the House of Lords—where, incidentally, none was called upon to address the House), two of whom at each stage were Queen's Counsel. Success in the Court of Appeal and the House of Lords gave him his costs in those courts and at first instance. Then, as now, that would not have covered all his legal expenses. Even with the costs award in his favour in the House of Lords and below, it must have been a financial drain on Pickles. The cost of the litigation was enormous for the Corporation—Simpson estimates around £4,000.[110]

The cost of these extensive drilling and tunnelling operations must have broken Pickles financially. According to Brian Simpson, some time between 1900 and 1904 Edward Pickles (and his family) emigrated to Canada, much poorer for all the trouble. Edward apparently never did extract any stone. The Corporation is alleged to have threatened to 'swamp' Pickles with litigation—and this it failed to do—but in the end he sank himself.

It has proved impossible to trace Pickles's descendants in Canada or Yorkshire. Pickles is an extremely popular name in Yorkshire,[111] and that has not helped in tracing the family. One has a mental picture of the man,[112] but alas we do not know his appearance or his ultimate fate.

Who was the Baddy in *Pickles*?

It is usually assumed that Edward Pickles was a greedy, grasping, and ruthless man, and that the Corporation was an innocent victim of his machinations, forced into litigation in a valiant attempt to avoid his

[109] M. Dockray, 'Guineas by Gaslight', in M. Dowrick (ed.), *City University Centenary Lectures in Law* (Blackstone Press Ltd, London, 1996), 27, 38. The statistics on wages and cost of living throughout Great Britain and in particular places are the subject of dispute, but for my purpose the figure gives a rough yardstick against which to measure Pickles's affluence.

[110] Simpson, above at note 56, 17.

[111] See the entry under 'Pickles' in G. Redmonds, *Yorkshire Surnames Series Pt 1: Bradford & District* (1990), 43.

[112] In his facetious essay 'In the Heaven of Legal Concepts', the great Romanist Rudolph von Jhering (1818–92) personifies the concept of Property in these terms, which fit exactly my mental picture of Edward Pickles: 'That can only be Property. It looks just as I thought it would look; squat, rough, with sturdy limbs, well fed and with a saturated satisfied expression on its face. You can see that it will not permit challenge by anybody, and feels perfectly secure.' Quoted in M. R. Cohen and F. S. Cohen, *Readings in Jurisprudence and Legal Philosophy* (Prentice-Hall Inc., New York, 1951), 678, 687.

blackmail. We may never know the truth, but there is at least some reason to reassess this black-and-white picture.

We know next to nothing about Edward Pickles the man. One thing we do know is that he did the right thing by his mother and his five siblings. As the oldest son, and hence heir in law, Edward made adequate provision for his mother, sisters, and younger brother by selling some of the land and mortgaging some. Edward was left with 140 acres; apparently he was determined to make the best of what he had left.

Edward was found to have lied about the purpose of his scheme. The caustic comment North J. passed on the evidence of Edward's engineer—'that the real facts must have escaped his memory'[113]—applied equally to Edward. In mitigation, Lord Macnaghten pleaded the monstrous claim of the Corporation that Pickles could not do what he liked on his own land.[114]

The correspondence reveals Edward to be quick to anger, stubborn, and intransigent. The archived papers tell of attempts by representatives of the Corporation to inspect the site (which were thwarted by Edward) and a desultory discussion of price. These point towards the possibility of a negotiated sale. But, as I have been at pains to point out, there is as much, if not more, in the papers to suggest that the Corporation would have no truck with Edward Pickles. The attitude of the Town Clerk was intransigent from the start. The Corporation did not take any of the opportunities offered to buy the land or the water rights, neither did it go to Parliament to acquire such rights compulsorily. Instead, it pursued expensive litigation as far it could go. And when the legality of the matter had been definitively sorted out, the Corporation refused to negotiate with Pickles. At one point it might have been able to negotiate a water right for less than the ultimate cost of the litigation, but that is to look at the matter with the benefit of considerable hindsight.

There is not much evidence that this was perceived by the courts as a 'David and Goliath' struggle, but Edward might well have thought it was. And this is the way it was portrayed in a local newspaper.[115] The actions and intransigence of both sides left a great deal to be desired. Ultimately the mighty pebble of absolute ownership in percolating underground water slayed the Corporation.

113 Above at note 4, 62–3. The evidence of Edward's engineer, John Woodhead, was essentially that in designing the scheme of shafts and tunnels he did not consider the impact on the Spring.

114 Above at note 76 and accompanying text.

115 *Leeds Evening Press*, Tuesday, 30 July 1895, p. 1, coll. 5 and 6.

Was Edward Acting Maliciously?

As we have seen, the appellate courts in *Pickles* said that Edward's actions were not actionably malicious because his motive was legally irrelevant, and hence not to be inquired into. The reasons why the common law took this approach are explored later in Chapters 6 and 7.

What needs to be emphasized here is that reasonable people differ over whether Edward was acting maliciously and should have been restrained from diverting the water. Boiled down to its most basic, the claim of the Corporation of Bradford was that Edward Pickles was acting maliciously in disregard of the interests of the public of Bradford. Pickles disagreed vehemently, and asserted his right to do with his own as he liked. If the Corporation wanted the water either it should purchase the right to use the water, or it should stop complaining.

Edward was not wasting the water for its own sake. His motive was to deprive the Borough of it in order to bring pressure to bear on the Corporation to bargain with him. He thought, as do many others, that that was legitimate. What if he had been offered a reasonable price by the Corporation but persisted in wasting the water because he simply enjoyed annoying the Corporation, or because he disliked the Town Clerk? Is it less legitimate to derive pleasure from the Corporation's annoyance than seeking to induce the Corporation to buy the water? If so, how—if at all—is the law to differentiate between those situations?

As far as we know, there was no rival water supply company seeking Edward's water, neither was there a nearby supply outlet to which Edward could divert the water for profit. If there had been a competitor, the element of competition seemingly would have legitimated his actions. But what if, even then, it could be proved that his real desire was to harm the Corporation, to put it out of the water business? What if he sold the water to the rival company for less than Bradford offered?

As we will see in Chapters 6 and 7, most common law jurisdictions in the United States, and all civil law legal systems, are able to reach at least some of this behaviour; but thanks to *Pickles*, the law in England and Wales and Northern Ireland is different. As we have seen earlier in this chapter, and as will be discussed in more detail in Chapter 6, the law of Scotland was otherwise, but it was mis-portrayed in *Pickles* and did not prevail.

4

Property and Statutory Interpretation

First and foremost, *Pickles* was a case about statutory interpretation. The Corporation took its stand against Edward Pickles on the statute first.[1] The Corporation sought an injunction in respect of the alleged breach of statutory duty by Pickles. The case illustrates the potency of the common law principle that whenever possible statutes will be interpreted by the courts to protect the property interests of individuals.

This chapter considers the structure and content of the Bradford Waterworks Act 1842 and its successors in order to place the key provision (section 49) in context. This is something that many of the judges in *Pickles* did not do. The differing approaches of the judges to the interpretation of section 49 are then summarized, and some comments are ventured about what *Pickles* illustrates about statutory interpretation and the common law mindset.

Discussions of statutory interpretation tend to induce the 'M.E.G.O effect': an abbreviation for 'my eyes glaze over'.[2] The difficulty of discussing interpretation issues carefully and clearly, within a reasonable compass, and in a way that does not lack interest or an appropriate sense of proportion to the overall story, must be acknowledged. But no treatment of *Pickles* can avoid the topic.

Bradford Waterworks Act 1842

The background to this Act was explored in Chapter 1. To recap, the purposes of the Act were to incorporate the Bradford Waterworks Company, to provide that Company with the powers necessary to construct the waterworks on Hewenden Beck and the pipeline to Bradford, and to protect the interests of other users of the water from

[1] The Corporation sought an injunction primarily in respect of the breach of statutory duty. As the Corporation was the beneficiary of the prohibition against interference with water in section 49 of the Bradford Waterworks Act 1854, it was probably taken for granted that the Corporation had standing to seek to enforce the prohibition by injunction, rather than being limited to seeking the liquidated damages provided for in the second half of that provision. No argument on *locus standi* was raised in any of the courts.

[2] M. R. Borick (ed.), *Acronyms, Initialisms & Abbreviations Dictionary* (Gale Research, Detroit, 21st edn, 1996), vol. 1, Pt 2: G–O, p. 2321 (described as '[a]n article, written about an important subject, that resists reader interest and has a soporific effect').

Many Wells Spring. This private Act runs to 368 sections, but it is necessary to refer to only a relatively small number of provisions.

Consensual and Compulsory Purchase

Several provisions deal with what can be broadly described as consensual and compulsory purchase. As to consensual purchase, the new Company was authorized to buy out the pre-existing and inadequate water undertaking, and its previous purchase of Trooper Farm and Many Wells Spring was confirmed.[3] Furthermore, as discussed below, the Company was authorized also to buy small parcels of land (up to a maximum of 50 acres) to gain access to spring water, or to protect such water from injury or deterioration.

The difficulty of negotiating rights of way or outright land purchases with the numerous landowners over whose land the seven-mile pipeline had to travel from Cullingworth to Bradford, necessitated obtaining statutory powers to purchase land compulsorily upon payment of fair compensation. The process of identifying all the lands touched by the waterworks and polling the owners is discussed in Chapter 1.[4] Suffice it to say that the Act of 1842 identifies and briefly describes all the properties (and the owners, lessees, and occupiers thereof) which are to be taken or affected by the proposed waterworks. It is made lawful for the Company to purchase absolutely every estate, interest, or encumbrance of any kind touching 'the Lands which they are hereby authorized to enter into and take for the Purposes of the Undertaking . . .'.[5] Provision is made for recalcitrant or unwilling owners of lands authorized to be taken by the Act to lose title to the Company upon bank deposit of the earlier agreed or awarded purchase price.[6] Extensive provision is made for settling the price of land authorized to be taken, or the amount of compensation to be paid for injurious affection, where the Company and landowner are unable to agree. The full panoply of jury trial was available for claims exceeding £50;[7] lesser claims were to be determined by two justices.[8] The Company had to pay the purchase price or compensation prior to entering the land, except where the purpose was surveying or with the permis-

[3] Bradford Waterworks Act 1842, sections 142–4. That Act authorized the Company to purchase Trooper's Farm (upon which the Spring arose), which the Company promoters had bought unconditionally in 1838.

[4] See Chapter 1.

[5] Bradford Waterworks Act 1842, section 145. The unvarying reference to 'Lands' throughout this Part of the Act is noteworthy. The interpretation section provides that, in the absence of contrary indication in the subject matter or context, the word 'Lands' extends to 'Messuages, Lands, Tenements and Hereditaments of any Tenure'. Ibid., section 360.

[6] Ibid., section 159.

[7] Ibid., sections 170–92.

[8] Ibid., section 171.

sion of the owner, upon pain of financial penalty for breach.[9] Parliament ensured that the Company did not drag its heels by placing a three-year time limit on the Company's powers to purchase or take land compulsorily pursuant to the Act.[10]

Mining Near Waterworks

An important group of provisions immediately follows authorizing compulsory purchase of lands. These provisions concern mining near the waterworks. Yorkshire is a famous mining area, and many farms at one time or another supported mining of some sort.[11] It is obvious that provision needed to be made for this. As was seen in Chapter 2,[12] the procedure laid down shaped the actions of Edward Pickles nearly 50 years later, so these provisions bear more detailed examination.

The marginal note to section 196 captures its flavour: '[m]ines lying near the Works not to be worked if the Company be willing to purchase them.' For the purpose of protecting the waterworks from apprehended danger from mining within 40 yards of any works, the owner, lessee, or occupier[13] desiring to mine within that proximity is required to give the Company notice. Within 30 days of receipt of notice the Company is empowered to inspect the mine to assess the likelihood of damage to the works, and if the Company thinks that damage is likely *and* is prepared to compensate the owner for his inability to work the mine then the owner is enjoined not to work the mine. In case of disagreement as to the amount of compensation, this is settled according to the procedure laid down earlier in the Act.[14] If the Company does not state its willingness to treat within the 30-day period, the owner is entitled to work the mines 'in such a Manner as may be proper and necessary for the beneficial working thereof . . .'.[15] However, 'improper working' of such mines within the 40-yard radius is a different matter entirely. In that event, the Company is given power to inspect, to give notice of remedial action required to prevent injury, and, in the face of inaction, to undertake that work at the owner's expense.[16] Furthermore, if the owner is put to any increased or additional expense in working the mines or minerals due to construction of any of the waterworks, the Company is required to make compensation.[17]

[9] Ibid., sections 164–5.
[10] Ibid., section 218.
[11] See Chapter 2.
[12] Ibid.
[13] In what follows I will refer simply to the 'owner', but it is intended to cover lessees and occupiers as well.
[14] Bradford Waterworks Act 1842, section 196.
[15] Ibid., section 197.
[16] Ibid., sections 198–9.
[17] Ibid., section 201.

These provisions concern only the working of mines within 40 yards of any waterworks.[18] Outside that radius any owner is free to mine or work existing mines without fear of restraint under this Part of the Act. [19] Outside that radius the owner desirous of mining is not required to give the Waterworks Company any notice of intent to commence mining operations. Should such operations come to the attention of the Company and cause concern, the Company has no statutory authority under this Part of the Act to elect to prevent the mining upon payment of compensation. That is a matter for negotiation, or of reliance by the Company on any other powers of acquisition in the Act of 1842 or elsewhere.

The mining provisions disclose an ingenious compromise of the competing interests. Clearly, however, the balance falls on the side of the owner of the mines or minerals, who either will be able to mine (properly) or will be compensated for not being able to do so where the Waterworks Company thinks damage to the works is likely. The decision lies with the Company to weigh up the risk of damage against the enforced expenditure of compensation, which if disputed will be determined by justices or a jury (depending on the amount claimed). If the Company weighs up the risk and decides within the time frame not to compensate the owner, the only limitation on the owner's working of the mine within 40 yards of the waterworks is that it be 'properly' mined.[20]

Springs

The next relevant provision is the first to mention 'Water from Springs', and provides in part:[21]

That for any of the following purposes it shall be lawful for the Company, in addition to the Lands authorized to be compulsorily taken by them . . ., to contract with any party willing to sell the same for the Purchase of any Land not exceeding in whole Fifty Acres, to be taken and used in such places as shall be deemed eligible for the Purpose of obtaining Water from Springs, or of protecting such Springs from Injury or Deterioration, or of making and providing additional Reservoirs, Tanks, Aqueducts, and other Buildings and Conveniences, or for

[18] The Act does not speak of mining operations, but rather of working Mines. This would have been suggestive of existing mines, but for the fact that section 196 requires the owner of 'any Mines or Minerals' desirous of working the same to give the Company notice. This points to the sections covering new mining operations to recover minerals as well as existing mines. Any other interpretation would frustrate the purpose behind the provisions. It should be noted that the words 'Mine' and 'Minerals' are not defined in the Act.

[19] There may, of course, be common law restrictions.

[20] The only indication of what might amount to 'improper working' appears from a juxtaposition in section 197 with lawful working in a proper and necessary manner for the beneficial working of the mines.

[21] Bradford Waterworks Act 1842, section 226.

making convenient Roads or Ways to the said Works, or for any other Purpose connected with the said Works which the Company may think beneficial to the Undertaking. . . .

The Company is authorized to acquire no more than 50 acres of land for any or all of these purposes and, while the Company can resell this land, it cannot hold more than 50 acres of such acquired land at any one time.[22]

As we will see below, the Act makes specific provision for the purchase of Many Wells Spring. So at this point the draftsman was unlikely to have that specific Spring in mind but, rather, was providing for the contingency of the discovery of new springs. On that basis, the referent 'such' would link protection from injury or deterioration back to newly discovered springs, and would not encompass the consensual purchase of some of the Pickles' farm in order to prevent injury to the Many Wells Spring water. However, the final clause in the quoted extract from section 226 is more general, and there is no reason to think that the Company could not have used this provision to buy up some of the Pickles' land,[23] if both parties were agreeable. No mention was made of this provision in the *Pickles* litigation, probably because the (successor) Corporation of Bradford was so patently unwilling to purchase any land at all.[24]

Many Wells Spring

The major provisions in sections 233 to 234 relating to Many Wells Spring were quoted in Chapter 1, but are set out again here owing to their importance and for the sake of convenient reference:

CCXXXIII. [section 233] And be it enacted, That, subject to the Restrictions and Provisions in this Act, it shall be lawful for the Company from Time to Time to divert or alter the Course of a certain Beck called *Hewenden Beck* or *Harden Beck*, and also to divert and to take the Water from the several Streams and Springs herein-after mentioned; (that is to say,)

The Springs and Streams of Water called '*Many Wells*,' arising or flowing in and through a certain Farm, Lands, and Grounds called *Trooper* or *Many Wells Farm*, situated in the Township of *Wilsden* in the Parish of *Bradford* in the West Riding of *Yorkshire*.

CCXXXIV. [section 234] And be it enacted, That after the said *Many Wells* Springs have been purchased by the Company, it shall not be lawful for any

22 Ibid., section 227.

23 Around 1842 the extent of the Pickles' landholding was probably closer to 300 acres than 200, and the estimated water catchment area for Many Wells Spring was 530 acres: see Chapter 1, note 32. So this authorization to contract for up to 50 acres of land to prevent injury to springs would not have allowed purchase of anything like the whole farm, let alone the entire catchment area.

24 See Chapter 2.

Person other than the said Company to divert, alter, or appropriate in any other Manner than by Law they may be legally entitled, any of the Waters now supplying or flowing from the same, or to sink any Well or Pit, or do any Act, Matter, or Thing whereby the Waters of the said Springs may be drawn off or diminished in Quantity; and if any Person shall illegally divert, alter, or appropriate the said Waters, or any Part thereof, or sink any such Well or Pit, or shall do any such Act, Matter, or Thing whereby the said Waters may be drawn off or diminished in Quantity, and shall not, immediately on being required so to do by the said Company, repair the Injury done by him, so as to restore the said Springs and the Waters thereof to the State in which they were before such illegal Act as aforesaid, they shall forfeit to the said Company any Sum not exceeding Five Pounds for every Day during which the said Supply of Water shall be diverted or diminished by reason of any Work done or Act performed by or by the Authority of such Person, in addition to the Damage which the Company may sustain by reason of their Supply of Water being diminished.

As we saw in Chapter 3, section 234 was at the forefront of the Corporation's case to prevent Edward Pickles digging shafts and tunnelling on his farm property in 1890.

Another provision—requiring the Company to construct a Reservoir to supply the mill-owners downstream on Hewenden Beck with a continuous supply of water in order to run their mills—speaks of 'the Water issuing from the Springs of Water before mentioned . . .' and authorizes its taking and diversion.[25]

Interference with Property

Several provisions in the Act of 1842 underline the importance Parliament placed on the necessity for clear statutory authorization for interference with property rights. Schedule H to the Act identifies and briefly describes all the properties (and the owners, lessees, and occupiers thereof) which are to be taken or affected by the proposed waterworks.[26] Except as so provided in Schedule H or with the consent of the owners, section 236 enjoins the Company from taking or injuring 'any Property of the following Kinds': any house or building erected before a specified date in 1840; and any ground enclosed or set aside as a garden, orchard, nursery, yard, paddock, plantation, planted wood, or avenue to a house before that same date. Significantly, this proviso follows: 'Provided always, that it shall not be lawful for the Company to take or diminish any water of any of the Becks or Streams of Waters mentioned in such Schedule, or any of the Springs or Feeders thereto, except as herein specif-

[25] Bradford Waterworks Act 1842, section 238.

[26] Twenty-eight owners are listed, although several own more than one property. Ninety-three properties are separately described in the Schedule.

ically authorized'. The becks or streams mentioned in the Schedule are Hewenden or Harden Beck, Denholme Beck, Sow Dyke Beck, Pyehole Beck, and Chellow Dean Beck. Two entries refer to 'Beck or Stream of Water' or 'Beck or Water', without identifying by name, but all the rest name the beck or stream. The only reference to 'Springs of Water' in the Schedule is under the entry for Seth Wright, who owned and occupied Trooper or Many Wells Farm, which the Company had agreed to buy for £2,000 in January 1838.

The importance of this proviso is that it recognizes that appropriation of water or use that diminishes the water flow is akin to a taking of property. As a consequence, such taking or diminishment must be clearly authorized by the incorporating Act and, by necessary implication, compensated for.

Schedule H to the Act makes no mention of the second Edward Pickles or his wife Mary or East Many Wells Farm. In order to understand why that is so, it is necessary to recall what was said earlier about the mechanics of the preparation of private Acts of incorporation. The Company planned to pipe water from Many Wells Spring to the Town of Bradford, some seven miles away. It was a prerequisite of Parliamentary approval that a plan describing the line of the works be prepared and a so-called 'Book of Reference' compiled, containing a list of the owners, lessees, and occupiers of 'such Lands' as the works went through. The referent for this book was the plan, which numbered every plot of land in every Township touched by the works. It was from those submitted plans and books that the list of properties and owners in Schedule H was compiled.

This examination of the provisions of the Act of 1842 reveals at least two matters of importance. The first is Parliament's solicitude about protecting private property as far as it was possible to do so while authorizing the proposed waterworks. This is of a piece with the protections built into the Parliamentary Standing Orders and the process of pre-legislative scrutiny, discussed in Chapter 2. The second is that, by one means or another, the Company had ample opportunity to acquire East Many Wells Farm compulsorily, or to secure the water right at that time.

The Acts of 1854

The story of the 'municipalization' of the Bradford Waterworks Company in 1854 has been told already and need not be repeated.[27] The focus here is on the legal technicalities relevant to the transfer of ownership and how

[27] See Chapter 1.

those impacted on the statutory powers and immunities of the Corporation of Bradford regarding Many Wells Spring.

As we have seen, the Bradford Waterworks Act 1854 repealed the earlier legislation of 1842 and established a new waterworks company.[28] All the property of the old Company (including specifically 'the springs of water called *Many Wells* in *Trooper* or *Many Wells Farm*') vested in the newly incorporated company.[29] Various provisions ensured that repeal of the previous Acts and disestablishment of the old company would neither advantage nor disadvantage the newly created company or disturb vested rights of other parties.[30] Importantly, section 49 of the 1854 Act re-enacted section 234 of the 1842 Act with only slight and legally insignificant alterations.[31] Whatever protection section 234 had granted the privately owned Bradford Waterworks Company from 1842–54 was transferred to the new Company, which was to be purchased by the Corporation of Bradford.

The companion legislation—Bradford Corporation Waterworks Act 1854—authorized the purchase of the new company by the Corporation. Upon purchase, the powers and rights of the old Company vested in the Corporation,[32] as well as all of the restrictions and limitations placed on the Company under the earlier statutes.[33] The only other relevant provision contains an echo of section 226 in the Act of 1842, and authorizes the Corporation to purchase either absolute title or rights of usage of any streams or springs, and to 'protect' such streams or springs from injury or deterioration.[34]

The Waterworks Clauses Act 1847

Both of the Acts of 1854[35] expressly incorporated almost all of the provi-

[28] Bradford Waterworks Act 1854, section 2.

[29] Ibid., section 6.

[30] Ibid., sections 5–9.

[31] The differences are: (1) of punctuation and capitalization which reflect the evolution of grammar and style, with a complete absence of commas and semi-colons (in contrast to 22 commas and 1 semi-colon in the original provision) and no capital letters within the provision except for proper nouns; (2) that the 1842 Act spoke of 'Waters now supplying' Many Wells Springs, whereas the new Act said simply 'waters supplying'; (3) that the recital of the details of the farm at the beginning of the old section is missing in the new one and so the description of the Springs is found later on in the new section. These differences were held to be immaterial by all of the judges in *Pickles*, and section 49 was treated as identical to section 234.

[32] Bradford Waterworks Act 1854, section 17.

[33] Ibid., section 21.

[34] Ibid., section 33. See the text accompanying note 21 above for section 226 of the Act of 1842.

[35] Bradford Waterworks Act 1854, section 3; Bradford Corporation Waterworks Act 1854, section 4.

sions of the Waterworks Clauses Act 1847.[36] The Act of 1847 was a general piece of legislation, designed to reduce the bulk of future private Waterworks Acts and to promote greater uniformity. Accordingly, the best-drawn provisions on every topic of general importance found in the numerous previous private Waterworks Acts were gathered together in the Act of 1847, and it was stipulated that later private Waterworks Acts could simply incorporate all or some of these provisions. If that was done, the general Act and the later incorporating special Act were to be construed as one Act.

Section 14 of the Act of 1847 was in broadly similar terms to section 234 of the Bradford Waterworks Act 1842.[37] As noted above, section 234 was re-enacted with immaterial alterations as section 49 of the Bradford Waterworks Act 1854. The superficial similarity is deceptive, however, for there were some significant differences in wording between section 14 and section 234.[38] The differences are such that, had section 14 been the operative provision in the *Pickles* dispute, it would have been much more difficult for the Corporation to have taken a plausible stand against Edward Pickles on the statute.[39] That never materialized, however, because the re-enactment of section 234 with only slight changes in section 49 of the 1854 Act displaced section 14 of the 1847 Clauses Act. Whether the re-enactment was intended to displace the clearer provision in the incorporated Waterworks Clauses Act, or was simply a blind following of the 1842 precedent, we will never know.[40] That cases can turn on such matters is no surprise to lawyers.

So the re-enacted provision continued with all its ambiguity. If anything, the absence of punctuation in the re-enacted provision in the 1854 Act made matters worse. All of these flaws came home to roost in the litigation 40 years later.

One final matter deserves noting. Section 14 did not stand alone in the

36 10 and 11 Vict. ch. xvii.

37 The marginal note to section 14 reads 'Penalty for illegally diverting Water'. Section 14 is reproduced in note 6 in the Appendix.

38 The differences between section 14 of the Clauses Act and section 234 of the Act of 1842 are listed in note 7 of the Appendix.

39 The Corporation's claim would have to have been that the diversion was 'illegal' at common law. It could not have relied, as it did, on the ambiguities in section 49.

40 There is the ring of truth to the first part of Lord Justice Lindley's comment that '[t]he preservation of [section 234 as section 49] . . . is probably due to a desire on the part of the corporation to keep the old section in their special Act so as not to lose any protection it might give beyond that afforded by section 14 of the *Waterworks Clauses Act*, which was made applicable to all companies whose special Acts might incorporate its provisions': [1895] 1 Ch 145, 161. What he failed to realize in the second part of that statement was that the presence of section 49 effectively displaced section 14 of the Act of 1847. The Corporation could not have its cake and eat it too.

Act of 1847. The very next provision is drafted in the form of a proviso to section 14, reserving existing water use rights.[41] Section 15 provides:

> Provided always, That nothing herein contained shall prevent the Owners and Occupiers for the Time being of Lands through or by which such Streams shall flow from using the waters thereof in such Manner and to such Extent as they might have done before the passing of the special Act, unless they shall have received Compensation in respect of their Right of so using such Water.

This makes explicit what is implicit in the Bradford Waterworks Act of 1842,[42] and is hardly surprising in either instance given the Victorian affection for private property. To be sure, this provision does not encompass underground water supplying a spring (as in *Pickles*), but the general approach anticipates by nearly 50 years the response of the late Victorian judges in *Pickles* case. If section 14 had not been displaced, the combination of sections 14 and 15 would surely have made the decision in *Pickles* a foregone conclusion in favour of Edward Pickles.

Statutory Interpretation in *Pickles*

In all its dealings with Pickles, from the first letter of protest in May 1890 to the final appeal, the Corporation took its stand on the statute. It defied belief, in the view of its officers and Councillors, that the original adventurers would have invested in the waterworks, and that the Corporation would have bought it for a princely sum, without adequate legal protection of the water supply. Against this, Edward Pickles's argument was simplicity itself: As my rights as an owner were not expressly mentioned in the Acts of 1842 and 1854, and neither my forebears nor I received any notice of or compensation for any loss of property right, it must be the case that the Act does not restrain my use of my property. If the arguments were simple, the woefully drafted section 234 *cum* section 49 drove simplicity away.

Let us begin with what little is undisputed. The section came into effect once the original Bradford Waterworks Company had purchased Many Wells Spring. It was clearly intended to protect the water supply from that Spring for the benefit of the Company and 'the Town and Neighbourhood of *Bradford*'.[43] The actions that were foreseen as potentially harming the

[41] The exact wording of the marginal note is 'Reservation of existing Rights'.

[42] An echo of section 15 can be heard in the proviso to section 236, discussed in the text above following note 26. But, as pointed out there, the requirement of compensation was implicit rather than explicit.

[43] The Long Title of the Act of 1842 explains it is '[a]n Act for better supplying with Water the Town and Neighbourhood of *Bradford* in the West Riding of the County of *York*.'

water supply were diversion, alteration, or appropriation of the water, or the sinking of any well, pit, or other act that drew off the water or diminished the quantity of water. Lastly, the Act made no provision for compensation for landowners whose rights were or might be affected by this section.

It will aid discussion if section 49 is reproduced with some annotations as reference points for the ensuing discussion:

> And be it enacted, That after the said *Many Wells* Springs have been purchased by the Company, <u>it shall not be lawful for any Person other than the said Company to divert, alter, or appropriate in any other Manner than by Law they may be legally entitled, any of the Waters now supplying or flowing from the same</u> **[Part A]**, or <u>to sink any Well or Pit, or do any Act, Matter, or Thing whereby the Waters of the said Springs may be drawn off or diminished in Quantity</u> **[Part B]**; and if any Person shall illegally divert, alter, or appropriate the said Waters, or any Part thereof, or sink any such Well or Pit, or shall do any such Act, Matter, or Thing whereby the said Waters may be drawn off or diminished in Quantity, and shall not, immediately on being required so to do by the said Company, repair the Injury done by him, so as to restore the said Springs and the Waters thereof to the State in which they were before such illegal Act as aforesaid, they shall forfeit to the said Company any Sum not exceeding Five Pounds for every Day during which the said Supply of Water shall be diverted or diminished by reason of any Work done or Act performed by or by the Authority of such Person, in addition to the Damage which the Company may sustain by reason of their Supply of Water being diminished. (emphasis added)

The uncertainties and difficulties presented by section 49 abound. The section begins by combining in Part A a prohibition against diversion, alteration, or appropriation of the water 'supplying' the Spring or 'flowing' from it, with a clumsily worded exception for those with legal entitlement. This reads a little oddly, but the meaning seems clear enough: those persons with a legal entitlement to divert, alter, or appropriate the water flowing to or from the Spring are not affected by this prohibition.

The first real difficulty is whether this exemption for those with legal entitlement applied only to Part A or whether the exemption extended to Part B, covering the sinking of wells/pits and any actions drawing off water or diminishing quantity. That difficulty arose because the section was drafted in such a way as to treat diversion, alteration, or appropriation in Part A separately from the drawing off or diminishing of the supply by sinking holes or otherwise in Part B. (The advance made by the inapplicable Waterworks Clauses Act 1847 was that the exemption for those with legal entitlement to use of the water applied to all of the elaborated ways in which water could be drawn off.)

This uncertainty as to whether the existing water right exception applied to both Parts A and B, or just to Part A, was compounded by the absence of any such exception in the second half of the section, which prescribed a penalty for breach. There mention was made of 'illegal' diversion, alteration, or appropriation, but the other actions of sinking wells or pits, or drawing off water, or diminishing quantity were not so clearly qualified. There is a later reference to such 'illegal Act as aforesaid', but the use of the singular form continues to cast some doubt as to whether it applied to all the above eventualities or only to the explicitly designated 'illegal' acts of diversion, alteration, or appropriation. If the latter then the lawful sinking of a well or pit would seemingly not be covered by the penalty.

Another difficulty was what was meant by the phrase 'the Waters of the said Springs' in Part B. Did this refer back to the reference in Part A to 'any of the Waters now supplying or flowing from [*Many Wells* Springs]'? Or did the different wording mean that Part B applied only to the drawing off or diminution of water that had entered Trooper's Farm?

There is also uncertainty as to what significance, if any, to attach to the fact that section 49 combines a prohibition in the first half of the section with a penalty for unremedied 'illegal' acts in the second half.

High Court

Mr Justice North was the only judge of the eight who considered this case to find for the Corporation on the statute. He—along with all the others—treated section 49 of the Act of 1854 as the identical successor to section 234 of the original Bradford Waterworks Act 1842,[44] but he alone interpreted that provision as preventing Pickles's appropriation of the underground water before it entered the Corporation's land.

Counsel for Pickles argued that section 49 applied only to illegal acts done on the Corporation's land, and did not affect 'the rights of outside landowners'.[45] Opposing counsel denied that section 49 was limited to the acts done on the Corporation's land, observing a little later that section 14 of the Waterworks Clauses Act 1847 'would be meaningless if the Defendant is right'.[46] It is a pity that Mr Cozens-Hardy Q.C. put that submission in terms of the differently worded and inapplicable provision of the Waterworks Clauses Act, because that point could have been made with a good deal more conviction with respect to section 49 of the 1854

[44] *Pickles* [1895] 1 Ch 145,151, and 153 (Lord Herschell L.C.), 161 (Lindley L.J.) and 161 (A. L. Smith L.J.) (CA): [1895] AC 587, 595 (Lord Watson) and 601 (Lord Macnaghten).

[45] *Pickles* [1894] 3 Ch 53, 61.

[46] Ibid., 62–3. The Waterworks Clauses Act 1847 is referred to in argument at every level of court in this case, without it ever being pointed out that there were important differences between section 14 of the Waterworks Clauses Act 1847 and section 49 of the Act of 1854, or that the later provision displaced section 14. Perhaps it went without saying. There was certainly no judicial doubt that section 49 was the operative provision.

Act. Neither point was lost on North J., however. He was of the view that section 49 was much more strongly against Pickles than anything in the general Clauses Act.[47] The inference to be drawn from that being that the differences in wording were intentional and designed to meet the situation that had arisen. According to North J., it was 'absurd to say that the section is merely aimed at preventing the . . . [Corporation] from doing acts to their own prejudice, or forbidding such acts from being done by trespassers on the . . . [Corporation's] land'.[48]

North J. interpreted Parts A and B literally, and implicitly took the phrase 'the Waters of the said Springs' in Part B to refer back to the waters referred to in Part A (namely, 'the Waters now supplying and flowing from the same'). North J. found Pickles to be in breach of Part B of the section, prohibiting drawing off water and diminishing the flow of water to the Spring. He refused to see this Part as qualified by the exception for persons with legal entitlement. If the exception qualified both Parts A and B, North J. said scornfully, the provision would say no more than 'it is . . . illegal to do certain things except so far as it is legal to do them'.[49] He explained away the use of the exception in Part A as intending to preserve the rights of upper and lower riparian owners in an open stream, whereby the upper riparian owner was permitted to divert, or alter, or even appropriate to a certain extent, but not abstract, the whole supply. It was pointed out that the Act of 1842 pre-dated *Acton v Blundell* (1843), 'and the differences between the rights in waters flowing in a defined stream and other waters were not so well ascertained as they have since been'.[50]

What North J. appears to be saying here is that the exception applied only to reasonable use of surface streams by riparian owners and was not intended to apply to percolating underground water passing under properties. North J. is correct to point out that in 1842 there was no English law settling the point who owned or had the use of percolating underground water not in a defined stream. This was decided for the first time in *Acton v Blundell* in 1843, and was not finally affirmed by the highest Court until 1859. This was discussed briefly in Chapter 3 and is the subject of extended discussion in Chapter 5. Suffice it to say here that it is possible, but not likely, that a draftsman would have thought that way and drafted the section accordingly.[51]

North J. did not pretend that this interpretation gave a clear or satisfactory meaning to every word in the section, but thought it was preferable to the alternative.[52] Pickles's counsel argued strenuously that private

[47] Ibid., 65. [48] Ibid., 64–5. [49] Ibid., 64. [50] Idem.

[51] See Chapter 5. In the Court of Appeal, Lord Herschell L.C. said there was no justification in the language of section 49 for this interpretation: [1895] 1 Ch 145, 154.

[52] *Pickles* [1894] 3 Ch 53, 64.

Acts had to be very strictly construed and prima facie were not to be interpreted as to affect property rights, where the land had not been taken and no compensation was ever paid for the abridgement of those rights.[53] North J. recognized this as 'a very weighty argument', supported by considerable authority, but held that it had to give way to Parliamentary sovereignty in this case as the statute was so clearly worded.[54]

North J.'s claim that the clarity of the wording of section 49 displaced the common law presumption of no expropriation without compensation is not consistent with his admission that the provision was ambiguous. What *is* clear, however, is that North J. disapproved of Edward Pickles's actions. He made findings of fact against him at every point, and credibility findings against his key witness. Edward's actions were characterized as taken 'in bad faith'. According to Pickles's counsel, the reason for the 11-month delay in the judgment appearing after the trial, was the trial judge's unsuccessful hunt for common law authority against Pickles.[55] Little surprise, if that were true, that North J. would interpret the statute to achieve that end. Neither did North J. think that his interpretation of section 49 caused any injustice to Pickles. He thought that Pickles was not deprived thereby 'of anything which was of the slightest value',[56] because the judge accepted evidence that the flagstone deposits were either non-existent or worthless. The only other judge to express disapproval of Pickles's actions was Lord Justice Lindley, but he did not let that affect his decision.[57] In contrast, Lords Halsbury and (seemingly)[58] Macnaghten painted Edward as a heroic figure.

Court of Appeal

The three judges in the Court of Appeal unanimously rejected the trial judge's interpretation. They agreed that the provision was 'very ill-drawn' and that no interpretation was entirely satisfactory,[59] but insisted that any ambiguity or uncertainty of meaning must be interpreted against the *proferens* (the Corporation). Lord Herschell L.C. put the point most clearly:[60]

[53] *Pickles* [1894] 3 Ch 53, 65. [54] Idem. [55] See Chapter 3.

[56] *Pickles* [1894] 3 Ch 53, 67.

[57] It should not be overlooked that the Court of Appeal did offer to adjourn the case so that the Corporation could seek Parliamentary powers to acquire a water right compulsorily: see Chapter 3. That may have been influenced in part by a negative view of Pickles's actions.

[58] Lord Macnaghten was a master of irony and so it is possible that his seemingly straight-faced defence of Edward Pickles's words and actions is deceiving. See G. H. L. Fridman, 'Motive in the English Law of Tort' (1954) 40 Va LR 583, 595.

[59] *Pickles* [1895] 1 Ch 145, 154 (Lord Herschell L.C.); 160 (Lindley L.J.).

[60] Ibid., 152–3.

Having regard to the nature of the Act and its provisions generally, I think there is a strong presumption that the section in question was not intended to interfere with the rights of any person without compensation. The language of the Act is presumably that of those who promoted it, and there is nothing to bring its provisions to the notice of any person whose land or rights were not mentioned in the plan or the book of reference. It was urged that the Act recites that a supply of pure water would be of advantage to the town of *Bradford*. This, no doubt, was a justification for conferring the power of taking the property of private persons by compulsion, even though on terms of making compensation. But the undertaking was constituted with the view of making profit, and it would not be in accordance with the ordinary course of legislation to take away without compensation the private rights of individuals for the benefit of the undertakers, or even the inhabitants of *Bradford*. . . .

No doubt, if the language of the enactment reasonably admits only of a construction which would involve . . . [this] consequence . . ., effect must be given to it notwithstanding the presumption that there may be against the Legislature so enacting; but if, on the other hand, it is capable of a construction which would avoid such a consequence, I have no hesitation in saying this is the construction to be adopted.

Against this background, Lord Herschell proceeded to interpret section 49. He viewed the primary object of the section to be the imposition of a special penalty for illegal diversion of the company's water, and viewed the first half of the section to be merely introductory to the latter half, which imposed the penalty. He saw 'great difficulty, as a matter of grammatical construction', in reading the exception as applying to both Part A and Part B, and would have been prepared to do so only *in extremis*, in order to avoid inconsistency or absurdity. But it was not necessary to do so as he reached the same result by another route.

Lord Herschell drew a distinction between the phrase 'Waters now supplying or flowing from [the Springs]' (in Part A) and the phrase 'Waters of the said Springs' (in Part B). The Corporation had argued that the latter phrase included water supplying the Spring before it reached the Corporation's land. This was the only way it could catch the digging by Pickles within the statutory net. North J. had implicitly accepted that argument. The Lord Chancellor held that digging on Pickles' land did not draw off or diminish 'Waters of the said Springs', giving two reasons. The first was that if the Corporation was correct then the drawing off/diminishment resulting from digging would in effect 'divert, alter, or appropriate' water supplying the Spring and render 'nugatory' the protection for existing rights indisputably given in Part A of the section. This would create an 'absurdity'. Secondly, it was in accordance with sound interpretation to assume that the different words were intended to have different meanings. So Part A was held to deal with diversion, etc., of water flowing under Pickles' land, whereas Part B was confined to the waters of the Spring on Trooper's Farm.

This interpretation is far from ideal. It ignores the natural referents of the phrase 'said Waters' in the second half of the section, which imposed a financial penalty, and thereby created a mismatch between the prohibitions in Parts A and B, and the actions penalized in the second half of the section.

For his part, Lord Justice Lindley's starting point was the common law right of Pickles to dig on his own land established by *Chasemore v Richards*. If, as the Corporation argued, Pickles was not entitled to dig and drain the water away it could only be due to 'some special legislation, and not by reason of the ordinary law of the country'.[61] Lindley L.J. searched the Acts of 1842 and 1854 in vain for evidence of any compensation paid to Pickles's predecessors for any restriction on their common law rights. 'The absence of all provisions for such compensation', he said, 'is very material when we construe an obscure clause which is said to curtail the Defendant's ordinary rights'.[62]

Lord Justice Lindley admitted that this obscure provision contained words which could be interpreted to restrict the rights of a neighbour to dig on his own land, but, in the absence of compensation, he refused to read it that way. He viewed it as a penal provision, levying up to £5 a day penalty on any person who unlawfully interfered with the supply of water to which the company was entitled, and not intended to limit the use neighbours could make of their land. The word 'illegally' qualified both Parts A and B, and was to be determined by what could be lawfully done irrespective of the section. In effect, this reached the same result as saying that the lawful exception qualified Parts A and B: an interpretation, as we saw above, that Lord Herschell had 'great difficulty' accepting.

The remaining member of the Court, A. L. Smith, L.J., agreed that 'upon first reading this badly drawn section' it appeared that the exception for lawful acts qualified Part A but not Part B, but he did not feel driven to accept that view.[63] Like the Lord Chancellor, A. L. Smith L.J. thought that reading Part A as qualified by lawfulness but not Part B was 'meaningless'.[64] In order to make the section intelligible, it was suggested that the lawful qualification be read before the phrase beginning 'divert, . . .', thereby qualifying both parts of the section. This accounted for why no compensation was paid to Pickles's predecessors. The appellate judge thought that the trial judge had failed to appreciate that the paramount object of the section was to impose a penalty for what could not be lawfully done.[65]

Both Lord Herschell L.C. and A. L. Smith L.J. grasped the point that it is impossible to draw off or diminish the quantity of water without simul-

[61] *Pickles* [1895] 1 Ch 145, 159.
[62] Ibid., 160.
[63] Ibid., 164–5.
[64] Ibid., 165.
[65] Ibid., 166.

taneously diverting, or altering, or appropriating the water; and vice versa. The sinking of wells or pits is just one way in which water may be drawn off or the water supply diminished, and that is why other acts ('... any Act, Matter, or Thing ...') that would have the same result are prohibited as well. So there was an inextricable connection in fact between the actions and effects in both Parts A and B of the section, which the grammar seemingly denied.

House of Lords

Lord Halsbury's interpretation was in stark contrast to the detailed analyses in the courts below. To Lord Halsbury, the purpose of the provision was obvious. It was to protect from interference the 'property' of the Waterworks Company, being such streams, springs, and water supplies as the Company had bought.[66] Since, according to *Chasemore v Richards* (1859), the Waterworks Company had no right to the flow of the water, the Company did not 'own' the water before it reached its land and so the section did not protect that supply from prior interference. The Lord Chancellor thought that this was the true construction of the words themselves, but the absence of any payment of compensation to the Pickles was 'conclusive' against the interpretation proffered by the Corporation.

Lord Watson adopted basically the same approach. The only difference was that, whereas the Lord Chancellor implicitly held interference by sinking a well to be qualified by the exception for existing lawful entitlements, Lord Watson interpreted the phrase in Part B ('Waters of the said Springs'), which attached to sinking a well etc., as applying only to waters which reached the Spring on the Corporation's land. 'The prohibition gives effective protection against the withdrawal or diminution, either by the adjacent proprietor or any other person, of waters which have come within the dominion of the [Corporation]'.[67] That interpretation was just as plainly influenced as the Lord Chancellor's by the combination of *Chasemore v Richards* and the common law presumption against the expropriation of property without compensation.[68]

To Lord Ashbourne's mind, the case was straightforward, turning on 'considerations sufficiently simple and far from obscure'.[69] He could 'see nothing in the statutes to interfere with or prejudice' Pickles' legal rights as laid down in *Chasemore v Richards*.[70] 'Very clear words would be required to support the contention that legal rights have been swept away without compensation'.[71] The section protected waters that had come under the control of the Corporation.

66 *Pickles* [1895] AC 587, 593.
67 Ibid., 597.
68 Ibid., 596–7.
69 Ibid., 598.
70 Ibid., 599.
71 Idem.

Lord Macnaghten doubted whether the section was 'so unsatisfactory, so ill-drawn, as so difficult to construe as it seemed to be to the Court of Appeal'.[72] He, like Lord Herschell L.C. in the Court of Appeal and Lord Watson, interpreted the phrase 'the Waters of the said Spring' to mean the waters issuing from the Spring, and not underground sources that 'supplied' the Spring.[73] Echoing Lord Herschell again, Lord Macnaghten contended that this reading avoided the 'singular result' of Part A preserving entitlements and Part B taking them away.[74] This interpretation of the phrase was found to be supported by usage elsewhere in the Act.[75] Lord Macnaghten does not consider the other possible interpretation that the exception for legal entitlement qualified both Parts A and B. It can be inferred that he was not attracted to it.

In line with what Lords Halsbury and Watson had said, Lord Macnaghten was of the view that only when the water rose to the surface of Trooper's Farm did it become 'the absolute property of the company',[76] and thereby protected by the statute from interference by others. The penalty half of the section characterized '[a]ny such interference . . . as an illegal act'.[77]

The appellate judges each adopt one or other of two alternative interpretations of section 49. The first—supported most clearly by Lindley L.J. and more obliquely by A. L. Smith L.J.—is that the exception for legal entitlements, which explicitly qualified Part A, also implicitly qualified Part B. The other interpretation—supported by Lord Herschell L.C., and Lords Watson and Macnaghten—interpreted Part B as applying only to water which issued from Many Wells Spring. Due to the generality of the treatments by Lords Halsbury and Ashbourne it is difficult to categorize them, but their strong emphasis on property rights suggest that they supported the second interpretation.

The manifest difficulty with the second approach is that it denies the provision any meaningful, independent operation at all. This was North J.'s point, however obtusely he put it. The majority of the appellate judges (including at least two, if not all, of the Law Lords) interpreted the section to prohibit someone (presumably a trespasser) from digging or doing any other act *on the Corporation's land* so as to draw off water or diminish supply. Why anyone would have thought special statutory protection was needed to stop someone doing that is beyond comprehension. Lord Macnaghten intuited that his interpretation had reduced the provision to pointlessness. After concluding that the section protected the water that arose on Trooper's Farm from illegal interference, he said:[78]

72 *Pickles* [1895] AC 587, 601.

73 Ibid., 603.

74 Lord Herschell L.C. described this result as absurd: [1895] 1 Ch 145, 156.

75 Lord Macnaghten referred to sections 238 and 275.

76 [1895] AC 587, 603.

77 Idem.

78 Ibid., 604.

And, indeed, it seems to me very difficult to conceive how such an act could in any sense be legal, unless the company constructed their works in a perverse and foolish manner. No one from whom the company acquired land or even an easement for the purpose of the works could let down those works. No one else, it may be assumed, would be in a position to do so. No one could lawfully tap their aqueducts or conduits.

This can also be demonstrated by superimposing the language of section 49 on the environs of the Spring. It must be remembered that the Act of 1842 was 'purpose-built' to fit this particular waterworks project. As we know, the Spring arose less than 20 yards from the up-hill boundary with the Pickles' farm. It would have been as plain as a pikestaff (to any one who had inspected the property)[79] that the water gushing from the Spring came from underneath the upland farm.[80] The downhill overland flow of the water from the Spring to Hewenden Beck occurred entirely on Trooper's Farm, which was to be owned by the Company.[81] Nothing that occurred to the water down Hewenden Beck after it left the northern border of Trooper's Farm could possibly affect the supply or flow of Spring water, as gravity had done its work by then. And on Trooper's Farm, the 'flow' of the water overland to the Beck could not be diverted, altered, or appropriated by any means by anyone other than a trespasser. (Unless, as Lord Macnaghten said, the works had been most perversely constructed.) We can assume that the fact of possession backed by the law of torts and crimes would be sufficient to prevent trespass of this nature occurring, without the need for specific statutory protection.

So once the language of the section is superimposed upon the physical environment it appears that realistically the only scope for the operation of the section was in preventing the diversion, alteration, or appropriation of the water by any means whatsoever (including the sinking of wells or pits) *before* the water 'supplying' the Spring reached Trooper's Farm. If it did not apply to that it had no realistic sphere of operation and was useless. At bottom, North J. recognized that and was prepared to give the provision some effect rather than none. All the other judges sacrificed effect on the altar of property.

The real lesson of *Pickles* is that it is not a case of ambiguity at all. If the

[79] Ignoring this approach was made easier due to the fact that none of the judges (or counsel) would have ever visited the farm. Neither would the draftsman of the original Waterworks Bill put forward by the promoters in the early 1840s. The legislation would almost certainly have been drafted in London.

[80] North J. found this as a fact, notwithstanding that 'some witnesses said that it was impossible to be certain where the water at *Many Wells* came from': [1894] 3 Ch 53, 56–7 (summary of evidence and holdings extracted from the judgment by the official law reporter).

[81] I say 'to be owned' because the Bradford Waterworks Act 1842 proceeded on the basis that the Company it was incorporating did not yet own Trooper's Farm.

words were to have any meaningful operation they would have limited Pickles' property rights, without compensation. That could not be countenanced by the appellate judges, so, to a man, they 'interpreted' the section out of existence. This disobedience of the legislature is hidden by the 'smoke and mirrors' of interpretive word games.

Surreptitious Expropriation?

The uncompromising view taken by the Corporation in the litigation in the 1890s was that the successor to section 234 prevented Pickles from interfering with the water flowing under his farm to the detriment of the waterworks. Put another way, the Corporation's case was that the private promoters of the Bradford Waterworks Company inserted the original section 234 in their private Act of Parliament in order to ensure the continued flow of underground water to the Spring by restraining any neighbours (the Pickles family being the most obvious) from doing anything on their property that would disturb that flow. At bottom, such a view has to posit that the adventurers set out to deprive the Pickles family of the ordinary rights of usage of their neighbouring land without compensation or notice.[82] Such a stratagem would have depended for success upon the Pickles family not objecting before the Select Committees of either House of Parliament to the private Bill. No doubt, this would have been a safe bet because of the expense of doing so. To be sure, the promoters were not averse to saving money. Bob West has documented thoroughly their propensity for penny-pinching.[83] Nevertheless, there is an air of implausibility to any claim of surreptitious deprivation of the Pickles' rights as landowning neighbours.

First of all, as noted already, Many Wells Spring is less than 20 yards from East Many Wells Farm. One had only to look at the hillside to see where the waters supplying the Spring came from. Given the extremely close proximity to the boundary, it would be extraordinarily brazen of the promoters to attempt by statute surreptitiously to deprive the Pickles of any of their water rights. Secondly, the statutory provision was not pellucid on the point. It might be said that the ambiguity was carefully crafted

[82] An alternative view is that the adventurers believed, were advised, or simply assumed that the law guaranteed the downhill owner the continued flow of the percolating underground water—this topic is explored in Chapter 5—but, if that were, the case, surely there was no need for (at least parts of) section 234.

[83] R. West, 'Worstedopolis and the Water Works: Bradford Water Works Company 1837–1855' (unpublished B.A. dissertation, University of Bradford, 1980), *passim*. See also B. Thompson, 'Public Provision and Private Neglect: Public Health' in D. G. Wright and J. A. Jowitt (eds), *Victorian Bradford: Essays in Honour of Jack Reynolds* (City of Bradford Metropolitan Council, Bradford, 1981), 137, 146.

so as to disguise the promoters' intent, but this seems as implausible as it was risky. In 1842 the promoters could have no idea that they would sell within a decade to the Corporation, and probably looked forward to many years of profitable investment. A clandestine attempt to deprive the neighbouring Pickles family of water use rights through the insertion of a less-than-clear provision in a private Act is hardly a solid foundation upon which to proceed commercially. It would also fly in the face of the many protections of private property rights and, if not fully fledged property rights, rights to usage and flow of water contained in the rest of the Act.

Neither do the economics of the venture support the view of surreptitious expropriation without compensation. The capital of the Company was £44,000. The promoters bought Trooper's Farm for £2,000. The estimated cost of building the Hewenden compensation Reservoir was £6,500. The Pickles were landowning farmers, who leased out some of their land to other farmers. Plans and maps of the area show that some quarrying had been carried out on the farm some distance west of the boundary with Trooper's Farm. It is impossible to speculate as to what the Company would have had to pay the Pickles for a water right, but in the overall financial scheme of things it would have been a pittance: at a guess, a few hundred pounds at most. And if Holmes Pickles had proved obdurate in the face of such a request, the Company could have simply added his land to the list of affected properties in the Act. Moreover, the promoters were substantial landowners in their own right, and would have been as much willing captives of the prevailing private property rights-respecting ideology as the Parliamentarians and the judges. Is it plausible that they set out to deprive the Pickles family of some of their rights for the sake of a few hundred pounds?

To view the insertion of section 234 in the 1842 Act as a surreptitious expropriation makes little sense from a financial, political, legal, strategic, or ideological point of view. With the entire water supply scheme dependent on the continued outpouring of pure underground water from Many Wells Spring, it seems highly unlikely that the promoters trusted to the chance that, if neighbourly push came to shove in the future, a judge would interpret the less-than-clear section 234 so as to restrain the Pickles from making full use of their land, especially when no compensation had been paid for any such loss of rights. If the promoters did unwisely trust to chance then the gamble did not come off. Over 50 years later the Court of Appeal and the House of Lords interpreted this provision in favour of the Pickles family.

Many of the judges spoke of 'confiscation', 'arbitrary transfer' of property from one to another, or 'deprivation' of property. We have seen that they struggled to avoid any such consequence, and did so at the cost of depriving the provision of any meaningful effect. If it is implausible that the adventurers set out surreptitiously to deprive the Pickles of their rights, but that is the only meaningful interpretation to be given the section, how can this be explained? It is one of the purposes of Chapter 5 to explore this further.

A Time-honoured Technique

The plaintive plea of the Corporation of Bradford that such an interpretation rendered their considerable investment risky in the extreme fell on deaf judicial ears; and not for the first time. There was nothing novel in the general approach of the appellate courts in *Pickles*.

The cases are legion. For the purpose of illustration I have chosen *The South Shields Waterworks Company v Cookson*,[84] a little-noticed case involving a very similar dispute half a century earlier. The plaintiff Waterworks Company was established by a private Act of Parliament in 1788 in order to supply water from a spring on land it had acquired to the town of South Shields some distance away. The defendant was a soda manufacturer, which dug a well on its own land some 20 years later than the Waterworks Company and tapped into the same body of percolating underground water as fed the Waterworks' spring. The plaintiff pleaded that this well was 'near to' its spring, whereas in reply the defendant said that it was 'at a great distance'. The Court was not called on to resolve that factual issue. It appears that the defendant used water from the well initially to supply its soda manufacturing plant. At some point the defendant also used the water so acquired to supply another of its businesses manufacturing plate glass in the township, as well as distributing it to its workmen. The defendant is alleged to have extracted 'great quantities' of water, but there is no suggestion that this abstraction affected adversely the water supply to the plaintiff's spring. The plaintiff Waterworks, it appears, saw the activities of the defendant as an actual or potential competitive threat to its business in the township.

The Waterworks Company argued that the Act of 1788 gave it an 'exclusive right' to the water in the area surrounding the spring.[85] It pointed to provisions that protected sufficiency of supply of water for the use of landowners and their stock, and that required the company to supply water to those inhabitants of the town who requested it. Unless the Act was read to restrict the common law rights of landowners in the

[84] (1846) 15 LJ Ex. 315 (Ex.). The case is complicated somewhat by technical pleading points, which I have ignored for this purpose.
[85] Ibid., 317.

area to extract water for purposes other than for domestic use or watering stock, it was argued, the Act would be rendered 'illusory'. Counsel for the Waterworks Company acknowledged the *contra proferentem* approach to private Acts—that they are to be construed most strongly against those obtaining them—but argued that this should not be carried to the extreme of rendering such legislation illusory. After all, it was argued, this Act was a 'bargain with the public'; in consideration for being supplied with water by the company, the public gave up their individual right to abstract water for other than their own necessary domestic or farming purposes.[86] Baron Parke interrupted the argument to observe that there was nothing in this 'parliamentary contract' to deprive 'an adjoining landowner of the power to dig a well'.[87] Counsel discerned the shadow of *Acton v Blundell* behind that interjection and sought to distinguish that case on the ground that there the interference with the neighbour's water supply was incidental to mining, whereas here 'the well is sunk avowedly for the purpose of drawing off the water'.[88] Baron Alderson was unpersuaded also, interjecting that unless *Acton v Blundell* is held to be bad law it was fatal to the plaintiff's action.[89] In the result, that was the view of the Exchequer Court. Speaking for the Court, Baron Parke said simply that 'the defendants have a full right to sink a well on their own lands'.[90]

The Waterworks Company in the *South Shields* case was privately owned, as was the Bradford Waterworks Company initially, before it was taken over by the Corporation in 1854. On the other hand, the defendant in *Chasemore v Richards* was the Board of Public Health, drilling for water to supply the Town of Croydon. Does this show that the courts were neutral as between public and private public utilities? Did the application of the same law to all exemplify the equality between state and citizen, so admired by A. V. Dicey?

The full ramifications of those questions are beyond the scope of this study, but there is enough evidence to raise a doubt. The attitude of the courts exhibited in *Pickles* to municipal enterprise was not universally followed, and it contrasted starkly with the 'benevolent interpretation' afforded municipal authorities in their law-making capacity. The treatment by the courts of local authorities in the exercise of their expanding and multifarious functions in the nineteenth century, with particular reference to the role played by techniques of statutory interpretation, deserves more detailed attention than it has yet received.

[86] Idem. [87] Ibid., 318. [88] Idem. [89] Idem. [90] Idem.

Municipal Trading

Municipal trading was a controversial topic in the latter years of the nineteenth century.[91] An inexact phrase, 'municipal trading' usually refers to the provision by municipal authorities of water, gas, electricity, transportation, housing, and the like.[92] These activities expanded municipal functions beyond those of 'peace, order and good government' and were seen by many as trespassing directly on the province of private enterprise. Opponents described this as 'municipal socialism', but it must be borne in mind that in the last decades of that century no socialist party had control of any municipality.[93] The causes of municipal trading were industrialization and urbanization.[94] Its promoters 'were simply empirical Englishmen facing public needs, and trying to meet each of them in what appeared the most practical way'.[95] And so it was with the development of the public utility infrastructure in Bradford.[96] It began with the purchase ('municipalization') of the Water Company in 1854,[97] and the Corporation took up the opportunities offered later in the century to expand into gas, electricity, trams, etc.

For some, water municipalization may have been the thin end of the wedge, but many thought of water as *sui generis*. In a paper read before the Manchester Statistical Society in 1901, a lawyer made this point:[98]

[91] See generally H. Finer, *Municipal Trading: A Study in Public Administration* (George Allen & Unwin Ltd, London, 1941).

[92] See M. Falkus, 'The Development of Municipal Trading in the Nineteenth Century' (1977) 19 *Business History* 134, and B. Millward, 'Emergence of gas and water monopolies in nineteenth-century Britain: contested markets and public control', in J. Foreman-Peck (ed.), *New perspectives on the late Victorian economy: Essays in Quantitative Economic History 1860–1914* (Cambridge University Press, Cambridge, 1991), 96.

[93] B. J. Barber, 'Aspects of municipal government 1835–1914', in D. Fraser (ed.), *A history of modern Leeds* (Manchester University Press, Manchester, 1980), 301, 323–4. See also J. Sheldrake, *Municipal Socialism* (Avebury, Aldershot, 1989), chs 1 and 2.

[94] M. Loughlin, 'Municipal Socialism in a Unitary State', in P. McAuslan and J. F. McEldowney (eds), *Law, Legitimacy and the Constitution* (Sweet & Maxwell, London, 1985), 82, 83–6.

[95] R. Ensor, *England, 1870–1914* (Clarendon Press, Oxford, rev. edn 1941), 128.

[96] Indeed, the creation of 'a municipal social infrastructure' was a Victorian legacy: D. Fraser, 'Joseph Chamberlain and the Municipal Ideal', in G. Marsden (ed.), *Victorian Values: Personalities and Perspectives in Nineteenth-Century Society* (Longman, London, 1990), 135, 144.

[97] Its bigger eastern neighbour and rival, Leeds, bought the privately owned water company there in 1852, behind Manchester (1851) and Liverpool (1847). See W. H. Fraser, 'From Civic Gospel to Municipal Socialism', in D. Fraser (ed.), *Cities, Class and Communication: Essays in Honour of Asa Briggs* (Harvester/Wheatsheaf, New York, 1990), 58, 59.

[98] A. W. Fletcher, 'Municipal Trading' [1900–1901] *Transactions of the Manchester Statistical Society* 85, 86–7. The common law reflected the view expressed in the quotation that water is a 'prime necessity'. See *Minister of Justice for the Dominion of Canada v City of Lévis* [1919] AC 505 (PC, Canada) and generally M. Taggart, 'Public Utilities and Public Law' in P. A. Joseph (ed.), *Essays on the Constitution* (Brooker's, Wellington, 1995), 214, 239–49.

> Many people who are opposed to the general principle [of municipal trading] would concede the desirability of a municipal supply of water, and others would include also gas. With few exceptions, the only persons who appear to have any irreconcilable objection to the municipalization of water are the directors and shareholders of water companies. The supply of water, indeed, differs from that of other commodities for several reasons. Water, for instance, is a necessary of life, and an article of universal consumption, whereas gas and electricity are not. It is essential to the health of the community that the supply of water should be pure and plentiful, and that its use by certain classes of society should be encouraged. If these conditions be not fulfilled, dirt, disease, and death are the inevitable results. . . . Moreover, it is essential to good government that the municipality itself should have a constant and plentiful supply of water for public purposes. It is not surprising therefore to find that the balance of public opinion is in favour of local authorities, whose first consideration is to safeguard the public health, owning the water supply, rather than that it should be in the hands of companies, who naturally make it their first aim to secure a return on their capital. . . .

Some of the judges who decided *Pickles* appeared not to share that popular sentiment. As one might expect,[99] Lord Halsbury saw no reason why 'this trading company' should not purchase Pickles's interest in the water 'from which this trading company desires to make a profit'.[100] In a similar vein, Lord Macnaghten put this question in the mouth of Edward Pickles: 'Why should he, he may think, without fee or reward, keep his land as a store-room for a commodity which the corporation dispense, probably not gratuitously, to the inhabitants of Bradford?'[101] While hinting that the Corporation was making a profit on its water operation, there is no evidence that the Corporation did so; and even if it had, it would have gone into relief of rates.

An instructive case from the same period that exhibits a different attitude, albeit in another context but again involving Bradford Corporation (this time wearing the hat of electricity provider), is *Jeremiah Ambler & Sons Ltd v Bradford Corporation*.[102] There the Corporation was sued for flood damage to a factory allegedly caused by the Corporation's electricity generation plant on Bradford Beck. The action was unsuccessful due to an absence of proof that the damage was caused by the Corporation's electrical works, rather than by severe storm. The Corporation claimed from the unsuccessful plaintiff 'solicitor and client costs' pursuant to the Public Authorities Protection Act 1893. That statute required this higher level of costs to be awarded in any unsuccessful action against 'any

[99] The Liberty and Property League, with whose aims Lord Halsbury was in sympathy (see Chapter 5), presented over 400 petitions to Parliament in one year alone (1899), demanding an inquiry into the development and appropriate limits of municipal trading: Sheldrake, above at note 93, 3.

[100] *Pickles* [1895] AC 587, 595.

[101] Ibid., 600–1.

[102] [1902] 2 Ch 585 (CA).

person for any act done in pursuance, or execution, or intended execution of any Act of Parliament, or of any public duty or authority'. The issue before the Court of Appeal in this case was whether the Corporation of Bradford, in electing since 1883 to provide electricity to the public of Bradford pursuant to statutory powers, was acting under a 'public duty'.

A little background is necessary. To overcome the cumbrous private Bill industry with its delays and costs, Parliament experimented with what was called 'provisional order' procedure. The Act of Parliament, in this case the Electric Lighting Act 1882, permitted its provisions to be applied to particular localities by provisional order. Bradford was quick to take up the offered opportunity to provide electricity within the borough. Indeed, it was the first municipality in the country to do so in 1883.[103] Pursuant to these statutory powers it constructed sluices on Bradford Beck, which had been alleged to have caused the flooding during a storm.

Counsel for the unsuccessful plaintiff argued strenuously that the Corporation was not acting in the execution of any 'public duty' in lighting the town. The Corporation had simply opted to enter into 'a commercial enterprise', but was under no 'public duty' to do so. Counsel for the Corporation answered that the wording of the provision was wide and that the Corporation was providing electricity pursuant to statutory powers. This was the first time that the Court of Appeal had been required to address this question.[104]

Vaughan Williams L.J. put the case against the Corporation in these terms:[105]

> [Earlier authorities] do not necessarily affirm the proposition that the Act applies to municipal trading under the authority of a special Act or order which a corporation or other public body chooses to obtain just as any private person might do without being under any obligation so to do. The public authority in regard to such trading is, in fact, a mere volunteer; and, it may be urged that, as the public authority is under no obligation to exercise the statutory authority which it has obtained, and is at liberty to make a profit by the exercise of the authority, such profit, however, going of course in reduction of local taxation, there is no reason why a public authority trading in competition with private traders should be protected as to either costs or the time within which an action should be brought.

Notwithstanding the strength of those arguments, the Court of Appeal rather unconvincingly held that the Corporation was acting pursuant to statutory powers and fell within the protection of the Act. Romer L.J. said

[103] R. H. Parsons, *The Early Days of the Power Station Industry* (Babcock & Wilcox Ltd, Cambridge, 1939), 121–2.

[104] Incidentally, one of the earlier cases also involved the Corporation: *Chamberlain & Hookham Ltd v Bradford Corporation* (1900) 83 LT 518 (Ch).

[105] Above at note 102, 591.

that the Court was not concerned with the policy of the Act and should not approach its interpretation with any feeling that it was desirable to enlarge or curtail its application.[106] The Act was to be properly construed and applied, even if the result in certain cases appeared to bear hardly on plaintiffs.[107] Vaughan Williams L.J. said, in the closest the Court came to a policy justification of the result, 'the protection of the Act seems plainly to extend to a municipal authority supported primarily by the levy of rates, and which is bound to apply all the earnings of any undertaking authorized by statute in relief of the ratepayers'.[108]

'Benevolent Interpretation'

One of the hallowed administrative law cases of the late nineteenth century is *Kruse v Johnson*.[109] In its own time this case was as famous and influential as the mid-twentieth-century case of *Wednesbury*[110] that replaced it in the common law catechism.

Kruse's case involved a challenge to a newly created by-law prohibiting the playing of music in public within 50 yards of a dwelling-house. The two persons convicted of this offence were associated with the Salvation Army, and it seems clear that the police employed the by-law to stop Salvationists from singing hymns in public.[111] The primary challenge to the validity of the by-law was on the ground of unreasonableness. Despite considerable unease within the legal profession as to the potential tyranny by tinpot local bodies, each promulgating different local rules, a specially constituted Divisional Court (by a majority of six to one) upheld the by-law. The case is famous for its expression of judicial restraint, emphasizing the need for 'benevolent interpretation' of the by-laws of elected local authorities. What is less well known is that a sharp contrast was drawn between by-laws made by local authorities and those made by private bodies such as railway companies.

106 Ibid., 593.

107 Ibid., 593 (Vaughan Williams L.J.) and 593–4 (Romer L.J.).

108 Ibid., 593.

109 [1898] 2 QB 91 (DC—seven-judge bench).

110 *Associated Provincial Picture Houses Ltd v Wednesbury Corporation* [1948] 1 KB 223 (CA).

111 This paragraph draws heavily on the background to *Kruse v Johnson*, above at note 109, provided by D. G. T. Williams, 'Subordinate Legislation and Judicial Control' (1997) 8 PLR 77, 79–81. On the prominent role the Salvation Army has played in testing public disorder provisions, see V. Bailey, 'Salvation Army Riots, the "Skeleton Army" and Legal Authority in the Provincial Town', in A. P. Donajgrodzki (ed.), *Social Control in Nineteenth Century Britain* (Croom Helm, London, 1977), 231; R. Vorspan, '"Freedom of Assembly" and the Right to Passage in Modern English Legal History' (1997) 34 San Diego LR 921, 942–66; D. G. T. Williams, 'The Principle in *Beatty v Gillbanks*: A Reappraisal', in A. N. Doob and E. L. Greenspan (eds), *Perspectives in Criminal Law: Essays in Honour of John Ll. J. Edwards* (Canada Law Book Inc., Aurora, 1985), 105.

Lord Russell C.J., speaking for the majority of the Divisional Court, said:[112]

> The great majority of the cases in which the question of by-laws has been discussed are not cases of by-laws of bodies of a public representative character entrusted by Parliament with delegated authority, but for the most part cases of railway companies, dock companies, or other like companies, which carry on their business for their own profit, although incidentally for the advantage of the public. In this class of case it is right that the Courts should jealously watch the exercise of these powers, and guard against their unnecessary or unreasonable exercise to the public disadvantage. But when the Court is called upon to consider the by-laws of public representative bodies clothed with ample authority . . . I think the consideration of such by-laws ought to be approached from a different standpoint. They ought to be supported if possible. They ought to be, as has been said, 'benevolently' interpreted, and credit ought to be given to those who have to administer them that they will be reasonably administered. This involves the introduction of no new canon of construction.

Of course, this is not directly analogous to interpreting primary legislation, but cleaving democratically produced delegated legislation and privately produced by-laws, and the abandonment of the *contra proferentem* rule in the former category, suggests the glimmer of a public/private distinction.

The *Kruse* case pitted the majority's desire for public order against a religious minority's freedom of expression. It was an unequal struggle—as it almost always has been until very recent times—with freedom of expression the loser. Similarly, freedom of property was the much more valued right in popular (and legal) consciousness in the late Victorian period.

Property as Fundamental Right

There is little doubt that sanctity of property 'was (and indeed still is, however much weakened by modern political theory) one of the cardinal principles of English common law. Whatever rights were fundamental we may be sure they included the right to property.'[113] With the long battle for the sovereignty of Parliament won, these fundamental rights found expression in presumptions of legislative intent.[114] In theory, these

[112] Above at note 109, 98–9.

[113] G. W. Gough, *Fundamental Law in English Constitutional History* (Oxford University Press, Oxford, 1955), 54.

[114] See J. Bell and G. Engle, *Statutory Interpretation* (Butterworths, London, 3rd edn, 1995), ch. 7, and F. A. R. Bennion, *Statutory Interpretation: A Code* (Butterworths, London, 3rd edn, 1997), Parts XVI–XVII.

expressions of constitutional principle could be overcome by clear statutory wording, but in practice it seldom happened. As *Pickles* shows, the judges refused to countenance the prospect. The role of the 'constitutional' presumptions went beyond the role of preferring a right-respecting interpretation of an ambiguous provision to any other—although the judges were masters at creating uncertainty as to meaning when they wanted to—it operated as a floor below which the Legislature was not allowed to sink: constitutional bedrock, if you like.

Without a written Constitution, and in the face of Dicey's theory of Parliamentary supremacy, these constitutional protections could find expression only as rules of statutory interpretation.[115] In those countries with written Constitutions expressly protecting property, the taking of property for public purposes is an important aspect of constitutional law. In contrast, in the United Kingdom the subject has acquired the unglamorous name of 'compulsory purchase' and is a highly practical subject, attended by little constitutional fanfare or theorizing.[116]

The history of expropriation in the United Kingdom has yet to be written.[117] However, putting to one side the shadowy prerogative power to take private property in times of national emergency,[118] it has been a feature of land expropriation in the United Kingdom that statutory authorization is necessary (as well as sufficient) to acquire private property compulsorily. As F. A. Mann once noted with evident pride, and perhaps a touch of hyperbole, the 'early, unbroken and unqualified application' of the requirement of Parliamentary legislation, in relation to purposes which might have been seen to fall within the province of the Executive, 'remains a remarkable achievement'.[119]

The necessary authority to acquire land compulsorily was obtained from Parliament either directly by public general act or private act, or indirectly under Acts containing general powers of acquisition which are exercisable for particular purposes.[120] It is another remarkable feature of

115 I draw here from earlier work: M. Taggart, 'Expropriation, Public Purpose and the Constitution', in C. Forsyth and I. Hare (eds), *The Golden Metwand and the Crooked Cord: Essays on Public Law in Honour of Sir William Wade Q.C.* (Clarendon Press, Oxford, 1998), 91, 101–2.

116 W. B. Stoebuck, 'A General Theory of Eminent Domain' (1972) 47 Wash. LR 553, 554.

117 The best general treatment of the topic still is Stoebuck, ibid. For an illuminating study of expropriation and railway development in the United Kingdom, see R. W. Kostal, *Law and English Railway Capitalism, 1825–1875* (Clarendon Press, Oxford, 1994), ch. 4.

118 On the prerogative, see G. R. Rubin, *Private Property, Government Requisition and the Constitution, 1914–1927* (Hambledon Press, London, 1994), ch. 2; L. Scott and A. Hildesley, *The Case of Requisition: In re a Petition of Right of De Keyser's Royal Hotel Ltd.; De Keyser's Royal Hotel Ltd. v. The King* (Clarendon Press, Oxford, 1920), ch. III.

119 F. A. Mann, 'Outlines of a History of Expropriation' (1959) 75 LQR 188, 196.

120 W. D. McNulty, 'The Power of "Compulsory Purchase" Under the Law of England' (1912) 21 Yale LJ 639.

British expropriation law that over the centuries no one statute ever defined expropriation; rather, particular statutes provided for compulsory acquisition for particular purposes and prescribed the procedure by which land was to be acquired.[121] Until recent times, the closest thing to an expropriation statute was the Land Clauses Act 1845,[122] which simply brought together the best provisions from the numerous private acts then in force, better to ensure uniformity and to permit future Parliaments to legislate more economically. In the nineteenth century the large number of Acts—mainly private Acts delegating land acquisition powers to private for-profit companies for public works such as railway construction—simply authorized acquisition for specified purposes, and the power was not framed in constitutional terms. As Maitland once said of legislation in eighteenth-century Britain, but which rings true of expropriation statutes throughout their history, 'the British parliament seems rarely to rise to the dignity of a general proposition'.[123]

The history of the Bradford Waterworks Company illustrates the process of Parliament bestowing the power of compulsory purchase upon private companies in order to further the public interest. In that instance the public purpose was to improve the supply of water to 'the Town and Neighbourhood of *Bradford*'.[124] As the preamble to the Act of 1842 stated:

> WHEREAS the inhabitants of the Town of *Bradford* and the Neighbourhood thereof in the West Riding of the County of *York* are now inadequately supplied with Water: And whereas a sufficient and constant Supply of pure and wholesome Water would be of great Advantage to the Inhabitants of the said Town and Neighbourhood: And whereas it is ascertained that such a Supply can be obtained, and the several persons herein-after named, together with others, are willing, at their own Expence, to make and maintain all the necessary Works for affording such Supply to the said Inhabitants; but such Object cannot be effected without the Authority of Parliament. . .

But that public interest, which justified Parliament granting powers and immunities to private promoters, came at a price, and part of the price to be paid was full compensation for all property interference. As Lord Macnaghten said of section 49 of the Bradford Waterworks Act 1854 in *Pickles*:[125]

[121] H. Street and B. A. Wortley, 'State and Private Property in English Law', in *Staat and Privateigentum* (Max-Planck Institute, Carl Heymanns Verlag K.G., Berlin, 1960) 131, 132.

[122] 8 and 9 Vict. c. 18.

[123] Quoted by D. Lieberman, *The Province of Legislation Determined: Legal theory in eighteenth-century Britain* (Cambridge University Press, Cambridge, 1989), 16.

[124] From the Long Title of the Bradford Waterworks Act 1842.

[125] [1895] AC 587, 602. For an overview of how this idea of preventing the state from arbitrarily transferring the private property of A to B developed in the Constitutional soil of the United States, see J. V. Orth, 'Taking from A and Giving to B: Substantive Due Process and the Case of the Shifting Paradigm' [1997] *Constitutional Commentary* 337.

According to the ordinary course of legislation in this country, a clause of that sort is intended to protect property, rights, and interests which have been acquired by purchase, not to transfer arbitrarily from one person to another property and rights for which nothing has been paid, and for which no compensation is provided.

The Common Lawyer and Statute

The common lawyer has an ingrained resentment of statute law,[126] born first of superiority and latterly from insecurity. Statute law is everything the common law is not. Statutes are perceived of by the common lawyer as the product of fiat, not reason, incapable therefore of providing a source of ideas, and lacking the persuasive force and flexibility of case law.[127] Jack Beatson has described this view of the relationship between common law and legislation as one of 'oil and water'.[128] What is more, when the Legislature has the audacity to change the common law, it is inevitably for the worse.[129]

What began as a trickle of Acts hundreds of years ago has turned into an annual torrent of legislation almost completely engulfing the common law, so only the common law method remains.[130] And the methods of interpreting statutes developed against the common law backdrop: the preservation of property and liberty, and the minimalization of State interference. John Willis once described such principles of statutory interpretation as 'a sort of common law "Bill of Rights" '.[131] To learn 'to think like a lawyer'—one of the purposes of legal education—has meant adopting this common law mindset. By reading leading cases, such as *Pickles*, these attitudes and techniques are picked up almost by osmosis.

[126] See the excellent article by Roderick Munday, 'The Common Lawyer's Philosophy of Legislation' (1983) 14 *Rechtstheorie* 191.

[127] See, e.g., J. Landis, 'Statutes and the Sources of Law', in *Harvard Legal Essays* (Harvard University Press, Cambridge, 1934), 213 (reprinted in (1965) 2 Harv. J. on Legislation 7).

[128] 'Has the Common Law a Future?' [1997] CLJ 291, 300 and 308. See J. Beatson, 'The Role of Statute in the Development of Common Law Doctrine' (2000) 117 LQR 247.

[129] See, e.g., Sir Frederick Pollock, *Essays on Jurisprudence and Ethics* (Macmillan, London, 1882), 85 ('. . . Parliament generally changes the law for the worse . . . the business of judges is to keep the mischief of the interference within the narrowest possible bounds'). According to Lord Steyn, Pollock's statement was true until fairly recently, but is no longer: J. Steyn, 'Does Legal Formalism Hold Sway in England?' (1996) 49 Curr Leg. Probs 43, 48–9. Pollock's views on statutes and their interpretation are discussed by N. Duxbury, 'When We Were Young: Notes in the *Law Quarterly Review*, 1885–1925' (2000) 116 LQR 474, 496–500, and S. Hedley, 'Sir Frederick Pollock and the Teaching of English Law', in J. A. Bush and A. Wijffels (eds), *Learning the Law: Teaching and the Transmission of Law in England, 1150–1900* (The Hambledon Press, London, 1999), 407 (noting Pollock's support for codification). Pollock's views on *Pickles* are discussed in Chapter 5.

[130] Jack Beatson makes a similar point, above at note 128, 302.

[131] J. Willis, 'Statutory Interpretation in a Nutshell' (1938) 16 Can. BR 1, 17.

Times are changing, and there may well be a degree of caricature in this description of the legal mindset today.[132] But this 'small-minded attitude'[133] was alive and well in the late nineteenth century. 'English judges', Willis pointed out, 'have no power to declare Acts unconstitutional merely because they depart from the good old ways of thought; they can, however, use the presumptions to mould legislative innovation into some accord with the old notions.'[134] It must be borne in mind also that the 'statute book' up to the middle of the nineteenth century was a 'confused jumble' and an amateurish effort.[135] Both points are illustrated by the legislation at issue in *Pickles* and the way it was handled by the judiciary.

[132] Some judges nowadays view the common law and statute law coalescing in one legal system: *R v Secretary of State for the Home Department, ex p. Pierson* [1998] AC 539, 589, *per* Lord Steyn; quoted by W. M. C. Gummow, *Change and Continuity: Statute, Equity, and Federalism* (Oxford University Press, Oxford, 1999), 1.

[133] R. Zimmermann, '*Statuta Sunt Stricte Interpretanda*? Statutes and the Common Law: A Continental Perspective' [1997] CLJ 315, 319.

[134] Willis, above at note 131.

[135] Munday, above at note 126, 197.

5

Property and Water

The many different contexts in which water disputes have arisen—for example, drainage, building of mill dams, pollution, fishing, extraction of water for agrarian or other uses, the construction of bridges or weirs—make it difficult to generalize about the development of the rules of water right and use. The law evolved (with the inevitable 'lag' caused by the delays in litigation and the judges' perception of social reality)[1] as society developed and the demands on the water supplies increased. There were disputes about water use centuries before the Industrial Revolution.[2] However, the insatiable demand that industrialization and concomitant urbanization created for water vastly increased the number and importance of water disputes, and consequently the case law increased exponentially. The size of the literature on nineteenth-century water law warns against simplification, as does the contested modern scholarship seeking to understand that law, both as an autonomous body of law and in its social and economic context.[3]

Much of the best writing in both the nineteenth and twentieth centuries on water law has emanated from America. This adds to the difficulty of understanding the 'common law' of water, for few legal subjects are as sensitive to societal context, geography, and custom as that pertaining to water.[4] The water problems that arise in the United Kingdom—a relatively small nation populated early that suffers from too much water—are likely to differ (or to be resolved differently) from those encountered in a vast, largely undeveloped land with considerable variation in climatic conditions and a federal structure of government, as the United States was in the nineteenth century. This is the stuff of books rather than the

[1] What G. Edward White called 'social lag' in 'The Appellate Opinion as Historical Source Material' (1971) 1 *Journal of Interdisciplinary History* 491, 496.

[2] See, e.g., E. F. Murphy, 'English Water Law Before 1400' (1957) 1 Am J Leg His 103.

[3] See J. P. S. McLaren, 'Nuisance Law and the Industrial Revolution—Some Lessons from Social History' (1983) 3 OJLS 155; M. J. Horwitz, *The Transformation of American Law, 1780–1860* (Harvard University Press, Cambridge, 1977), ch. 2; C. Rose, 'The Comedy of the Commons: Custom, Commerce, and Inherently Public Property' (1986) 53 UChic LR 711 (reprinted in C. M. Rose, *Property and Persuasion: Essays on the History, Theory, and Rhetoric of Ownership* (Westview Press, Boulder, 1994)).

[4] This point has seldom been put better than in a Scottish work: J. Rankine, *A Treatise on the Rights and Burdens Incident to the Ownership of Lands and Other Heritages in Scotland* (William Blackwood & Sons, Edinburgh, 1st edn, 1879), 389.

fragment presented here. The best I can hope to achieve is to simplify drastically and to refer interested readers to some of the rich literature on these topics.

The aims of this chapter are twofold. First, to identify the uncertainty surrounding the law as regarding subterranean water at the time the Bradford Waterworks legislation was being promoted in 1840. This may explain why the Company, and later the Corporation, did not secure rights to the continued flow of the water under East Many Wells Farm. The second aim is to discuss the nineteenth-century development of water law in greater detail than was possible in Chapter 3. This permits the decision in *Pickles* to be put in a broader legal context. The absolute nature of the property right in underground water established in *Pickles* reverberates beyond the small corner of water law relating to appropriation of flowing underground water.

What was the Law in 1842?

One perspective from which to view water law in relation to the *Pickles* case is that of the participants in the establishment of the Bradford Waterworks Company *circa* 1840. In other words, what would legal advisers and Parliamentary counsel have understood the law to be relating to the use or diversion of percolating underground water in 1840? We know the first English case involving interference with subterranean water—*Acton v Blundell*—was not decided until after the enactment of the Bradford Waterworks Act in 1842. (Several of the judges in *Pickles* remarked upon this.)[5] A capable and industrious lawyer looking for an answer to the question of who owned or had the use right to the water flowing under Pickles's land would not have found an English case exactly on point, but that should not have been the end of the matter. The importance of the flow of water to the Bradford Waterworks Company, and the close proximity of the head of the Spring to the boundary with East Many Wells Farm, would have alerted even the dimmest of investors and their advisers to the need to ascertain the legal position and to make provision accordingly. The conscientious lawyer should have looked at Blackstone's *Commentaries* and case law dealing with analogous situations, and English treatises on water law; and might also have looked at American case law and commentary, as well as at the civil law.

[5] *Pickles* [1894] 3 Ch 53, 64 (North J.); [1895] 1 Ch 145, 156 (Lord Herschell L.C.); [1895] AC 587, 602–3 (Lord Macnaghten).

Blackstone on Property and Water

In the age before the modern textbook or treatise, William Blackstone's *Commentaries on the Laws of England* (published in four volumes between 1765 and 1769) was an easily accessible, readable, and manageable primer for lawyers (as well as laymen) on the laws of England as a whole.[6] It became the lawyers' bible. In the absence of more recent case law on any point, or the appearance of specialist works, it would have been professional negligence not to turn to the *Commentaries* to discover the law.[7]

To understand Blackstone's treatment of water law it is necessary to say something first about his conception of property. Blackstone described the right of private property as an 'absolute right' vested in individuals 'by the immutable laws of nature'.[8] Famously, he defined property as 'the sole and despotic dominion which one man claims and exercises over the external things of the world, in total exclusion of the right of any individual in the universe'.[9] But this focus on the 'absolute' nature of property can mislead.[10] As others have pointed out, Blackstone distinguished between two types of rights: 'absolute' rights, which were innate and possessed by individuals prior to the formation of civil society; and 'relative' rights, which belong to people who have joined together in a civilized community.[11] The price to be paid for the benefits of community was the giving

[6] Not surprisingly, a large amount has been written about Blackstone and his *Commentaries*. For a short but well-balanced introduction to both, see G. H. Jones, 'Blackstone, Sir William', in A. W. B. Simpson (ed.), *Biographical Dictionary of the Common Law* (Butterworths, London, 1984), 57–9. The *Commentaries* were intended to instruct the elite of English society as to their rights, and were not a specialist work. See C. E. Klafter, 'The Americanization of Blackstone's *Commentaries*', in E. A. Cawthorn and D. E. Narrett (eds), *Essays on English Law and the American Experience* (Texas A & M University Press, Texas, 1994), 42, 45–7.

[7] It is difficult to get a precise bead on how 'authoritative' the *Commentaries* were considered to be in Blackstone's lifetime and in the early nineteenth century. For his own time, see J. S. Waterman, 'Mansfield and Blackstone's Commentaries' (1933–34) 1 UChic LR 548.

[8] W. Blackstone, *Commentaries on the Laws of England* (Clarendon Press, Oxford, 1765–79), vol. 2, 2 (hereafter referred to as *Commentaries*). There has been much discussion of the genuineness of Blackstone's professed allegiance to natural law, but that need not be gone into here. See N. E. Simonds, 'Reason, History and Privilege: Blackstone's Debt to Natural Law' [1988] *Zeitschrift der Savigny-Stiftung für Rechsgeschichte* 200. For a useful discussion of the intellectual milieu in which Blackstone formulated his ideas about property, see C. S. Telly, 'The Classical Economic Model and the Nature of Property in the Eighteenth and Nineteenth Centuries' (1978) 13 Tulsa LJ 406. For an excellent discussion of the origins and influence of what is described as 'the creation story of property', see D. J. Siepp, 'The Concept of Property in the Early Common Law' (1994) 12 *Law & History Review* 29, 67–88.

[9] *Commentaries*, vol. 2, 2.

[10] See F. G. Whelan, 'Property as Artifice: Hume and Blackstone', in J. R. Pennock and J. W. Chapman (eds), *Property* (New York University Press, NOMOS XXII, 1980), 101, 118–21, and R. Willman, 'Blackstone and the "Theoretical Perfection" of English Law in the Reign of Charles II' (1983) 26 *The Historical Journal* 39, 64–67.

[11] See, e.g., R. P. Burns, 'Blackstone's Theory of the "Absolute" Rights of Property' (1985) 54 UCin LR 67, and A. W. Alschuler, 'Rediscovering Blackstone' (1996) 145 UPa LR 1, 28–36.

up of some part of the 'absolute' rights enjoyed in the state of nature; hence the rights enjoyed in the real world of a particular community (as opposed to an imagined state of nature) were 'relative'. 'Relative' rights could be limited by society (through legislation or the common law) whenever it was in the interests of society—'for the general advantage of the public'[12]—to do so.[13]

Blackstone divided all legal rights into two mutually exclusive categories—rights over persons and rights over things. The latter category was further divided into things real and things personal, and cascading subdivision ensued. It is well known that in this, as in much else, Blackstone borrowed from the civil law.[14]

In the subdivision of real property, Blackstone defined land as comprehending 'all things of a permanent, substantial nature'.[15] Lord Coke was quoted for the proposition that land 'comprehendeth in its legal signification any ground, soil, or earth whatsoever; as arable, meadows, pastures, woods, moors, waters, marshes, furzes, and heath'.[16] Blackstone went on to say:[17]

> It is observable that *water* is here mentioned as a species of land, which may seem a kind of solecism; but such is the language of the law: and I cannot bring an action to recover possession of a pool or other piece of water, by the name of the *water* only . . . but I must bring my action for the land that lies at the bottom. . . . For water is a moveable, wandering thing, and must of necessity continue common by the law of nature; so that I can only have a temporary, transient, usufructuary property therein: wherefore if a body of water runs out of my pond into another man's, I have no right to reclaim it. But the land, which that water covers, is permanent, fixed, and immoveable: and therefore in this I have a certain, substantial property; of which the law will take notice, and not of the other.

Blackstone then reverts back to Coke, quoting his maxim *cujus est solum*

12 *Commentaries*, vol. 1, 125.

13 For discussion of the relative and fragmented nature of property rights at that time, see R. Gordon, 'Paradoxical Property', in J. Brewer and S. Staves (eds), *Early Modern Conceptions of Property* (Routledge, London, 1995), 95, and D. Sugarman and G. R. Rubin, 'Towards a New History of Law and Material Society in England, 1750–1914', in G. R. Rubin and D. Sugarman (eds), *Law, Economy and Society, 1750–1914: Essays in the History of English Law* (Professional Books Ltd, Abingdon, 1984), 1, 31–6.

14 A. Watson, 'The Structure of Blackstone's Commentaries' (1988) 97 Yale LJ 795, 798.

15 *Commentaries*, vol. 2, 16.

16 Ibid., 17–18.

17 Ibid., 18 (italics in original). Blackstone went on to say: 'And therefore if a man grants all his lands, he grants thereby all his mines of metal and other fossils, his woods, his waters, and his houses, as well as his fields and meadows. Not but the particular names of the things are equally sufficient to pass them, except in the instance of water; by a grant of which, nothing passes but a right of fishing: but the capital distinction is this; that by the name of the castle, messuage, toft, croft, or the like, nothing else will pass, except what falls with the utmost propriety under the term made use of; but by the name of the land, which is *nomen generalissimun*, every thing terrestrial will pass' (ibid., 18–19).

ejus est usque ad coelum (whoever owns the soil owns all that lies above it), and added for the first time *et ad inferos* (and below it).[18]

In the subdivision of things personal, Blackstone conceived that a person had rights *over* 'external' things, which were either tangible or intangible.[19] Normally the rights of ownership over things would be 'absolute', but this was not always the case due to the nature of 'some few things'.[20] Blackstone included in this select list of what he called property in 'common' the elements of light, air, and water, and wild and untamable (*ferae naturae*) animals.[21] By the nature of these things a person could hold only a 'usufructory property', by which Blackstone meant that these things 'belong to the first occupant, during the time he holds possession of them, and no longer,' and if they escape or are abandoned, they return to the 'common stock'.[22]

Later in the same volume of the *Commentaries*, Blackstone described this as 'qualified property', in the sense that the limitations on the owner's dominion over light, air, water, and wild animals were inherent in the nature of the element or beast.[23] He wrote:[24]

> [Q]ualified property may subsist in the very elements, of fire, light, of air, and of water. A man can have no absolute permanent property in these, as he may in the earth or land; since these are of a vague and fugitive nature, and therefore can admit only of a precarious and qualified ownership, which lasts as long as they are in actual use and occupation, but no longer. If a man disturbs another, and deprives him of the lawful enjoyment of these; if one obstructs another's ancient windows, corrupts the air of his house or gardens, fouls his water, or unpens and lets it out, or if he diverts an ancient watercourse that used to run to the other's mill or meadow; the law will animadvert hereon as an injury, and protect the party injured in his possession. But the property in them ceases the instant they are out of possession: for, when no man is engaged in their actual occupation, they become again common, and every man has an equal right to appropriate them to his own use.

Blackstone extrapolated from this that 'the benefits of the elements' (namely, light, air and water) can be appropriated by the first occupant.[25] Ancient windows, existing walls, existing obnoxious industries, and existing use rights of flowing surface waters are all given as examples of

[18] Idem. Blackstone's innovation is discussed below at note 70.

[19] This is called the 'physicalist conception of property' by K. J. Vandevelde, 'The New Property of the Nineteenth Century: The Development of the Modern Concept of Property' (1980) 29 Buffalo LR 325, 331.

[20] *Commentaries*, vol. 2, 14. [21] Idem. [22] Idem.

[23] Ibid., 394–6. Property could also be qualified because of the particular circumstances of the owner: idem.

[24] Ibid., 395.

[25] This emphasis on possession/occupation and use reoccurs in Blackstone's discussion of a natural right to property in the state of nature. See Whelan, above at note 10, 116–18.

appropriation by first occupation. Blackstone went so far as to describe the first occupant and user of a stream as having 'acquired a property in the current'.[26]

Blackstone—like Bracton, Fleta, Britton, Callis, and Selden before him[27]—drew upon Roman law in his description of the elements of light, air, and water as everyone's by the law of nature.[28] It must be remembered that Blackstone 'was essentially a civilian and an academic . . . [whose] disappointed ambition was to become professor of civil law at Oxford'.[29] He became the Vinerian Professor of English Law on the rebound, so to speak, and the *Commentaries* grew out of his earlier lectures at Oxford.

By the 1830s, however, it was clear that the courts would not simply accept as representing the common law such 'leading principles' extracted from Roman law.[30] One of the cases that gave the warning was *Blundell v Catterall* (1821).[31] The issue there was whether there was a common law right to cross over privately owned seashore on foot, or with bathing machines, in order to reach the sea to bathe. In large part, the answer depended on whether or not this passage from *Bracton* accurately stated the common law:

[26] Above at note 20, 402.

[27] See S. C. Weil, 'Natural Communism: Air, Water, Oil, Sea, and Seashore' (1934) 47 Harv LR 425, 425, n. 2 for references. See also *Williams v Morland* (1824) 2 B. & C. 910, 913; 107 E.R. 620, 621, *per* Bayley J.; *Liggins v Inge* (1831) 7 Bing. 682, 692; 131 E.R. 263, 268, *per* Tindal C.J.

[28] In the second book of *Justinian's Institutes* it is said '[t]he things which are naturally everybody's are: air, flowing water, the sea, and the sea-shore. So nobody can be stopped from going on to the sea-shore. But he must keep away from houses, monuments, and buildings. Unlike the sea, rights to those things are not determined by the law of all peoples': P. Birks and G. McLeod (trans. and eds.), *Justinian's Institutes* (Duckworth, London, 1987), 55. This passage is adopted in *Bracton*. See S. E. Thorne (trans.), *Bracton on the Laws and Customs of England* (Belknap Press of Harvard University Press, Cambridge, 1965), vol. 2, 39–40. Although the exact date cannot be pinpointed, the complete *Corpus Juris Civilis* had certainly reached England by the third quarter of the twelfth century. However, it had less impact on the first common law book, called *Glanvill* (*circa* 1187–89), than on *Bracton*, because the main topics covered were feudal tenures and lord–tenant relations, topics upon which Roman law had little to say. See on this R. V. Turner, 'Who Was the Author of *Glanvill*? Reflections on the Education of Henry II's Common Lawyers' (1990) 8 *Law & History Review* 97, 105–6.

[29] A. W. B. Simpson, 'The Legal Treatise and Legal Theory', in E. V. Ives and A. H. Manchester (eds), *Law, Litigants and the Legal Profession* (Royal Historical Society, London, 1983), 11, 22.

[30] In the *Commentaries* Blackstone wrote of educating 'our gentlemen of independent estates and fortune' about 'a few leading principles, relating to estates and conveyancing': vol. 1, 7.

[31] (1821) 5 B. & Ald. 267; 106 E.R. 1190. See also *Ball v Herbert* (1789) 3 TR 253; 100 E.R. 560 (a case rejecting an alleged common law right to tow on the banks of navigable rivers), where *Bracton* was cited in argument and Buller J. observed that the passage could be traced to Justinian and was 'only part of the civil law', and, as it could not be found in 'our books', it was not part of the common law (ibid., 263; 565).

By natural law these are common to all: running water, air, the sea, and the shores of the sea, as though accessories of the sea. No one therefore is forbidden access to the seashore, provided he keeps away from houses and buildings [built there], for by the *jus gentium* shores are not common to all in the sense that the sea is, but buildings built there, whether in the sea or on the shore, belong by the *jus gentium* to those who build them.

Best J., in solitary dissent, described *Bracton* as 'no mean authority for what the common law was at the time he wrote'.[32] Best J. accepted that *Bracton* agreed with the civil law, but argued that *Bracton* adopted it into the common law, which was held to favour the common law right of way over the seashore to the beach. The majority, in contrast, saw the passage from *Bracton* as coming almost word for word from Justinian's *Institutes*, and not as representing the common law position. Sir Matthew Hale's treatise on *De Portibus Maris* was quoted extensively to illustrate the divergences between the civil law and the common law treatments of the foreshore, rivers, and banks.[33] The majority—Abbot C.J., Holroyd and Bayley JJ.—held that there was no common law right of way over the seashore to bathe in the sea.

What conclusion would someone reading the *Commentaries circa* 1840 reach as regards the law relating to percolating underground water? The first thing to note is that Blackstone never unambiguously addressed the issue of diversion of subterranean percolating water. Almost all the references to water—which were not numerous, in any event[34]—appear to refer to flowing surface water. There is the occasional reference to 'fouling water', but again this appears to relate to surface water. As noted earlier, the *Commentaries* were not a textbook in the modern sense, so it is misguided to look for minute detail on esoteric points of law. Nevertheless, Blackstone's emphatic support for the prior appropriation theory of surface water rights would have encouraged any legal adviser or Parliamentary agent to think that once the water flowing out of Many Wells Spring was 'appropriated' for the purpose of town supply by the Bradford Waterworks Company, it would be legally protected (by the common law) from interference by others.

32 Ibid., 282; 1195. See generally D. E. C. Yale, ' "Of No Mean Authority": Some Later Uses of Bracton', in M. S. Arnold, T. A. Green, S. A. Scully, and S. D. White (eds), *On the Laws and Customs of England: Essays in Honor of Samuel E. Thorne* (University of North Carolina Press, Chapel Hill, 1981), 383.

33 Ibid., 290–316; 1198–207.

34 T. E. Lauer described Blackstone's observations on watercourses as 'sparse': 'The Common Law Background of the Riparian Doctrine' (1963) 28 Missouri LR 60, 96.

Case Law and Literature between Blackstone and 1840

More than 70 years passed between the publication of the *Commentaries* and the promotion of the Bradford Waterworks Bill. Then, as now, a competent adviser would have surveyed the developments in the intervening period. There was, in fact, a good deal of case law to discover, although none was directly on point. The onslaught of the Industrial Revolution brought intensified water usage, as well as new uses for water, and disputes multiplied. During this period the English courts struggled to develop a workable system of water rights. Up until the early 1830s there was considerable uncertainty as to the rule that governed the use of flowing surface water. To simplify drastically the legal situation,[35] perhaps even to the point of caricature, the competing rules were referred to as 'prior appropriation' and 'natural flow'. There was support for both approaches in English law.[36]

The rule of 'prior appropriation' provided in essence that the first landowner to appropriate flowing surface water had the use of it to the detriment of all other subsequent users upstream or downstream. There were no restrictions as to how much water could be taken, or for what purpose. There is some suggestion that the use had to be 'beneficial', but this was hardly any restraint. For example, it was permissible to pipe the water off the first appropriator's land for the use of others.

The competing rule was known at this time by the term 'natural flow'. This rule gave the owners of land contiguous to flowing surface water the right to use that water, but only on land adjoining the stream and not so as to diminish the flow to their neighbours. A distinction was drawn between 'ordinary' and 'extraordinary' use of flowing water.[37] Water for 'ordinary uses' (such as household supply and water for animals) could be used without concern for downstream users. All other uses, called 'extraordinary uses', could be made only if they did not interfere with the upstream and downstream users.

The considerable case law over this period, and the doctrinal and policy twists and turns, are well analysed by others.[38] It suffices for my purpose to describe briefly the uncertain state of the law by the 1830s. The uncertainty is exemplified by two cases, decided within two years of each other, reaching diametrically opposed results. The first case, *Liggins v*

[35] For an exhaustive and nuanced treatment of the case law and its evolution, see J. S. Getzler, 'Rules Writ in Water: A History of Riparian Rights and Property Use Doctrine in England to 1870', unpublished D.Phil. thesis, University of Oxford, 1993.

[36] See Lauer, above at note 34, *passim*.

[37] The same distinction is sometimes expressed as natural and artificial uses.

[38] See Lauer, above at note 34, 99–106; Getzler, above at note 35.

Inge,[39] followed earlier case law in adopting the doctrine of prior appropriation. In the course of holding that an established downstream user could abandon by oral agreement his prior use right over flowing water in favour of a new upstream user, Tindal C.J. in the Court of Common Pleas began by saying that it was well settled in English law that flowing water was *publici juris*.[40] In Roman law, Chief Justice Tindal pointed out, running water was *res communis*, and so it belonged to no one but could be used by all.[41] But that was not the case in English law: 'by the law of England, the person who first appropriates any part of the water flowing through his land to his own use, has the right to the use of so much as he thus appropriates, against any other.'[42]

Two years later, in *Mason v Hill*,[43] the higher-ranking Court of King's Bench rejected the prior appropriation doctrine in favour of a natural rights theory. The Court drew support from precedent (unconvincingly, as the weight of authority favoured prior appropriation) and policy. Denman C.J., delivering the unanimous judgment of the Court, said:[44]

> [can the owner of the land who applies the stream that runs through it] take away from the owner of the land below, one of the natural advantages, which is capable of being applied to profitable purposes, and generally increases the fertility of the soil, even when unapplied; and deprive him altogether by anticipating him in its application to a useful purpose? If this be so, a considerable part of the value of an estate, which, in manufacturing districts particularly, is much enhanced by the existence of an unappropriated stream of water with a fall, within its limits, may at any time be taken away; and by parity of reasoning, a valuable mineral or brine water spring might be abstracted from the proprietor in whose land it arises, and converted to the profit of another.

The Court rejected any such consequence as a misconception of the principles, and set about 'reinterpreting' Blackstone and the cases favouring prior appropriation. The King's Bench surveyed Roman law and read down Blackstone's treatment to accord with their interpretation of Roman law, that running water may be used, but cannot be owned, and must be returned after use to the stream for the benefit of those downstream.

Such was the uncertain state of English water law in 1834, and so it remained in 1840.[45] Indeed, the divergence of opinion was not decisively

[39] (1831) 7 Bing. 682; 131 E.R. 263. The most significant earlier case to similar effect is *Bealey v Shaw* (1805) 6 East 208; 102 E.R. 1266.

[40] Ibid., 692; 268.

[41] Ibid., 692–3; 268.

[42] Ibid., 693; 268.

[43] (1833) 5 B. & Ad. 1; 110 E.R. 692. The members of the Court were Denman C.J., Littledale and Parke JJ.

[44] Ibid., 18; 698–9.

[45] For completeness it should be noted that the Court of Exchequer in 1839 held *Mason v Hill* to be inapplicable to a flow of surface water of artificial origin: *Arkwright v Gell* (1839) 5 M. & W. 203; 151 E.R. 87. This distinction between water flowing in artificial (man-made) channels and in natural watercourses—with riparianism applying to the latter but not the

settled in favour of the natural flow theory (increasingly by then called 'riparianism') until 1856 in *Embrey v Owen*.[46]

It will be recalled from Chapter 4 that several of the judges in *Pickles* made reference to the uncertain state of the law in 1842 as possibly explaining the drafting of the original section 234 of the Act of 1842. After quoting the first part of that section, Lord Macnaghten said:[47]

> Both as regards the underground sources of the springs and as regards the streams flowing from them in their natural course it forbids any act by any person in excess of his legal rights. At that time it must be remembered that the rights of landowners in regard to underground water had not been finally determined. If the view which commended itself to the Court of Exchequer in *Dickinson v Grand Junction Canal Company* had been established, the proposed action of Mr Pickles would, no doubt, have been illegal.

As late as 1852, the Court of Exchequer in *Dickinson v Grand Junction Canal Company*[48] held at common law that a landowner could not legally pump underground water from his well to the detriment of his neighbours; it was overruled in *Chasemore v Richards*.

These cases before 1843 all dealt with surface water. Our hypothetical adviser to the promoters of the Bradford Waterworks would not only have had to ascertain in 1840 the applicable theory as regards surface water—an uncertain matter—but also to decide whether that theory and the policy underlying it fitted best the situation of percolating underground water not in a defined stream. There were very few secondary sources to turn to for assistance.

As far as legal literature went there was only one contemporary English text on water or water rights,[49] and that added nothing to the case law. There was a brief and inconclusive discussion of subterraneous water in an 1839 work on easements, which quoted Marcellus and conveyed the (correct) impression that the law was uncertain and unset-

former—became established in the law of both England and America. See S. C. Weil, 'Mingling of Waters' (1915–16) 29 Harv LR 137.

46 (1856) 6 Ex. 353; 155 E.R. 579.

47 *Pickles* [1895] AC 587, 602–3.

48 (1852) 7 Ex. 282; 155 E.R. 953.

49 H. W. Woolrych, *A Treatise on the Law of Waters* (London, 1st edn, 1830). This book went to a second edition in 1851 (H. W. Woolrych, *Treatise of the law of waters: including the law relating to the rights in the sea, and rights concerning rivers, watercourses &c with a note concerning the rights of the Crown in the land between high and low water mark* (William Benning & Co., London, 2nd edn, 1851)), and thereafter other books appeared covering some of this ground: J. B. Phear, *Treatise on rights to sea and seashore* (Stevens & Norton, London, 1859); G. V. Yool, *An Essay on Waste, Nuisance, and Trespass, chiefly with reference to remedies in Equity; treating the law of Timber, Mines, Lights, Water, Support, The Construction of Public Works, &c., &c.* (W. Maxwell, London, 1863). Cf. the position in America discussed below at notes 53–61 and accompanying text.

tled.[50] The older style digests, abridgements, and encyclopedias—yet to be displaced by the treatise—attempted to bring some coherence (usually through focusing on remedies) to the heap of case law. They were of some help in finding cases, but provided little, if any, in the resolution of novel points.[51] Naturally, sewers and the drainage of land were of longstanding importance in England,[52] but (perhaps surprisingly) that case law and literature did not speak to the problem of interference with percolating underground water.

In the first half of the nineteenth century, the vacuum left by Blackstone's monumental achievement was filled in large part by American jurists such as Kent and Story, who combined distinguished judicial careers with the production of phenomenally successful treatises. In addition, a specialist literature on water law developed a little earlier in America than in England. The first specialist work on water law appeared there in 1824.[53] At this time Chancellor Kent was doing for American law what Blackstone had done for English law over 50 years earlier: he produced a multi-volume set of *Commentaries*. Kent's *Commentaries* gave prominence to the 1827 decision of the renowned American judge, Joseph Story, in *Tyler v Wilkinson*.[54] In that case, Justice Story, with a show of great learning, adopted the principle of riparianism in relation to flowing water. In an influential article, Lauer noted '[t]hat Story's opinion and Kent's treatise mark the inception of the 'reasonable use' doctrine of riparian rights in American law . . . [and] represents a substantial advance over earlier American and English law'.[55] Kent drew directly on the civil law (in particular French law) in promulgating the reasonable use doctrine,[56] and Story was influenced

[50] C. J. Gale and T. D. Whately, *A Treatise on the Law of Easements* (S. Sweet, London, 1839), 177–81. On the Roman law influences on this work and its influence, see A. R. Emmett, 'Roman traces in Australian law' (2001) 20 *Australian Bar Review* 205, 234–5, and Getzler, above at note 35, 273–6.

[51] I have in mind here *Viner's Abridgement* (23 vols, 1741–56) and J. Comyns, *Digest of the Laws of England* (1762–67).

[52] Commissioners of Sewers were among the earliest local authorities established in Britain. There were several early works. See *The Laws of Sewers; Or the Office and Authority of Commissioners of Sewers . . . To which are added, The Laws of Rumen-Marsh, and other Marshes and Fens* (Nutt & Gosling, London, 1726), and R. Callis, *Reading Upon the Statute of Sewers* (1647).

[53] J. K. Angell, *A Treatise on the Common Law in Relation to Watercourses* (Hilliard, Gray, Little and Wilkins, Boston, 1824). It went into several editions, the second of which in 1833 adopts Story J.'s use of the word 'riparian'. Joseph Angell was a prolific author.

[54] 24 Fed. Cas. 472 (No. 14, 312) (1827). See J. Kent, *Commentaries on American Law* (O. Halsted, New York, 1st edn, 1828), vol. 3, 439–42.

[55] Lauer, above at note 34, 61.

[56] On the influence of French law, see S. C. Weil, 'Waters: American Law and French Authority' (1919–20) 33 Harv LR 133. However, to my mind, Kent's accomplishments as a Romanist are marred forever by his admission in private correspondence that he used French and civil law references to impress and befuddle his less accomplished brethren so that they would agree with him! See S. C. Weil, 'Origin and Comparative Development of

by it indirectly.[57] American treatises and case law were referred to regularly in English courts during the nineteenth century, particularly where English common law was unsettled.[58] This was especially true of Kent's treatise and Story's judgment in *Tyler v Wilkinson*, as the reputation of both judges was very high in England. English works began to refer to the American jurisprudence.[59] There is no doubt that American law was highly influential in the ultimate acceptance of the natural flow theory (which amounted to riparianism) in the 1850s.[60]

Water law scholars have differed over how much credit to apportion between Roman law, later civil law, American law, and previous English law for the acceptance of riparianism in relation to flowing surface waters.[61] The strands are difficult to separate and lose their combined strength in the process. It is impossible to do that fascinating story justice here.

Our hypothetical adviser in 1840 should have read Blackstone's *Commentaries* and the subsequent English case law, and through that would have been aware of Roman and civil law influences. The truly conscientious might even have sought out the American position. All to no avail, however, in the search for a definitive answer. But in those circumstances, the one thing that would have stood out was the need to protect at all costs the Bradford Waterworks' legal position as regards the continued water flow under East Many Wells Farm. That could have been done by agreement to buy the land or the water right, or by coerced statutory purchase in the event of unwillingness to sell. It was shown earlier that what *was* done—the insertion of section 234—was manifestly inadequate for the protection of the water supply.[62] It is difficult to acquit the

the Law of Watercourses in the Common Law and Civil Law' (1918) 6 California LR 245, 250 (Part I of two-part article). See generally A. Watson, 'Chancellor Kent's Use of Foreign Law', in M. Reimann (ed.), *The Reception of Continental Ideas in the Common Law World, 1820–1920* (Duncker & Humblot, Berlin, 1994), 45 (many of Kent's citations to foreign law were merely window dressing, and he did not really use it to develop American law).

[57] Lauer, above at note 34, 62.

[58] See M. Hoeflich, 'The Americanization of British Legal Education in the Nineteenth Century' (1987) 8 J. Leg. Hist. 244, 249–51.

[59] Getzler refers to the approving reference to the American jurisprudence in the influential book by C. J. Gale and T. D. Whatley, op. cit. note 35 above, 273–6. That book also made extensive and influential use of Roman and continental authorities. See T. G. Watkin, *An Historical Introduction to Modern Civil Law* (Ashgate Dartmouth, Aldershot, 1999), 258–9, and above at note 50.

[60] See, e.g., the references to American jurisprudence in *Wood v Waud* (1849) 3 Ex. 748, 775; 154 E.R. 1047, 1058, and *Embrey v Owen* (1851) 6 Ex. 353, 368–72; 155 E.R. 579, 585–7.

[61] The remarkably prolific S. C. Weil highlighted the civil law contribution; T. E. Lauer excavated the common law foundations; and Roscoe Pound focused on the French legal connection. See R. Pound, 'The Influence of French Law in America' (1908) 3 Illinois LR 354, and also A. Watson, 'The Transformation of American Property Law: A Comparative Law Approach' (1990) 24 Georgia LR 163 (surveying Roman, French, and American Law).

[62] See Chapter 4.

actual legal advisers and Parliamentary agents of the promoters of the Bradford Waterworks Company of the charge of negligence in this respect.

Developments post-1840

The focus now moves to the developments between the time of incorporation of the Bradford Waterworks in 1842 and the *Pickles* litigation in the 1890s. This sets the legal scene in greater detail than was convenient in Chapter 3.

Subterranean Water

Amid the continuing uncertainty as to which theory of water right would apply to flowing surface waters, the first cases involving subterranean waters arose. At the remarkably late date of 1843, the case of *Acton v Blundell*[63] considered for the first time the question whether a landowner who dug in his property and disturbed the flow of percolating underground water to his neighbour's property was liable. The answer given was in the negative. If the subterranean water was not in a defined channel it was considered part of the soil, and hence as the property of the landowner to do with as he wished. For policy reasons the Court rejected the theory of natural flow (later called riparianism) as unsuited to the nature of percolating underground water, and supported this result with a number of technical legal arguments.

The facts of *Acton v Blundell* were straightforward. The plaintiff was a mill-owner, who for some years had drawn underground water from a well to power his mill. The defendant began mining for coal on a neighbouring property. The first mining took place three-quarters of a mile from the plaintiff's well, and this considerably diminished the flow from the well. Three years later the defendant dug for coal half a mile away from the well. This extinguished the plaintiff's water supply. In the ensuing litigation, the trial judge instructed the jury that, if the defendant mined in 'the usual and proper manner', the interference with the plaintiff's underground water supply was not actionable.[64] The jury found for the defendant. The plaintiff appealed unsuccessfully. The Exchequer Chamber upheld the direction as correct in law.

[63] (1843) 12 M. & W. 324; 152 E.R. 1223.
[64] Ibid., 348; 1233.

From Heaven to Hell

The spirit of the maxim *cujus est solum ejus usque ad coelum* figures prominently in *Acton*'s case. The essence of this maxim is that whoever owns the soil owns all that lies above it. The earliest reference to the doctrine in an English case is in 1586.[65] The best-supported view of the origin of the maxim is that it came from Jewish law and made 'a pseudo-Roman'[66] appearance as a gloss on the *Digest* by Accursius, whose eldest son lectured on law in England (possibly at Oxford) from about 1275 to 1280.[67] In a careful study, Yehuda Abramovitch concluded that '[t]he phrase came into English jurisprudence through the influence and usage of Jewish people, who used it for more than a thousand years',[68] and who came to England with the Normans in 1066.

The focal point of the maxim is the space above the ground. From its first judicial appearance in the sixteenth century until Blackstone's *Commentaries*, almost two centuries later, the maxim was applied to things above the land, rather than below it.[69] Blackstone appears to have broken new ground as far as English usage is concerned in 1767, when he wrote:[70]

> Land hath also, in its legal signification, an indefinite extent, upwards as well as downwards. *Cujus est solum, ejus est usque ad coelum*, is the maxim of the law upwards; . . . and, downwards, whatever is in a direct line between the surface of any land, and the center of the world; as is every day's experience in the mining countries. So that the word 'land' includes not only the face of the earth, but every thing under it, or over it.

65 *Bury v Pope* (1586) 1 Cro. Eliz. 118; 78 E.R. 375.

66 Y. Abramovitch, 'The Maxim "Cujus Est Solum Ejus Usque Ad Coelum" As Applied In Aviation' (1962) 8 McGill LJ 247, 253.

67 D. M. Walker, *The Oxford Companion to Law* (Oxford University Press, Oxford, 1980), 10. See also A. McNair, *The Law of the Air* (Butterworth, London, 1932), 17. The received view that Vacarius taught at Oxford has been doubted. See P. Birks and G. McLeod, 'Introduction', in P. Birks and G. McLeod (trans.), *Justinian's Institutes* (Cornell University Press, Ithaca, 1989), 7, n. 1.

68 Above at note 66, 253; F. A. L., Note: 'Cujus est Solum eius est usque ad coelum usque ad inferos' (1931) 47 LQR 14.

69 The most comprehensive treatment of the intervening cases and commentary is in Abramovitch, above at note 66, 254–6.

70 *Commentaries*, vol. 2, 18. Sir Edward Coke, on whom Blackstone relies in this passage, refers only to the upwards aspect: E. Coke, *The First Part of the Institutes of the Laws of England; or, a Commentary Upon Littleton* (London, 18th edn, 1823), vol. 1, para. 4(a). The Jewish law seems to have referred to both the heavens and the depths of the earth: F. A. L., above at note 68. By the mid-nineteenth century it was orthodoxy to state the maxim in terms of 'coelum' and 'inferos': G. F. Wharton, *Legal Maxims, Observations and Cases in Two Parts* (Law Times, London, 1865), 47. This was also the position in French law at that time. See R. S. Richards (trans.), *Code Napoleon; being the French Civil Code* (Wildy and Sons, London, n.d.), art. 552. For a modern comparison on this point, see R. Davies, 'A Comparative Study of Real Property Law in France and England', unpublished Ph.D. thesis, University of London, 1980, pp. 24–36.

What was required for the maxim to fit the case of percolating water was the acceptance of the notion that water percolating through the soil but not in a defined channel was part of the 'soil'. This is what the Court in *Acton v Blundell* decided, and in doing so it was the first occasion in which the maxim was directed downwards rather than upwards. In so doing, the Court did not ponder the incongruity that Blackstone long before pointed out in Lord Coke treating water as a species of land.[71]

The reliance on broad maxims was common in the nineteenth century, but began to fall out of favour towards the century's end. Goudy voiced a by-then-current and widespread suspicion of maxims:[72]

> [Maxims] are rather apt to be dangerous weapons in the armory of lawyers. They are apt to represent conclusions based on slender premises, or generalizations from an inadequate number of particulars, the exceptions to the rule being more or less regarded or left out of view in formulating the rule. Sometimes they have acted as Will-o'-the wisps to lead the Courts astray in their decisions.

What drove the Court in *Acton*'s case was policy. The brittle maxim simply justified, as best it could, the result.

Policy Arguments

The Exchequer Chamber in *Acton*'s case was confronted with a stark choice between three rules governing the use of underground percolating water: riparianism, prior appropriation, or absolute dominion. The judges knew they were making a choice that was unguided by precedent.[73] The Court came down firmly on the side of absolute dominion (subject, arguably, to a malice qualification) for two, interrelated reasons.

First, the movement of underground water was 'secret' and 'unknowable'.[74] An American court put this point best in the mid-nineteenth century:[75]

[71] *Commentaries*, vol. 2, 18; quoted above in the text accompanying note 17. Robert Callis, in his lectures on sewers at the Inns of Court *circa* 1647, pointed out the conflict between the Roman law relating to flowing surface water and the maxim *cujus est solum*. See S. C. Weil, 'Running Water' (1908–9) 22 Harv LR 190, 193–4.

[72] H. Goudy, 'Two Ancient Brocards', in P. Vinogradoff (ed.), *Essays in Legal History read before the International Congress of Historical Studies held in London in 1913* (Oxford University Press, Oxford, 1913), 215. See generally J. Williams, 'Latin Maxims in English Law' (1894–95) 20 *The Law Magazine & Law Review* (4th ser.) 283. Cf. P. Cook, 'Cujus Est Solum: More Than A Maxim' (1982) 7 Holdsworth LR 37.

[73] See E. F. Murphy, 'The Recurring State Judicial Task of Choosing Rules for Groundwater Law: How Occult Still?' (1987) 66 Nebraska LR 120, 121–2 and 125.

[74] *Acton v Blundell*, above at note 63, 350; 1233.

[75] *Chatfield v Wilson* (1856) 28 Vt 49, 54–5. See also *Frazier v Brown* (1861) 12 Ohio St. 294, 311.

[T]he existence of water underground, and its progress while there, are not uniform, and cannot be known with any degree of certainty, nor can its progress be regulated ... The secret, changeable and uncontrollable character of underground water in its operations, is so diverse and uncertain that we cannot well subject it to the regulations of law, nor build upon it a system of rules, as is done in the case of surface streams.

The science of hydrology was little developed at that time.[76] Consequently, very often one could not know with certainty how digging on one's own land might affect the movement of underground water to other, prior users of that water.

Secondly, that uncertainty and the consequent potential liability under either a riparian or a prior appropriation legal regime were viewed as unacceptable fetters on the economic development of land. Either legal regime would freeze (in the case of prior appropriation) or limit unpredictably (in the case of riparianism) development of one's own land. As Tindal C.J. pointed out in *Acton*'s case, the advantage to the first user of the water might bear no relation to the benefit of other, later users of the land. In the transition from an agrarian economy to an industrial one, subsequent uses were likely to be far more valuable. The Chief Justice said as much: 'The [first user's] well may be sunk to supply a cottage, or a drinking-place for cattle; whilst the owner of the adjoining land may be prevented from winning metals and minerals of inestimable value.'[77]

Roman and Civil Law

Acton v Blundell was a case of first impression, and so it was natural that counsel and the Court turned to Roman and civil law for guidance.[78] Counsel for the plaintiff referred to numerous Roman law texts in support of his client's claim to an undisturbed flow of water to the mill, until he

[76] See A. C. Skinner, 'Groundwater—legal controls and organizational aspects', in R. A. Downing and W. B. Wilkinson (eds), *Applied Groundwater Hydrology: A British Perspective* (Clarendon Press, Oxford, 1991) 8, and E. M. Shaw, 'Hydrology—a multidisciplinary subject', in A. D. M. Phillips and B. J. Turton (eds), *Environment, Man and Economic Change: Essays presented to S. H. Beaver* (Longman, London, 1975), 164.

[77] *Acton v Blundell*, above at note 63, 351; 1234.

[78] It was a time-honoured practice to resort to Roman and civil law for guidance where the common law was not settled. See L. Moccia, 'English Law Attitudes to the "Civil Law" ' (1981) 2 J Legal Hist 156, 163; D. T. Oliver, 'Roman Law in Modern Cases in English Courts', in *Cambridge Legal Essays Written in Honour of and Presented to Doctor Bond, Professor Buckland and Professor Kenny* (W. Heffer & Sons Ltd, Cambridge, 1926), 243, 246; B. Rudden, 'Comparative Law in England', in W. E. Butler and V. N. Kudriavtsev (eds), *Comparative Law and Legal System: Historical and Socio-Legal Perspectives* (Oceana Publications Inc., New York, 1985), 79, 81. Cf. R. H. Helmholz, 'Use of the Civil Law in Post-Revolutionary American Jurisprudence' (1992) 66 Tulane LR 1648. That was particularly true in relation to flowing and percolating water. See *Brown v Best* (1747) 1 Wils. K.B. 174; 95 E.R. 557; *Liggins v Inge* (1831) 7 Bing. 682; 131 E.R. 263; *Mason v Hill*, above at note 43.

was brought up short by Maule J.'s famous retort 'that what Marcellus says is against you'.[79] Counsel adroitly shifted ground, arguing that, understood in the context of his own time, Marcellus would have meant that use for occupational purposes was permissible but not for mining. 'Mining was then altogether unknown', counsel argued, adding '[t]hat the Romans knew little about cutting off or using under-ground currents of water appears from their use of aqueducts.'[80] To which Maule J. replied '[t]hat is not conclusive; it is certain they, in some instances, used water-pipes for their dwelling-houses.'[81]

The judge's observation is borne out by later historians of Roman water supply. The magnificence of the arched Roman aqueducts has distracted attention from the ubiquity of water supply from wells. Trevor Hodge pointed out recently:[82]

> [A]n ordinary Roman town was not supplied with water solely by its aqueduct: it also drew copious supplies from a great multiplicity of private wells and cisterns. . . . Nor should we think of the aqueduct as necessarily the senior partner of the two, and the wells a kind of auxiliary or supplement. In a way, it was the wells that provided essential services and the aqueduct that was a luxury. In a city's earliest days, drinking water was the personal and individual responsibility of the inhabitants, and they met it by sinking wells or cisterns, usually inside their houses, though local springs and fountains might also help. This normally provided enough water for essential human needs; some cities never had any other supply, and got by without any aqueduct right to the end of the Roman empire.

Water was extensively regulated in Roman law,[83] and, as noted above, this law undoubtedly influenced the development of the common law.[84] Of the 50 books (really chapters) of the *Digest*, discussion of water law clusters around urban water servitudes (Books 8 and 39), rural water servitudes, right and drainage laws (Books 8, 39, and 41), and large public rivers and watercourses (Books 41 and 43).[85] In addition, in other places in the *Digest*, some attention is given to springs, groundwater, sewage, and waterworks.[86]

79 *Acton v Blundell*, above at note 63, 336; above at note 63, 336; 1228.
80 Idem.
81 Idem.
82 A. T. Hodge, *Roman Aqueducts & Water Supply* (Duckworth, London, 1992), 48.
83 See, e.g., Note, 'Water Rights in Roman Law' (1903) 20 SALJ 266, and J. Plescia, 'The Roman Law on Waters' (1993) 21 *Index: International Survey of Roman Law* 433. See generally E. F. Ware, *Roman Water Law: Translated from the Pandects of Justinian* (West Publishing Co., St Paul, 1905) (a valuable collection and translation of all of the Roman law concerning fresh water).
84 See, e.g., A. Scott and G. Coustalin, 'The Evolution of Water Rights' (1995) 35 National Resources J. 821, 824.
85 J. L. Westcoat, 'Toward a Modern Map of Roman Water Law' (1997) 18 *Urban Geography* 100, 100–1.
86 Idem. Westcoat gives the examples of the treatment of the usufruct in Book 7, pouring things out of buildings in Book 9, and ownership and possession in Book 41.

The extensive control and regulation of water in Roman law focused almost entirely on surface running water. The paucity of legal treatment of subterranean water, especially given the importance of underground water supply, is a mystery.[87] Indeed, how much Roman law is taken to say about subterranean water depends on interpretation of the often difficult texts. The imposing and seemingly magisterial *Digest* is actually a 'cut and paste' job, preserving the best of the writing of the classical jurists and attempting—not always successfully—to synthesize their views.[88]

F. P. Walton, at the turn of the twentieth century, in an otherwise admirable article on abuse of right, says '[b]y Roman law it was clearly laid down that an owner of land had the right to sink wells or make excavations in his land, and if, in so doing, he cut the veins which fed the springs of his neighbour this was not a ground of liability in damages',[89] adding that 'this was subject to the limitation that the act must not be merely malicious.'[90] The passage from the *Digest* relied on for the first proposition is addressed to the different situation of diversion or extraction of surface water.[91] Chapter 3 of Book 39 is aptly titled 'Water and the Action to Ward Off Rainwater', and there is only the most incidental references to subterranean water. Walton, along with many others before and since, has taken the qualification of malicious exercise of right to be one such reference. As we saw in Chapter 3, this is a point of considerable importance in the *Pickles* litigation.

Recall the relevant passage of Marcellus from the *Digest*, quoted earlier:[92]

[87] Watson, above at note 61, 170–1. Alan Watson observed that the extraordinarily narrow scope for an action by a neighbour in relation to diminution of water supply in Roman law cannot be satisfactorily explained by prevalent social or economic conditions.

[88] See the elegant description in P. G. Stein, 'Justinian's Compilation: Classical Legacy and Legal Source' (1993) 8 *Tulane European & Civil Law Forum* 1, 1–2.

[89] F. P. Walton, 'Motive as an Element in Torts in the Common Law and in the Civil Law' (1909) 22 Harv LR 501, 510, citing D. 39.3.21. See also G. Stoner, 'The Influence of Social and Economic Ideals on the Law of Malicious Torts' (1910) 8 Mich LR 468, 471.

[90] Idem.

[91] This seems to me the most natural reading of the passage ('If water which has its sources on your land bursts on to my land and you cut off those sources . . .': D. 39.3.21), but note that the learned South African jurist, Innes C.J., was of the view that this covered underground water: *Union Government (Minister of Railways and Harbours) v Marais* 1920 A.D. 240, 246–7 (App. Div.).

[92] T. Mommsen, P. Krueger, and A. Watson, *The Digest of Justinian* (University of Pennsylvania Press, Pennsylvania, 1985), vol. 3, 396 (D. 39.3.1.12). Unless otherwise indicated, all translations of the *Digest* are taken from this source. It should be noted that doubts have been expressed as to: (1) the integrity of the text; (2) its authorship; and (3) whether it accurately represented classical law. As to (1), Alan Watson suggests the text may be corrupt at one point, relying on Mommsen: above at note 61, 170, n. 26. On the second point, there is South African authority which attributes the malice qualification to Ulpian rather than Marcellus: *Union Government (Minister of Railways and Harbours) v Marais*, above at note 91, 247. For discussion see F. Visser, 'Ground-water law in South Africa' (1987) 50 *Tydskrif Vir Hedendaage Romeins-Hollandse Reg* 412, 419–20. Certainly, Marcellus was one of Ulpian's

Next, Marcellus writes that no action, not even the action for fraud, can be brought against a person who, while digging on his own land, diverts his neighbour's water supply. And of course the latter ought not to have even the action for fraud, assuming that the other person acted not with the intention of harming his neighbour, but with that of improving his own field.

This has proved a puzzling passage for commentators, even in relation to diversion of surface water.[93] The possibility of an action for fraud (*actio de dolis*) in such circumstances, with its requirement of an intent to injure, appears not to have materialized in classical or later Roman law.[94]

In a less often noticed passage Ulpian asks: 'Suppose that I dig a well in my house and by doing so I cut off the sources of your well. Am I liable?' Trebanius is cited giving a negative answer on the ground that the landowner was simply exercising his rights.[95] There are other snippets in the *Digest* that may throw some light on the attitude of the Romans to the diversion, interception, or abstraction of underground water. There are several passages that say a landowner can retain rainwater on her property, and if that happens the downhill landowner cannot complain.[96] Similarly, Ulpian approves of Proculus' view that if a landowner diverts water by means of a channel and thereby deprives an adjoining landowner of water, this is simply 'the prevention of enjoyment of an advantage previously enjoyed' and does not create liability.[97]

On the related topic of polluting the underground water supply, Ulpian said that someone who pours something into a well and thereby pollutes the water is liable under the interdict against force or stealth to make restitution to an injured neighbour, 'for fresh water is part of the land, just as if someone had done a work connected with water'.[98] This reasoning resonates with that employed in *Acton v Blundell*. But, as Hans

favourite sources of reference. See T. Honoré, *Ulpian* (Clarendon Press, Oxford, 1982), 206 and 210. On (3), David Johnston has doubted whether the malice qualification represented classical Roman law: *Roman Law in Context* (Cambridge University Press, Cambridge, 1999), 73. *Accord*, F. H. Lawson, *Negligence in the Civil Law* (Clarendon Press, Oxford, 1950), 16. It is beyond my competence to evaluate these doubts.

93 See the discussion by D. Johnston, 'Owners and Neighbours: From Rome to Scotland', in R. Evans-Jones (ed.), *The Civil Law Tradition in Scotland* (The Stair Society, Edinburgh, 1995), 176, 180–1.

94 Ibid., 181.

95 D. 39.2.24.12.

96 D. 39.3.1.11; D. 39.3.1.21. See also D. 39.3.21 (if water, which has its source on the land of A and once 'burst' on to the property of B, is stopped due to A cutting off those sources there is no liability, in the absence of a servitude).

97 D. 39.2.26.

98 D. 43.24.11. H. W. Baade translates this passage as 'for percolating (live) water is to be viewed as part of the land': 'Springs, Creeks, and Groundwater in Nineteenth-Century German Roman-Law Jurisprudence with a Twentieth-Century Postscript', in D. S. Clark (ed.), *Comparative and Private International Law: Essays in Honor of John Henry Merryman on his Seventieth Birthday* (Duncker & Humblot, Berlin, 1991), 61.

Baade points out, Ulpian's appurtenance of underground water to the land in this passage conflicts directly with the Roman rules regarding flowing surface water, and if adopted would have had significant consequences in relation to water rights.[99]

The notion of proportionality in the exercise of property rights surfaces at several points in chapter 3 of Book 39. It is said that the action to ward off rainwater cannot be used to compel anyone to benefit their neighbour, but that an *actio utilis* or an interdict is available to allow the neighbour to restore a dam on the other owner's property where it will benefit the former and not harm the latter. This was supported on the ground of fairness: 'Equity supports this view even though we may lack a legal right.'[100] Also in the context of the action to ward off rainwater, Labeo is cited for the proposition that a person is not liable for diverting a torrent of water on to his neighbour. Paul agrees, 'provided that his actions were performed not with the intention of harming [the neighbour], but of avoiding damage himself'.[101]

At the end of the *Digest* some civil law maxims are found, one of which is '[n]o one is regarded as acting by fraud who makes use of his rights.'[102] This has been pointed to as evidence that Roman law did not recognize a notion of abuse of rights—that doctrine, it is said, was the product of the glossators. 'If a man did what he was entitled to', said Peter Stein, 'the Roman lawyers did not consider it right to inquire into his motives for acting.'[103] That may be so, but the prior question remains—what is a landowner entitled to do? The tensions evident in the above passages from the *Digest* are replicated in the common law.

This sketchy treatment of Roman law suffices for our present purpose. Of the surviving snippets relating to subterranean waters, arguably the most directly relevant is that of Marcellus. As we saw in Chapter 3, Marcellus' holding was referred to by counsel and followed by the Court of Exchequer Chamber in *Acton*'s case.[104] The qualification as to malice was seemingly approved in 1847, albeit again in *obiter dicta*, in another mine damage case.[105]

[99] Idem.

[100] D. 39.3.2.5. The Mommsen, etc. version translate this as: 'Considerations of fairness support this view even though we may lack a clear legal right'. See also the 'appeal to the considerations of fairness' in D. 39.2.6.

[101] D. 39.3.2.9.

[102] D. 50.17.55.

[103] P. G. Stein, 'Equitable Principles in Roman Law', in P. G. Stein, *The Character and Influence of the Roman Civil Law: Historical Essays* (Hambledon Press, London, 1988), 19, 27.

[104] *Acton v Blundell*, above at note 63, 353. Sir Frederick Pollock said that this was one of only two instances he was aware of where 'the opinion of a Roman lawyer, as embodied in the Digest, . . . [was] used and avowedly followed by an English Court of Common Law in a purely English litigation': *A First Book of Jurisprudence for Students of the Common Law* (Macmillan & Co., London, 2nd edn, 1904), 341.

[105] *Smith v Kenrick* (1849) 7 C.B. 515, 566; 137 ER 205, 225.

North J. correctly noted at first instance in *Pickles* that maliciousness was not alleged in *Acton*'s case, and so approval of the malice qualification in that case was only *obiter*.[106] Nevertheless, almost certainly unbeknownst to North J., but much more likely known to the earlier generations of judges, the malice qualification had featured prominently in the writings of the medieval European jurists and had been carried forward into the modern period.[107] It had support also in the early American case law, which antedated *Acton v Blundell*.[108]

The Road to *Chasemore v Richards*

Acton v Blundell is one of what can be called the mine drainage cases. The number of these cases, and the complexity of the issues raised, increased throughout the nineteenth century. Blundell was not digging a hole on his own land for the fun of it; he wanted to extract minerals. And by adopting the appropriation theory the Court of Exchequer Chamber encouraged such exploitation. It would have been possible to read *Acton*'s case in light of its facts and not to have viewed it as allowing a landowner to dig and appropriate for any purpose all the percolating underground water. Digging for minerals could have been viewed as a reasonable use of land justifying interference with neighbours' use of ground water, whereas other, less reasonable uses would not justify such interference.

In a little-noticed case, *The South Shields Waterworks Company v Cookson*,[109] decided less than three years after *Acton*'s case, the Court of Exchequer displayed an unwillingness to read down the holding. This case is discussed in detail in Chapter 4, but here it suffices to indicate that the defendant was abstracting underground water for a manufacturing purpose on its own land and piping the water off some distance to another of its businesses in a nearby town and to supply water to its employees living there. The plaintiff Waterworks Company claimed that this infringed its exclusive statutory right to supply water to that town. Baron Parke observed in the course of the argument that he could see nothing in the private Act establishing the Waterworks Company that deprived 'an adjoining landowner of the power to dig a well'.[110] Counsel

106 [1894] 3 Ch 53, 67.

107 See generally J. E. Scholtens, 'Abuse of Rights' (1958) 75 SALJ 39.

108 *Greenleaf v Francis* (1836) 18 Pick. 117, 122, *per* Putnam J. (Massachusetts) (*obiter*). In *Greenleaf's* case the Court cited the decision of Story J. in *Tyler v Wilkinson* (1827) 24 Fed. Cas. 472 (No. 14,312). In that case, Story J. sat as a judge in the United States Circuit Court for the District of Rhode Island. *Tyler*'s case is the bedrock American case establishing the principle that each riparian has a right to a reasonable use of the flowing water.

109 (1846) 15 LJ Ex. 315 (Ex.).

110 Ibid., 318.

responded by seeking to distinguish *Acton v Blundell* on the ground that there the interference with the neighbour's water supply was incidental to mining, whereas here 'the well is sunk avowedly for the purpose of drawing off the water'.[111] Baron Alderson was unpersuaded, interjecting that unless *Acton v Blundell* was held to be bad law it was fatal to the plaintiff's action.[112] And so it proved to be. The Exchequer Court held unanimously for the defendant. Speaking for the Court, Baron Parke said simply that 'the defendants have a full right to sink a well on their own lands'.[113] In this the judges foreshadowed the result nearly 20 years later in *Chasemore v Richards*.

In the earlier discussion in this chapter of what a hypothetical adviser to the Bradford Waterworks Company would have understood the law to be in 1840, I outlined the rival theories of 'prior appropriation' and 'natural flow'. It is necessary to develop that a little further in order to understand how the law stood by the 1860s.

The rule of 'prior appropriation' provided that the first landowner to appropriate flowing surface water had the use of it to the detriment of all other subsequent users upstream or downstream. There were no restrictions as to how much water could be taken, or for what purpose. There is some suggestion that the use had to be 'beneficial', but this was hardly any restraint. For example, it was permissible to pipe the water off the first appropriator's land for the use of others.

The competing rule was known historically by the term 'natural flow', but from the mid-nineteenth century increasingly went by the name that has stuck to this day—'riparianism' (deriving from the Latin word *ripa*, meaning 'bank of a river').[114] This rule gave the owners of land contiguous to flowing surface water the right to use that water, but only on the riparian tract and not so as to diminish the flow to their neighbours. A distinction was drawn between 'ordinary' and 'extraordinary' use of flowing water.[115] As the Privy Council said in an appeal from the civil law province of Lower Canada (now Quebec):[116]

[111] Idem. [112] Idem. [113] Idem.

[114] S. C. Wiel claims that the first use of the term 'riparian' in relation to the law of water in English law was in *Wood v Waud* (1849) 3 Ex. 748; 154 E.R. 1047: above at note 56, 246 (Pt I). Weil traces this use in English law back through the early American treatises by Joseph Angell (1824 and 1833) and Chancellor James Kent (1828), and a decision by Justice Joseph Story (1827), to the civil law: ibid., 247–57. In a later study Lauer apportions much more of the credit for the ascendancy of riparianism to the antecedent English case law and commentary: above at note 34.

[115] The same distinction is sometimes expressed as natural and artificial uses.

[116] *Miner v Gilmour* (1858) 12 Moore P.C. 131, 156; 14 E.R. 861, 870, *per* Lord Kingsdown; cited with approval by Lord Blackburn in *Orr Ewing v Colquhoun* (1876–77) 2 AC 839, 855. The law of France and England was considered to be identical on this point. It is interesting to note that the Court below (the Appeal Side of the Court of Queen's Bench in the District

By the general law applicable to running streams, every riparian proprietor has a right to what may be called the ordinary use of the water flowing past his land; for instance, to the reasonable use of the water for his domestic purposes and for his cattle, and this without regard to the effect which such use may have, in case of a deficiency, upon proprietors lower down the stream. But, further, he has a right to the use of it, or what may be deemed the extraordinary use of it, provided that he does not thereby interfere with the rights of other proprietors, either above or below him. Subject to this condition, he may dam up the stream for the purpose of a mill, or divert the water for the purpose of irrigation. But, he has no right to interrupt the regular flow of the stream, if he thereby interferes with the lawful use of the water by other proprietors, and inflicts upon them a sensible injury.

This distinction between ordinary and extraordinary uses was easily rendered as one between reasonable and (if objected to by other riparians) unreasonable uses. Indeed, Lord Kingsdown used the phrase 'reasonable use' to describe 'ordinary' use. So it is common to see riparianism described as the rule of reasonable use(r).

What is 'reasonable' has been contentious and has changed over time. In the late eighteenth century Lord Kames gave guidance by prioritizing uses as follows:[117]

A river or any running stream directs its course through the land of many proprietors; who are thereby connected by a common interest, being equally entitled to the water for useful purposes. Whence it follows, that the course of the river or running stream cannot be diverted by any one of the proprietors, so as to deprive others of it. Where there is plenty for all, there can be no interference; but many streams are so scanty, as to be exhausted by using it with discretion; though, hitherto, no rule has been laid down. To supply the defect in some measure, I venture to suggest the following particulars, which practice may in time ripen to a precise rule. . . . [I]f there be not a sufficiency of water for every purpose, those purposes ought to be preferred that are essential to the well-being of the adjacent proprietors. The most

of Quebec), whose judgment was affirmed by the Privy Council, had rejected for lack of proof an allegation that the defendant had abused his right of using the water: see (1859) 9 *Lower Canada Reports* 115, 117 (headnote). This makes sense of the passage in the Privy Council's advice suggesting that a malicious exercise of the right was assumed not to have been made out, 'otherwise, of course, the Plaintiff would have been entitled to damages' (ibid., 153; 869). Their Lordships noted that there was no appeal from this part of the judgment below. On the influence of *Miner v Gilmour* on Canadian law, see C. S. Burchill, 'The Origins of Canadian Irrigation Law' (1948) 29 *Canadian Historical Review* 353. The statement of the law in Canada by British judges is in identical terms to that expressed in the Massachusetts case, decided around the same time, of *Elliot v Fitchburg R.R.*, 64 Mass. (10 Cush.) 191 (1852).

117 Henry Home of Kames, *Principles of Equity* (Bell & Bradfute, Edinburgh, 5th edn, 1825), 33–4. An important qualification was entered a few pages later to this liberty to dig with immunity. It was subject to 'a limitation founded entirely upon equity'; namely, that a man cannot exercise his right to dig with the sole intention of hurting another, and, if he does so, a court of equity will restrain him from so acting: ibid., 36–7. This reflected the Roman law as captured by Marcellus in the *Digest*. See above in Chapter 3 and later in this chapter.

essential use is drink for man and beast; because they cannot subsist without it. What is next essential, is water for washing; because cleanness contributes greatly to health. The third is water for a corn-mill, which saves labour and cheapens bread. The fourth is watering land, for enriching it. The fifth is water for a bleach-field. And the lowest I shall mention, is water for machinery, necessary for cheapening the production of several arts. There may be more divisions; but these are sufficient in a general view. From this arrangement it follows, that one may use the water of a rivulet for drink, and for brewing and baking, however little be left to the inferior heritors [downstream users]. But a proprietor cannot be deprived of that essential use by one above him, who wants to divert the water for a mill, for a bleachfield, or for watering his land, unless he leaves sufficient for a mill below. According to this doctrine, I may lawfully dig a pit in my own field for gathering water to my cattle, though it happens to intercept a spring that run under ground into my neighbour's field and furnished him with water.

The decision by the Court of Exchequer in 1851 in *Embrey v Owen* finally established the rule of 'natural flow'/riparianism for flowing surface waters. Under this theory, flowing surface water could be used only by the riparian proprietor on the riparian tract, and even then (subject to 'ordinary' uses) not so as to diminish the flow.[118] Moreover, the riparian proprietor was not allowed to transfer his rights to use of the water to others.[119] Riparian water use rights are contingent on, and sensitive to, the use of others, and hence it is correct to speak of them as relative rights. This was the state of the law regarding flowing surface water when the English courts came to decide authoritatively in *Chasemore v Richards* which theory of water right—prior appropriation or 'natural flow'/riparianism—applied to percolating underground water. The issue boiled down to whether *Acton v Blundell* was correctly decided.

By this stage in the nineteenth century the House of Lords had emerged as a professional court of last resort, and the days of rivalry between the Courts of Exchequer, Common Pleas, King's Bench, and the composite Exchequer Chamber were numbered. Furthermore, as we will see, the doctrine of precedent was solidifying. But the 60 years prior to *Chasemore*'s case had seen an amazing diversity of views among the judges of the different courts on almost every aspect of water law. Many of the leading judges had distinct views as to what the cases stood for—both the cases they had participated in and the others. Particularly relevant because of the role he played in *Chasemore*'s case is the stance of Baron Parke, a dominating judicial figure for much of the period during which the competing theories of water right were being assessed.

118 *The Directors of the Swindon Waterworks Company Ltd v The Proprietors of the Wilts and Berks Canal Navigation Company* (1875) LR 7 HL 697; affirming sub. nom. *Wilts and Berks Canal Navigation Company v Swindon Waterworks Company Ltd* (1873–4) LR 9 Ch. 451 (CA).

119 *Omerod v Todmorden Mill Co.* (1883) 11 QBD 155 (CA).

Baron Parke, before his ennoblement as Lord Wensleydale in 1856, sat as a judge of King's Bench from 1828 to 1834—and was a member of the court that decided *Mason v Hill*—and then transferred to Common Pleas where he sat for 22 years. Not surprisingly, given his involvement in the case, Baron Parke had a definite view of what was, and was not, decided by *Mason v Hill*. *In arguendo* in a case in 1839, Parke B. said that the object of *Mason v Hill* was 'to set right the mistaken notion which had got abroad as a consequence of certain dicta in *Williams v Morland* [1824] . . ., that flowing water is publici juris, and that the first occupant of it for a beneficial purpose may appropriate it'.[120]

Baron Parke was wary of allowing riparians to use water for other than the ordinary and natural purposes of human sustenance and watering animals. He knew that the American brand of riparianism advocated by Kent and Story permitted water to be used for irrigation of land and industrial purposes, but he refused to approve or disapprove of that in cases that did not raise the question directly.[121] In giving the judgment in *Embrey v Owen*—the case that finally settled for riparianism in relation to flowing surface water—Baron Parke said *obiter* that it would be unreasonable to permit a riparian to irrigate 'many thousand acres of porous soil' abutting a stream.[122] It seems clear that Baron Parke consistently favoured traditional, small agrarian users over large-scale farms and industrialists.[123] In this he echoed the prioritization of Lord Kames laid down in the previous century.

Chasemore v Richards

This case was discussed briefly in Chapter 3, but more needs to be said here. It will be recalled that in *Chasemore v Richards* the plaintiff was a mill-owner who for a long time had enjoyed the use of a river, which was fed by percolating underground water. The defendant was the local Board of Health which had sunk a large well on its own land and extracted by steam-driven pumps a very large quantity of underground water for town supply, thereby diminishing the underground water supply to the river and causing damage to the plaintiff.

[120] *Arkwright v Gell*, above at note 45, 220; 94. The reference to *Williams v Morland* is (1824) 2 B. & C. 910; 107 E.R. 620 (KB).

[121] *Wood v Waud* (1849) 2 Ex. 748; 154 E.R. 1047, and *Embrey v Owen* (1851) 6 Ex. 353, 371–2; 155 E.R. 579, 586–7.

[122] *Embrey v Owen*, ibid., 371–2; 587.

[123] For American light on such an approach, see L. A. Halper, 'Christopher G. Tiedeman, "Laissez-Faire Constitutionalism" and the Dilemmas of Small-Scale Property in the Gilded Age' (1990) 51 Ohio State LJ 1349. In terms of one American writer's categorization, Parke had a 'static' view of property. See R. G. Bone, 'Normative Theory and Legal Doctrine in American Nuisance Law: 1850 to 1920' (1986) 59 SCal LR 1101, 1128–31.

The case received considerable judicial consideration by, in effect, four sets of judges. In the result, the near unanimous view was to affirm *Acton v Blundell*, and so the 'appropriation' theory was authoritatively applied to percolating underground water not in a known or defined channel. The only dissentient voices were Coleridge J. in the Exchequer Chamber and Lord Wensleydale in the House of Lords. Technically Lord Wensleydale did not formally register a dissent, but he found the issue much less clear-cut than his brethren and only reluctantly concurred, 'though not without very serious doubts as to the propriety of the conclusion' reached.[124] A small part of his difficulty was that he had been a party to a number of the allegedly conflicting decisions of the Court of Exchequer and he did not think they were in conflict.[125] More fundamentally, as discussed above, Lord Wensleydale was more attracted to the notion of 'reasonable user' of underground water than the others.

Lord Wensleydale came to this conclusion on the law:[126]

> Every man has a right to the natural advantage of his soil—the Plaintiff to the benefit of the flow of water in the river and its natural supplies, the Defendant to the enjoyment of his land, and to the underground waters on it, and he may, in order to obtain that water, sink a well. But according to the rule of reason and law, '*sic utere tuo ut alienum non laedas*,' it seems right to hold, that he ought to exercise his right in a reasonable manner, with as little injury to his neighbour's rights as may be. The civil law deems an act, otherwise lawful in itself, illegal if done with a malicious intent of injuring a neighbour, *animo vicino nocendi*. The same principle is adopted in the laws of Scotland, where an otherwise lawful act is forbidden 'if done *in aemulationem vicini*,' [Bell's Principles, section 966] but this principle has not found a place in our law.
>
> The question in this case, therefore as it seems to me, resolves itself into an inquiry, whether the Defendant exercised his right of enjoying the subterraneous waters in a reasonable manner.

To that question, Lord Wensleydale gave a resounding 'No'. Echoing a view he had expressed in relation to flowing surface waters, Lord Wensleydale was of the firm view that to extract large quantities of water for a purpose completely unconnected with the land under which it flowed or the inhabitants of that land, for the use of persons who had no right to use it directly and to the injury of neighbours who had an 'equal right' to the water, was unreasonable and hence unlawful.[127]

In the House of Lords in *Chasemore*'s case no doubt Lord Wensleydale

[124] *Chasemore v Richards* (1859) 7 HLC 349, 381; 11 E.R. 140, 152.
[125] Ibid., 381–2; 153.
[126] Ibid., 388; 155. The maxim *sic utere tuo ut alienum non laedas* translates in English as 'so use your own property as not to injure your neighbour's': G. F. Wharton, *Legal Maxims, with Observations in Two Parts* (Law Times, London, 3rd edn, 1903), 179.
[127] Ibid., 388–9; 156.

was bemused by the differing views of counsel and the judges below as to his views (as Baron Parke) on *Acton v Blundell*. The confusion arose from a reported interjection by Parke B. in the 1856 case of *Broadbent v Ramsbotham*. There counsel had referred to *Dickinson v Grand Junction Canal Company*, and Baron Alderson interjected by referring to *Acton v Blundell*. Before counsel could answer, Baron Parke piped up and said '[t]hat case decided that there is no right to a well unless the water has been used for twenty years. This Court, and I believe all Courts, disapprove of that part of the judgment that denies the natural right to the water.'[128] In argument before the Court of Exchequer Chamber in *Chasemore v Richards*, counsel for the plaintiff mill-owner took that interjection by Baron Parke to refer to *Acton v Blundell* (and not to *Dickinson v Grand Junction Canal Company*). Counsel submitted that Parke B. said that 'all the Courts disapproved of the judgment in *Acton v Blundell* which denies the natural right to the water'.[129] Erle J. responded immediately: 'From conversation I have had with the learned Baron, I believe he meant to say, that a person has a right to sink a well in his own land and get as much water as he pleased; and that he dissented from the notion that he could not get a right to a well under twenty years.'[130] That did not convince Coleridge J., who, in lonely dissent, drew satisfaction from the fact that Baron Parke disapproved of *Acton v Blundell*. Giving the judgment of the majority of the Exchequer Chamber, Cresswell J. cites another reported interjection by Parke B. in *Broadbent v Ramsbotham*, this time unambiguously referring to *Dickinson v Grand Junction Canal Company* and interpreting it narrowly.[131] Little wonder that Lord Wensleydale spends some time in his judgment in *Chasemore v Richards* clarifying his position.

In Chapter 3, I traced the treatment of Marcellus' morsel at the hands of Lord Wensleydale in *Chasemore v Richards* and the judges in *Pickles*. The point was made that the judges in *Pickles* had misunderstood Lord Wensleydale's rejection of Marcellus' malice qualification, and had quoted out of context his observation that the Scots law as to malicious exercise of right had not found a place in English law. Read in context, however, one can easily see the connection between a rule prohibiting malicious exercise of right and a rule of reasonable user. On the law as Lord Wensleydale thought it ought to be, there was no need for English law to find a place for the civilian doctrine. Everything that notion achieves in the civil law can be achieved within the balancing of interests under the rubric of reasonable user.[132] Without such balancing of interests

128 The exchange is recorded in the Law Journal series: *Broadbent v Ramsbotham* (1856) 15 L.J. Ex. 115, 121. The report of the exchange is different in the Exchequer Reports version, which is the one reproduced in the English Reports: (1856) 11 Ex. 602, 611; 156 E.R. 971, 975.

129 *Chasemore v Richards* (1857) 16 L.J. Ex. 393, 396.

130 Idem.

131 Ibid., 403.

132 This can be seen clearly in the later nuisance cases. See Chapter 7.

under a rule of reasonable user, however, the more necessary a doctrine like malicious exercise of rights would be. This can be seen clearly in Scots law (treated in Chapter 6) and the later American law, discussed below.

American Law in the Nineteenth Century

We have seen already the important, and perhaps decisive, influence American law had on the acceptance of riparianism by the English courts by the mid-nineteenth century. It is important to put those American developments in doctrinal context.[133] It is impossible in a small compass to do justice to the vast body of often-conflicting case law. In a country with so many state jurisdictions, the number of decisions can be overwhelming and creates considerable scope for disagreement as to what the majority position in the United States was at any point in time; let alone what was considered the most desirable position. American state jurisdictions can be crudely divided into those following the 'prior appropriation' rule, or the 'riparian' principle in relation to flowing surface water. There were three broad phases of legal developments in relation to percolating subterranean water.

In the initial phase American courts adopted the view that a landowner could dig in his own land with impunity. In other words, the American courts refused to draw an analogy between percolating underground water and flowing surface water, with the consequence that the rules governing reasonable use of surface water were not applied to percolating subterranean water. These cases, however, insisted that malicious exercise of the right to dig on one's own land was actionable.

The earliest American case antedated *Acton v Blundell* by seven years but was to like effect. In *Greenleaf v Francis* (1836)[134] the defendant drilled a well on his own land but within a few feet of his neighbour's well, to the detriment of the neighbour's water supply.[135] Applying the maxim *cujus*

[133] The case law is collected and discussed in the following sources: J. K. Angell, *A Treatise on the Law of Watercourses* (J. C. Perkins, ed.) (Little, Brown & Co., Boston, 6th edn, 1869), 178–96 (cited in argument before the House of Lords in *Pickles*: see (1895) 73 LT 353, 354); E. Washburn, 'Rights in Subterranean Waters' (1862–63) 11 *American Law Register* 65; H. Budd, 'The Law of Subterranean Waters' (1891) 39 *American Law Register* 236; E. W. Hatch, 'Property Rights in Percolating Waters' (1901) 1 Col LR 505; E. W. Huffcut, 'Percolating waters: The Rule of Reasonable User' (1903–4) 13 Yale LJ 222; S. Kenner, 'Some Observations on the Rights of Landowners in Subterranean Percolating Waters' (1908) 66 Central LJ 194; E. A. Lippman, 'Landowners' Rights in Percolating Water' (1909–10) 58 UPa LR 303; H. P. Farnham, 'Percolating Water and the Common Law' (1913) 19 *Case & Comment* 664; J. B. Clayberg, 'The Law of Percolating Water' (1915–16) 14 Mich LR 119.

[134] 18 Pick. 117; 35 Mass. 117 (1836).

[135] In an earlier case—*Panton v Holland*, 17 Johns. (N.Y.) 92 (1819)—an action was brought against a neighbour for digging so close to the boundary that it caused the collapse of a

est solum ejus est usque ad coelum et ad inferos, the Massachusetts Supreme Court held that the owner had 'absolute dominion of the soil', including the underground water. But the Court cautioned that '[t]hese rights should not be exercised from mere malice.'[136] A number of courts followed *Greenleaf v Francis,* supporting the result on the same policy grounds that persuaded the English judges in *Acton v Blundell* and *Chasemore v Richards* (these cases were frequently cited in American courts).[137] The *obiter* qualification of malice found in both *Greenleaf v Francis* and *Acton v Blundell* is also stressed in many of these cases, usually in *obiter dicta.*[138] For instance, in 1855 the Supreme Court of Pennsylvania declared that '[n]either the civil law nor the common law permits a man to be deprived of a well or spring or stream of water for the mere gratification of malice.'[139]

Some American courts rejected the malice qualification as incompatible with the 'absolute' right to dig in one's land and to use percolating water under one's land.[140] These courts recited the principle 'that an act legal in itself, violating no right, cannot be made actionable on the ground of the motive which induced it'.[141] An influential treatise writer on the law of torts, Judge Thomas Cooley of the Michigan Supreme Court, described this as a 'statement of . . . principle that is as old as the common

tenement on neighbouring land. It was alleged that this was done maliciously—which was not proved—nevertheless the New York Court accepted that '[i]n the exercise of a lawful right, a party may become liable to an action, where it appears that the act was done maliciously' (ibid., 98).

136 *Greenleaf v Francis,* above at note 134, 121–3, *per* Putnan J. The Court did not quote Marcellus from the *Digest,* although counsel referred to it in argument. At first instance the plaintiff had argued that the defendant was motivated by malice in placing his well so close to his neighbour's. The trial judge directed the jury as follows: (1) that if the defendant dug the well so close in order to obtain water for his own use, he was justified in doing so; (2) if the defendant dug the well where he did for the purpose of injuring the plaintiff and not in order to obtain water, then he was liable on the action in the case; (3) if the defendant dug the well to obtain water but at the same time wished to hurt the plaintiff, there was no liability. The jury returned a verdict for the defendant. The plaintiff appealed against the jury directions, but the directions and verdict were upheld. The Supreme Court approved of the trial judge's direction as to 'mere malice', but the jury's findings rejected it and that was the end of the matter. The case also stands for the proposition that mixed motivations do not render 'a lawful act' unjustified: ibid, 123.

137 See, e.g., *Ellis v Duncan,* 21 Barb. (N.Y.) 230 (1855); *Haldeman v Bruckhardt,* 25 Pa. 528 (1863); *Trustees and Inhabitants of the Village of Delhi & England v Youmans,* 50 Barb. (N.Y.) 316 (1867); *Chesley v King,* 74 Me 164 (1882).

138 See, e.g., *Trustees and Inhabitants of the Village of Delhi & England v Youmans,* ibid., 320.

139 *Wheatley v Baugh,* 25 Pa. 528, 533 (1855), *per* Lewis C.J.

140 *Chatfield v Wilson,* 28 Vt 49 (1855) is possibly the first and *Huber v Merkel,* 117 Wis. 355 (1903) is one of the last. See also *Phelps v Nowlen,* 72 N.Y. 39 (1878); D. L. Uelmen, 'The Law of Underground Water; A Half-Century of *Huber v Merkel*' [1953] Wis LR 491; K. F. Hostak, 'Wisconsin Ground Water Law—A New Era' [1957] Wis LR 309.

141 *Chatfield v Wilson,* 28 Vt 49, 55 (1855), *per* Bennett J. (refusing to follow the *obiter* statement in *Greenleaf v Francis*).

law'.[142] (This was the line taken by the appellate courts in *Pickles*, without reference to American jurisprudence.)

The rejection of a malice limitation highlighted the absolute nature of the right, and sparked a reaction. Some courts began to recant the initial rejection of the analogy to surface waters. It began with *dicta* in New Hampshire cases, applying the rule of 'reasonable use' to *all* water disputes.[143]

At this point it is necessary to split the simplistic coupling of the 'natural flow' theory and riparianism, which up to this point I have treated in discussion of the English cases as identical. American courts and commentators in discussing riparianism distinguished between the theory of 'natural flow' and what was called variously 'reasonable use(r)' or 'correlative rights'.[144] The first theory, as its name indicates, reflected the historically sanctioned approach. It focused on the use made of the water or land by the riparian landowner who had diminished his neighbour's water supply. The 'natural flow' theory prevented waste, or malicious diversion, or other extraordinary use of water, but did not invite any comparison with the use of water or land by the complaining neighbour.[145] In other words, there was no balancing of utility to ensure that the water was put to its most beneficial use. This is commonly juxtaposed with a rival theory, developed principally in America, which goes by the names of 'reasonable use' or the 'correlative rights' rule.[146] This rule allows each riparian owner to make reasonable use of surface water; but where the uses of neighbours conflict, the court compares the utility of conflicting uses and determines which is the most useful.[147] This version of the theory was reflected[148] in the *Restatement (First) of the Law of Torts* (1939), which purported to distil best judicial practice and doctrine from

[142] Quoted in Anon., 'Lawful Acts Maliciously Performed On One's Own Land' (1880) 21 Albany LJ 284, 286. See also T. Cooley, *A Treatise on the Law of Torts or the Wrongs Which Arise Independent of Contract* (1880), 497: 'Malicious motives make a bad case worse, but they cannot make that wrong which is in its essence lawful.'

[143] *Bassett v Salisbury Manufacturing Co.*, 43 N.H. 569, 578–9 (1862); *Hayes v Waldron*, 44 N.H. 580 (1863); *Swett v Cutts*, 50 N.H. 439, 446 (1870).

[144] For an excellent summary, see C. Donahue, T. E. Kauper, and P. W. Martin, *Cases and Materials on Property: An Introduction to the Concept and the Institution* (West Publishing Co., St Paul, 2nd edn, 1983), 322–4.

[145] P. N. Davis, 'Wells and Streams: Relationship at Law' (1972) 37 Missouri LR 189, 202.

[146] The confusion is compounded by the existence of two, different 'correlative rights' rules; one applying in the western arid states and another in the eastern states. For an excellent treatment, see Davis, at note 145, 203. The eastern 'correlative rights' doctrine is the one relevant to this discussion.

[147] Davis, ibid., 204.

[148] Somewhat uneasily, according to T. E. Lauer, who traces the influences in the drafting of the *Restatement*, and doubts that the case law justified the conclusion that there were two rival theories at play: 'Reflections on Riparianism' (1970) 35 Missouri LR 1, 3, n. 4.

the enormous body of American law.[149] Under the rule of reasonable use, malicious exercises of water rights are treated as cases of unreasonable use.[150]

Furthermore, the *Restatement* applied the principles which evolved in relation to surface water to subterranean water.[151] Because of the tendency of water to flow (whether on top or below the surface), and the impact that any substantial use of water by one is bound to have on the uses by neighbours, the *Restatement* declared the rights and privileges of users of subterranean waters as 'qualified rather than absolute'.[152] A possessor of land who, by using subterranean water, unintentionally causes substantial harm to another's use of the water is liable only if the former's use of the water was negligent, reckless, or ultrahazardous.[153] In contrast, a possessor whose use of water intentionally causes substantial harm to another user is liable if the harmful use was unreasonable.[154] In determining unreasonableness of use the *Restatement* dictates that to avoid liability the utility of the use must outweigh the gravity of the harm.[155] Important factors in determining utility are listed as: the social value which the law attaches to the primary purposes for which the use is made; the suitability of the use to the character of the locality; the impracticability of preventing or avoiding the harm; and the place where the water is used.[156]

The *Restatement* shows what the law was thought to have become by the 1930s.[157] It is safe to say, in my view, that by the time *Pickles* was decided the better-reasoned American cases were increasingly rejecting the doctrine of absolute ownership in percolating underground water, and were preferring a rule of reasonable use in relation to such water. This approach was supported by commentators. The case law discloses a shift in emphasis from the need to show malice to a showing of unreasonable

149 American Law Institute, *Restatement of the Law of Torts* (American Law Institute Publishers, St Paul, 1939).

150 See, e.g., *Springfield Waterworks Co. v Jenkins*, 62 Mo. App. 74 (St Louis Court of Appeal, 1895); *Gagnon v French Lick Springs Hotel Company*, 163 Ind. 687 (1904). In this category fell 'wanton waste' of water. See, e.g., *Runnels v Bullen*, 2 N.H. 532, 537–8 (1823) ('each may use his portion of the water, in any reasonable way he pleases, but neither can wantonly waste the water, to the prejudice of the other'), and *City of Corpus Christi v City of Pleasanton*, 276 SW 799, 80 (1955) (Supreme Court of Texas). Ernest Huffcut observed that '[l]ater American cases transfer the emphasis from the showing of "malice" to a showing of "unreasonable user" which may or may not be accompanied by malice': 'Percolating Waters: The Rule of Reasonable User' (1903–4) 13 Yale LJ 222.

151 Above at note 149, vol. IV, para. 858 and accompanying commentary.

152 Idem.

153 Ibid., para. 859.

154 Ibid., para. 860.

155 Ibid., para. 861.

156 Ibid., para. 862. Note that the motivation of the harmful user is not listed as an imporant factor.

157 See generally A. D. Tarlock, 'Supplemental Groundwater Irrigation Law: From Capture to Sharing' (1985) 73 Kentucky LJ 695.

user, which may or may not be accompanied by malice. Ultimately, as the *Restatement* shows, the doctrine of reasonable use/correlative rights supplanted the doctrine of absolute ownership qualified by a malice limitation.

But American legal developments were ignored by the judges in *Pickles*. Counsel to the Corporation referred in vain to the following statement from the leading American textbook, which was amply supported by American authority:[158]

> The Roman law, founded upon an enlightened consideration of the rights of property, declared that a man may dig for water on his own ground, and if he should thereby drain a well or spring in his neighbour's ground, he would be liable to no action for damages on that score. This principle of the Civil Law is also recognized doctrine of the Common Law. Neither the Civil Law nor the Common Law permits a man to be deprived of a well or stream for the mere gratification of malice.

None of the Law Lords rose to that bait in *Pickles*. In similar fashion to the treatment of Roman and civil law, having borrowed extensively from American law in the first half of the nineteenth century, by century's end these sources were ignored or marginalized by English judges.[159]

Subterranean Water in a Defined Stream

For the sake of completeness a few words must be said about the separate legal category of subterranean water which flows in a defined and known stream. The law applies to such water the same rules as apply to flowing surface water; namely, the riparian principle. Much turns, and certainly the results in several cases have, on whether the underground water tapped was in a defined and known underground stream or simply percolating through the soil. The leading case on this aspect of water law is from Ireland: *Black v The Ballymena Township Commissioner*.[160] The facts are a little complicated. The local Council sought to take water from a river for town supply, but riparian mill-owners objected and the dispute

[158] The reference to 'Angel [*sic*] on Watercourses, 6th edit: p. 182' in counsels' argument is found in the *Law Times* report of the case: *Corporation of Bradford v Pickles* (1895) 73 LT 353, 354. Joseph Angell's book, *A Treatise on the Law of Watercourses*, dated back to 1824, and went through many editions. The one referred to in argument is the 6th edn, by J. C. Perkins, and published in 1869 by the Boston publishing house, Little, Brown & Co.

[159] S. Hedley, 'Words, Words, Words: Making Sense of Legal Judgments, 1875–1940', in C. Stebbings (ed.), *Law Reporting in Britain* (Hambledon Press, London, 1995), 169, 170 ('References to US cases are not uncommon in the 1870s and 1880s but are rare thereafter'). See also A. Kiralfy, 'The Persuasive Authority of American Rulings in England' (1948) 23 Tulane LR 209.

[160] (1886) LR 17 Ir. 459.

went to arbitration. It was agreed that the town would not take water from the river until a compensation supply was provided for the mill-owners. The compensation project was beset by delay. In order to secure a temporary supply to the town of 9,000 inhabitants, the Council struck upon the idea of tapping one of the springs supplying a stream flowing to the river. This was done above the spring, before the water issued out of the ground. This yielded approximately 180,000 gallons a day for the town, but significantly diminished the river level to the detriment of the mill-owners, who issued suit. The case turned on whether the underground water was percolating or in a defined stream at the point it was tapped.

This was the first case to explore thoroughly what 'defined and known' stream or channel meant. The court held that it was a question of fact, with the onus of proof on the party asserting the right to the flow of water. What that party had to show in order to 'constitute the riparian relation' was knowledge of the underground stream. The existence of an underground stream was to be reasonably inferred 'from existing and observed facts in the natural, or rather the pre-existing, condition of the surface of the ground'. This had to be deducible by reasonable lay persons, 'without opening up the ground by excavation, or having recourse to abstruse speculations of scientific persons'. This stringent test was satisfied in this case, it being proved that the now underground stream had once flowed on the surface but in living memory had been covered over by falling rocks and dirt from above. This was undoubtedly a just result given the actions of the Council.

The relevance of this pocket of law for *Pickles* is that there was a possible argument that at the point Edward was poised to intercept the Spring, just over 40 yards from the mouth of the Spring, it could be reasonably deduced that the formerly percolating underground water was by then in a defined stream. There was absolute certainty at that point that Edward's second shaft would intercept the Spring water. This would have fallen within the spirit of the rule, but not the letter, as laid down in *Black*'s case, for the channel would not be 'known' in the relevant sense. It may be that not enough evidential attention was devoted to this issue by counsel for the Corporation at first instance. The focus instead was on portraying Edward's operations as so inefficient and ineffectual as to be maliciously inspired.[161] In any event, the findings of fact by the trial judge in relation to the status of the underground water did not help the Corporation's cause. Despite significant argument on this point before the Court of Appeal, the issue was really foreclosed by the findings below. Understandably, the point was not pursued to the House of Lords.

161 Recall that in *Acton v Blundell* the jury direction presumed that the digging (in that case, coal mining) was done in 'the usual and proper manner' (above at note 63, 348; 1233).

An interesting sidelight is that the Corporation of Bradford found itself on the wrong side of this doctrine a few years later in a dispute with another local landowner, William Ferrand. This gentleman and his mother, Lady Ferrand, had consistently opposed the Corporation's numerous applications for Waterworks Bills. Back in the 1840s, Lady Ferrand succeeded in gaining statutory protection for the water supply for her water fountain and ponds from Hewenden Beck.[162] Her attitude and that of her son to the competing and perhaps more pressing demands of the inhabitants of Bradford for an adequate water supply drew critical comment.[163] The Ferrand family had crossed legal swords with the Corporation before. This dispute concerned William Ferrand's attempt to 'do a Pickles'.

The Corporation of Bradford and others relied on water from Bradup Beck, which was supplied in large part from Sweet Well Spring, issuing from Ferrand's land. Ferrand granted permission to the Shipley Urban District Council to sink shafts above the point but 'in close proximity to the spot where the waters of the Sweet Well Spring flowed to the surface',[164] presumably for the purpose of town water supply to Shipley. This interception of the underground spring water significantly diminished supply to the Beck, and the Corporation and others who relied on that source suffered loss. They sought an injunction restraining the interruption of the supply.

The case—*The Mayor, Aldermen, and Burgesses of Bradford v Ferrand*[165]—was the first one in England to raise directly the question of water rights in a defined but unknown underground stream. The Corporation alleged that the intercepted underground water was in a defined stream. Prior to trial it had sought permission from the court to enter Ferrand's land to undertake tests and excavations in order to ascertain whether the underground waters flowed in a defined channel. The trial judge refused the motion. On appeal from that refusal it was agreed that the defendant should amend its statement of defence and raise a point of law for determination by the judge before the trial. The point of law was this: assuming that the underground water flows to the spring in a defined channel, but one the existence and course of which cannot be ascertained without excavation, the Corporation has no right to interfere with the abstraction of such underground water.

162 Sarah Ferrand and her son, William Busfield Ferrand, opposed the Bradford Waterworks Bill of 1841 (see Chapter 1, note 40) and succeeded in securing statutory protection. See sections 275–283 and 361 of the Bradford Waterworks Act 1842, 5 and 6 Vict. Ch. vi.

163 R. West, 'Worstedopolis and the Water Works: Bradford Water Works Company, 1837–1855' (unpublished B.A. dissertation, University of Bradford, 1980), 24–5.

164 *Mayor, Aldermen, and Burgesses of Bradford v Ferrand* [1902] 2 Ch 655, 657.

165 Ibid. The report in (1902) 87 LT 388 is fuller on the facts. I am grateful to Stuart Anderson for bringing this report to my attention.

Counsel for Ferrand and Shipley UDC were Butcher K.C. and Longstaffe, two of Edward Pickles's legal team in the House of Lords. They relied on Irish and American authorities and leading American textbooks for the proposition that underground water in a defined but unknown stream can be appropriated by the landowner without liability to others. Of course, *Black*'s case was relied upon. Opposing counsel, Buckmaster K.C. and Austen-Cartmell, argued that the requirement that the defined underground stream be 'known' had crept illegitimately into the law from the Irish cases. The foundation of the law, they argued, was not knowledge but *ex jure naturae*.

Farwell J. expressed in argument his distrust of such a general principle as 'the gift of nature'.[166] He endeavoured to give it more content by viewing it as akin to, if not derived from, the *jus naturale* of Roman law, which included the conception of *aequum et bonum*. Farwell J. regarded the natural law (*jus naturale*) on which the right to running water rests as meaning what is right and just (*aequum et bonum*) between upper and lower proprietors.[167] This repackaging of the argument did not take the judge very far. Ultimately, he relied on the identical policy arguments which had held sway in *Chasemore v Richards*. A defined stream might flow for miles underground, and it would be most 'startling' if an unsuspecting landowner should be liable for digging in his own land and interrupting the flow.[168] The fact that in this case the defendants knew exactly where to dig—just above the mouth of the Spring—was not alluded to and was ignored as irrelevant. It will be recalled, exactly the same thing occurred in *Pickles*.[169]

Pollution of Percolating Waters

A brief discussion of this topic may be in order.[170] It might be thought that if a neighbour can drain every drop of percolating underground water not in a defined and known stream—as the *Pickles* case held—that neighbour can pollute percolating underground water also with impunity. A decade before the House of Lords decided *Pickles* this issue fell for decision in *Ballard v Tomlinson*.[171]

166 (1902) 87 LT 388, 389.

167 Above at note 164, 660–1.

168 Ibid., 664. The quotation is from *Ewart v Belfast Poor Law Guardians* (1881) 9 LR Ir. 172, 194, *per* Palles C.B.

169 See Chapter 3.

170 For a full discussion of the Anglo-American case law regarding pollution of percolating underground water at the time Pickles was digging, see Budd, above at note 133, 255–60.

171 (1885) L.R. 29 Ch. 115 (CA); (1884) L.R. 26 Ch. 194 (Ch.). See also *Hodgkinson v Ennor* (1863) 4 B. & S. 229; 122 E.R. 446.

In this case the parties were neighbours, and each had a well sharing a common underground water supply. The defendant possessed the higher well, and when he drained a privy and industrial waste into his well it polluted the water that flowed into the plaintiff's lower well. Pearson J. found for the defendant on the ground that the plaintiff had no protectable property right in the percolating water. He reasoned that as the defendant was clearly entitled to pump every drop of water out of his well and leave the plaintiff with none, it would be no different in principle if he deprived him of the water by rendering it unfit.[172] The Court of Appeal unanimously rejected this reasoning. It was accepted that *Chasemore v Richards* permitted a landowner to extract all the water before it reached his neighbour, but if any did flow to his neighbour it must not arrive in a polluted state.[173] Lord Justice Lindley said that it took 'an inadequate view' of nuisance to think it was based exclusively on rights of property, and instanced the 'right' to receive light and pure air.[174]

The late Glanville Williams thought it 'odd that in *Bradford v Pickles* no argument seems to have been addressed to the House [of Lords] on discoloration'.[175] Certainly, on the facts of *Pickles* discoloration occurred during the digging, and well before the Corporation sought injunctive relief. Would the Corporation have had more success in the appellate courts relying on discoloration and arguing against *Ballard*'s case?[176]

It seems to me highly unlikely. Lord Justice Lindley sat in the Court of Appeal in both *Ballard* and *Pickles*, and in the latter case was the most critical of all the appellate judges of Pickles's behaviour. Reading his judgments together, there is no suggestion that he thought the contrasting results to be anomalous, inequitable, or unfair. There is no reason to believe that their Lordships would have decided any differently than they did. This was a case of disturbance or discoloration as a by-product of digging in one's own land in order to drain the water away.[177] Pickles was not 'fouling' or polluting the water with noxious substances, thereby creating health risks.

172 *Ballard v Tomlinson* (1884) L.R. 26 Ch. 194, 203.

173 (1885) L.R. 29 Ch. 115, 121 (Brett M.R.), 123 (Cotton L.J.) and 125 (Lindley L.J.).

174 Ibid., 126–7.

175 G. L. Williams, 'The Foundations of Tortious Liability' (1941) 7 CLJ 111, 128, n. 67. Williams referred to *Ballard*'s case. *Accord*, R. F. V. Heuston and R. A. Buckley, *Salmond & Heuston on the Law of Torts* (Sweet & Maxwell, London, 21st edn, 1996), 20, n. 15 ('Strangely enough, in *Bradford v Pickles* the rights arising from the pollution of the water, though clearly established, were not discussed').

176 At this time it appears that the Court of Appeal held itself bound by its own considered decisions (F. Pollock, *A First Book of Jurisprudence for Students of the Common Law* (Macmillan & Co., London, 2nd edn, 1904), 322–4), so the discoloration issue would have had to go to the House of Lords in any event.

177 At first instance in *Pickles*, in an unreported section of the judgment, Mr Justice North did not think that provisions prohibiting pollution assisted the Corporation: 'They forbid

Absolutism in Property

I want to end this chapter by touching on the broader theme of absolutism in property. When the conception of absolute property is discussed it usually refers to the individualistic philosophy which became dominant in the eighteenth and nineteenth centuries, both in Britain and on the Continent.[178] The finger is often pointed at William Blackstone for considering property as an 'absolute right',[179] although, as seen above, he ducked and weaved considerably in order to reconcile his absolutist rhetoric with reality.[180] Blackstone had a rather wide category of 'qualified property' into which was put all those things or substances which, by their nature or attributes, did not fit the absolute dominion model.[181] Water has always been difficult to classify in property terms. It has a unique 'publicness', because no person or community can exist without water in sufficient quality and quality: there is simply no substitute for water.[182]

There was a reaction to this absolutism, perhaps most famously articulated by the great German jurist von Jhering: 'There is no absolute property—property, that is, freed from taking into consideration the interest of the community, and history has taken care to engrave this truth upon the minds of all people.'[183] In a similar vein, but with typical English understatement, Sir William Holdsworth remarked that 'at no time can the state be wholly indifferent to the use that owners make of their property'.[184] The necessity for societal regulation of property rights and their exercise flows from the fact that property is an important means of social ordering. 'To permit anyone to do absolutely what he likes with his property in creating noise, smells, or danger of fire', Morris Cohen said in 1930,

the pollution of the Corporation Water but it is the permanent abstraction and not the mere temporary pollution of the water supply that is the important matter in this action'. A *Transcript of Shorthand Notes of Judgment of Mr Justice North* appears as Item No. 10 in Appendix A (pp. 22, 25) of the printed and bound Appeal Book filed with the House of Lords (undated) (hereafter referred to as *Case on Appeal, App. A*).

178 The literature is vast. For an introduction see P. S. Atiyah, *The Rise and Fall of Freedom of Contract* (Clarendon Press, Oxford, 1979), and E. F. Paul, *Moral Revolution and Economic Science: The demise of laissez-faire in British nineteenth century political economy* (Greenwood Press, Westport, 1979).

179 *Commentaries*, vol. 1, 134.

180 See, e.g., K. J. Vandevelde, 'The New Property of the Nineteenth Century: The Development of the Modern Concept of Property' (1980) 29 Buffalo LR 325, 332–3.

181 *Commentaries*, vol. 2, 389.

182 B. H. Thompson, 'Water Law as a Pragmatic Exercise: Professor Joseph Sax's Water Scholarship' (1998) 25 Ecology LQ 363, 367–8.

183 R. von Jhering, *Der Geist des Rechts: eine Auswahl aus seinen Schriften* (C. Schünemann, Bremen, 1965), 7.

184 W. Holdsworth, *History of English Law* (Little, Brown & Co., Boston, 1926) vol. 8, c. 4; quoted by M. R. Cohen, 'Property and Sovereignty' (1927–8) 13 Cornell LQ 8, 23.

'would be to make property in general worthless'.[185] Of course, the common law was not immune to that truth. It was reflected in the tussle between two maxims—*sic utere tuo ut alienum non laedas* (so use your own property as not to injure your neighbour's) and *damnum sine injuria* (loss befalling a person without any legal wrong being done).[186] But these maxims operated at such a high level of abstraction, and were in spirit so contradictory, that they provided little assistance in resolving clashes between the interests of neighbours .[187]

The emergence of the French doctrine of abuse of rights—discussed in the next chapter—was in large part a reaction to the rhetoric and reality of absolutism. This idea, as we will see, was taken up by 'enlightened'[188] judges in late nineteenth-century America, and by the end of the first quarter of the twentieth century it was firmly in place. Ironically, at about the time the tide was turning on absolutism in the United States, the House of Lords shored up the doctrine in *Pickles* and the force of precedent rendered it immune from significant judicial modification in Britain. The ball of reform in Britain was irretrievably passed thereby to the legislature. But the significant statutory modifications Parliament made simply overlaid the common law and did not change it. This reinforced the cleavage between private law and public law, and justified the continuation of the absolutist rhetoric.[189]

[185] Cohen, ibid., 21.

[186] The counter principle is often given as *qui jure suo utitur, nemini facit injuriam* (he who uses his legal rights harms no one). See F. H. Lawson, 'Notes on the History of Tort in the Civil Law' (1940) 22 *Journal of Comparative Legislation* (3rd ser) 136, 162, and V. E. Greaves, 'The Social-Economic Purpose of Private Rights: Section 1 of the Soviet Civil Code; A Comparative Study of Soviet and Non-communist Law' (1934) 12 NYUQR 165, 185–86 (Part I of two-part article).

[187] Idem ('Doctrine had to swing between the two poles').

[188] The word is Cohen's: above at note 184, 23.

[189] For further discussion of the divide between private law and public law, see the Epilogue.

6

Abuse of Rights

For more than a century the *Pickles* case has been accepted as slamming the common law door shut on the civil law doctrine of abuse of rights. Although the case concerned real property and water law, and possibly could have been confined to that sphere,[1] 'its simple and memorable facts, together with the generalized statements of principle to be found in the judgments of several of their Lordships, have meant that it is usually taken as authority for the much wider proposition that abuse of rights is unknown to English law'.[2] In this chapter we look at what the common law turned away from, and why.

The Doctrine of Abuse of Rights in French Law

The modern abuse of rights doctrine has its origins in French law.[3] It is viewed by many as a manifestation of equity, softening the absolutism of ownership in the interests of justice.[4] An early explanation of the doctrine was given by Larombière, who said that a person exercising a right must 'do so prudently, with ordinary precautions, without abusing it and without exceeding equitable (*justes*) limits'.[5] Despite the pervasive liberalism of nineteenth-century France, the courts applied the doctrine in a number of cases, and by the end of the century the abuse of rights doctrine occupied a 'modest place' in French law.[6] Up to that point, the doctrine had

1 See G. L. Williams, 'The Foundations of Tortious Liability' (1941) 7 CLJ 111, 144.

2 B. W. Napier, 'Abuse of Rights in British Law', in M. Rotondi (ed.), *L'Abus de Droit* (Padova, Italy, 1979), 267, 267–8.

3 The focus of this treatment of the doctrine of abuse of rights is on French Law and it is drawn entirely from English language sources. Furthermore, the reference to English language treatments of the doctrine has been selective. While I hope it approaches comprehensiveness regarding the application of the doctrine to the exercise of property rights, I have found little in the areas of abuse of contractual rights or abuse of rights in international law of direct relevance, and have not burdened the notes or the bibliography with those references.

4 B. Jeanneau, 'The Reception Of Equity in French Private and Public Law', in R. A. Newman (ed.), *Equity in the World's Legal Systems: A Comparative Study* (Établissements Émile Bruylant, Brussels, 1973), 223, 229.

5 L. L. Larombière, *Théorie et pratique des obligations* (1857), vol. V, p. 692; quoted by H. C. Leake, 'Abuse of Rights in Louisiana' (1932) 7 Tulane LR 426, 432 (italics in original).

6 A. Mayrand, 'Abuse of Rights in France and Quebec' (1974) 34 La LR 993, 994. See also F. P. Walton, 'Delictual Responsibility in the Modern Civil Law (More Particularly in the

been invoked most frequently in relation to misuse of property,[7] dismissal of employees, abuse of legal process, and boycotts.[8] In the twentieth century the doctrine evolved into one of general application and extends well beyond France. It has found its way, in one form or another, into most of the modern civil codes.[9]

The existence of the doctrine is beyond doubt, but its history has been dogged by terminological quibbling and ideological dispute.[10] One objection has been that the phrase is an oxymoron, in the sense that the right ends when its abuse commences. On this view the abusive behaviour is a legal wrong and as such unlawful;[11] so the objection is terminological only. But the reactions to the doctrine, and its extensions over time, transcend terminological quibbles and touch directly upon prevalent notions of the nature and functions of law.[12] The recognition and evolution of the abuse of rights doctrine is a mirror reflecting changing attitudes to property and other rights, and their justification. In the same way, the absence of such a doctrine in the common law system reflects a set of values.

Indeed, the contrast with the common law could not be more stark. Three French cases, all of which have some similarity to the facts in *Pickles*, provide comparative reference points.[13] One of the very earliest

French Law) as Compared with the English Law of Torts' (1933) 49 LQR 70, 86–9. The actual term 'abuse of rights' did appear in the judgments of French courts until the turn of the twentieth century: J. Voyame, B. Cottier, and B. Rocha, 'Abuse of Rights in Comparative Law (1)', in Council of Europe, *Abuse of rights and equivalent concepts: the principle and its present day application* (Council of Europe, Strasbourg, 1990), 23, 27.

[7] Although first developed in relation to abuse of real property rights, André Tunc noted that in the twentieth century the doctrine 'has become nearly useless in this field because of another doctrine, *troubles de voisinage*: whenever someone creates for his neighbour an inconvenience which exceeds what is normal between neighbours, he is liable, even though the inconvenience may be unavoidable and he may not have committed the slightest fault': 'The French Concept of *abus de droit*', in Canadian Institute of Advanced Legal Studies, *The Cambridge Lectures 1981* (Butterworths, Toronto, 1981), 151, 152.

[8] M. S. Amos, 'Abusive Exercise of Rights According to French Law' (1900) 2 J. Soc. of Comp. Leg. (2nd ser.) 453.

[9] An abuse of rights doctrine can be found operating in legal systems as diverse as those in Israel, Russia, the Arab states, and Japan. See S. Shilo, '*Kofin al midat S'dom*: Jewish Law's concept of abuse of rights' (1980) 15 Is. LR 49; E. L. Johnson, 'Abuse of rights in Soviet civil law' (1960) 1 *The Solicitor Quarterly* 320; A. Al-Qasem, 'The Unlawful Exercise of Rights in the Civil Codes of the Arab Countries of the Middle East' (1990) 39 ICLQ 396; A. R. R. Dawwas, 'Abuse of Rights in the Shari'a and under Modern Arab Civil Codes: A Study in Comparative Jurisprudence' (1993) 13 Islamic and Comparative LR 1; J. O. Haley, *The Spirit of Japanese Law* (The University of Georgia Press, Athens, 1998), ch. 7.

[10] See generally J. H. Crabb, 'The French Concept of Abuse of Rights' (1964) 6 Inter-American LR 1, 9–11.

[11] The best-known proponent of this view is M. Planiol, *Traité Élémentaire de Droit Civil* (11th edn, 1939), 312–13.

[12] V. Bolgár, 'Abuse of Rights in France, Germany, and Switzerland: A Survey of a Recent Chapter in Legal Doctrine' (1975) 35 La LR 1015.

[13] There is no originality in the selection or observed similarity to *Pickles*. See, e.g., H. C. Gutteridge, 'Abuse of Rights' (1933–5) 5 CLJ 22.

cases is *Badoit v André*,[14] decided three years before the House of Lords' decision in *Chasemore*'s case. In this case the plaintiffs and defendants both had access through springs on their respective properties, to a common source of mineral water, and, accordingly, each had a right to use a pump at his spring. The defendants were shown to have pumped the water out and into a river. It was inferred from this act of waste that the pump owner's sole purpose was to harm the plaintiffs. This was held to be an abuse of right giving rise to an action for damages.

The second case, decided by the Court of Cassation in 1902, concerned a landowner who started hydraulic works with the avowed intent of draining his own land.[15] These works, however, also drained neighbouring sources of water, to the plaintiff's detriment. Expert evidence indicated that the hydraulic work was useless for the purpose of drainage. The Court awarded damages, but only from the time that the expert testimony became known to the defendant.

The last case, *Coquerel v Clément-Bayard*,[16] was decided in 1915. The plaintiff was experimenting with airships, and his neighbour, intent on forcing the plaintiff to buy his land, erected high wooden scaffolds replete with iron spikes, so placed as to make it highly dangerous to launch or land the airships.[17] Indeed, one airship had already been punctured by the spikes. The plaintiff sued to have the defendant remove the structures, and sought damages as well. The defendant answered the suit by saying that he was only pursuing his own economic interest as owner. He was not trying to hurt the plaintiff for its own sake, but rather was motivated by the aim of obtaining a speculative profit. All three tribunals involved in the case considered the actions abusive, and the defendant was ordered to remove the structures and to pay damages.

It is difficult to give a brief and clear exposition of the doctrine of abuse of rights for it is a relatively young and evolving concept, and there are several divergences between the many civil law jurisdictions which have embraced it.[18] The function of the doctrine, said Chris Brunner in relation

14 Lyons, 1856, D.P. 1856. 2. 199. For a somewhat fuller account, see J. Cueto-Rua, 'Abuse of Rights' (1975) 35 La LR 965, 965–6.

15 Req., 10 June 1902, D.P. III. 1902. 1. 454, S. 1903. 1. 11; cited and discussed by Cueto-Rua, ibid., 989. This case is identified by the name *Fdorissier v Chaverot* in Z. L. Zile, 'Judicial Control of Land Use in France' (1960) 45 Cornell LQ 288, 301.

16 3 August 1915, S.1920.1.300, D.P.1917.1.79. The fullest account in English, upon which I have relied, is given by Cueto-Rua, ibid., 981. The author also notes the similarity with *Pickles*. For a more recent French-Canadian case with similar facts and identical result, see *Air-Rimouski Ltée v Gagnon* [1952] Que. SC 149 (in French).

17 Elspeth Reid points out that M. Coquerel had paid an inflated price for the field as a speculative investment, and he was using this rather extreme tactic to induce M. Clément-Bayard to buy it from him: 'Abuse of Rights in Scots Law' (1998) 2 Edinburgh LR 129, 136, n. 35.

18 Cueto-Rua, above at note 14, 971–2. In addition to the other specific references, starting

to Dutch law but in terms susceptible of extrapolation to the civil law in general,[19]

> is to delineate the limits of private rights. It does so by restricting them because of the interests of others, which would be unnecessarily harmed by the exercise of those rights to the fullest extent that the words of the statute would appear to allow. The revival of the doctrine in the 20th century shows that in formulating the rights of the individual, the French Civil code . . . overstressed the freedom of the individual to make use of his rights at his discretion, in so much as it underrated the social aspect of the exercise of those rights, namely, that the interests of others may not be completely disregarded. Insufficient regard for the interests of others may render the exercise of the right unacceptable.

The paradigm case of abuse of right, however, involves a malicious act. Malice has the chameleon quality of taking its meaning from context. Here its primary sense is of an act intended to harm or annoy the other party. Proof of that intention is required, and it will be inferred more readily if there is little or no advantage or benefit to the owner.[20] There is more difficulty where there is a legitimate, or less illegitimate, motive as well, such as in *Coquerel v Clément-Bayard*.[21] In these cases of so-called 'mixed motivation'[22] the balance of opinion in civil law systems appears to be that the doctrine will be invoked if the dominant purpose was the intention to harm.[23] In some civil law jurisdictions the doctrine of abuse of right is no longer restricted to situations where there is proof of intent to injure. There courts have refused to enforce claimed rights or to award

points for the study of abuse of rights in a number of civil law countries are: Voyame, Cottier, and Rocha, above at note 6; M. Rotandi (ed.), *L'Abus de Droit* (Padova, Italy, 1979) (English language treatments of the law in Britain, USA, Israel, Scandinavia, and Hungary: French, German, or Spanish language treatments of the law in France, Quebec, Yugoslavia, Germany, Spain, Italy, Czechoslovakia, Belgium, The Netherlands, Japan, Poland, Switzerland, and Latin America); A. M. Rabello (ed.), *Aequitas and Equity: Equity in the Civil Law and Mixed Jurisdictions* (The Harry and Michael Sacher Institute for Legislative Research and Comparative Law, The Hebrew University of Jerusalem, Jerusalem, 1997), 632 ff. (English language treatments of the law in Israel, Switzerland, Turkey, Quebec, and Louisiana).

[19] C. J. H. Brunner, 'Abuse of Rights in Dutch Law' (1977) 37 La LR 729, 731. For the current version of the Dutch abuse of rights doctrine, see P. P. C. Haanappel and E. MacKaay (eds), *New Netherlands Civil Code: Patrimonial Law (Property, Obligations and Special Contracts)* (Kluwer, Deventer), 6 (Art. 13).

[20] P. Catala and J. A. Weir, 'Delict and Torts: A Study in Parallel' (1964) 38 Tulane LR 221, 224 (Part II).

[21] Crabb, above at note 10, 13; Cueto-Rua, above at note 14, 989; R. B. Schlesinger, H. W. Bade, P. E. Herzog and E. M. Wise, *Comparative Law: Cases–Text–Materials* (Foundation Press, New York, 6th edn, 1998), 827.

[22] Cueto-Rua, ibid., 989.

[23] See Cueto-Rua, ibid., 990–1. This is similar to the position in Anglo-Australasian administrative law where power is exercised for a mixture of proper and improper purposes. See *Poananga v State Services Commission* [1985] 2 NZLR 385 (CA).

damages for breach where the holder of the right is shown simply to have no serious or legitimate interest in exercising the right.[24]

It is not clear why the highly individualistic French law—with the proud proclamation in its Civil Code of the absolute nature of property rights[25]—came to recognize and then embrace the abuse of rights doctrine, whereas the equally individualist common law refused to do so. Moreover, as the various formulations of the modern doctrine disclose, there is considerable woolliness of thought about what behaviour it catches, and why.[26] That does not explain fully why the common law decisively, indeed dismissively, turned its back on any such doctrine. After all, there was precedent in Scotland.

Abuse of Rights in Scots Law

In *Pickles,* Lord Watson denied that Scots law contained an abuse of rights notion, or at least one that might assist the Corporation in that case.[27] This remark was *obiter* and is 'unsound' in so far as it purported to reject the well-established doctrine of *aemulatio vicini* in Scots law.[28] This doctrine has been described in the following terms: 'In Scots law a proprietor of

24 See generally Cueto-Rua, ibid., 992–6.

25 French Civil Code, art. 544: 'Ownership is the right to enjoy and dispose of things in the most absolute manner, provided that use is not made of them which is prohibited by law or regulations': J. H. Crabb (trans.), *The French Civil Code Revised Edition (as amended to 1 July 1994)* (Fred B. Rothman & Co., Colorado, 1995), 127. Roscoe Pound spoke of the 'emphatic generalization' of this article in the Code: 'The French Civil Code and the Spirit of Nineteenth Century Law' [1955] BULR 77, 87.

26 The best discussion of this is in S. Herman, 'Classical Social Theories and the Doctrine of "Abuse of Right"' (1977) 37 La LR 747. See also Voyame, Cottier, and Rocha, above at note 6, 23, 24 ('the abuse of rights . . . is a general principle of hazy outline').

27 [1895] AC 587, 597. In argument, the disappearing Lord Shand is reported to have said that he did not think the doctrine 'goes very far in Scotland'. See 'The Manywells Springs Dispute. The Case in the House of Lords. Judgment Reserved.', *The Bradford Observer,* Friday, 10 May 1895, p. 5. On Lord Shand's fleeting appearance in the case, see Chapter 3.

28 See *Green's Encyclopaedia of the Laws of Scotland* (W. Green & Son Ltd, Edinburgh, 1931), vol. XII, para. 1078, and W. M. Gordon, *Scottish Land Law* (W. Green & Son Ltd, Edinburgh, 1989), 174. The Sherriff Court in *More v Boyle* [1967] SLT 38 held Lord Watson's view in *Pickles* to be 'inconsistent' with the weight of authority and affirmed the doctrine of *aemulatio vicini* as part of the law of Scotland. *Accord,* P. Robson and K. Miller, *Property* (W. Green/Sweet & Maxwell, Edinburgh, 1991), 97, n. 86 ('cannot be reconciled with later Scottish decisions'); N. R. Whitty, 'Nuisance', in *The Laws of Scotland: Stair Memorial Encyclopaedia* (The Law Society of Scotland & Butterworths, Edinburgh, 1988), vol. 14, paras 2033–5. In *The Law of Delict in Scotland* (W. Green & Son Ltd, Edinburgh, 2nd rev. edn, 1981), 51, D. M. Walker opines that the decision in *Pickles'* might well have been otherwise in Scotland'. Cf. D. M. Walker, 'Equity in Scots Law' (1954) 66 *Juridical Review* 103, 118 (where, speaking of Lord Kames's list of equitable maxims, Walker said: '[o]ne or two are probably not the law and possibly never have been, as, for example, that "Justice will not permit a man to exercise his right where his intention is solely to hurt another."' (See further, Appendix, note 8.)

land may make any lawful use of his land, however offensive or harmful to a neighbour, but not if he does so *in aemulationem vicini*, mainly for pure spite or other oblique motives.'[29]

As David Johnston has observed, early Scottish cases display 'a bewildering diversity of views on an owner's right to make unrestricted use of his own property'.[30] The concept of *aemulatio vicini*, however, surfaces enigmatically in a line of Scottish cases in the seventeenth and eighteenth centuries.[31] Three things seem reasonably clear from Johnston's thorough treatment of the early jurisprudence: that *aemulatio* was a well-established restraint on use of one's own property; that it applied only in the narrow sphere of indirect (non-physical) harm; and that it was difficult to prove. This case law antedated the full acceptance of the tort of nuisance into Scots law, and that nineteenth-century development further restricted the role for *aemulatio*.[32] Nevertheless, acceptance of the notion 'never faltered, and . . . it became an established doctrine in Scots law'.[33]

The fullest discussion of the doctrine in the eighteenth century is in Lord Kames's *Principles of Equity*, in which he described the right of a landowner to dig for water or to build as subject to 'a limitation founded entirely on equity'.[34] '[J]ustice will not permit a man to exercise his right where his intention is solely to hurt another; which in law-language is termed acting *in aemulationem vicini*. In all cases of this nature, a court of equity will give redress. . . .'[35] Although it is clear that this doctrine did not spring fully formed from Roman law, Kames's reference to equity in the sense of justice and fairness resonates with the following opinion of Paulus, uttered in the context of a dam destroyed by natural forces on a neighbouring property:[36]

[29] D. M. Walker, *The Oxford Companion to Law* (Clarendon Press, Oxford, 1980), 38. See also G. Watson (ed.), *Bell's Dictionary and Digest of the Law of Scotland* (Bell & Bradfute, Edinburgh, 7th edn, 1889), 29–30, and generally Reid, above at note 17.

[30] D. Johnston, 'Owners and Neighbours: From Rome to Scotland', in R. Evans-Jones (ed.), *The Civil Law Tradition in Scotland* (The Stair Society, Edinburgh, 1995), 176.

[31] See Johnston, idem, for case references and analysis. For a hostile view of the provenance of *aemulatio vicini*, see J. Rankine, *A Treatise on the Rights and Burdens Incident to the Ownership of Lands and Other Heritages in Scotland* (William Blackwood & Sons, Edinburgh, 1879), 300–2.

[32] Johnston, ibid., 194–7. For a brief but useful discussion of the decline in influence of Roman law and the rise in importance of English law in the 19th century, see P. G. Stein, 'The Influence of Roman Law on the Law of Scotland', in P. G. Stein, *The Character and Influence of the Roman Civil Law: Historical Essays* (Hambledon Press, London, 1988), 319, 357–8.

[33] Johnston, ibid., 197. See also the comprehensive recent treatment by Reid, above at note 17.

[34] (Kincaid & Bell, Edinburgh, 2nd edn, 1767), 59–60. This exact passage does not appear in the first edition (1760) but it appears in all subsequent editions.

[35] Ibid., 60.

[36] D. 39.3.2.5.

Labeo . . . holds that if the dam is man-made . . . an action can be brought to ensure that the neighbour allows its replacement though not one to compel him to replace it. For . . . [the action to ward off rainwater] cannot be used to compel anybody to benefit his neighbour, but can be used to stop him damaging his neighbour or interfering with him if the latter is acting legally. However, even though the action to ward off rainwater may be inapplicable, nonetheless, I hold the view that an *actio utilis* or an interdict is available to me against my neighbour if I wish to restore a dam on his land whose construction will be to my advantage and will not harm him in any way. Considerations of fairness support this view even though we may lack a clear legal right.

Kames's discussion alerts us to the potential for confusion in modern treatments if the three senses of 'equity' are not kept firmly in mind: equity as fairness; equity as a body of English law (as distinct from the common law); and the Courts of Equity, which administered that law. Scots law never had a separate system of equity, administered by a separate court.[37] Consequently, equitable notions directly influenced the principles of Scots law applied by the civil courts of Scotland.[38]

The reception of *aemulatio* into Scots law may seem somewhat arcane and distant from our inquiry, but that is far from the truth. Roman law was at bottom a system of remedies, which were infused with the notion of reasonableness.[39] Commentators threaded together diverse remedial snippets in the *Digest* and the numerous glosses,[40] and created a garment of principle, which had no equivalent in Roman law.[41] By this process the objective reasonableness underpinning the remedial superstructure in Roman law was transmogrified into the subjective focus on intention in *aemulatio vicini*.[42] The importance of this insight is that, as regards exercise of rights over subterranean water, *aemulatio vicini* approximates a reasonable user rule. This, of course, is simply shorthand for riparianism, which applies to surface waters. As we have seen, riparianism has its roots in

[37] D. M. Walker, 'Equity in Scots Law', in Newman, above at note 4, 187, 188.

[38] J. M. Thomson, 'The Role of Equity in Scots Law', in S. Goldstein (ed.), *Equity and Contemporary Legal Developments* (The Harry and Michael Sacher Institute for Legislative Research and Comparative Law, The Hebrew University of Jerusalem, Jerusalem, 1992), 911.

[39] Johnston, above at note 30, 194.

[40] The best treatment of medieval sources supporting the doctrine of abuse of rights is in J. E. Scholtens, 'Abuse of Rights' (1958) 75 SALJ 39.

[41] This conclusion has been expressed with different emphases by various writers. Contrast H. R. Hahlo and E. Kahn, *The South African Legal System and Its Background* (Juta & Co., Cape Town, 1968), 94 ('the prevailing view is that, though there may have been a few specific cases where "abuse of rights" was actionable [most of them involving water rights], there was no general doctrine of abuse of rights in Roman law') with Crabb, above at note 10, 5 ('[p]robably the soundest conclusion . . . is that the concept of abuse of rights did exist [in Roman law], but in terms of a number of partial applications, rather than as a general theory of law. No Roman jurist ever gathered these segments together and fashioned them into a generic principle of law').

[42] Johnston, above at note 30, 198.

Roman law. The common law took a long time in choosing decisively between the competing doctrines of prior appropriation and riparianism. The common law courts did a U-turn on this issue between 1831 and 1833, and the triumph of riparianism was not beyond doubt until 1856.[43] Scots law settled upon riparianism in relation to surface water much earlier.[44]

When the English courts rejected riparianism in relation to underground water not in a defined channel (for essentially policy reasons), first in 1843 and authoritatively in 1859, the nebulous prohibition against the malicious exercise of the otherwise absolute right to use subterranean water in an owner's soil went some way to inject reasonableness into the legal equation, albeit in a subjective form.

Equity and Abuse of Rights

Tony Weir has pointed out that the 'natural views' of the common lawyer and the chancery lawyer towards the use of rights differed fundamentally. The common law position, epitomized by *Pickles*'s case—that a legal right can be exercised for good, bad, or for no reason at all—is diametrically opposed to the stance of equity that people ought not to be allowed to behave badly.[45] Historically the primary roles of equity were to correct men's consciences for the wrongs they had committed and to temper the rigidity and universality of the common law.[46] Many sweeping propositions of the common law were qualified (in some instances considerably) by equity, and the common law notion that an owner could do what he pleased with his property was no exception.[47]

It is no coincidence that the fullest discussion of *aemulatio vicini* in Scots law is found in Kames's *Principles of Equity* (1760). An overview of Kames's view of equity throws into relief deep and enduring tensions within equity jurisprudence,[48] which helps to explain why a body of law that (on one view) seems so suited to preventing a landowner from acting badly towards another in close proximity has not developed in that way.

[43] See Chapter 5.

[44] See *Magistrates of Linlithgow v Elphinstone of Cumbernauld* (1768) 3 Kames's Decisions 331; W. M. Morison (ed.), *The Decisions of the Court of Sessions* (Bell & Bradfute, Edinburgh, 1805), vol. XXIX, p. 12805 (No. 28).

[45] T. Weir, 'The Common Law System', in R. David *et al.* (eds.), *Structures and the Divisions of the Law* (J. C. B. Mohr, Tubingen,1975), para. 2–93 (being ch. 2 of volume II of R. David (ch. ed.), *The Legal Systems of the World: Their Comparison and Unification*).

[46] See A. W. B. Simpson, *A History of the Common Law of Contract: The Rise of the Action of Assumpsit* (Clarendon Press, Oxford, 1975), 396–402.

[47] See the discussion of Weir, above at note 45, paras 2-97 to 2-108.

[48] In what follows I rely heavily on D. Lieberman, *The Province of Legislation Determined: Legal theory in eighteenth-century Britain* (Cambridge University Press, Cambridge, 1989), esp. chs 3, 7, and 8. For an overview of the life and work of Lord Kames, see D. M. Walker, *The Scottish Jurists* (W. Green & Son Ltd, Edinburgh, 1985), ch. 7.

Lord Kames wrote his work on equity with the avowed intention of influencing English law.[49] The book was well received in England, and Blackstone used it as a foil for his own views on equity.[50] Kames's ambition for equity knew few bounds. He saw it as the mechanism by which the judges could modernize and improve the law. Parliament was incapable of prosecuting vitally necessary reforms, in Kames's view, leaving the field of law reform to the judges. Equity took over where the common law left off, enforcing 'the principle of justice'.[51] The deficiencies of the common law were so numerous and glaring, according to Kames's diagnosis, that 'a massive dose of equitable correction'[52] was called for.

In this regard Kames occupied the extreme end of a position well supported in the history of equity jurisprudence.[53] This school of thought viewed equity as a flexible judicial instrument attuned to achieve justice in individual cases. Legal principle held primacy over precedent, and aphorisms guided but hardly constrained judicial discretion. But the rival school of thought viewed such wide, uncontrolled discretion as negating the rule of law (in the sense of officials applying, and citizens relying upon, known and settled rules), and placed much greater weight on certainty and precedent. At base these rival schools exemplify the perennial tension between discretion and rule. As Lieberman intimates, it was difficult to hold true to the historically sanctioned equitable notion of individuated justice while rebutting charges of uncertainty, arbitrariness, and judicial subjectivity.[54] At the time Kames wrote, equity had already 'attained a considerable degree of fixity and certainty both in statement of principles and of their application',[55] and it may have been unrealistic to expect to turn that tide. Under the influence of Jeremy Bentham, legislation became the preferred instrument of law reform.

The story of the hardening of equity's arteries has been often told. In outline the story goes like this. In the course of the eighteenth century the equitable jurisdiction to do justice (or, if there be a difference, to avoid

[49] Notwithstanding the fact that Scots law knew nothing of a separate system of equity, administered by a separate court, Kames observed that 'in Scotland, and other countries where equity and common law are united in one court, the boundary [between common law and equity] varies imperceptibly': *Principles of Equity* (Kincaid & Bell, Edinburgh, 1760), xiii.

[50] See J. S. Waterman, ' Mansfield and Blackstone's Commentaries' (1933–34) 1 UChic LR 549, 560–1.

[51] Lieberman, above at note 48, 167. Problematically, Kames subordinated this principle to that of utilitarianism. As Lieberman demonstrates, this undercut the very rationale of equitable intervention: ibid., 170–2. It is unnecessary to pursue this important point in the present context.

[52] Lieberman, ibid., 167.

[53] For a critical examination of Lord Kames's views and influence, see Walker, above at note 28, 116–25.

[54] Lieberman, above at note 48, 80.

[55] D. M. Walker, 'Equity in Scots Law', in Newman, above at note 4, 187, 190. See also W. S. Holdsworth, 'Blackstone's Treatment of Equity' (1929) 43 Harv LR 1.

undue hardship)[56] veered towards the pole of fixed rules. This process continued in the nineteenth century, particularly under the long tenure of the Woolsack by Lord Eldon. Ironically, the Judicature Act of 1873, which expressly gave equity priority over the common law in cases of conflict, had the effect of further marginalizing equity. The almost-coincident beginnings of modern university legal education in Britain and the appearance of the systematizing treatise or textbook tradition further elevated common law method over that of equity. It was in that milieu that *Pickles* fell to be decided. By this time, 125 years after *Principles of Equity* appeared, Kames's conception of wide-ranging equitable intervention to prevent injustice had been completely displaced by narrow and rigid categorization of equitable relief. It was not surprising, then, to read another famous Scottish lawyer[57] deny in *Pickles* precisely the jurisdiction that Lord Kames had advocated extra-judicially.

In a dictum in *Pickles*, Lord Watson said this:[58]

> If a landowner proceeded to burn limestone close to his march so as to cause annoyance to his neighbour, there being other places on his property where he could conduct the operation with equal or greater convenience to himself and without causing offence, the Court probably would grant an interdict. But the principle of aemulatio has never been carried further.

The example of burning lime appears to draw upon the case of *Dewar v Fraser*,[59] which involved the siting of a lime kiln adjacent to a boundary. Such activity had long since been considered a nuisance under English law.[60] Lord Watson's use of it as an illustration of the metes and bounds of *aemulatio* demonstrates both the domineering influence of English law in Scotland and the power of precedent over principle.

The tortured history of the separate development and coexistence of common law and equity is said to have 'retarded independent moral growth' in the larger common law field.[61] The result of the limited province of equitable remedies and the narrowing of equity's arteries,

[56] Cf. R. A. Newman, *Equity and Law: A Comparative Study* (Oceana Publications Inc., New York, 1961), 11: 'Early law, which is primarily concerned with rules designed for general application, allows little room for variation in individual cases, and relief from hardship emanates from an authority external to the law itself. Viewed at this stage of the evolution of law, equity corrects the law by applying, in circumstances where the ordinary rules would lead to unwarranted hardship, considerations of what is fair and just.'

[57] D. M. Walker—yet another Scot—said that Lord Watson is 'regarded as one of the greatest lawyers who ever sat on the British bench': above at note 29, 1293.

[58] [1895] AC 587, 598.

[59] (1767) Mor. 12803. Discussed by Johnston, above at note 30, 191.

[60] See C. Viner, *An Abridgement of Law and Equity* (Dublin, 1793), vol. 16, 26, para. 13: 'If a *limekiln* be erected so near my house, that when it burns, *the smoke* of it so *enters into the house, that none can inhabit there*, this is a nuisance. Co. 9.59. William Aldred's Case'(emphasis in the original).

[61] Newman, above at note 56, 13.

according to Ralph Newman, has been 'that equitable principles of what is fair and just are less widely used in . . . Anglo-American law than in any of the other great legal systems of the world'.[62] General equitable principles of fairness and justice never took hold. Of the so-called maxims of equity, some sound promising and potentially resonate with some of the concerns of an abuse of rights doctrine—for instance, he who comes to equity must come with clean hands; equity will not allow a statute to be used as an instrument of fraud; equity will not suffer a wrong to be without a remedy; he who seeks equity must do equity[63]—but either they are restricted to the discretion to grant equitable remedies (and therefore out of the mainstream of monetary compensation), or the animating and universalizing moral spirit was somehow diminished or entirely lost.

Why an Abuse of Rights Doctrine Did Not Develop

The common law was beginning to turn its back on Roman and civilian law at the time the modern law of abuse of rights was forming in France. As Sir Frederick Pollock observed, 'as our modern authorities become fuller, cases where it is needful or desirable to recur to the *Corpus Juris* are less and less likely to present themselves'.[64] Moreover, as Dicey's writings demonstrate, things French were not popular.[65] As discussed above, the wizened state of equity at the time denied the law a source of general moral principles.

It must be remembered that this was the heyday of legal positivism. The requirement in *Pickles* and the other cases, that immoral behaviour must be unlawful before it is actionable, was one with which positivists would have been entirely comfortable. Speaking of the work of the utilitarian legal theorists—Jeremy Bentham and John Austin—on a theory of legal liability, H. L. Pohlman observed:[66]

> The utilitarian theory of legal liability required an illegal, overt act that caused injury before an intelligent, rash, or negligent agent could incur legal liability. No doubt this was accepted tradition. Bentham's and Austin's contribution in the development of legal liability was to shift attention from the vicious will of the

[62] Idem.

[63] For a useful modern survey, see P. Jackson, 'The Maxims of Equity Revisited', in Goldstein, above at note 38, 72.

[64] F. Pollock, *A First Book of Jurisprudence for Students of the Common Law* (Macmillan & Co. Ltd, London, 2nd edn, 1904), 342.

[65] I have in mind here his famous rejection of *droit administratif*. See R. A. Cosgrove, *The Rule of Law: Albert Venn Dicey, Victorian Jurist* (University of North Carolina Press, Chapel Hill, 1980), ch. 5.

[66] H. L. Pohlman, *Justice Oliver Wendell Holmes & Utilitarian Jurisprudence* (Harvard University Press, Cambridge, 1984), 45–6.

agent to the general tendency of the act. But none of the earlier utilitarians imagined that this tendency alone sufficed for liability. The act must also be prohibited.

Moreover, the Benthamite-inspired drive for certainty in the law, which incidentally but not unrelatedly had transformed the doctrine of precedent in this period,[67] pointed strongly against such a vague exemption for malicious acts.[68]

An abuse of rights doctrine would require proof of intention to cause harm before a jury. Reliance has been placed on Chief Justice Brian's aphorism that 'the thought of man may not be tried for the devil himself knoweth not the thought of man'.[69] But that carries the argument no distance. More weighty was the considerable distrust of juries in the late nineteenth century. In many contexts the courts reformulated the law to reduce the discretionary power of the jury, especially in relation to potentially emotive issues.[70] Fear of leaving determination of a rather vague standard in the hands of a jury struck terror into the heart of at least Lord Herschell, who could 'imagine no greater danger to the community than that a jury should be at liberty to impose the penalty of paying damages for acts which are otherwise lawful, because they choose, without any legal definition of the term, to say they are malicious. No one would know what his rights were.'[71] Neither did the rapid decline of civil jury trial in the twentieth century overcome this concern. At mid-century Arthur Goodhart wrote that 'it is morally desirable that every man should know exactly what his rights and duties are without subjecting them to the equitable opinion of another, even if that other is a judge'.[72]

Furthermore, recognition of abuse of rights required a form of generalization entirely foreign to the dominant conception of the English law of *torts*. I use the plural form advisedly, for the dominant conception of the subject has been of a definite number of discrete torts, outside of which liability does not exist.[73] In the late nineteenth century, Holmes in

[67] See J. Evans, 'Change in the Doctrine of Precedent during the Nineteenth Century', in L. Goldstein (ed.), *Precedent in Law* (Clarendon Press, Oxford, 1987), 35, 65–8.

[68] The vagueness of the principle is still objected to in modern torts texts. See, e.g., R. F. V. Heuston and R. A. Buckley, *Salmond and Heuston on the Law of Torts* (Sweet & Maxwell, London, 21st edn, 1996), 20.

[69] R. O'Sullivan, 'Abuse of Rights' (1955) 8 Curr Leg Probs 61, 66. See also Gutteridge, above at note 13, 23.

[70] See generally P. S. Atiyah, *The Rise and Fall of Freedom of Contract* (Clarendon Press, Oxford, 1979), 391, and J. Getzler, 'The Fate of the Civil Jury in Late-Victorian England: Malicious Prosecution as a Test Case', in K. O'Donovan and G. R. Rubin (eds), *Human Rights and Legal History: Essays in Honour of Brian Simpson* (Oxford University Press, Oxford, 2001), 205.

[71] *Allen v Flood* [1898] AC 1, 118. See also Lord Macnaghten, ibid., 152–3.

[72] A. L. Goodhart, *English Law and the Moral Law* (Stevens & Sons Ltd, London, 1955), 145.

[73] For a novel alphabetical listing of all known torts (totalling 75), see B. Rudden, 'Torticles' (1991–92) 6/7 *Tulane Civil Law Forum* 105.

America and Pollock in England battled that orthodoxy by laying down general principles of liability at common law. They championed the principle that all injuries to another are torts unless justified. As we will see in Chapter 7, this principle easily accommodated maliciousness. The battle continued well into the twentieth century,[74] and has been stilled rather than resolved only by the imperialistic tort of negligence overrunning many of the others. But the fact remains that the particularism of the common law works against the Continental legal method of making individual cases cohere to the often sparse requirements of a Code text. The French lawyer asks if there was *faute* in the form of an abuse of right, whereas the common lawyer inquires whether a particular tort has been committed.[75] The Continental tendency and incentive towards systemic coherence are absent in the common law.[76]

The history of the common law is of the remedial tail wagging the substantive dog. The focus has been on wrongs and remedies, and less often on rights. This is cause and effect of the many-centredness (polycentricity) of our *torts* law. As Geoffrey Samuel perceptively observed:[77]

> [T]he problem of the right versus wrong dichotomy never quite reached the level of political debate achieved on the Continent for two main reasons. First, because equity . . . became emasculated with the rise of *laissez-faire* capitalism and so never became a forum for a legal-political debate. Secondly, because neither the common law nor equity formally recognised a doctrine of abuse of rights and, as a result, the whole political and social use of 'rights' never really emerged from the remedy-orientated cases. The question 'Ought a person be able to exercise a right in an unsocial way?' tended to remain hidden behind other questions operating at much lower levels of abstraction; and only very occasionally, usually with regard just to specific cases about landowners and contractors, did the concept of a right and its exercise emerge at all. When it did emerge, of course, its novelty carried such persuasive force that it would be virtually a contradiction to talk in terms of an abuse of the right. The social consequence of the exercise of a right thus became subjected to the prevailing private law ideology that rights were something that transcend both politics and social purpose; society was (still is?) about individual interests, about power on a 'personal' (including, importantly, legal persons) level, and any legal attempt to subject this power to some overriding social purpose was likely to be regarded by the courts with suspicion.

[74] See further Williams, above at note 1, 111, and Rudden, above at note 73, 108–10.

[75] K. Zweigert and H. Kötz (trans. by T. Weir), *Introduction to Comparative Law* (Clarendon Press, Oxford, 3rd rev. edn, 1998), 623.

[76] Idem. See also Crabb, above at note 10, 23 (Anglo-American tort law is resistant to 'any kind of unifying theme').

[77] G. Samuel, 'Classification of Law—IV' [1984] City of London LR 3, 34. See also G. Samuel and J. Rinkes, *Law of Obligations and Legal Remedies* (Cavendish Publishing Ltd, London, 1996), 308.

At the time *Pickles* was decided the suspicion took several forms—suspicion of novelty, of 'rights' talk, of things foreign, of social purpose tempering proprietary interests, and possibly even of 'socialism'.[78] Writing in the 1930s, a Professor of Comparative Law in the University of Cambridge harboured the 'grave' objection to the abuse of rights doctrine that 'it may get out of hand and result in serious inroad on individual rights, thus becoming an instrument of dangerous potency in the hands of the demagogue and the revolutionary'.[79] Any sense—however vague or ill-formed—that abuse of rights was potentially 'destructive of the liberty of the subject'[80] would have been anathema to late nineteenth-century judges. Indeed, *Pickles* is usually explained as simply reflecting the prevalent *laissez-faire* individualism of the age.[81]

Laissez-faire is a portmanteau term, often not defined or contextualized.[82] Generations of lawyers raised on the propaganda of A. V. Dicey absorbed that 'an age of *laissez-faire*' existed up to 1870, and thereafter Individualism gave way increasingly to Collectivism.[83] The Victorian age, howsoever its start and end points are determined,[84] encompassed enormous and unparalleled social and economic change. The thinking in all

[78] F. H. Lawson, *Negligence in the Civil Law* (Clarendon Press, Oxford, 1950), 18–19: 'it is clear that as soon as the theory of abuse of rights passes the stage where subjective malice is the sole test, it is really a socialist doctrine. It implies that a man's right is no longer, as it were, a sphere within which he is sovereign, over which he may dispose according to his own view of his interests and his ideas of right and wrong; it is to be subject to the control of society in the person of the judge, who exercises a veto over his decisions in accordance with what he considers to be the purpose for which society has conferred the right'. See also F. H. Lawson, 'Notes on the History of Tort in the Civil Law' (1940) 22 *Journal of Comparative Legislation* (3rd ser.) 136, 164–5; reprinted in F. H. Lawson, *The Comparison: Selected Essays: Volume II* (North Holland, 1977), 242. Geoffrey Samuel disputes this characterization: above at note 77, 34–5. Cf. G. Eörsi, *Comparative Civil (Private) Law: Law Types, Law Groups, The Roads to Legal Development* (Akadémiai Kiadó, Budapest, 1979), 78–80. (See further, Appendix, note 9.)

[79] Gutteridge, above at note 13, 43–4. See the more balanced treatment by a Russian emigrant comparing the laws of the USSR, Britain, USA, France, Germany, and Switzerland at about the same time: V. E. Greaves, 'The Social-Economic Purpose of Private Rights: Section 1 of the Soviet Civil Code; A Comparative Study of Soviet and Non-communist Law' (1934) 12 NYUQR 165 and 438 (two-part article).

[80] Gutteridge, above at note 13, 45.

[81] See, e.g., A. W. B. Simpson, *Victorian Law and the Industrial Spirit* (Selden Society, London, 1995), and W. Friedmann, *Legal Theory* (Stevens & Sons Ltd, London, 4th edn, 1960), 507.

[82] P. W. J. Bartrip, 'State Intervention in Mid-Nineteenth Century Britain: Fact or Fiction?' (1983) 23 J of Brit Stud 63.

[83] A. V. Dicey, *Lectures on the Relation between Law and Public Opinion in England During the Nineteenth Century* (Macmillan & Co., London, 1st edn, 1905), Lecture VII. See generally C. Harvie, *The Lights of Liberalism: University Liberals and the Challenge of Democracy, 1860–86* (Allen Lane, London, 1976).

[84] See R. Price, 'Does the Notion of Victorian England Make Sense?', in D. Fraser (ed.), *Cities, Class and Communications: Essays in Honour of Asa Briggs* (Harvester/Wheatsheaf, New York, 1990), 152.

disciplines advanced considerably over this period,[85] but often the older and newer ideas coexisted uneasily for many years.[86] Modern historians have attacked Dicey's periodization and established that legislative (state) intervention was both more pervasive and earlier in time.[87] There can be no doubt, however, that a strong strain of individualism still existed in political, social, economic, and legal thought by century's end.[88] This was particularly influential on the judges, and hence on judge-made law.[89] Not only were the ideological frames of reference of the late Victorian judges formed many decades before they ascended the bench, when *laissez-faire* thought was at its most pure, but also a major condition for judicial appointment—successful practice at the bar—ensured that they had had neither time nor incentive to re-evaluate those reference points; and on the bench these predilections played a part (how big a part is a controversial issue even today) in the adjudication of cases.[90]

Of the judges who decided *Pickles* in the House of Lords,[91] Lord Halsbury, the recently reappointed Lord Chancellor, was an arch Conservative[92] and a known sympathizer of the Liberty and Property Defence League.[93] This League was established in 1882 (with the assistance and devoted support of Lord Bramwell, among others) in order to defend the principles of freedom of contract, rugged individualism, and *laissez-faire*.[94] Moreover, as Lord Chancellor, Halsbury appointed 'many

[85] For developments in economic thought, for example, compare E. F. Paul, *Moral Revolution and Economic Science: The demise of laissez-faire in nineteenth-century British political economy* (Greenwood Press, Westport, 1979) with M. Evans, 'The Classical Economists, Laissez-Faire and the State', in M. Moran and M. Wright (eds), *The Market & the State: Studies in Interdependence* (St Martin's Press, New York, 1991), 1.

[86] Atiyah, above at note 70, 226.

[87] See Bartrip, above at note 82, 64–5 for references. See also on the other side of the Atlantic, W. J. Novak, *The People's Welfare: Law and Regulation in Nineteenth-Century America* (University of North Carolina, Chapel Hill, 1996).

[88] J. P. S. McLaren, 'Nuisance Law and the Industrial Revolution—Some Lessons from Social History' (1983) 3 OJLS 154, 190 (referring to D. Roberts, *Victorian Origins of the Welfare State* (1960), 22–34).

[89] Atiyah, above at note 86, 235.

[90] Elsewhere I have called this phenomenon 'social lag': M. Taggart, 'Outside Canadian Administrative Law' (1996) 46 UTLJ 648, 658, borrowing from G. E. White, 'The Appellate Opinion as Historical Source Material' (1971) 1 *Journal of Interdisciplinary History* 491, 496.

[91] A footnote has to suffice for the judges in the lower courts. Lord Herschell L.C. was every bit as political as a Liberal as Lord Halsbury was as a Conservative, but Lord Justices A. L. Smith and Lindley, and Mr Justice North were not 'political lawyers'.

[92] In his own lifetime Lord Halsbury was described as 'a Tory to the finger-tips; one of those favoured spirits to whom in the sphere of politics and religion doubt is unknown and unthinkable': J. B. Atlay, *The Victorian Chancellors* (Smith, Elder, & Co., London, 1908), vol. 2, p. 439.

[93] N. Solden, '*Laissez-Faire* as Dogma: The Liberty and Property Defence League, 1882–1914', in K. D. Brown (ed.), *Essays in Anti-Labour History: Responses to the Rise of Labour in Britain* (The Macmillan Press Ltd, London, 1974), 208, 224.

[94] Ibid., 212.

undistinguished men to the bench because of their political services to the Conservative Party'.[95] Of the other three Law Lords, politics featured in the careers of all of them. Lord Watson spent four years in the House of Commons—although it is said 'he took little part in general politics, either within its walls or on the platform'[96]—immediately prior to his appointment as a Lord of Appeal in Ordinary. Edward Macnaghten was actively involved in politics as Conservative MP for Antrim for seven years prior to his elevation to the House of Lords.[97] The remaining judge, Lord Ashbourne, had been appointed by the Liberals as Lord Chancellor of Ireland, and was retained by the Conservatives and made a life peer. Although not a Law of Appeal in Ordinary, Lord Ashbourne took an active role in the House of Lords.[98]

This was unexceptional at the time.[99] Lawyers were commonly involved in politics, and stints in the House of Commons could be fitted around barristerial practice; indeed, it was a common path to judicial preferment.[100] As a result the 'political lawyers' were in close touch with the sentiments of their communities regarding the issues of the day. Moreover, these men could not avoid what Ivor Jennings once referred to as 'the floating ideas' of their time.[101] 'It is scarcely possible', observed Patrick Atiyah in his magisterial study of freedom of contract,[102]

[95] D. Pannick, *Judges* (Oxford University Press, Oxford, 1987), 66. The late R. F. V. Heuston casts doubt on this in his entry for 'Gifford, Hardinge Stanley (First Earl of Halsbury)' in A. W. B. Simpson (ed.), *Biographical Dictionary of the Common Law* (Butterworths, London, 1984), 204, 205: 'Halsbury's judicial appointments, and to a lesser extent his judicial opinions, were once criticized as displaying an undue Conservative bias, but modern research takes a more balanced view of his efforts'. For an extended treatment of these topics see, R. F. V. Heuston, *Lives of the Lord Chancellors, 1885–1940* (Clarendon Press, Oxford, 1964), 36–66 and 73–6, and 'Lord Halsbury's Judicial Appointments' (1962) 78 LQR 504. I think Pannick is justified in saying 'many' if you include the county court appointments (which Heuston deliberately puts to one side). See on this P. Polden, *A History of the County Court, 1846–1971* (Cambridge University Press, Cambridge, 1999), 99, 247 and 250. (See further, Appendix, note 10.)

[96] M. T. Stormonth-Darling, 'Lord Watson' (1899) 11 *Juridical Review* 272, 275. William Watson was MP for Glasgow and Aberdeen Universities 1876–80.

[97] J. A. Wightman, 'Macnaghten, Sir Edward', in Simpson, above at note 95, 337–40. He was politically active in the House of Lords as well: Walker, above at note 29, 793. The Antrim seat was held at one time by Edward Macnaghten's father.

[98] R. Stevens, *Law and Politics: The House of Lords as a Judicial Body, 1800–1976* (Weidenfeld & Nicolson, London, 1979), 111–12.

[99] See A. H. Manchester, *A Modern Legal History of England and Wales, 1750–1950* (Butterworths, London, 1980), 80.

[100] See D. Duman, *The English and Colonial Bars in the Nineteenth Century* (Croom Helm, London, 1983), 179–91. See also H. J. Laski, 'The Technique of Judicial Appointment', in H. J. Laski, *Studies in Law and Politics* (George Allen & Unwin Ltd, London, 1932), 163, 169 ('membership of Parliament is a distinct assistance to a lawyer who desires judicial appointment').

[101] W. I. Jennings, 'In Praise of Dicey, 1885–1935' (1935) 13 *Public Administration* 123, 124.

[102] Atiyah, above at note 70, 293.

that any educated man growing to maturity between (say) 1800 and 1850 would not have read a good deal of the new political economy and radical political utilitarianism. Many were profoundly influenced by it, and many more were influenced by simplified versions of these bodies of thought. Amongst those there were certainly a number of the most important legal figures in the nineteenth century, including many leading judges.

Every judge who heard the *Pickles* case between 1893 and 1895 was born before 1840.[103] Atiyah's point is nicely illustrated by Edward Macnaghten, born in 1830, whose father at various times was a judge in India, Deputy-Lieutenant of Antrim, a Conservative politician, and, shortly after retiring from the House of Commons, author of a book entitled *The Elements of Political Economy* (1854).[104]

The progressive decline in appointment of 'political lawyers' to the higher judiciary in the twentieth century has been linked to the now dominant view that the operation of the law should be divorced from politics, unattractive judicial salaries, and the longer hours of Parliamentary work being less congenial to combining careers.[105] Today, 'exclusive devotion to the law'[106] is the norm. This movement has followed in the wake of the increasing formalism in English law, and the two processes mutually reinforced each other.

Formalism is another catch-all term, given different meanings at various times for various purposes. The characteristics relevant to this discussion are: the outward rejection of policy issues in legal analysis; denial of judicial law-making; a belief that law was a deductive science of principles drawn from cases; a hostility to legislation; and an increasing insularity.[107] The citadel of formalism was stormed by the legal realists in the 1930s in the United States. Unlike its common law cousin, the pragmatic and untheoretical English common law has never been systematically accosted by Legal Realism. Formalism has hung on in England. The reasons why are complex, and beyond the scope of this study.[108] But this

[103] In ascending order of court: North (1830); Herschell (1837), Lindley (1828), Smith (1836); Halsbury (1823), Watson (1827), Macnaghten (1830), Ashbourne (1837). This confirms the popular impression that Victorian office-holders were elderly, although this was not the case earlier in the century. See R. F. V. Heuston, 'Judicial Law-Making in Victorian England' (1987) 12 Holdsworth LR 16, 19.

[104] M. Stenton, *Who's Who of British Members of Parliament: Volume I 1832–1885: A Biographical Dictionary of the House of Commons* (The Harvester Press, Sussex, 1976), 254.

[105] D. Podmore, 'Lawyers and Politics' (1977) 4 Brit. J. of Law & Soc. 155, 178. See also R. Megarry, 'Seventy-Five Years On: Is the Judiciary What It Was?', in D. C. Hoath (ed.), *75 Years of Law at Sheffield 1909–1984* (University of Sheffield, Sheffield, 1984), 1, 8–10.

[106] As Lord Haldane (1856–1928) described it: quoted in Heuston, above at note 95, 215.

[107] I have drawn here mainly on Atiyah, above at note 70, 660.

[108] See, e.g., P. S. Atiyah, *Pragmatism and Theory in English Law* (Stevens & Sons, London, 1987) and W. Twining, *Blackstone's Tower: The English Law School* (Sweet & Maxwell, London, 1994).

helps to explain why *Pickles*, accepted on all sides as the product of *laissez-faire* individualism, has never been reconsidered by the courts in the collectivist era which characterized English political thought and action for much of the last century. The contrast with the position in America is striking.

In the early years of the twentieth century the focus in the United States shifted away from conceptualism towards policy, and the courts there increasingly considered 'the social needs of the community' in developing the law.[109] The sense that this was an inevitable step in the forward march of civilization is nowhere better captured than in a lecture in 1928 by the great American judge, Benjamin Cardozo:[110]

> For society at large as well as for the family, the changing *mores* have brought changing law. A new sense of the significance of social solidarity has engendered a new conception of the duty to refrain from anti-social conduct. Ancient precedents gave support to the view that conduct harmful to one's neighbor did not depend for its legality upon the animating motive. Modern decisions have set bounds to the license theretofore accorded to 'disinterested malevolence.' A growing altruism, or if not this, a growing sense of social interdependence, is at the bottom of the change. Power may be exercised with brutal indifference to the many when society was organized on a basis of special privilege for the few. Democracy has brought in its wake a new outlook, and with a new outlook a new law. The social forces contributing to the change did not write their message down into the set paragraphs of a statute. They left it in the air where the pressure was more effective because felt by all alike. At last, the message became law.

The gulf between this conception of common law adjudication and the formalism prevalent in Britain could hardly have been wider.[111] The site of social change in Britain was the legislature, not the courts. There the 'new social forces' wrote the cooperative message down in statute. At best suspicious and at worst resentful of this legislative invasion into the

[109] *Tuttle v Buck*, 107 Minn. 145, 148; 119 N.W. 946, 947 (1909) (Supreme Court of Minnesota). This is one of the leading cases in the development of the prima facie tort doctrine (discussed in Chapter 7).

[110] 'The Paradoxes of Legal Science', in M. E. Hall (ed.), *Selected Writings of Benjamin Nathan Cardozo* (Matthew Bender, Albany, 1947), 262. See also a similar passage in Cardozo's famous Storrs Lectures entitled 'The Nature of the Judicial Process': ibid., 24–5. For commentary, see A. L. Kaufman, *Cardozo* (Harvard University Press, Cambridge, 1998), 214–15. Characteristically, Roscoe Pound is almost as glowing in his praise of this development and made the direct comparison with the French abuse of rights doctrine: R. Pound, *The Spirit of the Common Law* (Beacon Press, Boston, 1963 reprint; originally published in 1921), 184–6. (For a discussion of Pound's achievements as a Romanist, see M. H. Hoeflich, *Roman and Civil Law and the Development of Anglo-American Jurisprudence in the Nineteenth Century* (University of Georgia Press, Athens, 1997), 125–30.) For a somewhat similar discussion about the same time on the other side of the Atlantic, see C. K. Allen, 'Legal Morality and the *Ius Abutendi*' (1924) 40 LQR 164.

[111] See G. Stoner, 'The Influence of Social and Economic Ideals on the Law of Malicious Torts' (1910) 8 Mich LR 468.

common law domain, the English judges responded by narrowly construing the message.

The foundations of the common law laid in the last quarter of the nineteenth century remain, notwithstanding statutory modification or outright reversal. The legislative responses to the inadequacy of the common law or the perceived need to redistribute wealth and power have not penetrated the common law or changed the psyche of the common lawyer. Legal education continues to inculcate these common law values through the curriculum (what is taught, when and how, and by whom). That generations of law students have been exposed, in one way or another, to the 'leading case' of *Pickles* proves the point. The statutory provisions preventing that type of situation arising date back to the mid-1940s, and, if noticed at all, are scarcely likely to be accorded the epithet 'leading'. Indeed, the notion of 'leading legislation' is an oxymoron to the common lawyer.

For most of the twentieth century judges and lawyers have known far less about economics than their nineteenth-century predecessors, and this has arguably exacerbated the influence in the law of *laissez-faire* thought.[112] Moreover, the ideology of *laissez-faire* has never been simply an economic issue in any narrow sense. Indeed, as Patrick Atiyah pointed out, individualism in the nineteenth century was 'asserted most emphatically as a moral principle, and as a highly desirable principle to be observed in social and political reform'.[113] It was and is emblematic of liberty.[114]

The work of Tony Weir illustrates this point.[115] Few English lawyers know more about the abuse of rights doctrine than Weir; he co-authored an influential treatment of the topic in the mid-1960s, has translated German works touching on the subject, undertaken comparative law study, and more recently published a book on the cognate area of economic torts. The economic torts are largely beyond the scope of this work, but I think that Weir's views on that law can be fairly taken to reflect those of a person of a traditional bent to a doctrine of abuse of rights.[116]

112 Atiyah, above at note 70, 293–4 and 666.

113 Atiyah, ibid., 260.

114 The classic *cri de coeur* is F. A. Hayek, *The Road to Serfdom* (University of Chicago Press, Chicago, 1944).

115 See also Gutteridge, above at note 13, 43–4 and 45.

116 In much earlier work Weir said that if rights are generously defined there may be more need for a doctrine preventing abuse than if the rights are carefully qualified to begin with; the latter being characteristic of the common law system. As the English courts declare rights so restrictively he opined 'there is little need for an equitable temperance of their exercise'. See Catala and Weir, above at note 20, 237. Percolating waters may be exceptional, but in that limited sphere there does not appear to be any careful qualification of the rights.

The beauty of *Pickles* is that it simply involves property and is uncomplicated by contract, ruinous competition, or trade union disputes. However, the proposition that *Pickles* is famous for establishing—that a lawful act does not become unlawful due to the (bad) motive of the person so acting—was reiterated in and applied to unfair competition and trade union boycott cases around the same time. The leading case is *Allen v Flood*.[117] There the House of Lords, comprising several of the Law Lords who sat on *Pickles*, held that there was no cause of action against a defendant who wilfully did an act with the intention of harming the plaintiff and succeeded in doing so. For liability to arise the act of the defendant had to be unlawful, which it was not in that case. 'That decision established it as law in England, that one is free to cause deliberate economic harm to another—whatever one's motive—provided that the means one employs are not unlawful in themselves.'[118] The decision has few supporters today, but Tony Weir is one. He wants to hold the line at inducing breach of contract as that is clearly unlawful, and deprecates modern extensions of that tort to embrace prevention of performance where there is no breach of contract.[119]

Weir's objections could equally be written about a doctrine of abuse of rights.[120] They relate to uncertainty in the law and the 'gross restriction on liberty' that a rule punishing behaviour which is not unlawful would have.[121] Using as a foil the German Civil Code provision that a person may not deliberately cause harm to another in a manner repugnant to good morals,[122] Weir indicates that it has given rise to 'an awesome amount of litigation', created uncertainty as to what amounts to 'immorality', and given rise to suspicion of judicial subjectivity.[123] In

117 [1898] AC 1. See also *Mogul Steamship Co. v McGregor Gow & Co.* [1892] AC 25 (HL).

118 T. Weir, *Economic Torts* (Clarendon Press, Oxford, 1997), 21.

119 Weir, ibid., 37–8; tilting at *Torquay Hotel Co. v Cousins* [1969] 1 All ER 522 (CA) and *Merkur Island Shipping v Lawton* [1983] 2 All ER 189.

120 See A. Gambaro, 'Abuse of rights in civil law tradition' (1995) 4 Eur. Rev. of Private Law 561; reprinted in A. M. Rabello (ed.), *Aequitas and Equity: Equity in Civil Law and Mixed Jurisdictions* (The Harry & Michael Sacher Institute for Legislative Research and Comparative Law, The Hebrew University of Jerusalem, Jerusalem, 1997), 632.

121 Weir, above at note 118, 38. See also T. Weir, *A Casebook on Tort* (Sweet & Maxwell, London, 1996), 600: '[*Allen v Flood*] holds that, whatever morality may say, in law one is free to beggar one's neighbours provided one neither does anything unlawful one's self nor gets anyone else to do anything unlawful.'

122 This is one of three provisions in the German Civil Code referred to in German abuse of rights cases: see Herman, above at note 26, 747–8. The German abuse of rights case law has been said to differ from that of the French courts in that the former focuses on the reasonableness of the act/result, whereas the latter focuses more on the subjective intention or behaviour: Voyame, Cottier, and Rocha, above at note 6, 32 and 35. Several of the critics of *Pickles* have pointed to the German example with approval: A. L. Goodhart, *Essays in Jurisprudence and the Common Law* (Cambridge University Press, Cambridge, 1931), 36–7.

123 Above at note 118, 50–5. Cf. Goodhart, above at note 122 (deploring the immortality of the law that allows someone to injure another intentionally without legal liability, and

concluding that the economic torts should not be extended to cover deplorable but lawful conduct (as the German, French, and American courts have done), Weir said:[124]

> There is the claim of freedom, the freedom to act badly, *le droit de nuire*. Provided that it is kept within limits, as it is by prohibiting illegal conduct, it is surely rather a desirable thing. The freedom to act virtuously is hardly worth fighting for. . . .
>
> [O]ne must ask whether our courts will readily accept and properly perform the role of determining whether conduct is moral or not. If equity is not a court of conscience, surely the common law should not be. . . .
>
> I end with a reminder of two matters already harped on. The first is the freedom aspect. It is not only that people must be able to know what the limits on their freedom are, but also that if the rules are loose, more suits will be brought and more defendants will have to answer. . . .
>
> But I do believe that in the economic sphere where some deliberate harm may unquestionably be caused, not just in self-defence as in the physical sphere but for self-aggrandizement, the common law should not, unless the law itself has outlawed the means used, impose liability; liberty of action should not be restrained by vaguer criteria, however inspiring their formulation.

Lord Macnaghten did not put the case better.

It is not my purpose here to argue that the common law should develop an abuse of rights doctrine,[125] or that such a doctrine should be introduced by statute, such as protection of moral rights has been in recent intellectual property legislation in many common law jurisdictions. Considerably more work would need to be done, both in understanding how the doctrine has operated across countries, cultures, and time, and in undertaking a cost/benefit analysis of 'transplantation' in the common law. Often such transplants do not take, mutate unexpectedly, or simply irritate.[126] It is, nevertheless, ironic that some common law jurisdictions seem poised to give birth to a generalized abuse of rights doctrine[127] at just the time when the ubiquitous modern doctrine is being diagnosed by some civilian scholars as terminally ill.[128]

commenting that 'sooner or later the English law will have to be changed' in line with the German Code).

[124] Ibid., 72, 74, and 76–7. *Accord*, Gambaro, above at note 120, 632, 644.

[125] Perillo has drawn on the following developments to demonstrate that American law now recognizes a doctrine of abuse of rights: abusive discharge of at-will employees, non-employment cases of retaliation, threat to the exercise of a right as duress, bad faith in the performance of a contract, abusive refusal to consent to the assignment of a lease or franchise, abusive terminations of contracts, bad faith in enforcement of a contract, abuse of rights as a crime, and a miscellany of abuse of rights cases. See J. M. Perillo, 'Abuse of Rights: A Pervasive Legal Concept' (1995) 27 Pacific LJ 37.

[126] See G. Teubner, 'Legal Irritants: Good Faith in British Law or How Unifying Law Ends Up in New Divergences' (1998) 61 MLR 11.

[127] See Perillo, above at note 125.

[128] See, e.g., Gambaro, above at note 120.

My interest in the abuse of rights doctrine lies in the reasons why the common law rejected it, and in the light this sheds on the different starting points of private law and public law. As Joseph Vining said once, 'we tend to forget how channeled we are by nothing more than a conceptual structure'.[129] The power of legal classification over the common law mind is often under-estimated.[130]

[129] J. Vining, *Legal Identity: The Coming of Age of Public Law* (Yale University Press, New Haven, 1978), 24.

[130] See G. Alexander, 'The Transformation of Trusts as a Legal Category, 1800–1914' (1987) 5 *Law & History Review* 303.

7

Malice and the Law of Torts

For a 20-year period spanning the turn of the twentieth century, the place of malice in the law of torts was a matter of considerable legal interest. It was a fashionable topic of conversation on both sides of the Atlantic at a time (regrettably long since passed) when British and American lawyers spoke much the same language and listened to one another.[1]

Sir Frederick Pollock

The English side of this exchange began with the pioneering work of Sir Frederick Pollock on *The Law of Torts*, first published in 1887.[2] The debt to American law is amply noted in the preface, which took the unusual form of an open letter to his friend, Justice Holmes (then of the Supreme Judicial Court of Massachusetts).[3] The influence of Holmes's theorizing can be seen in Pollock's tripartite division of the subject into causes of action based on intentional conduct, negligent conduct, and strict liability.[4] The book's just claim to fame is that it is the first English textbook to attempt to uncover the underlying principles of the subject and to

[1] See generally R. A. Cosgrove, *'Our Lady the Common Law': An Anglo-American Legal Community, 1870–1930* (New York University Press, New York, 1987). A legal commentator with an impeccable Anglo-American pedigree observed the 'parting of the ways' in 1930: A. L. Goodhart, 'Case Law in England and America' (1930) 15 Cornell LQ 173, 193. Goodhart was Editor of the *Law Quarterly Review* from 1926 to 1975. For a brief but insightful analysis of the rift, see R. Stevens, 'Basic Concepts and Current Differences in English and American Law' (1985) 6 J of Legal Hist 336. The fact that much of the debate about the place of malice in the law of torts took place in the pages of the *Law Quarterly Review* and the *Harvard Law Review* itself is noteworthy. The establishment of those reviews is symptomatic of the emergence of a modern, university-based academic professionalism. Peter Birks has pointed to the establishment of these Reviews (LQR (1885), Harv LR (1887)) as '[t]he beginning, or perhaps the end of the beginning' of 'serious and sustained thought about the common law': 'The Concept of a Civil Right', in D. G. Owen (ed.), *Philosophical Foundations of Tort Law* (Clarendon Press, Oxford, 1995), 31, 32, n. 5, and accompanying text.

[2] F. Pollock, *The Law of Torts: A Treatise on the Principles of Obligations Arising From Civil Wrongs in the Common Law* (Stevens & Sons, London, 1887).

[3] Ibid., v. The friendship began in 1874 and continued for the rest of their lives. See S. M. Novick, *Honorable Justice: The Life of Oliver Wendell Holmes* (Little, Brown & Co., Boston, 1989), 145–6.

[4] See K. J. Vandevelde, 'A History of Prima Facie Tort: The Origins of a General Theory of Intentional Tort' (1990) 19 Hofstra LR 447, 447–8 (hereafter referred to as 'Vandevelde I').

present a *Law* of *Torts*, rather than a collection of 'heterogeneous instances'.[5] Accordingly, the book was divided into two parts. The first part (headed 'General Part') dealt with generic principles—principles of liability, persons affected by torts, general immunities from tortious liability, and remedies. The second and longer part dealt with 'Specific Wrongs'.

Pollock began the second chapter (entitled 'Principles of Liability') with these words: 'There is no express authority that I know of for stating as a general proposition of English law that it is a wrong to do wilful harm to one's neighbour without lawful justification or excuse.'[6] Nevertheless, Pollock had no doubt that the law of torts had evolved to the stage where this abstract statement of principle was true. He saw as symmetrical fault-based causes of action and those based on intentionally inflicted harm. The positive duty to avoid causing negligent harm to others (negligence) was matched by the 'negative duty of not doing wilful harm' (intentional torts).[7] Both sets of duties were subject to necessary exceptions.[8] The emphasis was on duties rather than rights, again echoing Holmes.[9]

In his list of immunities (exceptions) from civil liability, Pollock included 'exercise of common rights'. He noted that any activity can cause loss or harm to others, but some activities are so desirable or commonplace that any loss caused is justified in law and does not occasion liability. The matter is *damnum sine injuria* (loss befalling a person without any legal wrong being done).[10] The examples given were loss of business caused by entry of a new business competitor, and harm to neighbours caused by the ordinary use of one's own land. As regards the latter, Pollock relayed the holdings of 'the leading cases' of *Acton v Blundell* and *Chasemore v Richards*. A little later he referred to Lord Wensleydale's dictum in *Chasemore*'s case that malice was not relevant to the common law; observing that while his Lordship cited no authority for that view, it reflected 'the general sense of English lawyers'.[11] This was contrasted with the Roman doctrine of *animus vicino nocendi* to

[5] Above at note 2, vi–vii.

[6] Ibid., 21.

[7] Ibid., 22.

[8] Idem.

[9] See generally Vandevelde I, 456–7 and 467. For Holmes, '[t]ort law consisted of a set of duties not to injure another imposed by government for reasons of public policy': ibid., 467. For discussion of the 19th-century debate over whether to have a jurisprudence of rights or of duties, see M. J. Horwitz, *The Transformation of American Law, 1870–1960: The Crisis of Legal Orthodoxy* (Oxford University Press, New York, 1992), 153–6.

[10] Ibid., 130. Pollock deprecated the conclusory tendency of such phrases, but correctly pointed out their long-standing usage: Vandevelde I, 462.

[11] Ibid., 136; citing for this last point Markby, *Elements of Law*, section 239, pp. 119–20. (For further details, see Appendix, note 11.)

some extent relied on in *Acton*'s case and followed in Scotland.[12] Pollock concluded:[13]

[Authorities on the law of Scotland] say that an owner using his own land must act not 'in mere spite or malice, *in aemulationem vicini*'. There seems on principle to be much to commend it. Certainly it would be no answer to say, as one is inclined to do at first sight, that the law can regard only intentions and not motives. For in some cases the law does already regard motive as distinct from purpose or intention, as in actions for malicious prosecution, and in the question of privileged communications in actions for libel. And also this is really a matter of intention. The motives for a man wishing ill to his neighbour in the supposed case may be infinite: the purpose, the contemplated and desired result, is to do such and such to him, to dry up his well, or what else it may be. If our law is to be taken as Lord Wensleydale assumed it to be, its policy must rest simply on the balance of expediency. *Animus vicino nocendi* would be very difficult of proof, at all events if proof that mischief was the only purpose were required (and it would hardly take less): and the evil of letting a certain kind of churlish and unneighbourly conduct, and even deliberate mischief, go without redress (there being no reason to suppose the kind a common one), may well be thought less on the whole than that of encouraging vexatious litigation. In Roman law there is nothing to show whether, and how far, the doctrine of Ulpian and Marcellus was found capable of practical application. I cannot learn that it had much effect in the law of Scotland. It seems proper, however, to point out that there is really no positive English authority on the matter.

So Pollock sat uneasily on the fence; the powerful pull of principle from Roman law was counteracted by the drag of pragmatic concerns. An important point, which relates to an earlier discussion, is that Pollock

[12] Ibid., 136–8. The running head at the top of these pages reads 'Malicious Exercise of Rights?'. On Scots law, see Chapter 6. Neil Duxbury points out that '[a]lthough adept as a Roman lawyer, Pollock often argued that the value of Roman law to those working within the common law tradition was distinctly limited': 'When We Were Young: Notes in the *Law Quarterly Review*, 1885–1925' (2000) 116 LQR 474, 487. A different picture is painted by Richard Cosgrove, who says that Pollock turned to Roman law at the behest of his pupil-master (the later Lord Lindley), and quotes Pollock as saying that thorough familiarity with Roman law throws 'a light without price on the dark places of our own doctrine'. See Cosgrove, above at note 1, 142. In his autobiography, Sir Frederick Pollock recalled that Lindley 'encouraged me to make some study of Roman law': *For My Grandson: Remembrances of an Ancient Victorian* (John Murray, London, 1933), 168.

[13] Ibid., 137–8. A consideration of Pollock's more general jurisprudential writings suggested to one writer that Pollock believed in natural right and viewed property rights as absolute, rather than relative. See R. G. Bone, 'Normative Theory and Legal Doctrine in American Nuisance Law: 1850–1920' (1986) 59 SCal LR 1101, 1120–1. That view does not sit very comfortably with the passage quoted in the text. The quoted passage was echoed 90 years later in Lord Reid's consideration of the common law principle that motive is irrelevant to civil liability: 'If we think that letting in proof of such motive as relevant would open the door to vexatious litigation against honest men, then policy would require us to support the principle. But otherwise there seems to me to be room for some fundamental rethinking about this principle of jurisprudence.' See J. S. C. Reid, 'The Law and the Reasonable Man' (1968) 54 *Proceedings of the British Academy* 189, 198.

viewed this still as an open (i.e. unsettled) question of English law.[14] That was not the way the judges in *Pickles* portrayed the issue.[15]

Despite the then-prevailing rule that the works by living authors were not authoritative,[16] Pollock was a major figure in the law in England.[17] His contemporary reputation among bench and bar was enormous.[18] Over the period of relevance to this study, Pollock was the Professor of Jurisprudence at Oxford, and authored several influential works. Moreover, he was a prime mover in establishing the *Law Quarterly Review* (which he edited from 1884 until 1919), edited the Revised Reports (a reprint of all the law of practical utility reported between 1785 and 1865), and became Editor in Chief of the Law Reports in 1895.

By the time the Pickles litigation reached the House of Lords, Pollock's treatise on *Torts* was in its fourth edition. The passage quoted above remained unchanged in any important respect, except that North J.'s following of Lord Wensleydale's dictum in *Pickles* was noted. More generally, since the first edition Pollock's theory of intentional torts had garnered the support of Lord Justice Bowen.[19] Ultimately that was to

[14] See Note, (1895) 11 LQR 108.

[15] See Chapter 5.

[16] On this rule of etiquette, which persisted well into the twentieth century, see P. Birks, 'Adjudication and Interpretation in the Common Law: A Century of Change', in B. S. Markesinis (ed.), *The Clifford Chance Lectures: Volume 1—Bridging the Channel* (Oxford University Press, Oxford, 1996), 135; I. Fletcher, 'An English Tragedy: The Academic Lawyer as Jurist', in T. M. Charles-Edwards, M. E. Owen, and D. B. Walters (eds), *Lawyers and Laymen: Studies in the History of Law Presented to Professor Dafydd Jenkins on his seventy-fifth birthday* (University of Wales Press, Cardiff, 1986), 316; K. G. C. Reid, 'The Third Branch of the Profession: The Rise of the Academic Lawyer in Scotland', in H. L. MacQueen (ed.), *Scots Law into the 21st Century: Essays in Honour of W. A. Wilson* (W. Green/Sweet & Maxwell, Edinburgh, 1996), 39; B. M. Komar, 'Textbooks As Authority in Anglo-American Law' (1922–3) 11 Cal LR 397; N. Duxbury, *Judges & Jurists: An Essay on Influence* (Hart Publishing, Oxford, 2001), 62–84. For a view that the convention appeared abruptly in the late nineteenth century and might well have been directed against the writings of Sir Frederick Pollock, see D. Pugsley, '*London Tramways* (1898)' (1996) 17 J Leg Hist 172, 172–4.

[17] '[Pollock's] writings were cited in court probably more than any other writings in their author's lifetime. They could claim, in Lord Wright's words, a place in the category of unwritten law': O. Hood Phillips, 'Legal Authors since 1800', in *Then and Now, 1799–1974: Commemorating 175 years of Law Bookselling and Publishing* (Sweet & Maxwell, London, 1974), 3, 23. Cf. Pugsley, above at note 16.

[18] Walker describes Pollock as 'outstandingly successful as a writer', but 'a poor lecturer who drew small audiences': D. M. Walker, *Oxford Companion to Law* (Clarendon Press, Oxford, 1980), 967. In the text I have drawn on this source and Gareth Jones' entry on 'Pollock, Sir Frederick' in A. W. B. Simpson, *Biographical Dictionary of the Common Law* (Butterworths, London, 1984), 421–3. See generally N. Duxbury, 'When We Were Young: Notes in the *Law Quarterly Review*, 1885–1925' (2000) 116 LQR 474, and S. Hedley, 'Sir Frederick Pollock and the Teaching of English Law', in J. A. Bush and A. Wijffels (eds), *Learning the Law: Teaching and the Transmission of Law in England, 1150–1900* (Hambledon Press, London, 1999), 407.

[19] See *Mogul Steamship Co. v McGregor, Gow & Co.* (1889) 23 QBD 598, 613–14 (CA) (decision affirmed on appeal, [1892] AC 25 (HL)); *Skinner & Co. v Shew & Co.* [1892] 1 Ch 413, 422, *per* Bowen L.J.; *Ratcliffe v Evans* [1892] 2 QB 524, 527–8, *per* Bowen L.J. (See further, Appendix, note 12.)

count for naught in Great Britain, but Bowen's dicta were much relied on in American jurisdictions.[20]

Oliver Wendell Holmes

On the American side the first shot was fired in the *Harvard Law Review* by none other than Oliver Wendell Holmes Jr, the doyen of American lawyers.[21] Holmes doubted the dogma that motive is always irrelevant to civil liability, and set out to show the relevance of malice in methodological terms.[22] Holmes began by referring to the 'familiar' example of the landowner using his land in some way harmful to a neighbour. Leaving to one side 'malice', Holmes considered the grounds upon which a person who is found objectively to intend to inflict harm on another can escape liability. Generally the former would be held liable unless he had acted 'with just cause'. Holmes denominated such justification a 'privilege'.[23] The extent of the privilege is a question of policy, and therefore a legislative question, 'and judges are shy of reasoning from such grounds'.[24] But when faced with such questions, as inevitably they would be, the judges were enjoined to eschew generalities and look at the particular circumstances.

To illustrate the point that 'privilege' may be recognized for very different reasons in different circumstances, Holmes discussed three instances: a person setting up a rival shop in a village big enough to support only one such shop, intent on ruining the existing business; a person building a house in such a way as to blight a neighbour's view; and an employer giving an honest but critical reference for an employee putting off a potential employer. Holmes described these as 'rights' as well as 'privileges',[25] and alluded to the reasons supporting each. Of particular relevance here is his discussion of the blighted view scenario:[26]

[20] It was one of only two cases that Oliver Wendell Holmes cited for his theory of intentional torts: Holmes, 'Privilege, Malice, and Internet' (1894) 8 Harv LR 1, 2–3. The other case was *Walter v Cronin*, 107 Mass. 555 (1871). See also *Aikens v Wisconsin*, 195 US 194, 204 (1904), *per* Holmes J. Much later, it also had an impact on the High Court of Australia in *Beaudesert Shire Council v Smith* (1966) 120 CLR 145. The action on the case for intentionally causing economic loss, recognized in that case, was a far cry from the American prima facie tort doctrine. Even that was too radical, however, and recently the High Court repudiated the *Beaudesert Shire* principle: *Northern Territory of Australia v Mengel* (1996) 185 CLR 307. And, more recently still, reaffirmed rejection of a prima facie tort doctrine: *Sanders v Snell* (1998) 196 CLR 329.

[21] Holmes, ibid.

[22] This is made clear repeatedly throughout the article: see ibid., esp. 14.

[23] Ibid., 3. [24] Idem. [25] Idem. [26] Ibid., 3–4.

[This rests] upon the fact that a line must be drawn between the conflicting interests of adjoining owners, which necessarily will restrict the freedom of each; upon the unavoidable philistinism which prefers use to beauty when considering the most profitable way of administering the land in the jurisdiction taken as one whole; upon the fact that the defendant does not go outside his own boundaries; and upon other reasons to be mentioned in a moment . . .

Some privileges are spoken of as if they were absolute. . . . For instance, in any common case, apart from statutory exceptions, the right to make changes upon or in a man's land is not affected by the motive with which the changes are made. Were it otherwise, and were the doctrine carried to its logical conclusion, an expensive warehouse might be pulled down on the finding of a jury that it was maintained maliciously, and thus a large amount of labor might be wasted and lost. Even if the law stopped short of such an extreme, still, as the motives with which the building was maintained might change, the question would be left always in the air. There might be other and better reasons than these and those mentioned before, or the reasons might be insufficient. I am not trying to justify particular doctrines, but to analyze the general method by which the law reaches its decisions.

Holmes went on, as the logic of his argument required, to take up the issue of malice, and had no doubt that in some circumstances malice would properly mark the limit of the privilege. Malice was defined as 'a malevolent motive for action, without reference to any hope of a remoter benefit to oneself to be accomplished by the intended harm to another'.[27] Despite the inconclusiveness of the above quotation, the distinct impression left is that the privilege attaching to the exercise of real property rights is absolute, and untempered by malice.[28] This is confirmed in Holmes's correspondence with Frederick Pollock, where he said that 'the nature of the motive may make all the difference, and the fact that motive makes no difference to land, has absolutely no bearing on the case of giving a character to a servant or destroying a man's business'.[29] It is also found in his judicial opinions.[30]

27 Ibid., 2.

28 This is a view found also in his earlier work, *The Common Law* (Brown & Little, Boston, 1881), 144.

29 M. de W. Howe (ed.), *The Pollock–Holmes Letters: Correspondence of Sir Frederick Pollock and Mr Justice Holmes, 1874–1932* (Cambridge University Press, Cambridge, 1942), vol. 1, 110. See also O. W. Holmes, 'Law in Science and Science in Law', in O. W. Holmes, *Collected Legal Papers* (New York, 1920), 210.

30 Holmes J. in *Aikens v Wisconsin*, 195 US 194, 204 (1904) said, 'it is obvious that justifications may vary in context, according to the principle of policy upon which they are founded, and that while some—for instance, at common law, those affecting the use of land are absolute (*Bradford v Pickles* [1895] AC 587), others may depend upon the end for which the act is done'. An early spite fence case in Massachusetts contains dicta by Holmes J. that support the view that he believed 'the power to use one's own property malevolently, in any way which would be lawful for other ends, is an incident of property . . .': *Rideout v Knox*, 148 Mass. 368, 372 (1889). It should be noted that Holmes J. did refer to the common law right to put up a fence for malevolent purposes as 'quasi accidental'!: ibid., 374.

Holmes's recognition of malice is at odds with his famous advocacy in *The Common Law*[31] of the 'external standard' of liability. By 'external' he meant that liability was incurred regardless of the motives of the actor, whether good or evil, and imposed if the danger of harm was foreseeable by a reasonably prudent person.[32] Vandevelde has shown convincingly that between the publication of *The Common Law* in 1881 and his 1894 essay, Holmes changed his mind on the irrelevance of actual motives in relation to intentional torts.[33] In his 1894 essay Holmes assumed that 'we have got past the question which is answered by the test of the external standard'; namely, that it is accepted 'that the manifest tendency of the defendant's act is to inflict temporal damage upon the plaintiff'.[34] Upon that assumption Holmes moved to assert that the intentional infliction of temporal damage is actionable unless done with just cause ('privileged'),[35] and that the defendant's actual motives could be relevant in determining the justification for the conduct.[36]

Note that Holmes disavowed any requirement that the action be unlawful. As we have seen, whether the action was 'privileged', or good cause made out, was a question of policy for the courts to resolve in all the circumstances. H. L. Pohlman has drawn attention to the debt Holmes owed the utilitarians—particularly Jeremy Bentham and John Austin—in fashioning a general theory of legal liability. But, as Pohlman helpfully explains, Holmes parted company with them over the necessity for the act to be unlawful:[37]

> the resemblances hide an important difference between Holmes' theory of legal liability and the utilitarians'. Both theories emphasised the factual tendency of the act (as opposed to the nature of the will), but the utilitarians required more for legal liability. According to them, an agent was not punished no matter the tendency of his act, unless he violated another person's legal right. The utilitarian

[31] Above at note 28.

[32] For a discussion of Holmes's external standard of liability, see H. L. Pohlman, *Justice Oliver Wendell Holmes & Utilitarian Jurisprudence* (Harvard University Press, Cambridge, 1984), ch. 2. The important point here is that Holmes's theory of tort law was that liability is imposed on grounds of public policy, rather than based on blameworthiness or subjective fault. See Vandevelde I, 458.

[33] K. J. Vandevelde, 'The Modern Prima Facie Tort Doctrine' (1991) 79 Kentucky LJ 519, 533–4 (hereafter referred to as 'Vandevelde II'). See also M. J. Horwitz, above at note 9, 132–3; M. J. Horwitz, 'The Place of Justice Holmes in American Legal Thought', in R. W. Gordon (ed.), *The Legacy of Oliver Wendell Holmes, Jr.* (Stanford University Press, Stanford, 1992), 31, 55–64; G. E. White, *Justice Oliver Wendell Holmes: Law and the Inner Self* (Oxford University Press, Oxford, 1993), 215–18 and 282. In his earlier article, Vandevelde shows that Holmes's belated recognition of the legal relevance of malice not only qualified his earlier position but problematically undercut his earlier theoretical aspirations: Vandevelde I, 475–6.

[34] Above at note 20, 2. [35] Ibid., 3. [36] Ibid., 5–6.

[37] Above at note 32, 45–6; quoting in support from O. W. Holmes, 'The Path of the Law' (1897) 10 Harv LR 457, 471 (omitted from this quotation).

theory of legal liability required an illegal, overt act that caused injury before an intelligent, rash, or negligent agent could incur legal liability. No doubt this requirement was accepted tradition. Bentham's and Austin's contribution in the development of legal liability was to shift attention from the vicious will of the agent to the general tendency of the act. But none of the earlier utilitarians imagined that this tendency alone sufficed for liability. The act must also be prohibited.

This was the requirement Holmes abandoned. By placing exclusive attention upon the tendency of the act, Holmes thought it possible to arrive at the simplest comprehensive theory of legal liability possible. . . . If the tendency or the danger of the act was manifest, then (but for a few exceptions and privileges) the agent was liable.

This is important not only in explaining Holmes's thought but also, perhaps, in shedding light on the thinking of the judges in cases like *Pickles* and *Allen v Flood*. Was the requirement of an unlawful act simply 'accepted tradition'—received by osmosis?[38] What part did positivism have to play in this? The requirement of unlawfulness before immoral behaviour becomes actionable is a line that a positivist would be not only comfortable drawing, but might also be compelled to draw.

Holmes was a positivist, but by the 1890s he had lost his earlier faith in formal conceptualization and embraced what Vandevelde calls 'a positivist instrumentalism'[39]—a belief that cases should be decided on policy grounds.[40] With such an open-ended theory of intentional tort, obviously much turned on what counted as justification. To Holmes this was an issue of policy pure and simple. Not surprisingly, then, given the subjectivity involved, Holmes often found himself at odds with his judicial colleagues when these issues arose in litigation. We have seen that Holmes believed that the rights of landowners should not be limited by such a tort, and so that ownership would be a justification for any harm inflicted on neighbours by digging in one's own land.[41] In contrast, he strongly favoured the right of organized labour to strike and picket peacefully, and held such behaviour justifiable in the cause of agitation for

[38] This throws some light on the extraordinary polarization in *Allen v Flood* as to the significance of *Keeble v Hickeringill* (as to which see the text accompanying notes 113–21 below). The judges were at odds over what was the true common law tradition.

[39] Vandevelde I, 496. On the changes in Holmes's thought, see Horwitz, above at note 9, 123–42. Cf. T. C. Grey, 'Holmes and Legal Pragmatism' (1988–9) 41 Stan LR 787, 816–26. As with every aspect of Holmes's thought, there is controversy over whether he lost his faith in conceptualization (however defined). For reference to additional readings on this see W. M. Treanor, 'Jam for Justice Holmes: Reassessing the Significance of *Mahon*' (1998) 86 Geo. LJ 813, 855, n. 253.

[40] On changes in Holmes's thinking as to the place of policy in the law, see M. Tushnet, 'The Logic of Experience: Oliver Wendell Holmes on the Supreme Judicial Court' (1977) 63 Va LR 975, 1044–49.

[41] There are also dicta to this effect in the American case law. See, e.g., *Plant v Woods*, 176 Mass. 492, 499; 57 NE 1011, 1014 (1900).

better pay and conditions.[42] Needless to say, this was not a fashionable judicial viewpoint at the time.[43] In contrast, some courts were not prepared to take for granted (as Holmes had done) the immunity of landowners for digging for water on their own land.[44]

There is no reason to believe that any of the Law Lords who decided *Pickles* had read the recent part of the *Harvard Law Review* containing Holmes's essay; certainly it was not referred to in the arguments or speeches. The Anglophilic Holmes incessantly nurtured his intellectual links to England, but none of the Law Lords in the *Pickles* case appear to have been in correspondence with him. Neither was Holmes's interest and familiarity with academic work in England necessarily reciprocated by most English judges of that time.[45] Moreover, if Holmes's essay had been read by the judges who decided *Pickles*, one suspects the reaction would have been one of horror.[46] The cleaving of law and morality was designed to leave such policy matters to the legislature, not the courts. Holmes's treatment made explicit what was implicit in Pollock's textbook treatment—which would assuredly have been consulted by the judges who decided *Pickles*—that setting the limits on justification was for the judges and juries.

The doctrine Holmes argued for—that the intentional infliction of injury without justification is actionable in tort—became well established in the United States, where it goes by the name of prima facie tort.[47] There

[42] See *Vegelahn v Guntner*, 167 Mass. 92, 109; 44 N.E. 1077, 1081–2 (1896) and *Plant v Woods*, ibid., 504–5; 1016 (both dissenting judgments).

[43] Indeed, Holmes is reported to have told a neighbour that his well-publicized dissent in *Vegelahn v Guntner* (ibid.) shut out the possibility of judicial promotion. See D. J. Slepp, 'Chief Justice Holmes in the Science and Art (and Politics) of Judging' (1999) 5 *Massachusetts Legal History* 19, 26–7. Of course, it did no such thing, and in due course Holmes was appointed Chief Justice of the Supreme Judicial Court of Massachusetts (ibid., 29–30), and ultimately to the United States Supreme Court.

[44] See, e.g., dicta in the leading New York case of *Beardsley v Kilmer*, 236 N.Y. 80, 89–90; 140 N.E. 203, 205–6 (1923).

[45] For an insightful comparison between Holmes and the average English judge at the time, see P. S. Atiyah, 'The Legacy of Holmes Through English Eyes'(1983) 63 BULR 341, 377–82. Nor should we fall into the trap of thinking that Holmes was then as important a figure as he became by the 1920s. See P. D. Carrington, 'Law as "The Common Thoughts of Men": The Law-Teaching and Judging of Thomas McIntyre Cooley' (1997) 49 Stan LR 495, 499.

[46] A careful reader of Holmes's essay might have simply concluded that it did not apply to either the type of case or the particular facts in *Pickles*. As to the type of case, we have seen already that Holmes was strangely reluctant to deny the absolute nature of the rights of owners to use their land as they saw fit (see above at note 28). As to the particular facts, Holmes's definition of 'disinterested malevolence' was restricted to actions the sole purpose of which was to injure another without any benefit to the actor: above at note 21, 2, and *Aikens v Wisconsin*, above at note 30, 206. Holmes's version of prima facie tort doctrine did not apply in cases of mixed motivation, such as *Pickles*. This aspect of Holmes's approach (but not others) is faithfully recorded in New York prima facie tort law. See Vandevelde I, 485–91.

[47] See the excellent treatment in Vandevelde I.

are two competing modern formulations of the doctrine.[48] Under the dominant formulation in the *Restatement (Second) of Torts*, actual malice is only one of several factors to be weighed in determining the existence of justification,[49] whereas it is a requirement of the rival formulation long supported by the New York courts that the defendant must be solely motivated by malice.[50] The doctrine is a principal doctrinal vehicle for attacking malicious exercise of legal rights.[51]

Within a year of the appearance of Holmes's essay, the House of Lords in *Pickles* had slammed the door on any such development in British law. The cases subsequent to *Pickles* all involved trade competition, boycotts, and strikes; precisely the type of case where Holmes thought the proper balancing of factors would justify the infliction of economic harm by aggressive trade rivals or trade unionists.[52] Consequently, the prima facie tort doctrine never took hold in the United Kingdom and is virtually unheard of there.

The case Holmes had to meet in England had been put two years earlier in the pages of the *Law Quarterly Review* by Judge W. E. Ormsby of the High Court in Travancore, India.[53] Judge Ormsby's purpose was to eradicate the concept of malice from the law of torts. He pointed to its uncertain and variable meaning,[54] the difficulty of proving evil motive (especially in cases of mixed motivation), and to its anomalous character even in relation to the handful of minor torts in which it featured (namely, malicious prosecution, qualified privilege in defamation, inducing breach of contract, and slander of title). He concluded in no uncertain terms that malice should be legally irrelevant:[55]

Motive, which is all-important in morals, has properly no place in the law of Torts. The cases in which it has been ruled otherwise are admittedly exceptional, and it may be added more or less anomalous. The term malice, with all respect for certain *dicta* to the contrary, is in the last degree obscure and misleading. At first

[48] See generally Vandevelde II, 535, 537, and 540–3.

[49] See *Restatement (Second) of Torts* (American Law Institute, 1979), para. 870: 'one who intentionally causes injury to another is subject to liability to the other for that injury, if his conduct is generally culpable and not justifiable under the circumstances. This liability may be imposed although the actor's conduct does not come within a traditional category of tort liability.' Vandevelde points out that this formulation 'differs little' from that first penned by Pollock and Holmes: Vandevelde II, 528.

[50] See J. G. Duport, 'Disinterested Malevolence as an Actionable Wrong' (1953) 22 Fordham LR 185. This aspect of the New York formulation of the doctrine is much criticized and appears to stem from a misunderstanding of Holmes's position: Vandevelde II, 544.

[51] See G. Shapiro, 'The Prima Facie Tort Doctrine: Acknowledging the Need for Judicial Scrutiny of Malice' (1983) 63 BULR 1101.

[52] See above at note 20.

[53] W. E. Ormsby, 'Malice in the Law of Torts' (1892) 8 LQR 140. Holmes does not cite this article in his.

[54] See also D. A. Stroud, 'What is Malice?' (1898–99) 24 *The Law Magazine & Review* (5th ser) 341.

[55] Above at note 53, 149.

denoting hatred or personal ill-will, it loses by degrees its original meaning, till at last it reaches its vanishing point in its identification with 'intention' or 'knowledge'.

As Pollock had noted in his treatise, this was the prevalent professional opinion in England at the time.[56] The House of Lords put its stamp of approval on this stance in *Pickles*. As the House was then bound by its own decisions, the issue became academic in Great Britain; but the academics on the other side of the Atlantic did not let up.

The reaction of Sir Frederick Pollock demonstrates the closure of argument induced in English legal circles by the infallibility rule of precedent. In the next edition of his *Torts* treatise in 1897, Pollock acquiesced in the House of Lords' decision by excising all references to what principle might have required, and the promising line of Scottish authority was explained away as Lord Watson had done in *Pickles*.[57] The vacuum in English authority had been filled, and that was an end to the matter. And, for good measure, Pollock said '[t]he law is believed to be understood to the same effect in the United States.'[58]

Later American Discussion

The American law, however, was less settled than Pollock led his readers to believe. Attempting to rebut what he called the 'mischievous' dicta of Lords Watson and Macnaghten in *Allen v Flood*,[59] that motive is irrelevant to civil liability, James Barr Ames assembled considerable case law to show that in some circumstances motive was relevant.[60] As in Holmes's earlier treatment, the unfair competition and trade boycott cases were focal points. But, unlike Holmes, Ames saw no reason in public policy or the nature of real property rights to insulate exercise of such rights from tortious liability for maliciously imposed harm. Against the result in *Pickles*, Ames pitted the law in 13 of 15 American state jurisdictions, which were said to have held malevolent drainage of a neighbour's spring to sound in tort, as well as French and German authorities to like effect.[61]

56 See above at note 11 and accompanying text. Coincidentally the source of that opinion is Markby, who also wrote (initially) from India.

57 *The Law of Torts* (Stevens & Sons, London, 5th edn, 1897), 139–40. See also Pollock's editorial postscript to M. de Villiers, 'Nuisances in Roman Law' (1897) 13 LQR 387, 394, noting that except for the doctrine of *aemulatio vicini* there is 'a remarkable agreement between the Roman Law and the Common Law'.

58 Ibid., 140.

59 [1898] AC 1, 92 and 151, respectively.

60 J. B. Ames, 'How Far an Act may be a Tort because of the Wrongful Motive of the Actor' (1905) 18 Harv LR 411.

61 See the cases cited ibid., 414–15. Ames referred to 'a strange inconsistency in the

The comparative law aspect was fully examined a few years later, again in the pages of the *Harvard Law Review*.[62] F. P. Walton demonstrated that the abuse of right doctrine was well established in French law, and paid particular attention to the historical development of that doctrine in relation to the use of real property. This brought out clearly the contrast with *Pickles*. Furthermore, Walton saw more inconsistency in the American cases involving the malicious draining of springs than Ames had done.[63] In his conclusion Walton sought to align English law more closely with French law by changing the starting point of analysis. Rather than starting with the proposition that 'malice will not make a lawful act unlawful' (as in *Pickles* and *Allen v Flood*), Walton supported the alternative approach approved by Bowen L.J.[64] and Holmes J. that 'wilful damage done to another is actionable unless there is just cause or excuse'. This move away from the absolute nature of property rights (by definition, lawful) towards justification of the malicious exercise of those rights reflected a more general jurisprudential shift from right to duty.[65]

Walton used Holmes's methodology, but took it to its logical conclusion. No rights should a priori be sacrosanct; the degree of legal protection accorded each right had to be argued over and justified. As Holmes said in 1899:[66]

decided cases' because, in contrast to the state score card in relation to spite wells noted in the text, six out of the ten state courts which had considered the malevolent erection of spite fences had found against liability: ibid., 415. See also J. B. Ames, 'Law and Morals' (1908–9) 22 Harv LR 97, 111. On spite fences, see J. O'Meara and H. W. Santen, 'Legal Status of the Spite Fence in Ohio' (1928) 2 UCinn LR 164 and J. S. Freeland, 'Statutory Regulation of Spite Fences in American Jurisdictions' (1936–7) 25 Kentucky LJ 356. For useful comparative treatments of common law regulation of spite wells and spite fences, see Note, 'The Effect of Motive upon Actionability in the Exercise of Rights in Real Property—Spite Wells and Spite Fences' (1924–5) 11 Va LR 122 and R. T. Drukker, 'Spite Fences and Spite Wells: Relevancy of Motive in the Motive in the Relations of Adjoining Landownwers' (1938) 26 Cal LR 691. Ames is correct that the state courts showed more constancy in granting relief in spite well cases than in ones involving spite fences.

62 F. P. Walton, 'Motive as an Element in Torts in the Common and in the Civil Law' (1908–9) 22 Harv LR 501. Walton was an Englishman who had studied law at Oxford and Edinburgh. He taught first in Scotland, and from 1897 to 1914 was Dean of Law at McGill University, Quebec, Canada. He wrote extensively on Roman law, including a well-known book at the time entitled *Historical Introduction to Roman Law* (1906).

63 Ibid., 516 ('extreme'). In support, Walton refers to an article by Ames in (1892–3) 6 Harv LR 414. I think this must be a miscitation, as I cannot find anything by Ames there or thereabouts. However, in Ames's article in 1905 (referred to above at note 60) the vast majority of state courts to have considered the point were said to favour liability. The inconsistency Ames referred to was as between the courts' holdings in relation to malicious drainage and erection of spite fences: above at note 61.

64 Walton, above at note 62, 519: citing *Skinner & Co. v Shew & Co.* [1893] 1 Ch 413, 422, *per* Bowen L.J., and *Aikens v Wisconsin*, above at note 30, 204, *per* Holmes J.

65 Horwitz, above at note 9, 152–6.

66 'Law in Science and Science in Law', in O. W. Holmes, *Collected Legal Papers* (Peter Smith, New York, 1952), 210, 241.

If the scope of the right is already determined as absolute and irrespective of malice, *cadit quaestio*, there is nothing to argue about. So if all rights have that scope. But if different rights are of different extent, if they stand on different grounds of policy and have different histories, it does not follow that because one right is absolute, another is—and if you say all rights should be so, that is only a pontifical or imperial way of forbidding argument.

But, as noted earlier, Holmes viewed the right to dig for water on one's own land as absolute, regardless of motivation. In this respect Holmes did not apply his own methodology and never explained why policy and history demanded that this right be absolute in nature. He simply assumed that to be the case and moved on to issues like trade competition and union boycotts that interested him more. It fell to others, like Walton, to put the absolute right of ownership to the sword of policy and history. Increasingly, American courts refused to assume the absolute nature of ownership rights in relation to draining water and the erection of spite fences.[67]

The emphasis on policy rather than conceptualism and the shift in focus from rights to duties moved American courts increasingly to consider 'the social needs of the community'.[68] The American judges thought that this was an inevitable step in the forward march of civilization.[69] This was in marked contrast to the formalistic conception of adjudication prevalent in Britain.[70]

Economic Torts

Anyone who has occasion to wander into the field of economic torts learns quickly that the historical development has been rather haphazard and far from consistent.[71] The great but somewhat unloved case of *Allen v Flood*[72] sharply divided judicial opinion, and the ultimate result

67 The treatment of spite fences is a fascinating chapter in legal history. As we have seen, some of the leading French abuse of rights cases involved the spite fence scenario: above in Chapter 6. Spite fences case law and legislation are considered by both Ames and Walton in their articles.

68 *Tuttle v Buck*, 107 Minn. 145, 148; 119 N.W. 946, 947 (1909) (Supreme Court of Minnesota). This is one of the leading cases in the development of the prima facie tort doctrine. The Court held, relying in part on Pollock's treatise and dicta of Bowen L.J., that someone who conducted a business with the sole objective of destroying the business of another, without any interest in profiting himself, committed an intentional tort.

69 See, e.g., B. Cardozo, 'The Paradoxes of Legal Science', in M. E. Hall (ed.), *Selected Writings of Benjamin Nathan Cardozo* (Matthew Bender, Albany, 1947), 262.

70 See G. Stoner, 'The Influence of Social and Economic Ideals on the Law of Malicious Torts' (1910) 8 Mich LR 468.

71 See generally J. D. Heydon, *Economic Torts* (Sweet & Maxwell, London, 2nd edn, 1978).

72 [1898] AC 1. See T. Weir, *Economic Torts* (Clarendon Press, Oxford, 1997).

reflected the view of a minority of the judges who heard the case or advised upon it.[73] Much case law has followed, some of it not true to the spirit of the great case, and lines have been drawn which are difficult to defend. On these shifting sands the modern house of economic torts has been built. The temptation to be drawn into the fascinating history of the economic torts will be sternly resisted here. In what follows I will sketch only as much as is necessary to understand the choice made in *Allen v Flood*[74] not to recognize a tort of maliciously exercising rights. The result and the reasoning behind it 'harmonize[d] perfectly'[75] with *Pickles*. In *Allen*'s case the House of Lords not only affirmed its stance in *Pickles*, but also generalized it beyond those particular facts to include the exercise of other legal rights.[76]

Despite its longevity in the law, the term 'malice' has never acquired a settled meaning. Indeed, the extraordinarily large range of meaning—sliding from spite or ill will all the way to simply intentionally doing an action—was a regular cause of criticism whenever the term was used.[77] There were, however, cases that supported the view that a malicious motive or purpose rendered an otherwise lawful act unlawful.[78] By and large these early cases concerned actions on the case. The leading case in this group was at the forefront of the Bradford Corporation's argument before the House of Lords.[79]

[73] The case was decided by the House of Lords by a margin of six judges to three. All the judges below and six of the eight judges who were summoned to advise the House favoured liability. North J. was the only Chancery judge to be summoned, and he favoured liability. The judicial head count was 13:8 in favour of liability, but the minority position against liability prevailed in the House of Lords and became the law. For an intriguing discussion of the head count, see R. F. V. Heuston, 'Judicial Prosopography' (1986) 102 LQR 90.

[74] I am aware that this cuts off an interesting discussion of *Quinn v Leatham* [1901] AC 495 and the subsequent cases, but it is a digression.

[75] A. V. Dicey, Note (1902) 18 LQR 1.

[76] See D. Howarth, 'Is there a Future for the Intentional Torts?', in P. Birks (ed.), *The Classification of Obligations* (Clarendon Press, Oxford, 1997), 233, 263.

[77] See, e.g., W. Markby, *Elements of Law considered with reference to Principles of General Jurisprudence* (Clarendon Press, Oxford, 5th edn, 1896), sections 686–94, and G. H. L. Fridman, 'Malice in the Law of Torts' (1958) 21 MLR 484.

[78] *Bowen v Hall* (1881) 6 QBD 333, 338, *per* Brett L.J. (CA); *Temperton v Russell* [1893] 1 QB 715; *Flood v Jackson* [1895] 2 QB 21 (CA).

[79] There is no extant verbatim record of counsels' arguments before the House. The Official Law Report account is skimpy, covering less than a page, and, despite some minor variations, the record of argument in the other report series is no better. Reliance was placed first and foremost on *Keeble v Hickeringill* (below at note 81), for the proposition that 'a user which would otherwise be justifiable ceases to be so when the subject is to injure another': [1895] AC 587, 590. In a newspaper account of the argument Lord Halsbury L.C. is reported to have retorted: 'That is rather an alarming proposition'. See 'The Manywells Springs Dispute. The Case in the House of Lords. Judgment Reserved.', *The Bradford Observer*, Friday, 10 May 1895, p. 5.

Of Ducks, Rooks, and Grouse

The earliest cases involved duck decoys. To the modern eye, reference to a duck decoy is most likely to conjure up the image of replica ducks floating on a pond. But in the eighteenth century duck decoys were elaborate man-made ponds representing a considerable investment of money, time, skill, and ingenuity.[80] In *Keeble v Hickeringill*,[81] the defendant discharged a gun on his own land close to the plaintiff's decoy and frightened some of the ducks away. The allegation was that the defendant knew of the existence of the decoy and the fact that the plaintiff earnt his livelihood thereby, and created gunfire intending to damnify the plaintiff by driving the ducks away. The action on the case succeeded; the jury found the defendant guilty and awarded damages of £20. The Court of Queen's Bench upheld this award on appeal.[82]

The judgment of Holt C.J. puts great stress on the fact that duck catching via the decoy was the plaintiff's trade from which he derived profit. This was seen clearly as a property interest protectable by law from intentional injury. Not all intentional injury was actionable, however. The Chief Justice drew a distinction between this case and legitimate competition by the same method of capture. If the defendant had caused the same loss to the plaintiff's duck-catching business by the establishment of a rival decoy, that would not have been actionable. In modern language, the legitimate objective of competition in business would have justified the interference. The action seems then to have lain for hindering the plaintiff in the enjoyment of his trade.[83] Moreover, it was a trade of social benefit, ensuring the provision of food to markets, and hence to be encouraged.[84] The action was not to recover 'for the loss of the fowl, but

[80] See generally A. W. B. Simpson's fascinating account of the history of duck decoys in ch. 3—'The Timeless Principles of the Common Law: *Keeble v Hickeringill* (1707)'—of his *Leading Cases in the Common Law* (Clarendon Press, Oxford, 1995).

[81] (1707) 11 Mod. 73, 130; 88 E.R. 898, 945: 3 Salk. 9; 91 E.R. 659: Holt K.B. 14, 17, 19; 90 E.R. 906, 907, 908: W. Kel. 273; 25 E.R. 610. The spelling of the case name varies a good deal but I have used the generally accepted modern spelling.

[82] The case was argued twice before the Court. The first round of argument and discussion by the judges is reported at (1706) 11 Mod. 73, 88 E.R. 898; Holt K.B. 14, 90 E.R. 906 and Holt K.B. 17, 90 E.R. 906. It is not clear why the case was stood over to the next term for further argument. Holt C.J. alone is reported as expressing dissatisfaction with the case: (1706) 11 Mod. 73, 74, 88 E.R. 898. The arguments of counsel were couched in terms of property in the ducks. The comments of the judges, apart from the Chief Justice, centred on property in the ducks. The inference I draw is that the Chief Justice did not think the answer to this problem lay in property analysis.

[83] (1707) 11 Mod. 130, 131; 88 E.R. 945 ('in the nature of disturbing him from exercising his trade').

[84] Also duck decoy ponds 'bring money into the country' and hence are not unlawful: Holt K.B. 18, 18–19; 90 E.R. 907, 908.

for the disturbance' to trade.[85] In other words, the property interest at stake was not in the ducks but rather in the exercise of the duck catcher's profitable trade.

This account of the reasoning comes from Chief Justice Holt's manuscript account of the case he heard, attached as a note to another case reported a century later by the law reporter Sir Edward East. The contemporaneous reports of the case were incomplete and in poorly regarded law reports,[86] and hence East decided to publish for the first time Holt's manuscript version. What the manuscript version does not disclose, but which is adverted to in one of the four contemporaneous reports, is that there were two decoys.[87] Both the defendant and the plaintiff had decoys in operation on their own land in close proximity to each other. This sheds light on what occurred and Lord Holt's reaction to it. The obvious inference is that the defendant sought to disturb by gunfire ducks at the plaintiff's decoy in an attempt to destroy his competitor's business.[88] In other words, *Keeble v Hickeringill* is an early case of unfair competition.

Without the additional fact that both parties had decoys in close proximity, one could not be so sure as to the defendant's motivation. He might have been malevolent, or he might have been simply shooting ducks on his own land and inadvertently scared the ducks at the plaintiff's decoy. The additional facts make sense also of the allegation that the defendant's gunfire 'prevented' ducks from entering the plaintiff's decoy. They also give real point to Chief Justice Holt's discussion of competition. In the manuscript version of the judgment Holt discusses competition by another decoy in a hypothetical way. The hypothetical nature of that discussion carries over into the following, much-quoted extract:[89]

> This is like the case of 11 H. 4, 47. One schoolmaster sets up a new school to the damage of an ancient school, and thereby the scholars are allured from the old school to come to his new. (The action was held there not to lie.) But suppose Mr Hickeringill should lie in the way with his guns, and fright the boys from going to school, and their parents would not let them go thither; sure that schoolmaster might have an action for the loss of his scholars.

[85] (1809) 11 East 571, 578; 103 E.R. 1126, 1129.

[86] For caustic criticism of each set of reports, see J. W. Wallace, *The Reporters* (4th rev. edn, 1882), 387–8 (11 Mod.), 398–9 (Holt K.B.), 399–400 (Salk.), and 431 (W. Kel.).

[87] The fact that there were two duck decoys 'pretty near' each other is reported in the reports bearing Holt's name: (1707) Holt 14; 90 E.R. 906. (However, as Wallace pointed out, '[a] few of the cases *may* be from Lord Holt's manuscripts, but the book is not his': Wallace, above at note 86, 399.) The full story is told by Simpson, above at note 80. I have not availed myself of that wonderful account here because my purpose is to sketch the facts as they would have appeared to counsel and judges with nothing more to go on than the original reports and, after 1809, Lord Holt's published manuscript account.

[88] The other possibility is that the defendant hoped that the disturbed or diverted ducks would settle on his decoy, but that seems less likely given the close proximity of the decoys.

[89] Above at note 85, 576; 1128.

The rivalry between old and new schools is a very close analogy to that of two duck decoys.[90]

The legacy of the poor contemporaneous reporting of the case and the publication of the less-than-complete manuscript account a century later has been to cloud considerably the holding and the importance of the case. As we will see, it polarized judicial opinion in *Allen v Flood*. For the 13 judges who decided or advised in favour of liability in that case, *Keeble v Hickeringill* was viewed as a leading case, which had often been followed in spirit if not name. Whereas, for the eight judges who opposed visiting liability upon the trade-union official—which included a majority of the House of Lords—it was a rather ancient and awkward precedent which had been seldom followed, and was to be read down in order to conform with the then-prevailing spirit of the common law.

The merits of the next case, *Carrington v Taylor*,[91] also involving a duck decoy, were not so clear-cut.[92] The plaintiff owned an ancient decoy and he brought an action on the case against the defendant, a licensed fisherman who supplemented his income by shooting wild fowl from his boat. The defendant fired at ducks on a public river and the gunfire disturbed birds at the plaintiff's decoy some hundreds of yards away.[93] He did not fire into the decoy. On those facts the jury found the defendant guilty of wilfully disturbing the plaintiff's decoy and awarded damages of £2. The Court of King's Bench refused to disturb the verdict, referring to the 'old precedent' of *Keeble v Hickeringill*. Le Banc J. recalled that that case had been followed in one or two unidentified cases on the Norfolk circuit.[94] Once in possession of the full facts in *Keeble*'s case and Holt's manuscript judgment (the latter of which would not likely have been available to the Court), the distinguishing features between the two cases should have been obvious. No wonder this case was roundly condemned by some of the judges who took part in *Allen v Flood*.[95] Unless there was some special

90 In the passage Lord Holt does not describe who the gun-wielding Hickeringill is. The impression given is that he is an interloper. To make the analogy very close and that much more powerful, the gun-wielding Hickeringill should have been depicted as the master from the old school. From other reports of the case it is clear that this is what Holt C.J. intended. See (1707) 3 Salk. 9; 91 E.R. 659 and Holt K.B. 19; 90 E.R. 908, 909.

91 (1809) 11 East 571; 103 E.R. 1126. The case of *Tarleton v M'Gawley* (1793) Peake 270; 170 E.R. 153 is often cited in this series of cases, but for my purpose it adds little and it is omitted.

92 I say that on the basis of the reports. Once again Brian Simpson has shown that things may not have been what they seem, and that the true facts may have been much closer to those in *Keeble*'s case. See Simpson, above at note 80, 67–70.

93 The only indication from the reports that the defendant might have been acting other than innocently is that he fired a second time a little further down the river, after his first shot had disturbed a considerable number of birds.

94 See further Simpson, above at note 80, 65–7.

95 *Allen v Flood* [1898] AC 1, 20 (Hawkins J.: disagreeing with *Carrington*'s case despite approval of *Keeble*'s case), 103 (Lord Watson: 'a decision I venture to think that no English Court would at this day care to repeat'), 136 (Lord Herschell), and 169 (Lord Shand).

privilege which attached to ancient decoys and warded off disturbance in the surrounding area,[96] on the reported facts it is difficult to see what the defendant had done wrong or what right of the plaintiff had been infringed. We cannot know what impact the true facts of this case, unearthed by Brian Simpson nearly a century after *Allen v Flood*,[97] might have had on the judges' thinking about the place, if any, for malice in the law of torts. What we do know is that it made *Carrington v Taylor* an easy target and made it much easier to discredit the authority of *Keeble*'s case.

Hannam v Mockett[98] was much closer to the fact situation in *Keeble*'s case. There the defendant discharged guns close to his neighbour's property in order to drive away the rooks[99] that nested in the trees there. The plaintiff alleged that this behaviour deprived him both of the profitable opportunity to kill the birds and of enjoyment of their presence in his trees. At trial the plaintiff won an award of £10, but the Court of King's Bench reversed. The judges reasoned that the birds were not the plaintiff's property but were wild (unappropriated) animals, not protected from disturbance by common law or statute. The plaintiff had no economic right in relation to the birds that the law recognized, so the defendant was not attempting to deprive him of anything of legal consequence. In short, the plaintiff had a hope or expectation as to profit but nothing more.

There were several factors that appear to have influenced the decision. First, rooks were obviously not as valuable or as prized as ducks. Indeed, they are portrayed as a nuisance.[100] Although no one went so far as to characterize the defendant's actions as an abatement of nuisance, the judges seemed to sympathize with the defendant. Secondly, there was no evidence of any substantial investment in machinery etc., to lure or harvest the rooks, in contrast to the situation with duck decoys.[101] Thirdly, and relatedly, the plaintiff did not seem to be in a trade or established business. This seems to be the decisive difference. The focus in *Keeble*'s case was not on property in the unappropriated ducks attracted by the decoy. Rather, it was on the unjustified disturbance to the business. In the absence of a legally recognized business interest—which Lord Holt called 'property' at one point in *Keeble*'s case—the plaintiff had to claim a right in the disturbed birds. The law was against him on that point.

Nevertheless, in these cases involving disturbance to birds, arguments and dicta about degrees of proprietary interests are quite noticeable. This

[96] For discussion of ancient decoy, introduced by the trial judge, see Simpson, above at note 80, 69.

[97] See above at note 72.

[98] (1824) 2 B. & C. 934; 107 E.R. 629.

[99] A 'rook' is defined in the *Oxford English Dictionary* as '[a] black, raucous-voiced European and Asiatic bird . . . , nesting in colonies; one of the commonest of the crow-tribe, and in the north of Britain usually called a *crow*.'

[100] Above at note 98, 938; 630.

[101] Idem.

can be seen in *Ibbotson v Peat*.[102] There the plaintiff, who lived next to a grouse moor, put out food to attract the grouse from the moor on to his own property so that he could kill them. The moor owner's gamekeeper foiled this plan by setting off fireworks and frightening the birds away from the lure. The plaintiff sued in nuisance, and the defendant relied on the improper behaviour of the plaintiff to justify the action taken.

The Court of Exchequer found for the plaintiff. In argument, opposing counsel agreed that a landowner had 'a qualified property in the game whilst on his land',[103] but none of the judges directly addressed this property argument. Pollock C.B. said, in effect, that two wrongs do not make a right. If the defendant felt aggrieved by the plaintiff's action, he should have obtained redress in a lawful manner, and not taken the law into his own hands. The implication from the Chief Baron's judgment is that the plaintiff had done something unlawful in luring the grouse. In contrast, Baron Bramwell insisted that the plaintiff had done nothing wrong. All that was involved was good old competition. In the course of counsel's argument and again in his judgment, Bramwell B. cited *Chasemore v Richards* and drew the analogy of a neighbour digging in his own land and thereby draining a neighbouring well. In such an instance the only remedy of the neighbour is to dig his well deeper.[104] So, here, the defendant should have offered the grouse 'stronger inducements to return to his land'.[105] Martin B. thought that the case was covered by *Carrington v Taylor*. The remaining judge, Pigott B., simply concurred.

The tort of inducing breach of contract, which visits liability on a person who persuades another by unlawful means to breach a contract with a third party, emerged in the mid-nineteenth century. In the leading case, *Lumley v Guy*,[106] the concept of malice appeared in some of the formulations of when persuasion became unlawful. The requirement that the actionable inducement to breach of contract be 'malicious' meant only that the inducer was aware of the contract's existence. However, in *Bowen v Hall*[107] the Court of Appeal appeared to misinterpret this requirement, holding that the purpose of the inducer must be to injure the plaintiff or benefit himself at the plaintiff's expense.[108] Later cases of this sort placed great stress on the presence of a purpose to injure.[109] So much so that a

102 (1865) 3 H. & C. 644; 159 E.R. 684.

103 Ibid., 647–8; 686. This echoes Blackstone's analysis: see Chapter 5.

104 Ibid., 647 and 650; 686.

105 Baron Bramwell's besottment with *laissez-faire* ideology makes it impossible to suppress the image of the grouse being fed out of the invisible hand.

106 (1853) 2 El. & Bl. 749; 118 E.R. 749.

107 [1881] 6 QBD 333.

108 M. J. Klarman, 'The Judges versus the Unions: The Development of British Labour Law, 1867–1913' (1989) 75 Va LR 1487, 1518–19.

109 See *Temperton v Russell* [1893] 1 QB 715.

contemporary commentator said that by the mid-1890s the law seemed poised on the brink of accepting that malice (in the sense of intention to harm) did render otherwise lawful acts unlawful.[110] In *Allen v Flood* the House of Lords pulled back from the brink. There the House, comprising several of the Law Lords who sat on *Pickles*, held that there was no cause of action against a defendant who wilfully did an act with the intention of harming the plaintiff and succeeded in doing so. For liability to arise the act of the defendant had to be unlawful, which it was not in that case. As Tony Weir notes, *Allen v Flood* 'established it as law in England, that one . . . is free to cause deliberate economic harm to another—whatever one's motive—provided that the means one employs are not unlawful in themselves'.[111] Malice in and of itself does not give rise to a cause of action. The House of Lords not only affirmed its stance in *Pickles*, but also generalized it beyond those particular facts to include the exercise of other legal rights.[112]

The two cases discussed above, *Keeble v Hickeringill*[113] and *Carrington v Taylor*,[114] figured prominently in the argument in *Allen v Flood*. They were cited for the proposition that malice by itself constitutes a cause of action. In particular, stress was put on the general rule laid down by Chief Justice Holt in *Keeble*'s case: '[w]here a violent or malicious act is done to a man's occupation, profession or way of getting a livelihood; there an action lies in all cases.'[115] Although influential upon judges in the lower court and those advising the House, the majority there 'passed over [*Keeble*'s case] lightly'.[116] Lord Macnaghten did not find the earlier cases helpful, 'not even, I think, . . . the great case about frightening ducks in a decoy, whatever the true explanation of that decision may be'.[117] Lord Watson was unwilling to rely upon such an old authority unless it was directly on point and its principle had been acted upon.[118] He sought to show that neither condition was satisfied, by reading Holt's dictum as applying to unlawful acts and denigrating the result in the successor case, *Carrington v Taylor*.[119] To similar effect is the judgment of Lord Herschell, who added that if *Keeble*'s case really stood for this wide proposition then one would have expected it to be treated as a 'leading case', but it had not been so

110 J. H. Henderson, 'Malicious Motive as a Ground of Action' (1901) 13 Juridical Review 452, 453.

111 Weir, above at note 72, 21.

112 Howarth, above at note 76, 263.

113 Above at note 81.

114 (1809) 11 East 571; 103 E.R. 1126.

115 *Keeble v Hickeringill* (1809) 11 East 574, 576; 103 E.R. 1127, 1128.

116 E. Freund, 'Malice and Unlawful Interference' (1897–98) 11 Harv LR 449, 455.

117 Above at note 72, 153.

118 Ibid., 101.

119 Ibid., 101–3. Lord James abstained from reviewing the older authorities as that had been done by others, and was content to say that they did not 'establish more than that the interference which is itself unlawful constitutes a cause of action': ibid., 180.

treated.[120] Several Law Lords reinterpreted *Keeble v Hickeringill* as properly a nuisance case, and hence as irrelevant to the issue before the Court.[121]

What appeared to be lacking in *Keeble*'s case was a clear holding as to what legal right was infringed by the unneighbourly action. To the majority in *Allen*'s case there could be no legal wrong without infringement of a legal right, and a right to be protected against malicious action was altogether too vague.[122] In the Court of Appeal Lord Esher refused to define malice, saying in effect that it had an elephantine quality that any jury would be able to identify easily. That was anathema to Lord Herschell. To him, precise legal definition of the term was essential so that juries could be properly directed. It was abhorrent that a person might be found liable for behaviour that could not be precisely defined and hence avoided.

Many commentators have taken exception to the generality of the language in *Allen v Flood* and *Pickles* about the irrelevance of malice in English law.[123] Nevertheless, the House of Lords in these two cases aborted the embryonic prima facie tort doctrine in English law. Perhaps surprisingly this view quickly spread to Scotland. The similarity of developments in English and Scots law is noteworthy.

We have seen already that the Scottish doctrine of *aemulatio vicini* was clearly capable of developing into a general abuse of rights doctrine.[124] Lord Watson's error (unforgivable for a Scot) as to the scope of that doctrine in *Pickles*,[125] combined with the results and other reasoning in *Pickles* and *Allen*'s case—both cases were quickly followed in Scotland—retarded the development of an indigenous Scottish doctrine of abuse of rights.[126] South of the border the line of cases stemming from *Keeble v Hickeringill* had provided support for a tort of malicious injury. But, notwithstanding significant judicial support for such a doctrine, the

[120] Ibid., 132–6. Lord Shand agreed with the views of Lords Herschell and Watson on the older cases: ibid., 169.

[121] Ibid., 101 (Lord Watson), 133 (Lord Herschell), and 174 (Lord Davey).

[122] See the excellent discussion by Freund, above at note 116. In 1904, Henry Terry argued that the right interfered with in such cases was 'the right of pecuniary condition', which he defined as 'the protected position of fact being the holding of value or purchasing power in some form': 'Malicious Torts' (1904) 20 LQR 10, 14.

[123] See, e.g., J. F. Lever, 'Means, Motives, and Interests in the Law of Torts', in A. G. Guest (ed.), *Oxford Essays in Jurisprudence (First Series)* (Clarendon Press, Oxford, 1964), 50; G. L. Williams, 'The Foundation of Tortious Liability' (1941) 7 CLJ 111: J. Finnis, 'Intention in Tort Law', in Owen, above at note 1, 229, 237–42; G. H. L. Fridman, 'Motive in the English law of Tort' (1954) 40 Va LR 583, 586–8; G. H. L. Fridman, 'Malice in the Law of Torts' (1958) 21 MLR 484; Howarth, above at note 76, 263.

[124] See Chapter 6.

[125] See Chapter 6.

[126] J. M. Thomson, 'An Island Legacy—The Delict of Conspiracy', in D. L. Carey Miller and D. W. Meyers (eds), *Comparative and Historical Essays in Scots Law: A Tribute to Professor Sir Thomas Smith QC* (Butterworths & the Law Society of Scotland, Edinburgh, 1992), 137, 150–51. See also E. Reid, 'Abuse of Rights in Scots Law' (1998) 2 Edinburgh LR 129, 154–5.

majority in *Allen v Flood* turned its back decisively on any such tort. In both Scotland and England the law of nuisance was left to catch such malicious behaviour as it could.

Nuisance

Basically, nuisance is a tort against the land,[127] and the great majority of cases concern disputes between neighbours.[128] At its most basic, the law of nuisance restricts what one person can do on her land in order that her neighbour can enjoy the use of his land. The core of the nuisance doctrine is captured by the Latin phrase *sic utere tuo ut alienum non laedas* (use your own property in such a manner as not to injure that of another). Or, as that paragon of *laissez-faire* virtue, Baron Bramwell once remarked '[t]he convenience of such a rule may be indicated by calling it a rule of give and take, live and let live.'[129] The institution of property is supported by such limitations, to say nothing of the maintenance of social order.[130]

As with the economic torts, this is not the place for an extended discussion of nuisance. However, something must be said about nuisance for two reasons. First, malice does play a role in the law of nuisance. Secondly, and relatedly, it is sometimes supposed that the law of nuisance could have provided the answer to the Corporation's predicament in *Pickles*. *Keeble v Hickeringill*, reinvented as a nuisance-type case by some of their Lordships in *Allen v Flood*, is pointed to as a useful precedent in this regard.[131] But the law of nuisance did not avail the Corporation of Bradford, and it is important to know why.

It is one of the delightful accidents of legal history that six months prior to hearing the argument at first instance in *Pickles*, North J. decided *Christie v Davey*,[132] one of the leading cases on the relevance of malice in nuisance. It took North J. 11 months to render judgment in *Pickles*, a delay which Pickles' counsel thought was caused by the judge's futile search for authority against Pickles on the malice point.[133] It would be extraordinary if North J. had overlooked an authority that was right under his nose and pen. The same thing goes for Cozens-Hardy Q.C., who appeared in both cases. The fact is that neither North J. nor counsel saw the relevance of nuisance or *Christie v Davey* to the problem at hand in *Pickles*.[134] Nor did

[127] F. Newark, 'The Boundaries of Nuisance' (1949) 65 LQR 480, 489.

[128] J. R. L. Milton, 'The Law of Neighbours in South Africa' [1969] *Acta Juridica* 123, 129.

[129] *Bamford v Turnley* (1862) 3 B. & S. 62, 84; 122 E.R. 27, 33. See also *Cambridge Water Co. v Eastern Counties Leather plc* [1994] 2 AC 264, 299, *per* Lord Goff (HL).

[130] See M. R. Cohen, 'Property and Sovereignty' (1927–28) 13 Cornell LQ 8.

[131] See above at note 121 and accompanying text.

[132] [1893] 1 Ch 316.

[133] See Chapter 3.

[134] *Contra*, A. MacDonald, 'Hollywood Silver Fox Farm v Emmett' (1937) 2 Alberta LQ 99, 100 ('The most probable conclusion is that [*Christie v Davy*] was overlooked [in *Pickles*]').

any of the judges in the higher courts. The doctrinal reason for this is plain.[135]

Historically, nuisance cases, almost without exception, concerned the spread of something—be it odours, noise, water, gunshots, or whatever—from one property to another so as to interfere unreasonably with the use and enjoyment of the latter property.[136] What happened in *Pickles* was the prevention of something (there percolating water) which the neighbour had no right to receive escaping from one property to another.[137] *Pickles* stands for the proposition that it is not tortious in such circumstances to deprive someone of emanations from your property, even if maliciously motivated.

Of course, the law may yet develop beyond these confines. Technological developments have resulted in situations where signals and the like emanating from a distance, which a landowner desires to receive, are blocked or otherwise interfered with by a neighbouring property. These types of situations move closer to that in *Pickles*. The classic example is television reception, which was the subject of much discussion in *Hunter v Canary Wharf Ltd*.[138] The relevant aspect of this well-known case was whether the interruption of residents' television reception caused by the construction of a large tower on nearby land was capable of being a nuisance. Both the Court of Appeal and the House of Lords answered in the negative, on the basis that (absent an easement or statutory regulation) at common law an owner is free to build what she likes on her land and the neighbours can like it or lump it.[139] Moreover, Lord Goff said that 'for an action of private nuisance to lie in respect of interference with the plaintiff's enjoyment of his land, it will generally arise from something emanating from the defendant's land'.[140]

A quick word should be said about malice in the law of nuisance

[135] Gerry Cross has suggested that *Pickles* and *Christie v Davey* are irreconcilable unless there is a special rule in relation to maliciously inspired noise: 'Does only the careless polluter pay? A fresh examination of the nature of private nuisance' (1995) 111 LQR 445, 453–5. I disagree for the reasons given in the text. See also J. Wightman, 'Nuisance—the Environmental Tort? *Hunter v Canary Wharf* in the House of Lords' (1998) 61 MLR 870, 873, n. 16. My purpose here is simply to explain why nuisance was not considered relevant in *Pickles*, not to defend the policy behind the law.

[136] *Accord*, *Hunter v Canary Wharf Ltd* [1997] AC 655, 685, per Lord Goff: 'for an action in private nuisance to lie in respect of interference with the plaintiff's enjoyment of his land, it will generally arise from something emanating from the defendant's land. Such an emanation may take many forms-noise, dirt, fumes, obnoxious smell, vibrations, and such like.' See also, ibid., 700, per Lord Lloyd of Berwick. See also de Villiers, above at note 57, 391.

[137] *Pratt v Young* (1952) 69 WN 214, 218, per Brereton D.C.J. (NSW District Court). See D. Elvin and J. Karas, *Unlawful Interference With Land* (Sweet & Maxwell, London, 1995), para. 2-028 and Reid, above at note 126, 129.

[138] [1997] AC 655.

[139] Ibid., 685–86 (Lord Goff), 709–11 (Lord Hoffman), 725–27 (Lord Hope of Craighead).

[140] Ibid., 685, per Lord Goff.

because this is a much discussed topic in relation to *Pickles*. The holding that ill motive does not convert a lawful act into an unlawful one has not stood in the way of the courts preventing persons from maliciously making noise or other emanations in order to harm or annoy their neighbours. The principle of reasonable user in the law of nuisance factors the motive of the defendant into the reasonableness calculus. Two cases are invariably cited in support of this proposition.[141] In the first case, *Christie v Davey*,[142] North J. issued an injunction against an occupier of a house who made a considerable amount of noise by banging trays together with the intention of causing annoyance to his musical neighbour. The noise would have had to be tolerated if generated in the course of a legitimate use of the land, but not when created 'for the purpose of vexing and annoying his neighbours'.[143] Forty years later, in *Hollywood Silver Fox Farm Ltd v Emmett*,[144] Macnaghten J. issued an injunction against the defendant, who, by firing guns on his own property, intentionally disturbed breeding foxes on his neighbour's property, which foxes then displayed cannibalistic behaviour. Counsel for the plaintiff relied on *Keeble*'s case and distinguished *Pickles* on the ground that it did not concern the law of nuisance. Opposing counsel took his stand on *Pickles* as the later case, overruling the earlier authorities. In a brief judgment Macnaghten J. held that *Pickles* had no bearing in nuisance, and that malice was a determinative factor in weighing up the competing interests of the neighbours.[145]

It is common in comparative law discussions of abuse of rights and analogous common law doctrines and remedies to read that the civil law and common law systems reach much the same results but by different routes.[146] In particular, it is said that the law of nuisance is capable of

[141] To which, no doubt, will be added Lord Cooke of Thorndon's dictum in his dissenting judgment in *Hunter v Canary Wharf Ltd*, ibid., 721, that malice qualifies the exercise of property rights, such that the malicious erection of a structure to interfere with television reception would be actionable. In addition to the two cases discussed in the text, Lord Cooke cites *Attorney-General of Manitoba v Campbell* (1983) 26 CCLT 168. Lord Cooke's position has been criticized as contrary to the holding in *Pickles*: W. V. H. Rogers, *Winfield & Jolowicz on Tort* (Sweet & Maxwell, London, 15th edn, 1998), 506. (See further, Appendix, note 13.)

[142] [1893] 1 Ch 316.

[143] Ibid., 326. North J. said he would have taken 'an entirely different view of the case' if the neighbours were 'both perfectly innocent': ibid., 326 and also 328.

[144] [1936] 2 KB 468. The judge, Macnaghten J., was the son of Lord Macnaghten and the grandson of Baron Martin. See Pollock, above at note 12, 171–2.

[145] The brevity of the judgment caused confusion as to the basis of the decision, and led to an exchange between Sir William Holdsworth and Arthur Goodhart. See (1937) 53 LQR 1–4. For the view that *Pickles* overruled *Christie v Davey*, and hence *Hollywood Silver Fox Farm* was wrongly decided, see A. MacDonald, 'Hollywood Silver Fox Farm v Emmett' (1937) 2 Alberta LQ 99.

[146] See, e.g., J. H. Crabb, 'The French Concept of Abuse of Rights' (1964) 6 Inter-American LR 1; U. Mattei, *Basic Principles of Property Law: A Comparative Legal and Economic Introduction* (Greenwood Press, Westport, 2000), 148.

dealing with most, if not all, of the situations involving maliciously-motivated unneighbourly behaviour.[147] But that is true only up to a point, and the *Pickles* situation is presently beyond that point. The absence of a property right in the water to be received denied the Corporation in that case the protection of nuisance law and injunctive relief.[148] The courts in *Pickles* were unwilling to elevate the presence of malicious behaviour over that lack of a property right. So Marcellus was rejected,[149] the expansive dictum of Holt C.J. in *Keeble*'s case was ignored, and anything like a prima facie tort doctrine aborted.

One can also hear the rattle of the chains of the old forms of action here. For historical reasons, property law relies for its enforcement upon tort law. There is no remedy for abuse of property right, unless it can be fitted within an existing tort.[150] As we have seen, the only likely contender—nuisance—did not extend this far. The equitable remedies might have developed to prevent the malicious exercise of property rights, but did not do so (for the reasons given in Chapter 6). As F. H. Lawson observed about *Pickles*, '[i]t is arguable that the Bradford Corporation failed merely because they could find no appropriate form of action'.[151]

'Bad Motive Cannot Make a Lawful Act Unlawful'

Motive was declared irrelevant to the law of torts in *Pickles*. If doing an unlawful act with a good motive cannot excuse tortious liability, it was said, then doing a lawful act with a malicious motive cannot render it tortious.[152] This mantra—that bad motive cannot make a lawful act unlawful—was repeated time and again both in England and in the United States.[153]

[147] See, e.g., J. R. L. Milton, 'The Law of Neighbours in South Africa' [1969] *Acta Juridica* 123, 130.

[148] See L. A. Sheridan, *Injunctions and Similar Orders* (Barry Rose Law Publishers Ltd, Chichester, 1999), 120.

[149] See Chapters 3 and 6.

[150] In other words, the definition of common law property rights is found partly in property law and partly in tort law: P. Cane, 'Fault and Strict Liability for Harm in Tort Law', in W. Swadling and G. Jones (eds), *The Search for Principle: Essays in Honour of Lord Goff of Chieveley* (Oxford University Press, Oxford, 1999), 171, 173.

[151] F. H. Lawson, 'Notes on the History of Tort in the Civil Law' (1940) 22 *Journal of Comparative Legislation* (3rd ser.) 136, 165; reprinted in F. H. Lawson, *The Comparison: Selected Essays: Volume II* (North Holland, Amsterdam, 1977), 210.

[152] *Pickles* [1895] AC 587, 594, *per* Lord Halsbury.

[153] See *Stevenson v Newnham* (1853) 13 C.B. 285, 297; 138 E.R. 208, 213 (Baron Parke); *Allen v Flood* [1898] AC 1, 172 (Lord Watson) and 151 (Lord Macnaghten); *Quinn v Leathem* [1901] AC 495, 510 (Lord Macnaghten); *South Wales Miners' Federation v Glamorgan Coal Co. Ltd* [1905] AC 239, 246 (Lord Macnaghten). In the late 1880s Judge Thomas Cooley, 'the most respected lawyer in America and among the most widely respected persons in American public life' (P. D. Carrington, 'Law as "The Common Thoughts of Men": The Law-Teaching

Several leading torts scholars have described this axiom as 'question-begging'. The question is, or should be: Is the conduct lawful in light of the purpose or motive? William Prosser distinguished between those situations where the passage of centuries had crystallized rules that applied irrespective of motive, and those more modern situations where the interests are recognized as interdependent and relative, and more finely balanced. In the latter situations, the courts have realized that the defendant's motivation is an important factor in the balance.[154] This line of thinking is similar to that of Holmes, and leads inevitably to the justification of any loss suffered by another. Malice, of course, negating just cause or excuse.[155] This, then, is the prima facie tort doctrine.[156]

Glanville Williams has described the supposed symmetry of the irrelevance of good motivation on unlawful conduct and bad motivation on lawful conduct as fallacious; an 'insidious platitude' which says nothing, and certainly does not prove what it sets out to prove.[157] Nonetheless, it remains the 'general rule' in tort law that 'the motive with which conduct was done is irrelevant to its tortiousness' (subject to a few well-established exceptions).[158]

Time for Reconsideration?

There has been no shortage of critics of *Pickles* over the last century. The list includes Lords Denning[159] and Reid,[160] Professors Roscoe Pound,[161]

and Judging of Thomas McIntyre Cooley' (1997) 49 Stan LR 495, 495), wrote in his influential *Treatise on the Law of Torts* that '[m]alicious motives make a bad act worse, but they cannot make that wrong which in its essence is lawful' (T. M. Cooley, *A Treatise on the Law of Torts or the Wrongs which arise Independent of Contract* (Callaghan & Co., Chicago, 1st edn, 1879), 690). This was repeated many times in American cases. See the cases referred to in the 4th edn, of Cooley's *Treatise* (Callaghan & Co., Chicago, 1932) (D. A. Haggard, ed.), para. 534.

154 W. L. Prosser, *Handbook on the Law of Torts* (West Publishing Co., St Paul, 1955), 21–2.

155 Shapiro, above at note 51.

156 Prosser, above at note 154, 23; Walton, above at note 62, 519.

157 Williams, above at note 123, 127, esp. n. 65.

158 P. Cane, *The Anatomy of Tort Law* (Hart Publishing, Oxford, 1997), 35.

159 A. T. Denning, *Freedom Under the Law* (Stevens & Sons Ltd, London, 1949), 68–9. Brian Napier described Lord Denning as 'the leading exponent of [an] English doctrine of abuse of rights', referring to the following judgments: *Morgan v Fry* [1968] 2 QB 710, 729; *Cory Lighterage v Transport and General Workers Union* [1973] 2 All ER 558, 567; *Re Brocklehurst* [1978] 1 All ER 767, 775 (dissent); *Chapman v Honig* [1963] 2 QB 502, 510–14 (dissent). See B. W. Napier, 'Abuse of Rights in British Law', in M. Rotondi (ed.), *L'Abus de Droit* (Padova, Italy, 1979), 265, 282.

160 Reid, above at note 13, 198.

161 R. Pound, *The Spirit of the Common Law* (Beacon Press, Boston, 1963 reprint; originally published in 1921), 184–6 and 197–8.

A. L. Goodhart,[162] Glanville Williams,[163] Wolfgang Friedmann,[164] and C. K. Allen.[165] The legal position set out in *Pickles* was described in the 1930s as 'the consecration of the spirit of unrestricted egoism',[166] and many since then have seen it as the 'apogee' of the absolutism of property exploitation.[167] It is commonplace to observe that the tide had turned against *laissez-faire* ideology for much of the last century, leaving the *homo economius* (personified by Edward Pickles) high and dry. Successive waves of regulatory legislation have left little room for such behaviour.[168] Is it time to heed these persistent calls for a reconsideration of the common law position?

[162] A. L. Goodhart, *Essays in Jurisprudence and the Common Law* (Cambridge University Press, Cambridge, 1931), 36–7. Cf. A. L. Goodhart, *English Law and the Moral Law* (Stevens & Sons Ltd, London, 1955), 144–7.

[163] Williams, above at note 123, 126–8.

[164] W. Friedmann, *Legal Theory* (Stevens & Sons Ltd, London, 4th edn 1960), 507.

[165] C. K. Allen, 'Legal Morality and the *Ius Abutendi*' (1924) 40 LQR 164.

[166] H. C. Gutteridge, 'Abuse of Rights' (1933–35) 5 CLJ 22.

[167] J. S. Getzler, 'Rules Writ in Water: A History of Riparian Rights and Property Use Doctrine in England to 1870', unpublished D.Phil. thesis, University of Oxford, 1993, p. 327; J. Harris, *Private Lives, Public Spirit: Britain, 1870–1914* (Penguin Books, London, 1994), 117.

[168] The restrictions on ground water abstraction in the Water Act 1945 (UK) were replaced by the licensing system established by the Water Resources Act 1963 (UK). See R. Megarry and H. W. R. Wade, *The Law of Real Property* (Clarendon Press, Oxford, 5th edn, 1984), 65 and 843; and for the background see H. F. Cook, 'Groundwater Development in England' (1999) 5 *Environment and History* 75.

Epilogue:

Pickles and the Public/Private Law Divide

Local history and single case-centred legal historical research[1] share the pitfall of 'boosterism', of accentuating or overestimating the importance of a particular area or case.[2] The danger is perhaps even greater in relation to a 'leading' case, for influence or reputation of a particular case may be more difficult to trace and quantify than that of a particular town or locality. Like an iceberg, one imagines that the still visible tip of a leading case conceals a large mass of subterranean influence, but this is difficult to prove from the surface. Indeed, it is easy simply to dismiss *Pickles* as a hangover from a highly individualistic age, now overridden by statute—a museum piece. But it remains an integral part of the common lawyers' private law mindset. The case continues to appear in the desiccated footnotes of tort and property textbooks. One of the innumerable victims of the lawyerly ritual of bloodletting, whereby the facts, complexity, contingency, and interest is drained away. The case itself, although still accorded the exalted status of a 'leading' one, these days is seldom cited in court; although when it is, it is still accepted as authoritative and capable on occasions of aiding meritless decisions.[3]

The case of *Stephens v Anglian Water Authority*[4] comes to mind. There a water authority abstracted ground water that otherwise would have flowed to the plaintiff's land. The discontinuance of the underground flow led to subsidence on the plaintiff's land. The plaintiff sued unsuccessfully in negligence. In denying the claim the court drew assistance from the *Pickles* case, observing that if the neighbour would not be liable for maliciously abstracting percolating underground water then he could

[1] C. W. Nyguist has described this as 'single case scholarship' and 'single case research': 'Contract, Single Case Research and the Massachusetts Archives' (1997) 3 *Massachusetts Legal History* 53. The pioneer in this genre is A. W. B. (Brian) Simpson, and it is known around the world 'as doing a Simpson': R. H. Helmholz, 'Brian Simpson in the United States', in K. O'Donovan and G. R. Rubin (eds), *Human Rights and Legal History: Essays in Honour of Brian Simpson* (Oxford University Press, Oxford, 2001), 285, 288.

[2] J. A. Jowitt, 'Late Victorian and Edwardian Bradford', in J. A. Jowitt and R. K. S. Taylor (eds), *Bradford, 1890–1914: The Cradle of the Independent Labour Party* (Bradford Centre Occasional Papers No. 2, Bradford, 1980), 4, 21.

[3] P. G. Stein and J. Shand, *Legal Values in Western Society* (Edinburgh University Press, Edinburgh, 1974), 212 (restrictive effect of *Pickles* still being felt).

[4] [1987] 3 All ER 379. See also *Langbrook Properties Ltd v Surrey County Council* [1969] 3 All ER 1424 (Ch).

not be liable for doing so carelessly. This result has raised the ire of torts lawyers.[5]

But to pursue such issues further, and to answer the question deliberately left hanging at the end of the last chapter, would require another book, and a different kind of book than this one has become. This is a different book than the one I set out to write. I first became interested in *Pickles* for the light it would shed on the public/private law divide, and the implications of (re)privatization of public utilities, such as water companies.[6] But I soon got drawn into the fascinating story, and realised the importance of understanding the case in the context of its own time and place. It dawned on me that by projecting contemporary concerns back into the past and looking for future guidance, I was misusing historical method in the cause of advocacy. The fact that lawyers habitually do this—indeed, abstraction and de-contextualization are part of the common law method—did not seem to me sufficient excuse. However, in closing I want to sketch the enduring significance of *Pickles* to the contemporary debate about the public/private law divide.

Property Rights: Stick or Club?

It has become fashionable to describe the concept of property as a 'bundle of sticks'.[7] One of those 'sticks', and arguably the most important, is the right of the owner to exclude others from his or her land. This right entails the exclusion or ejection of anyone for any reason—good or bad—or for no reason at all, without warning and without any obligation to explain why or to otherwise act fairly. As Kevin Gray has noted, '[i]n some deep sense the sustained exercise of exclusory power is perhaps all there is to the grand claim of proprietary ownership. Behind all the brave philosophical and political rhetoric of conventional property talk there lurks only the unattractive rumble of state-sanctioned *force majeure*.'[8]

The *fons et origo* of the modern law is the all but forgotten case of *Wood v Leadbitter*,[9] which subsequently legitimated many forms of discrimina-

[5] See, e.g., J. G. Fleming, 'Negligence and Property Rights' (1988) 104 LQR 183, and T. Weir, *A Casebook on Torts* (Sweet & Maxwell, London, 8th edn, 1996), 445.

[6] See M. Taggart, 'The Province of Administrative Law Determined?', in M. Taggart (ed.), *The Province of Administrative Law* (Hart Publishing, Oxford, 1997), 1.

[7] There is a large literature. See generally J. E. Penner, 'The "Bundle of Rights" Picture of Property' (1996) 43 UCLA Law Review 711.

[8] K. Gray, 'Property in Common Law Systems', in G. E. van Maanen and A. J. van der Walt (eds), *Property Law on the Threshold of the 21st Century* (Bureau JA Vormgevers, Tilburg, 1996), 265.

[9] (1845) 13 M. & W. 838; 153 E.R. 351. For an excellent study of this case in its racing context, see P. Polden, 'A Day at the Races: *Wood v Leadbitter* in Context' (1993) 14 J Leg Hist 28.

tion, particularly racial discrimination in the provision of services and entertainment to the public.[10] Importantly, there were a few islands of common law control of such discrimination amid this sea of private autonomy: in relation to railways, carriers, ferrymen, and inns for travellers (the so-called common callings); businesses 'affected with public interest'; and suppliers of 'prime necessities'.[11] Ultimately, and inevitably given the limitations of such common law regulation, the more obvious and socially unacceptable forms of discrimination have been prohibited by statute. But this has not stopped the continued portrayal of the common law as absolute in character.

The veneer of statutory overlay does not adhere to the pre-existing common law in a way that indelibly changes its character and future description. The common lawyer's deep-seated distrust of statute law, and the common law's innate superiority complex,[12] perpetuates the unreality of describing (usually with approval) theoretically absolute common law rights that bear no relationship whatsoever to the extensively regulated and controlled exercise of those rights in the modern society.[13] Jack Beatson has described this as the 'oil-and-water' approach because the common law and statute never mix: a process he rightly deprecated.[14] Failure to view property rights and restrictions in a holistic way perpetuates the ideology supporting the unreformed common law.[15] In other words, it denies or is blind to the fact that property rights are socially constructed.

That may appear a detour, but its relevance to the 'stick' of absolute and unfettered use of property right is this. The right to exclude was thought to be absolute and could be exercised maliciously. However, the common law limited that right in some circumstances and there was the potential to do more. Writers about bundles of sticks or rights, or the incidents of ownership often do not highlight the 'stick' of absolute unfettered use, which can

[10] See generally J. W. Singer, 'No Right to Exclude: Public Accommodations and Private Property' (1996) 90 NwULR 1283, and C. Backhouse, 'Racial Segregation in Canadian Legal History: Viola Desmond's Challenge, Nova Scotia, 1946' (1994) 17 Dal. LJ 299.

[11] See Taggart, above at note 6, 6–17. See also A. Reichman, 'Professional Status and the Freedom to Contract: Toward a Common Law Duty of Non-Discrimination' (2001) 14 *Canadian Journal of Law & Jurisprudence* 79 and A. Reichman, 'Property Rights, Public Policy and the Limits of the Legal Power to Discriminate', in D. Friedmann and D. Barak-Erez (eds), *Human Rights in Private Law* (Hart Publishing, Oxford, 2001), 245.

[12] See, e.g., R. Munday, 'The Common Lawyer's Philosophy of Legislation' (1983) 14 *Rechtstheorie* 191.

[13] A recent example of this unreality is the majority judgments in *Hunter v Canary Wharf Ltd* [1997] AC 655 (HL).

[14] J. Beatson, 'Has the Common Law a Future?' [1997] CLJ 291, 309. Once again, the contrast with the civil law is instructive. See R. Zimmermann, '*Statuta Sunt Stricte Interpretanda*? Statutes and the Common Law: A Continental Perspective' [1997] CLJ 315.

[15] See generally J. W. Singer, *Entitlement: The Paradoxes of Property* (Yale University Press, New Haven, 2000).

be used maliciously to hit others. Take, for example, the influential essay on 'Ownership' by A. M. Honoré.[16] There the discussion of the incident of 'the right to use' does not contain any reference to malicious use, although Honoré does consider more generally the prevention of harmful use and social control.[17]

One such control mechanism is the tort of nuisance. But, as we saw in Chapter 7, this did not help the Corporation of Bradford. For what *Pickles* stands for as far as nuisance is concerned is that it is not a nuisance to *prevent* the escape from your own property of something (there percolating water) that your neighbour has no right to receive. It is not a tort in such circumstances to deprive someone of emanations from your property, even if maliciously motivated.

This is a limitation of the common law system, going back to the forms of action. The law of property is enforced by actions for tort, breach of contract, and unjust enrichment. Unless malicious exercise of property is recognized as a tort, for example, there is no remedy available. The equitable remedies might have developed to prevent the malicious exercise of property rights, but did not (for the reasons given in Chapter 6).

The Private Law Paradigm

By and large, *Pickles* was viewed by the judges as a private law dispute over water between an individual landowner and a landowning company which ran a water supply business. The fact that the original adventurers (who had established the company for personal gain) had sold out to the local municipality, which was a creature of statute and guardian of the welfare of the inhabitants, was not treated as relevant. Indeed, Lord Halsbury referred to the Corporation (twice) as 'this trading company', and both he and Lord Macnaghten alluded to its profit-making capacity.[18] Any public interest in the continued supply of water to Bradford was trumped by Pickles's absolute property right.

It could be said that in this the law and the courts were consistent and properly blind to any distinction between private and public bodies. Recall the facts of *Chasemore v Richards*.[19] There the appropriator of the percolating underground water was a local Board of Public Health acting

[16] A. M. Honoré, 'Ownership', in A. G. Guest (ed.), *Oxford Essays in Jurisprudence (First Series)* (Clarendon Press, Oxford, 1961), 107; reprinted in T. Honoré, *Making Law Bind: Essays Legal and Philosophical* (Clarendon Press, Oxford, 1987), 161.

[17] Ibid., 123 (incorrectly citing prohibition of harmful use as an incident of property, rather than a limitation imposed upon the right of use: Penner, above at note 7, and C. Lewis, 'The Modern Concept of Ownership of Land' [1985] *Acta Juridica* 241, 254).

[18] *Pickles* [1895] AC 587, 595 and 600–1.

[19] (1859) 7 HLC 349; 11 E.R. 140 (HL).

pursuant to its statutory mandate to improve health. The Board pumped the water from a well to supply a nearby township. That, however, is not on all fours with *Pickles*. There was an express finding in *Chasemore's* case that there was no malice or ill-will directed to the complaining mill-owner, whose business was adversely affected by the pumping. The relevant enquiry is this: if the tables had been turned in *Pickles* and the Corporation owned the uphill land and threatened to divert the water in order to coerce Pickles into doing something he was not minded to do, would the courts have allowed the Corporation to be 'master of the situation' in the same way?

The answer, in my view, is 'No'.[20] The same Lord Macnaghten who seemingly so admired the enterprise of Edward Pickles believed that public authorities should be kept firmly in their statutory place. In *Westminster Corporation v London & North Western Railway*[21] he declared:

> It is well settled that a public body invested with statutory powers such as those conferred upon the corporation must take care not to exceed or abuse its power. It must keep within the limits of the authority committed to it. It must act in good faith. It must act reasonably. The last proposition is involved in the second, if not in the first.

In saying that if the places of Bradford Corporation and Edward Pickles were reversed so would the result have been, it must be admitted that the downhill Mr Pickles might have struggled to establish *locus standi* to sue in his own name.[22]

The classic modern statement of what divides private and public law remains that of Professor Sir William Wade, in successive editions of his textbook:[23]

> The powers of public authorities are . . . essentially different from those of private persons. A man making a will may, subject to any rights of his dependants, dispose of his property just as he may wish. He may act out of malice or a spirit

[20] The only other person I am aware of to reverse the parties in *Pickles* is Geoffrey Samuel, in an article that came to my attention some time after I wrote about this. In Part IV of a series of articles entitled 'Classification of Law', Samuel said that if the situation were reversed 'an action for damages—or, at least, an action for an injunction or declaration—by the citizen might well have succeeded given that the courts have for long taken the view that a public authority ought to exercise their rights in a reasonable way': [1984] City of London LR 1, 8.

[21] [1905] AC 426, 430.

[22] I owe this point to Stuart Anderson of the University of Otago. (See further, Appendix, note 14.)

[23] H. W. R. Wade and C. F. Forsyth, *Administrative Law* (Clarendon Press, Oxford, 8th edn, 2000), 357. Almost identical passages appear in earlier editions. The passage has been judicially approved. See, e.g., *Webster v Auckland Harbour Board* [1983] NZLR 646, 650, *per* Cooke and Jeffries JJ.; *Webster v Auckland Harbour Board* [1987] 2 NZLR 129, 131, *per* Cooke P. (CA); *R v Tower Hamlets London Borough Council, ex p. Chetnik Developments Ltd* [1988] 1 AC 858, 872, *per* Lord Bridge of Harwich (HL).

of revenge, but in law this does not affect his exercise of his power. In the same way, a private person has an absolute power to allow whom he likes to use his land, release a debtor, or, where the law permits, to evict a tenant, regardless of his motives. This is unfettered discretion. But a public authority may do none of these things unless it acts reasonably and in good faith and upon lawful and relevant grounds of public interest. . . . [U]nfettered discretion is inappropriate to a public authority, which possesses powers solely in order that it may use them for the public good.

Although the judges speak a great deal about bad faith or lack of good faith in administrative law cases, they almost always mean simply 'acting unlawfully' rather than spitefully or maliciously.[24] Instances of the latter behaviour by public bodies are thankfully rare. There is, however, a special public law tort available in that unlikely event.[25]

Does anything change when so-called public utilities (such as water), which have been in public ownership for a long period, suddenly are privatized? Privatization is an ugly word but an accurate one. The root of the word is private, and its original meaning was 'not holding public office or official position'.[26] So the derivation, privatization, properly captures the significance of the process: the shift from the public to the private sphere.[27] We say that these utilities are placed on the level playing field. The extra public law duties owed by these formerly public bodies have been 'bulldozed off' the field. The referees' rulebook comprises private law and statutory intrusions. The whistle can be blown for 'fouls'—more often declared so by statute than the common law—but malicious exercise of property rights still does not feature as one in the common law part of the rulebook. On the hoarding around the level playing field (assuming it has some bounds) one can imagine seeing the graffiti artist's deviant scrawl '*Pickles* Rules, Okay'. Perhaps . . .

As administrative law casts off the rope of *ultra vires* to voyage onto these uncharted seas of the ugly 'izations'—privatization, corporatization, globalization, and the like—the common law of common callings and businesses affected with a public interest is being looked to on all sides to justify the journey.[28] Some work has been done, but much

24 See Wade and Forsyth, above at note 23, 415. See also C. Hoexter, 'Administrative Justice and Dishonesty' (1994) 111 SALJ 700.

25 The tort of misfeasance in a public office.

26 A. O. Hirschman, *Shifting Involvements: Public Interest and Private Action* (Princeton University Press, New Jersey, 1982), 121.

27 See M. Taggart, 'Corporatisation, Privatisation and Public Law' (1991) 2 PLR 77, 94.

28 See specifically C. Forsyth, 'Of Fig Leaves and Fairy Tales: The Ultra Vires Doctrine, the Sovereignty of Parliament and Judicial Review' [1996] CLJ 122, 126; Sir John Laws, 'Public Law and Employment Law: Abuse of Power' [1997] PL 455. See generally M. Taggart, 'Public Utilities and Public Law', in P. A. Joseph (ed.), *Essays on the Constitution* (Brookers, Wellington, 1995), 214.

remains to be done.[29] There can be no doubt, however, that *Pickles* will have to be reckoned with. To private lawyers of a particular bent, *Pickles* is a talisman keeping public law and its collectivist values at bay. To public lawyers of various bents, *Pickles* is a symbol of the divide between private and public law that they question or attack.

The Public Dimension of Private Property

One approach to *Pickles* would be to see it as an anomalous case. In relation to a small subset of water law—percolating underground water not in a defined stream—the courts made a classification that in a few cases could be seen to lead to injustice.[30] Indeed, statutory intervention in the United Kingdom effectively has overridden the common law. Why, then, make a mountain out of a (non-existent) molehill?[31] There is more to it than this view allows.

By treating percolating water as part of the soil the courts converted it into a solid thing—reduced it from a flowing, fluid, living thing into an inert thing—thereby depriving it of its essential properties and disconnecting it from the powerful ideas of shared use that swirl around water. This was, I think, what counsel for the Corporation was groping to express in attempting to differentiate rights of use of flowing water from other rights of property.[32] The rejection of that argument was more than a wrong turning—although it was that—it underscored an attitude to property. The Victorians described it as showing who was 'master of the situation'.[33] Today we might describe it as an 'in your face' attitude, the revelling in ostentatious dominion. Carol Rose brilliantly captures all of this:[34]

[29] For a sample of some of the recent work, see the essays by M. Aronson, J. W. F. Allison, A. C. Aman, D. Mullan, J. McLean, P. Craig, and D. Dyzenhaus, in Taggart, above at note 6.

[30] Gutteridge was strongly opposed to wholesale introduction of the Continental abuse of rights doctrine, but he favoured a remedy (to be created by statute) in the very particular circumstances of *Pickles*: H. C. Gutteridge, 'Abuse of Rights' (1933–5) 5 CLJ 22, 44–5. Others would have cared less if *Pickles* had been confined to its facts, or limited in application to water or land law. See G. L. Williams, 'The Foundation of Tortious Liability' (1941) 7 CLJ 111, 128–9. Cf. G. Samuel, 'Reason, Logic and Morals in the Common Law' [1976] City of London LR 7, 12.

[31] One American writer put the question this way. Did *Pickles* involve 'a small corner of water law doctrine', or were the judges 'struggling over a normative theory with ramifications for all property disputes'? See R. G. Bone, 'Normative Theory and Legal Doctrine in American Nuisance Law: 1850 to 1920' (1986) 59 SCal LR 1101, 1203.

[32] See Chapter 5.

[33] The quote, of course, is from Lord Macnaghten in *Pickles* [1895] AC 587, 600.

[34] C. M. Rose, 'Property as the Keystone Right?' (1996) 71 Notre Dame LR 329, 351. If one goes back far enough in the history of the common law, goods and animals were the stuff of property, not land. See D. J. Siepp, 'The Concept of Property in the Early Common Law' (1994) 12 *Law & History Review* 29.

What is the symbol for property? It is easy to answer that *land* is that symbol. . . . But why is land—immovable, enduring land—the central symbol for property? Why not, say, water? Water, after all, is in fact the subject of important and valuable property rights, and, indeed, concerns about water can substantially modify the rules about land. If water was our chief symbol for property, we might think of property rights—and perhaps other rights—in a quite different way. We might think of rights literally and figuratively as more fluid and less fenced-in; we might think of property entailing less of the awesome Blackstonian power of exclusion and more of the qualities of flexibility, reasonableness and moderation, attentiveness to others, and cooperative solutions to common problems. Those qualities are in fact even a part of landed property—as in nuisance law—however little the *symbol* of landed property may suggest.

Water law is a particularly rich source of ideas about public use and the public interest tempering private rights of property. Powerful ideas of waters being *jus publici*, public use rights on navigable rivers and elsewhere, and the notion of a public trust over natural resources can be traced back far into legal history, and are resurfacing increasingly under the banner of environmentalism and in settlements with indigenous peoples. Extremely valuable work has been done by Harry Scheiber and Carol Rose, amongst others, in relation to water, navigable rivers, foreshore, and the like.[35] The language of *jus publici* or property affected with a public interest spans environmental law, water law, mining law, eminent domain/compulsory acquisition, constitutional law, and public utility law. Some of the ideas surface in the law of common callings.[36] It is an enormous task to bring these threads together—which probably explains why it has not been done—but it is a vital one. If the common law is to continue to have a role to play in the control of (public and private) power, it is vitally important to recognize the pervasiveness of the doctrines and ideas which limit the exercise of power in the interests of neighbours, the public, and the public good. Once again, the contested 'property model' exemplified in *Pickles* must be reckoned with.[37]

[35] See for a sample of the work: H. Scheiber, 'The Road to *Munn*: Eminent Domain and the Concept of Public Purpose in the State Courts', in D. Fleming and B. Bailyn (eds), *Law in American History* (Little, Brown & Co., Boston, 1971), 327; C. M. Rose, *Property & Persuasion: Essays on the History, Theory & Rhetoric of Ownership* (Westview Press, Boulder, 1994), chs 5–6; M. Selvin, 'The Public Trust Doctrine in American Law and Economic Policy, 1789–1920' [1980] Wisconsin LR 1403; G. J. MacGrady, 'The Navigability Concept in the Civil and Common Law: Historical Development, Current Importance, and Some Doctrines That Don't Hold Water' (1975) 3 Florida State ULR 511; P. Deveney, 'Title, Jus Publicum and the Public Trust: An Historical Analysis' (1976) 1 Sea Grant LJ 13. See also W. J. Novak, *The People's Welfare: Law and Regulation in Nineteenth Century America* (University of North Carolina, Chapel Hill, 1996).

[36] See above at note 28 and accompanying text.

[37] See generally Singer, above at note 15, and K. Gray and S. Gray, 'Private Property and Public Propriety', in J. McLean (ed.), *Property and the Constitution* (Hart Publishing, Oxford, 1999), 11.

It is appropriate that the last word concerns Edward Pickles. Despite considerable efforts, I have not been able to discover what became of the redoubtable Edward Pickles or his family after they emigrated to North America (probably Canada), considerably poorer for his dispute with the Corporation of Bradford. I harbour the hope that some reader may know and will contact me.

Appendix: Further Notes

Note

1. J. Wignall Leather and his father George (principal of the firm George Leather & Co.) were no strangers to controversy and political machinations. Shareholder dissatisfaction with their appointment as sole engineers by the fledgling Leeds Water Works Company in 1838 took the company to the brink of dissolution. The detractors cast aspersions on the Leathers' competence in relation to water engineering and alleged exorbitant charges. The story is told in D. Fraser, 'The Politics of Leeds Water' (1973) 53 *Thoresby Society Publications* 50, 62–4.

   George Leather engineered the Bilbury dam, which burst in 1852 killing 81 people. This disaster was topped by George Leather's nephew, J. Towlerton Leather, who served his articles with George Leather & Co. Towlerton was the water engineer responsible for the construction of the ill-fated Dale Dyke Dam, west of Sheffield, which collapsed on 11 March 1864, killing 250 people and causing considerable property damage. There is a thorough treatment of both disasters in G. M. Binnie, *Early Victorian Water Engineers* (Thomas Telford Ltd, London, 1981), chs 4 ('George Leather (1787–1870) and the Collapse of the Bilberry dam') and 13 ('John Towlerton Leather (1804–85) and the collapse of the Dale Dyke dam'). Towlerton was cleared of blame at the time, but in retrospect that seems too lenient a view. See G. M. Binnie, 'The collapse of the Dale Dyke dam in retrospect' (1978) 11 *Quarterly Journal of Engineering Geology* 305. About this time Wignall Leather had a falling out with the Corporation of Bradford, which may have been precipitated by the Dale Dyke dam disaster, and they parted company later in 1864: Binnie, ibid., 125.

2. Marcellus was cited in two cases during this period. In *Smith v Kenrick* (1849) 7 C.B. 515; 137 E.R. 205, Maule J.—who had interjected during argument in *Acton v Blundell* that 'Marcellus is against you' (see text accompanying note 19 in Chapter 3)—interjected in the argument of counsel for the plaintiff that the Court in *Acton v Blundell* 'seem to have adopted the doctrine there cited from Marcellus' (ibid., 552; 220). A little later, interjecting in argument once again, Maule J. said '[b]ut, if he acts negligently, or capriciously, and injury results, no doubt he is liable' (ibid., 559; 222). Delivering the judgment of the Court, Cresswell L.J. established the right of a landowner to mine his land without regard to the interests of neighbouring landowners, so long as the former does not act 'negligently or maliciously' (ibid., 565–6; 225). There was no evidence of negligence, or that the mining 'was done with any design to injure his neighbour's mine' (ibid., 561; 223). In *Dickinson v The Grand Junction Canal Company* (1852) 7 Exch. 282, 155 E.R. 953 (Ex.) counsel on both sides cite the passage from Marcellus with approval (at 294, 958; 297, 959).

In *Rawstron v Taylor* (1855) 11 Exch. 369; 156 E.R. 873, Martin B., both by way of interjection and in his judgment, went out of his way to say that motive was not relevant to the landowner's right to drain surface water from his land (378, 384; 879, 881). Neither *Acton v Blundell* nor Marcellus was cited by counsel or the Court. *Contra* R. O'Sullivan, 'Abuse of Rights' (1955) 8 Curr Leg Probs 61, 68, n. 68. In one report of *Broadbent v Ramsbotham* (1856) 25 L.J. Exch. 121, Parke B. disapproved of *Acton v Blundell*.

3. Watson was preaching to the converted, of course. The Town Clerk had written much the same thing to Mr Cozens-Hardy Q.C., when informing him of the Corporation's unwillingness to accept the Court of Appeal's offer to hold judgment until statutory power to take the water was sought from Parliament (typewritten copy of a letter from the Town Clerk to H. H. Cozens-Hardy Q.C., dated 7 November 1894):

If the Court is against us in the present Appeal it can only be on the ground that in their judgment the Section in the Acts of 1842 and 1854 which we claim to be in favour gives us nothing more than a right of action against anybody acting illegally in our land. We reply that the general law secured to us that far without the Enactment and that the Section gave us the protection we claim. The Court are asked by Pickles to say that though we paid £220,000 to get the water for Bradford—have enjoyed it for 40 years previously—and although the powers were got with Notice of the Bill to Pickles's ancestors without objection being made, we are to have nothing for the money—and bought nothing. The Corporation venture to hope that this is not the correct interpretation of the Section. . . .

4. The report in *The Times* of 11 December 1894, p. 14, notes:

Mr Cozens-Hardy Q.C., stated that the Corporation propose to appeal to the House of Lords, and asked that the injunction might be continued pending the appeal. If the defendant were allowed to prosecute his works, an injury might be done to the plaintiffs which could not be repaired, even if the decision of this Court should be reversed by the House of Lords.
The Court acceded to this application, and, instead of dismissing the action at once, they made an order declaring that the plaintiffs were not entitled to the relief they claimed, and giving the defendant costs as above mentioned, on the terms that the plaintiffs are to present their petition of appeal within ten days after the perfecting of the order of this Court, and to prosecute their appeal with due diligence. If this is not done, the defendant is to be at liberty to apply to the Court to dissolve the injunction. The continuance of the injunction is not to affect the payment of the costs.

The strictness of the conditions may indicate some judicial annoyance at the Corporation passing up the Lord Chancellor's offer of postponement while Parliamentary powers were sought.

5. It became evident to me when I inspected the tunnel in May 1999 that it went back into the hillside a considerable distance under East Many Wells Farm.

W. H. Leatham, J. Ruscoe, and G. F. Renton say 'Many Wells Springs . . . flows from a heading driven about half a mile into the hillside . . .': *Bradford Corporation Waterworks Department, 1855–1955* (Bradford, 1955), 52. It is inconceivable that this extensive tunnelling was undertaken in 1842–5, when the waterworks and Reservoir at Hewenden were constructed, without consent or Parliamentary authority and the payment of compensation. The plans produced for the litigation detailed only Pickles's plans and did not describe the Corporation's waterworks. It seems to have been assumed that the Corporation's works did not extend under Pickles's land. If such a tunnel had been there in 1892–5, surely Pickles's digging would have disturbed it?

There are drawings in the possession of Yorkshire Water, Bradford, which suggest that the tunnel goes back a long way and that a deep bore hole was made beside the Spring entrance. This is likely the hole Watson drilled to recoup the supply *circa* 1898. The only sensible explanation is that the heading was driven into the hillside sometime in the twentieth century, after Pickles sold the farm. It is impossible to confirm this due to historical vandalism.

I am grateful to David Varley of Yorkshire Water, Bradford, for arranging admittance to the tunnel and for showing me the surviving drawings relating to Many Wells Spring. He was also able to confirm that several interesting-looking items relating to Many Wells Spring indexed in *B.C.W.W. Waterworks Engineers Office: A to Y; Index to Papers and Plans Connected Therewith* (which I had not seen at W.Y.A.S.) had been thrown away in the late 1980s in order to free up space!

6. 'After the Streams or Supplies of Water hereby or by the special Act authorized to be taken by the Undertakers shall have been so taken, every person who shall illegally divert or take the Waters supplying or flowing into the Streams so taken, or any Part thereof, or who shall do any unlawful Act whereby the said Streams or Supplies of Water may be drawn off or diminished in Quantity, and who shall not immediately repair the Injury done by him, on being required to do so by the Undertakers, so as to restore the said Waters to the State in which they were before such Act, shall forfeit to the Undertakers any Sum which shall be awarded, in *England* or *Ireland*, by two Justices . . . not exceeding Five Pounds for every Day during which the said Supply of Water shall be diverted or diminished by reason of any Act done by or by the Authority of such Person, and any Sum so forfeited shall be in addition to the Sum which he may be lawfully adjudged liable to pay to the Undertakers for any Damage which they might sustain by reason of their Supply of Water being diminished; and the Payment of the Sum so forfeited shall not bar or affect the Right of the Undertakers to bring or raise an Action at Law against such Person for the Damage so committed.'

7. The differences between section 14 of the Clauses Act and section 234 of the Act of 1842 (referred to below for the sake of simplicity as the Bradford Act) are:

(1) the marginal note of the general Act refers to 'illegally' diverting water, whereas the Bradford Act does not;
(2) the Bradford Act is specific to Many Wells Springs, whereas obviously the general Act refers generically to 'Streams and Supplies of Water';
(3) the general Act replaces the clumsy expression of the Bradford Act 'it shall not be lawful for any Person . . . to divert, alter or appropriate in any manner than by Law they may be legally entitled . . .') with the straightforward phrase 'every Person who shall illegally divert . . .';
(4) there is no reference in the general provision to 'Well or Pit' (which is repeated twice in the Bradford Act), and that greatly simplifies the structure and grammar of the section;
(5) it is not clear in the Bradford Act that the situations which follow the one dealing with illegal diversion (namely, sinking a well or pit, and any act, etc., whereby the water is drawn off or diminished) are also conditioned by illegality. In contrast, the general Act explicitly states that any action in drawing off or diminishing the water must be 'unlawful' before it is penalized;
(6) this clear requirement in the general Act that both the diversion and the diminution must be the result of unlawful conduct also simplifies the drafting of the section. One of the difficulties with section 234 of the Bradford Act was uncertainty as to whether the phrase 'such illegal Act as aforesaid' applied to all three events (illegal diversion; sinking well or pit; and the act of drawing off or diminishing water flow) or just the 'Act' of drawing off (leaving the lawful sinking of a well or pit covered by the penalty);
(7) there is one minor respect in which the provision in the Bradford Act is clearer than the general Act. It clearly covers diversion, etc., of waters supplying Many Wells Springs. It is less clear that the general Act does cover diversion of water supplying springs before it hits the surface. 'Streams' is defined in the general Act to include Springs, but that definition raises an argument that it is restricted to running surface water. On the other hand, in the general Act 'Streams' is juxtaposed with the very general term 'Supplies of Water', which would cover underground water supplying a spring, and could be argued to displace the prima facie interpretations provided by the general Act. Whatever the correct approach, there is no doubt that on this point the Bradford Act is clearer;
(8) the general Act provision is even more emphatic that the statutory penalty does not displace a common law action to recover for damage caused by diminution of water supply.

8. It is frequently pointed out by commentators that Lord Watson in *Pickles* contradicted what he said two years earlier in *John Young and Company v The Bankier Distillery Company* [1893] AC 691, 697. There he said that a downhill landowner cannot object to the gravitational flow of surface or underground water from higher land 'unless it has been unduly and unreasonably increased by operations which are in aemulationem vicini'. One does not have to go into the intricacies of the law relating to the obligations of higher and lower landowners in this regard (as to which see D. P. Derham, 'Interference with Surface Waters by Lower Landholders' (1958) 74 LQR 361) to appreciate that the situation in *Pickles* was different. It must be remembered also that in *Pickles* Lord Watson did not deny the doctrine of *aemulatio vicini* altogether. This particular criticism appears to me to be unfounded.

9. Talk of socialism reminds us that Bradford was the birth place of the Independent Labour Party at the time this litigation was getting off the ground. See J. A. Jowitt and R. K. S. Taylor (eds), *Bradford, 1890–1914: The Cradle of the Independent Labour Party* (Bradford Centre Occasional Papers No. 2, Bradford, 1980); K. Laybourn and D. James (eds.), *'The Rising Sun of Socialism': The Independent Labour Party in the Textile District of Yorkshire between 1890 and 1914: A Collection of Essays* (West Yorkshire Archive Service, Bradford, 1991).

10. Despite Heuston's thorough-going research and defence, I remain unpersuaded that Halsbury should be acquitted of the charge. He departed from convention in not consulting the Chief Justices of the courts, he undoubtedly favoured friends, and he seemed impervious to, if not defiant of, professional opinion (although in one case not Prime Ministerial opinion) on the issue. Heuston isolates seven out of Halsbury's 30 High Court appointments as 'dubious', but explains away three as 'unlucky'; in the sense that they could have been expected to perform better than they did. That leaves four 'bad' appointees, who were as undistinguished on the bench as they were at the bar. Of the rest, 18 or 19 appointees had 'competent professional attainments', and some four or five had distinguished careers at the bar and on the bench. Even on Heuston's calculations, this seems a high 'failure' rate to me, given the tight legal circle of the time. See also J. A. G. Griffith, *The Politics of the Judiciary* (Fontana/Collins, London, 1st edn, 1977), 21–2. Putting Halsbury's selections in the context of judicial appointments by others in the second half of the nineteenth century, Daniel Duman concludes that 'other Lord Chancellors and Prime Ministers were less guilty of placing really incompetent lawyers on the bench' than Halsbury and Salisbury: *The English and Colonial Bars in the Nineteenth Century* (Croom Helm, London, 1983), 182. *Accord*, P. Polden, *A History of the County Court, 1846–1971* (Cambridge University Press, Cambridge, 1999), 99 as regards county court appointments.

11. This book, the full reference for which is W. Markby, *Elements of Law Considered with Reference to Principles of General Jurisprudence* (Clarendon Press, Oxford), was first published in 1871, and ran through six editions (the last in 1901). It was 'a very successful book' in its day: A. W. B. Simpson, 'Book Review' (1997) 41 Am J Leg His 481, 482. Pollock's reference must be to the first edition, as it is the only one to contain anything relevant at that section number. Indeed, Markby there all but anticipates the fact situation that arose in *Pickles*, and concludes that the answer depends on whether the town had gained or not a right to the water.

The author, Sir William Markby, was at the time a puisne judge in India, but he returned to teach at Oxford in 1878. He was acquainted with Pollock.

It was at a meeting in Markby's rooms at Oxford, attended by Pollock amongst others, that the *Law Quarterly Review* was initiated: T. G. Watkins, 'Markby, Sir William', in A. W. B. Simpson (ed.), *Biographical Dictionary of the Common Law* (Butterworths, London, 1984), 352–3. Markby was a 'foremost champion' of John Austin's separation of law and morality: see R. A. Cosgrove, 'The reception of analytical jurisprudence: the Victorian debate on the separation of law and morality, 1860–1900' (1981–2) 43 *Durham University Journal* 47, 49. Indeed, Markby had assisted John Austin's widow to prepare her husband's lectures on jurisprudence for publication: F. H. Lawson, *The Oxford Law School 1850–1965* (Clarendon Press, Oxford, 1968), 174. The 'general sense' of English lawyers on the irrelevance of malice to legal liability, reported by Markby and relayed by Pollock, sat comfortably with the separation thesis of analytical jurisprudence. For his part, Pollock was very ambivalent about Austinian analytic jurisprudence: see ' "This Living Temple of Justice": Sir Frederick Pollock, First Citizen of the Anglo-American Legal Community' in R. A. Cosgrove, *'Our Lady the Common law': An Anglo-American Legal Community, 1870–1930* (New York University Pres, New York, 1987), 144–8.

For praise of Markby's work by Pollock, see F. Pollock, 'Oxford Legal Studies (1886)', reprinted in M. H. Hoeflich (ed. and compiler), *The Gladsome Light of Jurisprudence: Learning the Law in England and the United States in the 18th and 19th Centuries* (Greenwood Press, New York, 1988), 254, 258.

12. That is not to suggest that Bowen L.J. would have supported an abuse of rights doctrine. He was in the majority of the Court of Appeal in the *Mogul Steamship* case ((1889) 23 QBD 598; affirmed by the House of Lords), which rejected any liability for malicious exercise of economic power. In the following passage, Bowen L.J. presaged the higher courts' reasoning in *Pickles*: 'But there is surely no doctrine of law that compels him to use his property in a way which judges and juries may think reasonable: see *Chasemore v Richards*. If there is no such fetter upon the use of property known to English law, why should there be any such fetter on trade?' (ibid., 616). For a characteristically lively discussion of the *Mogul Steamship* case, see T. Weir, 'Abstraction in the Law of Torts—Economic Loss' [1974] City of London LR 15, 22–4; and for the wider context see M. Cooper, 'McGregor Gow and the Glen Line: The rise and fall of a British shipping firm in the Far East trade, 1870–1911' (1989) 10 *Journal of Transport History* 166.

Brian Simpson has observed of Bowen that 'his undoubted brilliance never fulfilled itself in the law' and that he did not rank as one of the great Victorian judges. See the entry under 'Bowen, Charles Synge Christopher' in A. W. B. Simpson (ed.), *Biographical Dictionary of the Common Law* (Butterworth, London, 1984), 68–9. This view was not shared by Sir Frederick Pollock, who put Bowen amongst the three greatest English judges he had encountered: F. Pollock, *For my Grandson: Remembrances of an Ancient Victorian* (John Murray, London, 1933), 172–3. Also Pollock's old pupil-master, Lord Lindley, said of Bowen that he was 'by far the most brilliant man of us all [on the Court of Appeal] and his good patience endeared him to all who knew him': N. Lindley, 'Autobiography' (unpublished manuscript, *circa* 1918), p. 108. Bowen was promoted to the House of Lords in 1893 after 11 years on the Court of Appeal, but died shortly thereafter in April 1894.

13. See also *Palmar v Loder* [1962] CLY 2233 (Havers J. granted a perpetual injunction to restrain the defendant from interfering with the plaintiff's enjoyment of her flat by the defendant's shouting, banging, crying, laughing, ringing doorbells, etc.); *MacGibbon v Robinson* (1953) 2 DLR 689 (BCCA) (noise disturbing whelping mink—the *Hollywood Silver Fox* case is referred to at first instance ((1952) 4 DLR 142) but not in Court of Appeal judgments, strengthening the suspicion that it was perceived as a negligence case); *Stoakes v Bridges* [1958] *Queensland Weekly Notes* #6, pp. 9–11 (Qd S.C.) (*Weekly Notes* are to be found in the back of the [1958] volume of the *Queensland Reports*) (campaign of disruptive telephone calls in retaliation for a real or imagined injury held to be a nuisance). Cf. the rough treatment of the harassing telephone calls case of *Khorasandjian v Bush* [1993] QB 727 by the House of Lords in *Hunter v Canary Wharf Ltd* [1997] AC 655.

    There are dicta in nineteenth-century nuisance cases not dealing with water that suggest that the presence of malice will affect reasonableness. See *Gaunt v Fynney* (1872) L.R. 8 Ch. 8, 12, *per* Lord Selborne; *Bamford v Turley* (1862) 3 B. & S. 66, 83; 122 E.R. 27, 33, *per* Baron Bramwell.

14. In *Pudsey Coal Gas Co. v Corporation of Bradford* (1873) LR 15 Eq. 167, the plaintiff unsuccessfully applied for an injunction to stop the Bradford Corporation from supplying gas to a mill outside the area which Bradford was authorized by statute to supply and within the area which Pudsey Coal Gas Company was authorized to supply. Apparently there was no statutory monopoly enjoyed by the Pudsey Company; and Bradford Corporation did not need the cloak of statutory powers to effect supply to the mill. In those circumstances, Sir Richard Malins V.C. found for Bradford on the grounds that (i) there was nothing to prevent the Corporation from supplying gas to the mill if it could do so without causing inconvenience, and (ii) Pudsey Coal Gas Company had not suffered any 'private injury' and so had no cause of action. In the twentieth century this and like cases were interpreted as holding that trade competitors have no standing to challenge the actions of rivals in the absence of a breach of 'private right'. See *Birr (No. 1) Rural District Council v Birr Urban District Council* [1915] 1 Ir. R 413; *Dundee Harbour Trustees v Nicol* [1925] AC 550; S. M. Thio, *Locus Standi and Judicial Review* (Singapore University Press, Singapore, 1971), 196. The argument against a downhill individual having standing to obtain an injunction against an uphill local authority maliciously cutting off the flow of underground water is that there is no 'private right' interfered with—neither property right nor tortious act. Although in our hypothetical situation there is not the element of trade rivalry or the focus on particular statutory authorization, it would involve *ultra vires* in a broader sense of unreasonableness and bad faith.

Select Bibliography

Abramovitch, Y., 'The Maxim "Cujus Est Solum Ejus Usque Ad Coelum" As Applied in Aviation' (1962) 8 *McGill Law Journal* 247.

Addy, T. and Renton, G. F., 'Bradford Corporation Waterworks 1855–1955: A Review' (1956) 38 *Journal of the Association of British Waterworks* 302.

Alexander, G., 'The Transformation of Trusts as a Legal Category, 1800–1914' (1987) 5 *Law & History Review* 303.

Allan, C. E., *The Rights of Local Authorities as regards Private Bills* (Shaw & Sons, London, 1900).

Allen, C. K., 'Legal Morality and the *Ius Abutendi*' (1924) 40 *Law Quarterly Review* 164; reprinted in C. K. Allen, *Legal Duties and Other Essays in Jurisprudence* (Clarendon Press, Oxford, 1931), 95.

Al-Qasem, A., 'The Unlawful Exercise of Rights in the Civil Codes of the Arab Countries of the Middle East' (1990) 39 *International and Comparative Law Review* 396.

Alschuler, A. W., 'Rediscovering Blackstone' (1996) 145 *University of Pennsylvania Law Review* 1.

American Law Institute, *Restatement of the Law of Torts* (American Law Institute, St Paul, 1939).

—— *Restatement (Second) of Torts* (American Law Institute, St Paul, 1979).

Ames, J. B., 'How Far an Act may be a Tort because of the Wrongful Motive of the Actor' (1905) 18 *Harvard Law Review* 411; reprinted in *Selected Essays on the Law of Torts* (1924), 155.

—— 'Law and Morals' (1908–9) 22 *Harvard Law Review* 97.

Amos, M. S., 'Abusive Exercise of Rights According to French Law' (1900) 2 *Journal of the Society of Comparative Legislation* (2nd ser.) 453.

Angell, J. K., *A Treatise on the Common Law in Relation to Watercourses* (Hilliard, Gray, Little and Wilkins, Boston, 1824).

—— *A Treatise on the Law of Watercourses* (J. C. Perkins, ed.) (Little, Brown & Co., Boston, 6th edn, 1869).

Anon., *The Law of Sewers; Or the Office and Authority of Commissioner of Sewers . . . To which are added, The Laws of Rumney-Marsh, and other Marshes and Fens* (Nutt & Gosling, London, 1726).

Anon., 'Lawful Acts Maliciously Performed on One's Own Land' (1880) 21 *Albany Law Journal* 284.

Anon., 'Malicious Exercise of Rights' (1894) 68 *Justice of the Peace* 814.

Anon., Note, 'Water Rights in Roman Law' (1903) 20 *South African Law Journal* 266.

Anon., *The Centenary Book of Bradford* (William Byles & Sons, Bradford, 1947).

Atiyah, P. S., *The Rise and Fall of Freedom of Contract* (Clarendon Press, Oxford, 1979).

—— 'The Legacy of Holmes Through English Eyes' (1983) 63 *Boston University Law Review* 341.

—— *Pragmatism and Theory in English Law* (Stevens & Sons Ltd, London, 1987).

Baade, H. W., 'Springs, Creeks, and Groundwater in Nineteenth-Century German Roman-Law Jurisprudence with a Twentieth-Century Postscript', in D. S. Clark (ed.), *Comparative and Private International Law: Essays in Honor of John Henry Merryman on his Seventieth Birthday* (Duncker & Humblot, Berlin, 1991), 61.

Backhouse, C., 'Racial Segregation in Canadian Legal History: Viola Desmond's Challenge, Nova Scotia, 1946' (1994) 17 *Dalhousie Law Journal* 299.

Bailey, V., 'Salvation Army Riots, the "Skeleton Army" and Legal Authority in the Provincial Town', in A. P. Donajgrodzki (ed.), *Social Control in Nineteenth Century Britain* (Croom Helm, London, 1977), 231.

Baines, T., *Yorkshire, Past and Present: A History and a Description of the Three Ridings of the Great County of York, from the Earliest Ages to the Year 1875* (William Mackenzie, London, 1877), 2 vols.

Barber, B. J., 'Aspects of municipal government, 1835–1914', in D. Fraser (ed.), *A History of Modern Leeds* (Manchester University Press, Manchester, 1980), 301.

—— 'Municipal government in Leeds, 1835–1914', in D. Fraser (ed.), *Municipal Reform and the Industrial City* (Leicester University Press, Leicester, 1982), 62.

Beatson, J., 'Has the Common Law a Future?' [1997] *Cambridge Law Journal* 291.

—— 'The Role of Statute in the Development of the Common Law' (2000) 117 *Law Quarterly Review* 247.

Bickley, A., 'The Sowden Watercolours', in G. Firth (ed.), *Street Characters of a Victorian City: John Sowden's Bradford* (Arts, Museums and Libraries Division, City of Bradford Metropolitan Council, Bradford, 1993), ix.

Binnie, G. M., 'The collapse of the Dale Dyke dam in retrospect' (1978) 11 *Quarterly Journal of Engineering Geology* 305.

—— *Early Victorian Water Engineers* (Thomas Telford Ltd, London, 1981).

Birks, P., 'The Concept of a Civil Right', in D. G. Owen (ed.), *Philosophical Foundations of Tort Law* (Clarendon Press, Oxford, 1995), 31.

—— 'Adjudication and the Interpretation in the Common Law: A Century of Change', in B. S. Markesinis (ed.), *The Clifford Chance Lectures: Volume 1—Bridging the Channel* (Oxford University Press, Oxford, 1996), 135.

—— and McLeod, G. trans. and eds, *Justinian's Institutes* (Cornell University Press, Ithaca, 1987).

Blackstone, W., *Commentaries on the Laws of England* (Clarendon Press, Oxford, 1765–69).

Bolgár, V., 'Abuse of Rights in France, Germany and Switzerland: A Survey of a Recent Chapter in Legal Doctrine' (1975) 35 *Louisiana Law Review* 1015.

Bone, R. G., 'Normative Theory and Legal Doctrine in American Nuisance Law: 1850 to 1920' (1986) 59 *Southern California Law Review* 1101.

Brenner, J. F., 'Nuisance Law and the Industrial Revolution' (1974) 3 *Journal of Legal Studies* 403.

Briggs, A., *Victorian Cities* (published in 1970; rep. University of California Press, Berkeley, 2nd edn, 1993).

Brown, L., *Victorian News and Newspapers* (Clarendon Press, Oxford, 1985).

Brunner, C. J. H., 'Abuse of Rights in Dutch Law' (1977) 37 *Louisiana Law Review* 729.

Buchanan, R. A., 'Engineers and government in nineteenth-century Britain', in R.

MacLeod (ed.), *Government and Enterprise: Specialists, administrators and professionals, 1860–1919* (Cambridge University Press, Cambridge, 1988), 41.

Buckland, W. W. and McNair, A. D. (rev. by F. H. Lawson), *Roman Law & Common Law: A Comparison in Outline* (Cambridge University Press, Cambridge, 1952).

Buckley, R. A. (1996), *The Law of Nuisance* (Butterworths, London, 2nd edn, 1996).

Budd, H., 'The Law of Subterranean Waters' (1891) 39 *American Law Register* 237.

Burchill, C. S., 'The Origin of Canadian Irrigation Law' (1948) 29 *Canadian Historical Review* 353.

Burns, R. P., 'Blackstone's Theory of the "Absolute" Rights of Property' (1985) 54 *University of Cincinnati Law Review* 67.

Calabresi, G. and Melamed, A. G., 'Property Rules, Liability Rules and Inalienability: One View of the Cathedral' (1972) 85 *Harvard Law Review* 1089.

Cane, P., *The Anatomy of Tort Law* (Hart Publishing, Oxford, 1997).

—— 'Fault and Strict Liability for Harm in Tort Law', in W. Swadling and G. Jones (eds), *The Search for Principle: Essays in Honour of Lord Goff of Chieveley* (Oxford University Press, Oxford, 1999), 171.

Carrington, P. D., 'Law as "Common Thought of Men": The Law-Teaching and Judging of Thomas McIntrye Cooley' (1997) 49 *Stanford Law Review* 495.

Catala, P. and Weir, J. A., 'Delict and Torts: A Study in Parallel: Part II' (1964) 38 *Tulane Law Review* 221.

Chandelie, J. M. N., 'Property, Absolute Right But Limited Immunity. A Theory Illustrated by Comparative Study of Conflicts between Neighbouring Landowners', unpublished Ph.D. thesis, University of Cambridge, 1979.

Clayberg, J. B., 'The Law of Percolating Water' (1915–16) 14 *Michigan Law Review* 119.

Clifford, F., *A History of Private Bill Legislation* (Butterworths, London, 1885–7), 2 vols.

Cohen, M. R., 'Property and Sovereignty' (1927–8) 13 *Cornell Law Quarterly* 8.

Cook, H. F., 'Groundwater Development in England' (1999) 5 *Environment & History* 75.

Cook, P., 'Cujus Est Solum: More Than A Maxim?' (1982) 7 *Holdsworth Law Review* 37.

Cooley, T. M., *A Treatise on the Law of Torts or the Wrongs which arise Independent of Contract* (Callaghan and Company, Chicago, 1st edn, 1879).

Cornish, W. R. and Clark, G. de N., *Law and Society in England 1750–1950* (Sweet & Maxwell, London, 1989).

Cosgrove, R. A., *The Rule of Law: Albert Venn Dicey, Victorian Jurist* (University of North Carolina Press, Chapel Hill, 1980).

—— 'The reception of analytical jurisprudence: the Victorian debate on the separation of law and morality, 1860–1900' (1981–82) 43 *Durham University Journal* 47.

—— *'Our Lady the Common Law': An Anglo-American Legal Community, 1870–1930* (New York University Press, New York, 1987).

Crabb, J. H., 'The French Concept of Abuse of Rights' (1964) 6 *Inter-American Law Review* 1.

—— trans., *The French Civil Code Revised Edition (as amended to 1 July 1994)* (Fred B. Rothman & Co., Colorado, 1995).

Crépeau, P-A., 'Abuse of Rights in the Civil Law of Quebec', in A. M. Rabello (ed.), *Aequitas and Equity: Equity in Civil Law and Mixed Jurisdictions* (The Harry and Michael Sacher Institute for Legislative Research and Comparative Law, The Hebrew University of Jerusalem, 1997), 583.

Cross, G., 'Does only the careless polluter pay? A fresh examination of the nature of private nuisance' (1995) 111 *Law Quarterly Review* 445.

Cudworth, W., *Round About Bradford: A Series of Sketches (Descriptive and Semi-Historical) of Forty-Two Places Within Six Miles of Bradford* (T. Brear, Bradford, 1876; reprinted by Mountain Press, Queensbury, 1968).

—— *Historical Notes on the Bradford Corporation* (T. Brear, Bradford, 1881).

—— *Bradford Portraits* (Bradford, 1892).

—— 'Bradford in 1759' (1895) 2 *Bradford Antiquary* 216.

—— 'The First Bradford Waterworks' (1905) 4 *Bradford Antiquary* 353.

Cueto-Rua, J., 'Abuse of Rights' (1975) 35 *Louisiana Law Review* 965.

Dawwas, A. R. R., 'Abuse of Rights in the Shari'a and Under Modern Arab Civil Codes: A Study in Comparative Jurisprudence' (1993) 13 *Islamic & Comparative Law Review* 1.

Daude, D., 'Doves and Bees', in *Droits de l'Antiquité et Sociologie Juridique: Mélanges Henri Lévy-Bruhl* (l'Instititut de Droit Roman, Paris, 1959), 63.

David, R., 'Supereminent Principles in French law', in J. Dainow (ed.), *The Role of Judicial Decisions and Doctrine in Civil Law and in Mixed Jurisdictions* (Louisiana State University Press, Baton Rouge, 1974), 119.

Davis, P. N., 'Wells and Springs: Relationship at Law' (1972) 37 *Missouri Law Review* 189.

Davies, R., 'A Comparative Study of Real Property Law in France and England', unpublished Ph.D. thesis, University of London, 1980.

Denning, A. T., *Freedom Under the Law* (Stevens & Sons Ltd, London, 1949).

Derham, D. P., 'Interference with Surface Water by Lower Landholders' (1958) 74 *Law Quarterly Review* 361.

Deveney, P., 'Title, *Jus Publicum* and the Public Trust: An Historical Analysis' (1976) 1 *Sea Grant Law Journal* 13.

de Villiers, M., 'Nuisances in Roman Law' (1897) 13 *Law Quarterly Review* 387.

Devine, D. J., 'Some Comparative Aspects of the Doctrine of Abuse of Rights' [1964] *Acta Juridica* 148.

Dewhurst, I., *A History of Keighley* (Keighley Corporation, Keighley, 1974).

Dicey, A. V., Note, (1902) 18 *Law Quarterly Review* 1.

—— *Lectures on the Relation between Law and Public Opinion in England During the Nineteenth Century* (Macmillan & Co., London, 1st edn, 1905).

Dockray, M., 'Savigny and the Squatter' (1985) 6 *Journal of Legal History* 109.

—— 'Guineas by Gaslight', in M. Dowrick (ed.), *City University Centenary Lectures in Law* (Blackstone Press Ltd, London, 1996), 27.

Donahue, C., 'Noodit, Titius and the Natural Law School: The Occupation of Wild Animals and the Intersection of Property and Tort', in J. A. Ankum *et al.* (eds), *Satura Roberta Feenstra: sexagesimum quintum annum aetatis complenti ab alumnis collegis amicis oblata* (Éditions universitaires, Fribourg, 1985), 609.

—— '*Animalia Ferae Naturae*: Rome, Bologna, Leyden, Oxford and Queen's County, N.Y.', in R. S. Bagnall and W. V. Harris (eds), *Studies in Roman Law in Memory of A. Arthur Schiller* (E. J. Brill, Leiden, 1986), 39.

—— Kauper, T. E. and Martin, P. W., *Cases and Materials on Property: An Introduction to the Concept and the Institution* (West Publishing Co., St Paul, 2nd edn, 1983).

Drewry, G., 'Lawyers and statutory reform in Victorian Government', in R. MacLeod (ed.), *Government and Expertise: Specialists, administrators and professionals, 1860–1919* (Cambridge University Press, Cambridge, 1988), 27.

Drukker, R. T., 'Spite Fences and Spite Wells: Relevancy of Motive in the Relations of Adjoining Landowners' (1938) 26 *California Law Review* 691.

Duman, D., *The English and Colonial Bars in the Nineteenth Century* (Croom Helm, London, 1983).

Duport, J. G., 'Disinterested Malevolence as an Actionable Wrong' (1953) 22 *Fordham Law Review* 185.

Duxbury, N., 'When We Were Young: Notes in the *Law Quarterly Review*, 1885–1925' (2000) 116 *Law Quarterly Review* 474.

—— *Judges & Jurists: An Essay on Influence* (Hart Publishing, Oxford, 2001).

Elliott, A., 'The Establishment of Municipal Government in Bradford 1837–57: An analysis of the political and social factors which gave rise to the incorporation of Bradford: the foundations of municipal activity and their relationship to a changing society', unpublished Ph.D. thesis, University of Bradford, 1976.

—— 'The Incorporation of Bradford' (1979) 15 *Northern History* 156.

—— 'Municipal government in Bradford in the mid-nineteenth century', in D. Fraser (ed.), *Municipal Reform in the Industrial City* (Leicester University Press, Leicester, 1982), 111.

Elvin, D. and Karas, J., *Unlawful Interference With Land* (Sweet & Maxwell, London, 1995).

Emmett, A. R., 'Roman traces in Australian law' (2001) 20 *Australian Bar Review* 205.

Eörsi, G., *Comparative Civil (Private) Law: Law Types, Law Groups, The Roads to Legal Development* (Akadémiai Kiadó, Budapest, 1979).

Evans, J., 'Change in the Doctrine of Precedent during the Nineteenth century', in L. Goldstein (ed.), *Precedent in Law* (Clarendon Press, Oxford, 1987), 35.

Farnham, H. P., 'Percolating Water and the Common Law' (1913) 19 *Case and Comment* 664.

Fawcett, R. H., 'The Story of Wilsden' (1976) 11 *Bradford Antiquity* 1–28, 131–150, 187–209.

Ferguson, R., 'The Horwitz Thesis and Common Law Discourse in England' (1983) 3 *Oxford Journal of Legal Studies* 34.

Fieldhouse, J., *Bradford* (Longman Group Ltd, London, 1972).

Finnis, J., 'Intention in Tort Law', in D. G. Owen (ed.), *Philosophical Foundations of Tort Law* (Clarendon Press, Oxford, 1995), 229.

Firth, G., *Bradford and the Industrial Revolution: An economic history, 1760–1840* (Ryburn Publishing, Halifax, 1990).

Fletcher, A. W., 'Municipal Trading' [1900–01] *Transactions of the Manchester Statistical Society* 85.

Fletcher, I., 'An English Tragedy: The Academic Lawyer as Jurist', in T. M. Charles-Edwards, M. E. Owen and D. B. Walters (eds), *Lawyers and Laymen: Studies in the History of Law presented to Professor Dafydd Jenkins on his seventy-fifth birthday* (University of Wales Press, Cardiff, 1986), 316.

Fraser, D., 'The Politics of Leeds Water' (1973) 53 *Thoresby Society Publications* 50.
—— *Power and Authority in the Victorian City* (St Martin's Press, New York, 1979).
—— 'Introduction: Municipal reform in historical perspective', in D. Fraser (ed.), *Municipal Reform and the Industrial City* (Leicester University Press, Leicester, 1982), 2.
—— 'Joseph Chamberlain and the Municipal Ideal', in G. Marsden (ed.), *Victorian Values: Personalities and Perspectives in Nineteenth-Century Society* (Longman, London, 1990), 135.
Fraser, W. H., 'From Civic Gospel to Municipal Socialism', in D. Fraser (ed.), *Cities, Class and Communication: Essays in Honour of Asa Briggs* (Harvester/Wheatsheaf, New York, 1990), 58.
Freund, E., 'Malice and Unlawful Interference' (1897–98) 11 *Harvard Law Review* 449.
Fridman, G. H. L., 'Motive in the English Law of Tort' (1954) 40 *Virginia Law Review* 583.
—— 'Malice in the Law of Torts' (1958) 21 *Modern Law Review* 484.
Friedmann, W., *Legal Theory* (Stevens & Sons Ltd, London, 4th edn, 1960).
Gale, C. J. and Whately, T. D., *A Treatise on the Law of Easements* (S. Sweet, London, 1st edn, 1839).
Gambaro, A., 'Abuse of Rights in civil law tradition' (1995) 4 *European Review of Private Law* 561; reprinted as 'Abuse of Rights in Civil Law Tradition' in A. M. Rabello (ed.), *Aequitas and Equity: Equity in Civil Law and Mixed Jurisdictions* (The Harry and Michael Sacher Institute for Legislative Research and Comparative Law, The Hebrew University of Jerusalem, 1997), 632.
Garrand, J., *Leadership and power in Victorian industrial towns, 1830–80* (Manchester University Press, Manchester, 1983).
Getzler, J. S., 'Rules Writ in Water: A History of Riparian Rights and Property Use Doctrine in England to 1870', unpublished D.Phil. thesis, University of Oxford, 1993.
—— 'The Fate of the Civil Jury in Late-Victorian England: Malicious Prosecution as a Test Case', in K. O'Donovan and G. R. Rubin (eds), *Human Rights and Legal History: Essays in Honour of Brian Simpson* (Oxford University Press, Oxford, 2001), 205.
Goldstein, R. (ed.), *Equity and Contemporary Legal Developments* (The Harry and Michael Sacher Institute for Legislative Research and Comparative Law, Jerusalem, 1992).
Goodhart, A. L., 'Case Law in England and America' (1930) 15 *Cornell Law Quarterly* 173.
—— *Essays in Jurisprudence and the Common Law* (Cambridge University Press, Cambridge, 1931).
—— *English Law and the Moral Law* (Stevens & Sons Ltd, London, 1955).
Gordon, R., 'Paradoxical Property', in J. R. Brewer and S. Staves (eds), *Early Modern Conceptions of Property* (Routledge, London, 1995), 95.
Gordon, W. M., *Scottish Land Law* (W. Green & Son Ltd, Edinburgh, 1989).
Gott, C., 'On the Bradford Waterworks', in *Report of the British Association for the Advancement of Science* (1873), 451.
Goudy, H., 'Two Ancient Brocards', in P. Vinogradoff (ed.), *Essays in Legal History*

read before the International Congress of Historical Studies held in London in 1913 (Oxford University Press, Oxford, 1913), 231.

Gray, K., 'Property in Common Law Systems', in G. E. van Maanen and A. J. van der Walt (eds), *Property Law on The Threshold of the 21st Century* (Maklu, Antwerp, 1996), 235.

—— and Gray, S., 'Private Property and Public Propriety', in J. McLean (ed.), *Property and the Constitution* (Hart Publishing, Oxford, 1999), 11.

Graziadei, M., 'Changing Images of the Law in XIX Century English Legal Thought (The Continental Impulse)', in M. Reimann (ed.), *The Reception of Continental Ideas in the Common Law World, 1820–1920* (Duncker & Humblot, Berlin, 1993), 115.

Greaves, V. E., 'The Social-Economic Purpose of Private Rights: Section 1 of the Soviet Civil Code; A Comparative Study of Soviet and Non-communist Law' (1934) 12 *New York University Quarterly Review* 165, 438 (two parts).

Grey, T. C., 'Holmes and Legal Pragmatism' (1988–89) 41 *Stanford Law Review* 787.

Grinling, C. H., *The History of the Great Northern Railway, 1845–1922* (George Allen & Unwin Ltd, London, rev. edn, 1903).

Gutteridge, H. C., 'Abuse of Rights' (1933–35) 5 *Cambridge Law Journal* 22.

Hahlo, H. R. and Kahn, E., *The South African Legal System and Its Background* (Juta & Co., Cape Town, 1968).

Haldane, R. B., 'Lord Watson' (1899) 11 *Juridical Review* 269.

Hall, M. E. (ed.), *Selected Writings of Benjamin Nathan Cardozo* (Fallon Publications, New York, 1947).

Halper, L. A., 'Christopher G. Tiedeman, "Laissez-Faire Constitutionalism" and the Dilemmas of Small Scale Property in the Gilded Age' (1990) 51 *Ohio State Law Journal* 1349.

Hamlin, C., 'Muddling in Bumbledon: On the Enormity of Large Sanitary Improvements in Four British Towns, 1855–1885' (1988) 32 *Victorian Studies* 55.

Harris, J., *Private Lives, Public Spirit: Britain, 1870–1914* (Penguin Books, London, 1994).

Harrison, J. F. C., *The Early Victorians 1832–1851* (Weidenfeld & Nicolson, London, 1971).

Hartley, W. P., 'The Development of Coal Mining in the Heavy Woollen District of West Yorkshire During the Nineteenth Century' (1994–5) 14 *Journal of Regional & Local Studies* 25.

Hartog, H., *Public Property and Private Power: The Corporation of the City of New York in American Law, 1730–1870* (University of North Carolina Press, Chapel Hill, 1983).

Hassan, J. A., 'The impact and development of the water supply in Manchester, 1568–1882' (1983–84) 133 *Transactions of the Historic Society of Lancashire & Cheshire*, 25.

—— 'The Growth and Impact of the British Water Industry in the Nineteenth Century' (1985) 38 *Economic History Review*, 2nd ser. 531.

—— *A history of water in modern England and Wales* (Manchester University Press, Manchester, 1998).

—— and Taylor, P., 'The Politics of Water in early and Mid-Victorian Britain: The Experience of Bolton' (1998) 148 *Transactions of the Historic Society of Lancashire and Cheshire* 119.

Hassan, J. A. and Wilson, E. R., 'The Longdendale water scheme, 1848–1884' (1979) 14 *Industrial Archaeology* 102.

Hatch, E. W., 'Property Rights in Percolating Waters' (1901) 1 *Columbia Law Review* 505.

Hayek, F. A., *The Road to Serfdom* (University of Chicago Press, Chicago, 1944).

Headrick, T. E., *The Town Clerk in English Local Government* (George Allen & Unwin Ltd, London, 1962).

Hedley, S., 'Words, Words, Words: Making Sense of Legal Judgments, 1875–1940', in C. Stebbings (ed.), *Law Reporting in Britain* (Hambledon Press, London, 1995), 169.

—— 'Sir Frederick Pollock and the Teaching of English Law', in J. A. Bush and A. Wijffels (eds), *Learning the Law: Teaching and the Transmission of Law in England, 1150–1900* (Hambledon Press, London, 1999), 407.

Helmholz, R. H., 'Use of the Civil Law in Post-Revolutionary American Jurisprudence' (1992) 66 *Tulane Law Review* 1648.

—— 'Brian Simpson in the United States', in K. Donovan and G. R. Rubin (eds), *Human Rights and Legal History: Essays in Honour of Brian Simpson* (Oxford University Press, 2001), 285.

Henderson, J. H., 'Malicious Motive as a Ground of Action' (1901) 13 *Juridical Review* 452.

Hennock, E. P., *Fit and Proper Persons: Ideal and Reality in Nineteenth-Century Urban Government* (Edward Arnold, London, 1973).

Herman, S., 'Classical Social Theories and the Doctrine of "Abuse of Rights"' (1977) 37 *Louisiana Law Review* 747.

Heuston, R. F. V., 'Lord Halsbury's Judicial Appointments' (1962) 78 *Law Quarterly Review* 504.

—— *Lives of the Lord Chancellors, 1885–1940* (Clarendon Press, Oxford, 1964).

—— 'Parke, James (First (and last) Lord Wensleydale)', in A. W. B. Simpson (ed.), *Biographical Dictionary of the Common Law* (Butterworths, London, 1984), 401.

—— 'Judicial Prosopography' (1986) 102 *Law Quarterly Review* 90.

—— 'Judicial Law-Making in Victorian England' (1987) 12 *Holdsworth Law Review* 16.

—— and Buckley, R. A., *Salmond and Heuston on the Law of Torts* (Sweet & Maxwell, London, 21st edn, 1996).

Heydon, J. D., *Economic Torts* (Sweet & Maxwell, London, 2nd edn, 1978).

Hird, H., *How a City Grows: Historical Notes on the City of Bradford* (Horace Hird, Bradford, 1966).

—— *Bradford in History: Twenty-four Essays on the Life by the Broad Ford from the Celtic Age to the Present Day* (Horace Hird, Bradford, 1968).

Hodge, A. T., *Roman Aqueducts & Water Supply* (Duckworth, London, 1992).

Hoeflich, M. H., 'The Americanization of British Legal Education in the Nineteenth Century' (1987) 8 *Journal of Legal History* 244.

—— ed. and compiler, *The Gladsome Light of Jurisprudence: Learning the Law and the United States in the 18th and 19th Centuries* (Greenwood Press, New York, 1988).

—— *Roman and Civil Law and the Development of Anglo-American Jurisprudence in the Nineteenth Century* (University of Georgia Press, Athens, 1997).

Hoexter, C., 'Administrative Justice and Dishonesty' (1994) 111 *South African Law Journal* 700.

Holdsworth, W. S., 'Blackstone's Treatment of Equity' (1929) 43 *Harvard Law Review* 1.

—— *A History of English Law* (Methuen & Co., London, 1965), vol. XV.

Holmes, O. W., *The Common Law* (Brown & Little, Boston, 1881).

—— 'Privilege, Malice, and Intent' (1894) 8 *Harvard Law Review* 1.

—— 'The Path of Law' (1897) 10 *Harvard Law Review* 457.

—— *Collected Legal Papers* (Harcourt, Brace & Co., New York, 1921).

Holroyd, A. (ed.), *Collectanea Bradfordiana: A Collection of Papers on the History of Bradford and the Neighbourhood* (A. Holroyd, Saltaire, 1873).

Home, Henry (Lord Kames), *Principles of Equity* (Kincaird & Bell, Edinburgh, 2nd edn, 1767).

—— *Principles of Equity* (Bell & Bradfute, Edinburgh, 5th edn, 1825).

Honoré, A. M., 'Ownership', in A. G. Guest (ed.), *Oxford Essays in Jurisprudence (First Series)* (Clarendon Press, Oxford, 1964), 107: reprinted in T. Honoré, *Making Law Bind: Essays Legal and Philosophical* (Clarendon Press, Oxford, 1987), 161.

—— *Ulpian* (Clarendon Press, Oxford, 1982).

Hood Phillips, O., 'Legal Authors since 1800', in *Then and Now, 1799–1974: Commemorating 175 Years of Law Bookselling and Publishing* (Sweet & Maxwell, London, 1974), 3.

Horwitz, M. J., *The Transformation of American Law, 1780–1860* (Harvard University Press, Cambridge, 1977).

—— 'The Place of Justice Holmes in American Legal Thought', in R. W. Gordon (ed.), *The Legacy of Oliver Wendell Holmes, Jr.* (Stanford University Press, Stanford, 1992), 31.

—— *The Transformation of American Law, 1870–1960: The Crisis of Legal Orthodoxy* (Oxford University Press, New York, 1992).

Hostak, K. F., 'Wisconsin Ground Water Law—A New Era' [1957] *Wisconsin Law Review* 309.

Howarth, D., 'Is There a Future for the Intentional Torts?', in P. Birks (ed.), *The Classification of Obligations* (Clarendon Press, Oxford, 1997), 233.

—— and O'Sullivan, J. A. , *Hepple, Howarth and Matthews' Tort: Cases and Materials* (Butterworths, London, 2000).

Howarth, W., *Wisdom's Law of Watercourses* (Shaw & Sons Ltd, Crayford, 1992).

Howe, M. de W. (ed.), *The Pollock-Holmes Letters: Correspondence of Sir Frederick Pollock and Mr Justice Holmes, 1874–1932* (Cambridge University Press, Cambridge, 1942).

Huffcut, E. W., 'Percolating Waters: The Rule of Reasonable User' (1903–4) 13 *Yale Law Journal* 222.

Ittman, K., 'Family Limitation and Family Economy in Bradford, West Yorkshire, 1851–81' (1991–2) 25 *Journal of Social History* 547.

Jackson, P., 'The Maxims of Equity Revisited', in R. Goldstein (ed.), *Equity and Contemporary Legal Developments* (The Harry and Michael Sacher Institute for Legislative Research and Comparative Law, Jerusalem, 1992), 72.

James, D., 'William Byles and the *Bradford Observer*', in D. G. Wright and J. A. Jowitt (eds), *Victorian Bradford: Essays in Honour of Jack Reynolds* (City of Bradford Metropolitan Council, Bradford, 1981), 115.

James, D., *Bradford* (Ryburn Publishing, Halifax, 1900).

James, J., *The History and Topography of Bradford* (C. Stanfield, Bradford, 1841).

Jeanneau, B., 'The Reception of Equity in French Private and Public Law', in R. A. Newman (ed.), *Equity in the World's Legal Systems: A Comparative Study* (Établissements Émile Bruylant, Brussels, 1973), 223.

Jenkins, D., 'Early factory development in the West Riding of Yorkshire, 1770–1800', in N. B. Hart and K. G. Ponting (eds), *Textile History and Economic History: Essays in Honour of Miss Julia de Lacy Mann* (Manchester University Press, Manchester, 1973), 247.

Johnson, E. L., 'Abuse of Rights in Soviet Civil Law' (1960) 1 *The Solicitor Quarterly* 320.

Johnston, D., 'Owners and Neighbours: From Rome to Scotland', in R. Evans-Jones (ed.), *The Civil Law Tradition in Scotland* (The Stair Society, Edinburgh, 1995), 176.

—— *Roman Law in Context* (Cambridge University Press, Cambridge, 1999).

Jones, G. H., 'Blackstone, Sir William', in A. W. B. Simpson (ed.), *Biographical Dictionary of the Common Law* (Butterworths, London, 1984), 57.

Josserand, L., *De L'esprit des Droit et Leur Relativité: Théorie De L'Abus des Droit* (2nd edn, 1939).

Jowitt, J. A., 'Late Victorian and Edwardian Bradford', in J. A. Jowitt and R. K. S. Taylor (eds), *Bradford, 1890–1914: The Cradle of the Independent Labour Party* (Bradford Centre Occasional Papers No. 2, Bradford, 1980), 4.

—— 'A Review of Recent Writings on the History of the Town', in D. G. Wright and J. A. Jowitt (eds), *Victorian Bradford: Essays in Honour of Jack Reynolds* (City of Bradford Metropolitan Council, Bradford, 1981), 245.

Kenner, S., 'Some Observations on the Rights of Landowners in Subterranean Percolating Waters' (1908) 66 *Central Law Journal* 194.

Kent, J., *Commentaries on American Law* (O. Halsted, New York, 1826–30), 4 vols.

Kersley, R. H. (ed.), *Broom's Legal Maxims* (Sweet & Maxwell Ltd, London, 10th edn, 1939).

Klarman, M. J., 'The Judges versus the Unions: The Development of British Labor Law, 1867–1913' (1989) 75 *Virginia Law Review* 1487.

Klafter, C. E., 'The Americanization of Blackstone's *Commentaries*', in E. A. Cawthorn and D. E. Narrett (eds), *Essays on English Law and the American Experience* (Texas, A & M University Press, Texas, 1994), 42.

Koditschek, T., 'The dynamics of class formation in nineteenth-century Bradford', in A. L. Beier, D. Cannadine and J. M. Rosenheim (eds), *The First Modern Society: Essays in English History in Honour of Lawrence Stone* (Cambridge University Press, Cambridge, 1989), 511.

Komar, B. M., 'Textbooks As Authority in Anglo-American Law' (1922–3) 11 *California Law Review* 397.

Kostal, R. W., *Law and English Railway Capitalism, 1825–1875* (Clarendon Press, Oxford, 1994).

Langbein, J. H., 'Chancellor Kent and the History of Legal Literature' (1993) 93 *Columbia Law Review* 547.

Laski, H. J., 'The Technique of Judicial Appointment', in H. J. Laski, *Studies in Law and Politics* (George Allen & Unwin Ltd, London, 1932), 163.

—— 'The Committee System in Local Government', in H. J. Laski, W. I. Jennings and W. A. Robson (eds), *A Century of Municipal Progress, 1835–1935* (George Allen & Unwin Ltd, London, 1935), 82.

Lauer, T. E., 'The Common Law Background of the Riparian Doctrine' (1963) 28 *Missouri Law Review* 60.

—— 'Reflections on Riparianism' (1970) 35 *Missouri Law Review* 1.

Law, M. C. D., *The Story of Bradford* (Sir Isaac Pitman & Sons Ltd, London, 1912).

Lawson, F. H., 'Notes on the History of Tort in the Civil Law' (1940) 22 *Journal of Comparative Legislation* (3rd Ser) 136; reprinted in F. H. Lawson, *The Comparison: Selected Essays; Volume II* (North Holland, Amsterdam, 1977), 210.

—— *Negligence in the Civil Law* (Clarendon Press, Oxford, 1950).

Leake, H. C., 'Abuse of Rights in Louisiana' (1933) 7 *Tulane Law Review* 426.

Leatham, W. H., Ruscoe, J., and Renton G. F., *Bradford Corporation Waterworks Department: 1855–1955 Centenary* (Bradford Corporation, Bradford, 1955).

Lennertz, J. E., 'Property Rights in France and America: The Resolution of Incompatible Uses' (1984) 12 *Proceedings of the Annual Meeting of the Western Society for French History* 200.

Lever, J. F., 'Means, Motives, and Interests in the Law of Torts', in A. G. Guest (ed.), *Oxford Essays in Jurisprudence (First Series)* (Clarendon Press, Oxford, 1964), 50.

Lewin, J. L., '*Boomer* and the American Law of Nuisance: Past, Present and Future' (1990) 54 *Albany Law Review* 189.

Lewis, A. D. E., ' "What Marcellus says is against you": Roman Law and Common Law', in A. D. E. Lewis and D. J. Ibbetson (eds), *The Roman Law Tradition* (Cambridge University Press, Cambridge, 1994), 199.

Lieberman, D., *The Province of Legislation Determined: Legal theory in eighteenth-century Britain* (Cambridge University Press, Cambridge, 1989).

Lippman, E. A., 'The Landowner's Rights in Percolating Water' (1909–10) 58 *University of Pennsylvania Law Review* 303.

Loughlin, M., 'Municipal Socialism in a Unitary State', in P. McAuslan and J. F. McEldowney (eds), *Law, Legitimacy and the Constitution* (Sweet & Maxwell, London, 1985), 82.

McCord, N., 'Ratepayers and Social Policy', in P. Thane (ed.), *The Origins of British Social Policy* (Croom Helm, London, 1978), 21.

MacDonald, A., 'Hollywood Silver Fox Farm v Emmett' (1937) 2 *Alberta Law Quarterly* 99.

MacGrady, G. J., 'The Navigability Concept in the Civil and Common Law: Historical Development, Current Importance, and Some Doctrines That Don't Hold Water' (1975) 3 *Florida State University Law Review* 511.

McLaren, J. P. S., 'Nuisance Law and the Industrial Revolution—Some lessons from Social History' (1983) 3 *Oxford Journal of Legal Studies* 155.

Maltby, H. J. M., 'The Coal Industry of the Bradford District', in *The Book of Bradford* (W. H. Brocklehurst, Bradford, 1924), 99.

Manchester, A. H., *A Modern Legal History of England and Wales, 1750–1950* (Butterworths, London, 1980).

Markby, W., *Elements of Law Considered with Reference to the Principles of General Jurisprudence* (Clarendon Press, Oxford, 1871).

Mattei, U., *Basic Principles of Property Law: A Comparative Legal and Economic Introduction* (Greenwood Press, Westport, 2000).

Mayrand, A., 'Abuse of Rights in France and Quebec' (1974) 34 *Louisiana Law Review* 993.

Megarry, R., 'Seventy-Five Years On: Is the Judiciary What It Was?', in D. C. Hoath (ed.), *75 Years of Law at Sheffield, 1909–1984* (University of Sheffield, Sheffield, 1984), 1.

Mignault, P. B., 'L'Abus des Droits' (1939–40) 3 *University of Toronto Law Journal* 360.

Milton, J. R. L., 'The Law of Neighbours in South Africa' [1969] *Acta Juridica* 123.

—— 'The Concept of Nuisance in English Law: A study of the origins and historical development of the concept of nuisance from its earliest beginnings to the end of the nineteenth century', unpublished Ph.D. thesis, University of Natal, 1978.

Moccia, L., 'English Law Attitudes to the "Civil Law" ' (1981) 2 *Journal of Legal History* 156.

Mommsen, T., Krueger, P. and Watson, A., *The Digest of Justinian* (University of Pennsylvania Press, Pennsylvania, 1985).

Mukhopadhyay, A. K., *Politics of Water Supply: The Case of Victorian London* (The World Press Private Ltd, Calcutta, 1981).

Munday, R., 'The Common Lawyer's Philosophy of Legislation' (1983) 14 *Rechstheorie* 191.

Murphy, E. F., 'English Water Law Before 1400' (1957) 1 *American Journal of Legal History* 103.

—— 'The Recurring State Judicial Task of Choosing Rules for Groundwater Law: How Occult Still?' (1987) 66 *Nebraska Law Review* 120.

Napier, B. W., 'Abuse of Rights in British Law', in M. Rotondi (ed.), *L'Abus des Droit* (Padova, Italy, 1979), 265.

Newark, F., 'The Boundaries of Nuisance' (1949) 65 *Law Quarterly Review* 480.

Note , 'The Effect of Motive upon Actionability in the Exercise of Rights in Real Property—Spite Wells and Spite Fences' (1924–5) 11 *Virginia Law Review* 122.

Novak, W. J., *The People's Welfare: Law and Regulation in Nineteenth-Century America* (University of North Carolina, Chapel Hill, 1996).

Novick, S. M., *Honorable Justice: The Life of Oliver Wendell Holmes* (Little, Brown & Co., Boston, 1989).

Oliver, D. T., 'Roman Law in Modern Cases in English Courts', in *Cambridge Legal Essays: Written in Honour of and Presented to Doctor Bond, Professor Buckland and Professor Kenny* (W. Heffer & Sons Ltd, Cambridge, 1926), 243.

Ormsby, W. E., 'Malice in the Law of Torts' (1892) 8 *Law Quarterly Review* 140.

Orth, J. V., 'Taking from A and Giving to B: Substantive Due Process and the Case of the Shifting Paradigm' [1997] *Constitutional Commentary* 337.

O'Sullivan, R., 'Abuse of Rights' (1955) 8 *Current Legal Problems* 61.

Pannick, D., *Judges* (Oxford University Press, Oxford, 1987).

Paul, E. F., *Moral Revolution and Economic Science: The demise of laissez-faire in nineteenth British political thought* (Greenwood Press, Westport, 1979).

Pemberton, E. L., 'Private Bill Legislation' (1885) 38 *Fortnightly Review* (new ser.) 228.

Penner, J. E., 'The "Bundle of Rights" Picture of Property' (1996) 43 *University of California at Los Angeles Law Review* 711.

Perillo, J. M., 'Abuse of Rights: A Pervasive Legal Concept' (1995) 27 *Pacific Law Journal* 37.

Phear, J. B., *Treatise on rights to sea and seashore* (Stevens & Norton, London, 1859).

Philbrick, F. S., 'Changing Conceptions of Property' (1938) 86 *University of Pennsylvania Law Review* 691.

Pisani, D. J., *Water, Land and Law in the West: Limits of Public Policy, 1850–1920* (University Press of Kansas, Lawrence, 1996).

Planiol, M., *Traité Élémentaire de Droit Civil* (11th edn, 1939).

Plescia, J., 'The Roman Law on Waters' (1993) 21 *Index: International Survey of Roman Law* 433.

Podmore, D., 'Lawyers and Politics' (1977) 4 *British Journal of Law and Society* 155.

Pohlman, H. L., *Justice Oliver Wendell Holmes & Utilitarian Jurisprudence* (Harvard University Press, Cambridge, 1984).

Polden, P., 'A Day at the Races: *Wood v Leadbitter* in Context' (1993) 14 *Journal of Legal History* 28.

—— *A History of the County Court, 1846–1971* (Cambridge University Press, Cambridge, 1999).

Pollock, F., 'Oxford Legal Studies (1886)', reprinted in M. H. Hoeflich (ed. and compiler), *The Gladsome Light of Jurisprudence: Learning the Law and the United States in the 18th and 19th Centuries* (Greenwood Press, New York, 1988), 255.

—— *The Law of Torts: A Treatise on the Principles of Obligations Arising From Civil Wrongs in the Common Law* (Stevens & Sons, London, 1887).

—— *The Law of Torts* (Stevens & Sons, London, 5th edn, 1897).

—— *A First Book of Jurisprudence for Students of the Common Law* (Macmillan & Co. Ltd, London, 2nd edn, 1904).

Pound, R., 'The Influence of French Law in America' (1908) 3 *Illinois Law Review* 354.

—— *The Spirit of the Common Law* (Beacon Press, Boston, rep. 1963).

—— 'The Influence of the Civil Law in America' (1938) 1 *Louisiana Law Review* 1.

—— 'The French Civil Code and the Spirit of Nineteenth Century Law' (1955) 52 *Boston University Law Review* 77.

Powell, R., 'Roman Law in Common Law Courts' (1958) 11 *Current Legal Problems* 19.

Prest, J., *Liberty and Locality: Parliament, Permissive Legislation, and Ratepayers' Democracies in the Nineteenth Century* (Clarendon Press, Oxford, 1990).

Pringsheim, F., '*Animus* in Roman Law' (1933) 49 *Law Quarterly Review* 43.

Pugsley, D., '*London Tramways* (1898)' (1996) 17 *Journal of Legal History* 172.

Pulling, A., *Private Bill Legislation: Can Anything Be Now Done to Improve It?* (Longman, Brown, Green, Longmans & Roberts, London, 1859).

Rabello, A. M. (ed.), *Aequitas and Equity: Equity in Civil Law and Mixed Jurisdictions* (The Harry and Michael Sacher Institute for Legislative Research and Comparative Law, The Hebrew University of Jerusalem, Jerusalem, 1997).

Rankine, J., *A Treatise on the Rights and Burdens Incident to the Ownership of Lands and Other Heritages in Scotland* (William Blackwood & Sons, Edinburgh, 1st edn, 1879).

Reichman, A., 'Professional Status and the Freedom to Contract: Toward a Common Law Duty of Non-Discrimination' (2001) 14 *Canadian Journal of Law and Jurisprudence* 79.

—— 'Property Rights, Public Policy and the Limits of the Legal Power to Discriminate', in D. Friedmann and D. Barak-Erez (eds), *Human Rights in Private Law* (Hart Publishing, Oxford, 2001).

Reid, E., 'Abuse of Rights in Scots Law' (1998) 2 *Edinburgh Law Review* 129.

Reid, J. S. C., 'The Law and the Reasonable Man' (1968) 54 *Proceedings of the British Academy* 189.

Reid, K. G. C., 'The Third Branch of the Profession: The Rise of the Academic Lawyer in Scotland', in H. L. MacQueen (ed.), *Scots Law into the 21st Century: Essays in Honour of W. A. Wilson* (W. Green/Sweet & Maxwell, Edinburgh, 1996), 39.

Reimann, M. (ed.), *The Reception of Continental Ideas in the Common Law World 1820–1920* (Duncker & Humblot, Berlin, 1994).

Renton, G. F., 'Water Supply of Bradford', undated and unpublished typescript, deposited in the Bradford Central Library.

Richardson, C., *A Geography of Bradford* (University of Bradford, Bradford, 1976).

Robins, F., *The Story of Water Supply* (Geoffrey Cumberlege, Oxford, 1946).

Robson, P. and Miller, K., *Property* (W. Green/Sweet & Maxwell, Edinburgh, 1991).

Robson, W. A., 'The Public Utility Services', in H. J. Laski, W. I. Jennings and W. A. Robson (eds), *A Century of Municipal Progress, 1835–1935* (George Allen and Unwin Ltd, London, 1935), 299.

Rodger, A., *Owners and Neighbours in Roman Law* (Clarendon Press, Oxford, 1972).

Rogers, W. V. H., *Winfield & Jolowicz on Tort* (Sweet & Maxwell, London, 15th edn, 1998).

Rose, C. M., 'Energy and Efficiency in the Realignment of Common Law Water Rights' (1990) 19 *Journal of Legal Studies* 261.

—— *Property & Persuasion: Essays on the History, Theory & Rhetoric of Ownership* (Westview Press, Boulder, 1994).

—— 'Property as the Keystone Right' (1996) 71 *Notre Dame Law Review* 329.

—— 'The Shadow of *The Cathedral*' (1997) 106 *Yale Law Journal* 2175.

Ross, W. D., 'Bradford Politics, 1880–1906: A detailed study of the fortunes of the political parties in Bradford as shown in parliamentary elections and by the movement of public opinion', unpublished Ph.D. thesis, University of Bradford, 1977.

Rotherham, C. I., 'The Allocation of Remedies in Private Nuisance: An Evaluation of the Judicial Approach to Awarding Damages in Lieu of an Injunction' (1989) 4 *Canterbury Law Review* 185.

—— 'Conceptions of Property in Common Law Discourse', unpublished Ph.D. thesis, University of Cambridge, 1996.

—— 'Proprietary Relief for Enrichment by Wrongs: Some Realism about Property Talk' (1996) 19 *University of New South Wales Law Journal* 378.

—— 'Conceptions of property in common law discourse' (1998) 18 *Legal Studies* 41.

Rotondi, M. (ed.), *L'Abus de Droit* (Padova, Cedam, 1979).

Round, O. S., *Riparian Rights; Being A Concise Review of the Law Relating to Running Streams, Angling, and the Sea Shore* (William Amer, London, 1859).

Rudden, B., 'Comparative Law in England', in W. E. Butler and V. N. Kudriavtsev (eds), *Comparative Law and Legal System: Historical and Socio-Legal Perspectives* (Oceana Publications Inc., New York, 1985), 75.

—— *The New River: A Legal History* (Clarendon Press, Oxford, 1985).

—— 'Torticles' (1991–92) 6/7 *Tulane Civil Law Forum* 105.

Rumble, H. H., 'Limitations on the Use of Property By Its Owner' (1918) 5 *Virginia Law Review* 297.

Rydz, D. L., *The Parliamentary Agents: A History* (Royal Historical Society, London, 1979).

Sainty, J., *A List of English Law Officers, King's Counsel and Holders of Patents of Precedence* (Selden Society, London, 1987).

Samuel, G., 'Reason, Logic and Morals in the Common Law' [1976] *City of London Law Review* 7.

—— 'Classification of Law—IV' [1984] *City of London Law Review* 3.

—— and Rinkes, J., *Law of Obligations and Legal Remedies* (Cavendish Publishing, London, 1996).

—— *Law of Obligations and Legal Remedies* (Cavendish Publishing, London, 2nd edn, 2001).

Samuel, R., 'Mrs Thatcher's Return to Victorian Values' (1992) 78 *Proceedings of the British Academy* 9.

Scheiber, H., 'The Road to *Munn*: Eminent Domain and the Concept of Public Purpose in the State Courts', in D. Fleming and B. Bailyn (eds), *Law in American History* (Little, Brown & Co., Boston, 1971), 327.

Schlesinger, R. B., Bade, H. W., Herzog, P. E., and Wise, E. M., *Comparative Law: Cases-Text-Materials* (Foundation Press, New York, 6th edn, 1998).

Schofield, A. B., *Dictionary of Legal Biography, 1845–1945* (Barry Rose Law Publishers Ltd, Chichester, 1998).

Scholtens, J. E., 'Abuse of Rights' (1958) 75 *South African Law Journal* 39.

Scott, A. and Coustalin, G., 'The Evolution of Water Rights' (1995) 35 *Natural Resources Journal* 821.

Selvin, M., 'The Public Trust Doctrine in American Law and Economic Policy, 1789–1920' [1980] *Wisconsin Law Review* 1403.

Shapiro, G., 'The Prima Facie Tort Doctrine: Acknowledging the Need for Judicial Scrutiny of Malice' (1983) 63 *Boston University Law Review* 1101.

Sheldrake, J., 'The Water Industry: A Brief Review of its Development and Prospects' (1985) 17 *London Review of Public Administration* 8.

—— *Municipal Socialism* (Avebury, Aldershot, 1989).

Shephard, V., *Historic Wells In and Around Bradford* (Heart of Albion Press, Loughborough, 1994).

Sheridan, L. A., *Injunctions and Similar Orders* (Barry Rose Publishers, Chichester, 1999).

Shilo, S., '*Kofin Al Midat S'dom*: Jewish Law's concept of the abuse of rights' (1980) 15 *Israel Law Review* 49.

Siepp, D. J., 'The Concept of Property in Early Common Law' (1994) 12 *Law & History Review* 29.

Siepp, D. J., 'Chief Justice Holmes in the Science and Art (and Politics) of Judging' (1999) 5 *Massachusetts Legal History* 19.

Sigsworth, E. M., *Black Dyke Mills: A History* (University of Liverpool, Liverpool, 1958).

Simpson, A. W. B. (Brian), *A History of the Common Law of Contract: The Rise of the Action of Assumpsit* (Clarendon Press, Oxford, 1975).

—— 'The Legal Treatise and Legal Theory', in E. V. Ives and A. H. Manchester (eds), *Law, Litigants and the Legal Profession* (Royal Historical Society, London, 1983), 11.

—— ed., *Biographical Dictionary of the Common Law* (Butterworths, London, 1984).

—— *Leading Cases in the Common Law* (Clarendon Press, Oxford, 1995).

—— *Victorian Law and the Industrial Spirit* (Selden Society, London, 1995).

—— 'Land Ownership and Economic Freedom', in H. N. Scheiber (ed.), *The State and Freedom of Contract* (Stanford University Press, Stanford, 1998), 13.

Singer, J. W., 'No Right to Exclude: Public Accommodations and Private Property' (1996) 90 *Northwestern University Law Review* 1283.

—— *Entitlement: The Paradoxes of Property* (Yale University Press, New Haven, 2000).

Skinner, A. C., 'Groundwater—legal controls and organizational aspects', in R. A. Downing and W. B. Wilkinson (eds), *Applied Groundwater Hydrology: A British Perspective* (Clarendon Press, Oxford, 1991), 8.

Smith, D. J., 'Victorian Valuations' (1995–6) 18 *Transactions of the Hunter Archaeological Society* 35.

Solden, N., '*Laissez-Faire* as Dogma: The Liberty and Property Defence League, 1882–1914', in K. D. Brown (ed.), *Essays in Anti-Labour History: Responses to the Rise of Labour in Britain* (Macmillan Press Ltd, London, 1974), 208.

Stein, P. G., 'Equitable Principles in Roman Law', in P. G. Stein, *The Character and Influence of the Roman Civil Law: Historical Essays* (Hambledon Press, London, 1988), 19.

—— 'The Influence of Roman Law on the Law of Scotland', in P. G. Stein, *The Character and Influence of the Roman Civil Law: Historical Essays* (Hambledon Press, London, 1988), 319.

—— 'Maine and Legal Education', in A. Diamond (ed.), *The Victorian Achievement of Sir Henry Maine: A centennial reappraisal* (Cambridge University Press, Cambridge, 1991), 195.

—— 'Justinian's Compilation: Classical Legacy and Legal Source' (1993) 8 *Tulane European & Civil Law Forum* 1.

Steinberg, T., *Nature Incorporated: Industrialization & the Waters of New England* (Cambridge University Press, Cambridge, 1991).

Stern, W. M., 'Water Supply in Britain: The Development of a Public Service' (1954) 74 *Journal of the Royal Sanitary Institute* 998.

Stevens, R., *Law and Politics: The House of Lords as a Judicial Body, 1800–1976* (Weidenfeld & Nicolson, London, 1979).

—— 'Basic Concepts and Current Differences in English and American Law' (1985) 6 *Journal of Legal History* 336.

Steyn, J., 'Does Formalism Hold Sway in England?' (1996) 49 *Current Legal Problems* 43.

Stoebuck, W. B., 'A General Theory of Eminent Domain' (1972) 47 *Washington Law Review* 553.

Stoner, G., 'The Influence of Social and Economic Ideals on the Law of Malicious Torts' (1910) 8 *Michigan Law Review* 468.

Stormonth-Darling, M. T., 'Lord Watson' (1899) 11 *Juridical Review* 272.

Stroud, D. A., 'What is Malice?' (1898–99) 24 *The Law Magazine & Review* (5th ser) 341.

Sugarman, D., 'Legal Theory, the Common Law Mind and Making of the Textbook Tradition', in W. Twining (ed.), *Legal Theory & Common Law* (Basil Blackwell, London, 1986), 26.

—— and Rubin, G. R., 'Towards a New History of Law and Material Society in England, 1750–1914', in G. R. Rubin and D. Sugarman (eds), *Law, Economy and Society, 1750–1914: Essays in the History of English Law* (Professional Books Ltd, Abingdon, 1984), 1.

—— ' "A Hatred of Disorder": Legal Science, Liberalism and Imperialism', in P. Fitzpatrick (ed.), *Dangerous Supplements: Resistance and Renewal in Jurisprudence* (Pluto, London, 1991), 34.

Taggart, M., 'Public Utilities and Public Law', in P. A. Joseph (ed.), *Essays on the Constitution* (Brooker's, Wellington, 1995), 214.

—— 'The Province of Administrative Law Determined?', in M. Taggart (ed.), *The Province of Administrative Law* (Hart Publishing, Oxford, 1997), 1.

—— 'Expropriation, Public Purpose and the Constitution', in C. Forsyth and I. Hare (eds), *The Golden Metwand and the Crooked Chord: Public Law Essays in Honour of Professor Sir William Wade Q.C.* (Clarendon Press, Oxford, 1998), 91.

Tann, J., 'The Bleaching of Woollen and Worsted Goods, 1740–1860' (1968–70) 1 *Textile History* 158.

Tarlock, A. D., 'Supplemental Groundwater Irrigation Law: From Capture to Sharing' (1985) 73 *Kentucky Law Journal* 695.

Teclaff, L. A., 'Private Water Rights in France and in the Eastern United States' (1962) 11 *American Journal of Comparative Law* 560.

Telly, C. S., 'The Classical Economic Model and the Nature of Property in Eighteenth and Nineteenth Centuries' (1978) 13 *Tulsa Law Journal* 406.

Terry, H., 'Malicious Torts' (1904) 20 *Law Quarterly Review* 10.

Thompson B., 'Public Provision and Private Neglect: Public Health', in D. G Wright and J. A. Jowitt (eds), *Victorian Bradford: Essays in Honour of Jack Reynolds* (City of Bradford Metropolitan Council, Bradford, 1981), 137.

—— 'Infant mortality in nineteenth-century Bradford', in R. Woods and J. Woodward (eds), *Urban Disease and Mortality in Nineteenth-Century England* (St Martin's Press, New York, 1984), 120.

Thompson, B. H., 'Water Law as a Pragmatic Exercise: Professor Joseph Sax's Water Scholarship' (1998) 25 *Ecology Law Quarterly* 363.

Thomson, J. M., 'An Island Legacy—The Delict of Conspiracy', in D. L. Carey Miller and D. W. Meyers (eds), *Comparative and Historical Essays in Scots Law: A Tribute to Professor Sir Thomas Smith QC* (Butterworths & the Law Society of Scotland, Edinburgh, 1992), 137.

—— 'The Role of Equity in Scots Law', in S. Goldstein (ed.), *Equity and Contemporary Legal Developments* (The Harry and Michael Sacher Institute for Legislature Research and Comparative Law, Hebrew University of Jerusalem, Jerusalem, 1992), 911.

Thorne, S. E., *Bracton on the Laws and Customs of England* (Belknap Press of Harvard University Press, Cambridge, 1965).

Treanor, W. M., 'Jam for Justice Holmes: Reassessing the Significance of *Mahon*' (1998) 86 *Georgetown Law Journal* 813.

Tunc, A., 'The French Concept of *abus de droit*', in Canadian Institute of Advanced Legal Studies, *The Cambridge Lectures 1981* (Butterworths, Toronto, 1981), 151.

Turner, J. H., *Ancient Bingley: or, Bingley, Its History and Scenery* (Thomas Harrison & Sons, Bingley, 1897).

Turner, R. V., 'Who Was the Author of *Glanvill*? Reflections on the Education of Henry II's Common Lawyers' (1990) 8 *Law & History Review* 97.

Tushnet, M., 'The Logic of Experience: Oliver Wendell Holmes on the Supreme Judicial Court' (1977) 63 *Virginia Law Review* 975.

Twining, W., *Blackstone's Tower: The English Law School* (Sweet & Maxwell, London, 1994).

Uelmen, D. L., 'The Law of Underground Water; A Half Century of *Huber v Merkel*' [1953] *Wisconsin Law Review* 491.

Vandevelde, K. J., 'The New Property of the Nineteenth Century: The Development of the Modern Concept of Property' (1980) 29 *Buffalo Law Review* 325.

—— 'A History of Prima Facie Tort: The Origins of a General Theory of Intentional Tort' (1990) 19 *Hofstra Law Review* 447.

—— 'The Modern Prima Facie Tort Doctrine' (1991) 79 *Kentucky Law Journal* 519.

Vining, J., *Legal Identity: The Coming of Age of Public Law* (Yale University Press, New Haven, 1978).

Visser, F., 'Ground-water law in South Africa' (1987) 50 *Tydskrif Vir Hedendaage Romeins-Hollandse Reg* 412.

Voyame, R., Cottier, B. and Rocha, B., 'Abuse of Rights in Comparative Law (1)', in Council of Europe, *Abuse of rights and equivalent concepts: The principle and its present day application* (Council of Europe, Strasbourg, 1990), 23.

Wade, H. W. R. and Forsyth, C., *Administrative Law* (Clarendon Press, Oxford, 8th edn, 2000).

Walker, D. M., 'Equity in Scots Law' (1954) 66 *Juridical Review* 103.

—— *The Oxford Companion to Law* (Clarendon Press, Oxford, 1980).

—— *The Law of Delict in Scotland* (W. Green & Son Ltd, Edinburgh, 1981).

—— *The Scottish Jurists* (W. Green & Son Ltd, Edinburgh, 1985).

Wallace, J. W., *The Reporters* (Soule & Bugbee, Boston, 4th rev. edn, 1882).

Walton, F. P., 'Motive as an Element in Torts in the Common and in the Civil Law' (1909) 22 *Harvard Law Review* 501.

—— 'Delictual Responsibility in the Modern Civil Law (more particularly in the French Law) as compared with English Law of Torts' (1933) 49 *Law Quarterly Review* 70.

Ward, J. T., 'West Riding landowners and mining in the nineteenth century', reprinted in J. Benson and R. G. Neville (eds), *Studies in the Yorkshire Coal Industry* (Manchester University Press, Manchester, 1976), 45.

Ware, E. F., *Roman Water Law: Translated from the Pandects of Justinian* (West Publishing Co., St Paul, 1905).

Washburn, E., 'Rights in Subterranean Waters' (1862–3) 11 *American Law Register* 65.

Waterman, J. S., 'Mansfield and Blackstone's Commentaries' (1933–4) 1 *University of Chicago Law Review* 549.

Watkins, T. G., 'Markby, Sir William', in A. W. B. Simpson (ed.), *Biographical Dictionary of the Common Law* (Butterworths, London, 1984), 352.

—— *An Historical Introduction to Modern Civil Law* (Ashgate Dartmouth, Aldershot, 1999).

Watson, A., 'The Structure of Blackstone's Commentaries' (1988) 97 *Yale Law Journal* 795.

—— 'The Transformation of American Property Law: A Comparative Law Approach' (1990) 24 *Georgia Law Review* 163.

—— 'Chancellor Kent's Use of Foreign Law', in M. Reimann (ed.), *The Reception of Continental Ideas in the Common Law World, 1820–1920* (Duncker & Humblot, Berlin, 1993), 45.

Watson, J., *Water Supply with a description of the Bradford Waterworks (Old and New)* (Peter Lund, Humphries & Co., Bradford, 1900).

Weil, S. C., 'Running Water' (1908–09) 22 *Harvard Law Review* 190.

—— 'A Short Code of Underground Water' (1913) 2 *California Law Review* 25.

—— 'Theories of Water Law' (1913–14) 27 *Harvard Law Review* 530.

—— 'The Mingling of Waters' (1915–16) 29 *Harvard Law Review* 137.

—— 'Origin and Comparative Development of the Law of Watercourses in the Common Law and Civil Law' (1918) 6 *California Law Review* 245 and 342 (two parts).

—— 'Waters: American Law and French Authority' (1919–20) 33 *Harvard Law Review* 133.

—— 'Natural Communism: Air, Water, Oil, Sea, and Seashore' (1934) 47 *Harvard Law Review* 425.

—— 'Fifty Years of Water Law' (1936) 50 *Harvard Law Review* 252.

Weir, T., 'The Common Law System', in R. David *et al.* (eds.), *Structures and the Divisions of the Law* (J. C. B. Mohr, Tubingen, 1975), 77.

—— 'Abstraction in the Law of Torts—Economic Loss' [1974] *City of London Law Review* 15.

—— *A Casebook on Tort* (Sweet & Maxwell, London, 8th edn, 1996).

—— *Economic Torts* (Clarendon Press, Oxford, 1997).

West, B., 'Worstedopolis and the Water Works: Bradford Water Works Company 1837–1855', unpublished B.A. dissertation, University of Bradford, 1980.

Westcoat, J. L., 'Toward a Modern Map of Roman Water Law' (1997) 18 *Urban Geography* 100.

Wharton, G. F., *Legal Maxims, with Observations & Cases in Two Parts* (Law Times, London, 1863).

Whelan, F. G., 'Property as Artifice: Hume and Blackstone', in J. R. Pennock and J. W. Chapman (eds), *Property* (New York University Press, NOMOS XXII, 1980), 101.

White, G. E., 'The Appellate Opinion as Historical Source Material' (1971) 1 *Journal of Interdisciplinary History* 491.

—— *Justice Oliver Wendell Holmes: Law and the Inner Self* (Oxford University Press, Oxford, 1993).

Whitty, N., 'Water Law Regimes', in K. Reid and R. Zimmermann (eds), *A History of Private Law in Scotland: Volume 1: Introduction and Property* (Oxford University Press, Oxford, 2000), 420.

Wightman, J., 'Nuisance—the Environmental Tort? *Hunter v Canary Wharf* in the House of Lords' (1998) 61 *Modern Law Review* 870.

Williams, D. G. T., 'Subordinate Legislation and Judicial Control' (1997) 8 *Public Law Review* 77.

Williams, G. L., 'The Foundation of Tortious Liability' (1941) 7 *Cambridge Law Journal* 111.

Williams, J., 'Latin Maxims in English Law' (1894–95) 20 *The Law Magazine & Law Review* (4th Ser.) 283.

Willis, J., 'Statutory Interpretation in a Nutshell' (1938) 16 *Canadian Bar Review* 1.

Willman, R., 'Blackstone and the "Theoretical Perfection" of English Law in the Reign of Charles II' (1983) 26 *The Historical Journal* 39.

Winder, W. H. D., 'The Development of Blackmail' (1941) 5 *Modern Law Review* 21.

Winfield, P. H., *Select Legal Essays* (Sweet & Maxwell, London, 1952).

Wisdom, A. S., *Aspects of Water Law* (Barry Rose Publishers, Chichester, 1981).

Witting, C., 'Of Principle and Prima Facie Tort' (1999) 25 *Monash University Law Review* 295.

Woolrych, H. W., *A Treatise on the Law of Waters* (London, 1st edn, 1830).

—— *Treatise of the law of waters: including the law relating to rights in the sea, and rights concerning rivers, watercourses & with a note concerning the rights of the Crown in the land between high and low water mark* (William Benning & Co., London, 2nd edn, 1851).

Wright, D. G., 'Mid-Victorian Bradford: 1850–1880' (1982) 47 *Bradford Antiquary* (new ser.) 65.

Yale, D. E. C., ' "Of No Mean Authority": Some Later Uses of Bracton', in M. S. Arnold, T. A. Green, S. A. Scully, and S. D. White (eds), *On the Laws and Customs of England: Essays in Honor of Samuel E. Thorne* (University of North Carolina Press, Chapel Hill, 1981), 383.

Yiannopoulos, A. N., 'Civil Liability for Abuse of Right: Something Old, Something New . . .' (1994) 54 *Louisiana Law Review* 1173.

Zimmermann, R., '*Statuta Sunt Stricte Interpretanda*? Statutes and the Common Law: A Continental Perspective' [1997] *Cambridge Law Journal* 315.

Zweigert, K. and Kötz, H. (Weir, T. trans.), *Introduction to Comparative Law* (Clarendon Press, Oxford, 3rd rev. edn, 1998).

Index